ISBN 0-8373-5015-8

15 ADMISSION TEST SERIES

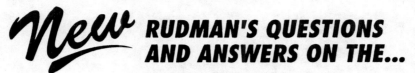 **RUDMAN'S QUESTIONS AND ANSWERS ON THE...**

NTE

NATIONAL TEACHER EXAMINATION

CORE BATTERY

Intensive preparation for the examination including...

Professional Knowledge
- Teaching Principles and Practices
- Psychological Foundations of Education
- Societal Foundations of Education

General Knowledge
- Social Studies, Literature and Fine Arts
- Science and Mathematics

Communication Skills
- Listening Comprehension
- Reading Comprehension
- Writing

NATIONAL LEARNING CORPORATION

Copyright © 1999 by

National Learning Corporation

212 Michael Drive, Syosset, New York 11791
(516) 921-8888

(800) 645-6337
Fax (516) 921-8743
www.passbooks.com

PRINTED IN THE UNITED STATES OF AMERICA

PASSBOOK SERIES®

THE *PASSBOOK SERIES*® has been created to prepare applicants and candidates for the ultimate academic battlefield—the examination room.

At some time in our lives, each and every one of us may be required to take an examination—for validation, matriculation, admission, qualification, registration, certification, or licensure.

Based on the assumption that every applicant or candidate has met the basic formal educational standards, has taken the required number of courses, and read the necessary texts, the *PASSBOOK SERIES*® furnishes the one special preparation which may assure passing with confidence, instead of failing with insecurity. Examination questions—together with answers—are furnished as the basic vehicle for study so that the mysteries of the examination and its compounding difficulties may be eliminated or diminished by a sure method.

This book is meant to help you pass your examination provided that you qualify and are serious in your objective.

The entire field is reviewed through the huge store of content information which is succinctly presented through a provocative and challenging approach—the question-and-answer method.

A climate of success is established by furnishing the correct answers at the end of each test.

You soon learn to recognize types of questions, forms of questions, and patterns of questioning. You may even begin to anticipate expected outcomes.

You perceive that many questions are repeated or adapted so that you gain acute insights, which may enable you to score many sure points.

You learn how to confront new questions, or types of questions, and to attack them confidently and work out the correct answers.

You note objectives and emphases, and recognize pitfalls and dangers, so that you may make positive educational adjustments.

Moreover, you are kept fully informed in relation to new concepts, methods, practices, and directions in the field.

You discover that you are actually taking the examination all the time: you are preparing for the examination by "taking" an examination, not by reading extraneous and/or supererogatory textbooks.

In short, this PASSBOOK®, used directedly, should be an important factor in helping you to pass your test.

NATIONAL TEACHER/PRAXIS EXAMINATIONS (NTE)

INTRODUCTION

I. WHAT ARE THE PRAXIS EXAMINATIONS?

The Praxis Series Examinations comprise standardized tests that measure the academic achievement and proficiency of teaching applicants. Developed and administered by the Educational Testing Service (ETS), these examinations evaluate the ability and knowledge of college seniors completing teacher education programs and advanced candidates who have received additional professional training in specific fields.

State departments of education and local school systems in this country that do not administer their own examinations for teaching positions may require teaching applicants to submit scores on the National Teacher Praxis Examination Series. These professional assessments of beginning teachers are designed to provide objective measurements of the knowledge, skills, and abilities required in the teaching profession. These test results are then used for certifying teachers as initial, qualifying, validating, statutory, incremental, promotional and/or supervisory.

Additionally, many colleges use the Praxis Examinations in their teacher education programs at graduate and undergraduate levels, to provide student guidance and allow self-assessment by individual students. The Praxis tests have also been used as comprehensive examinations for undergraduate students and as qualifying examinations for graduate students.

Three groups of tests at three different levels of assessment, Praxis I, II, and III, constitute the Praxis Examinations. Praxis I and II evaluate the mental ability, professional knowledge, and general cultural level of candidates, and the Praxis III Examination assesses the practical skills demonstrated by the teaching applicant in a required classroom performance.

While Praxis I and II are jointly administered nine times a year, nation-wide, the Praxis III Examination is a requirement in certain states only.

II. WHAT ARE THE PRAXIS I EXAMINATIONS?

Also described as Academic Skills Assessments, this section of the examination uses Pre-Professional Skills Tests (PPST), and the Computer Based Testing Program (PI-CBT), to measure the candidate's proficiency in the basic academic skills of reading, writing, and mathematics.

The PPST tests comprise objective-type, short-answer questions in the paper-and-pencil format, as well as the writing test, a 30-minute essay. The PI-CBT tests are of an *adaptive* nature, which means that the computer selects questions for the candidate based on his answers to previous questions. These are objective-type questions to which the candidate must respond with single or multiple-choice answers, as well as answers written in their own words on the computer, an IBM or compatible PC with a mouse. This section of the Praxis I examination also requires the candidate to either handwrite or use a word processor to compose a 40-minute essay.

The PI-CBT program provides year-round testing by appointment at a network of Sylvan Technology Centers, ETS Field Service Offices, as well as centers at selected colleges and universities.

III. WHAT ARE THE PRAXIS II EXAMINATIONS?

Also categorized as Subject Assessments, the Praxis II Examinations evaluate the candidate's knowledge of his professional area. The Praxis II Examinations continue to utilize the National Teacher Examination's Core Battery Tests, as well as the NTE Specialty Area Tests.

Additionally, the Praxis II Examinations include the Multiple Subject Assessment for Teachers or MSAT, and the Content Area Performance Assessment or CAPA tests.

A. WHAT ARE THE CORE BATTERY EXAMINATIONS?

Core Battery Examinations consist of a battery of three (3) discrete tests, which attempt to give a picture of the teacher-candidate's general ability and mental equipment. They are designed to measure the general educational background of college students, not to evaluate advanced preparation. The tests cover three categories: professional education (knowledge), general education (knowledge), and communication skills. Professional Knowledge includes questions related to the social and cultural forces that influence curriculum and teaching, as well as questions related to general principles of learning and instruction. General Knowledge includes subtests on Science and Mathematics, and Social Studies, Literature, and Fine Arts. Communication Skills measures Listening, Reading, and Written English Expression. These examinations are described in more detail in Section E.

Usually, all candidates are required to take the Core Battery Examinations since it is reasonable to expect that teachers should possess a high order of basic mental, cultural, and professional abilities and traits.

B. WHAT ARE THE SPECIALTY EXAMINATIONS?

The Specialty Examinations enable the candidate to demonstrate competence in a special field. These are described in Section E below.

C. WHICH TESTS SHOULD YOU TAKE?

Candidates for positions in the elementary school area usually take either Specialty Examination #1 - EDUCATION IN THE ELEMENTARY SCHOOL (1-8) or Specialty Examination #2 - EARLY CHILDHOOD EDUCATION (Kg.-3). Some school systems and colleges, however, require prospective elementary school teachers to take both Specialty Examinations #1 and #2.

Those who are candidates for secondary school positions customarily take the one Specialty Examination covering their teaching specialty, although they are also sometimes asked to indicate another specialty - either in secondary education or even in elementary education.

Where school systems require teacher-candidates to take their own examinations in addition to the National Teacher Examinations, these local examinations are usually given at the same time. The school system to which application is made will notify the candidate whether such additional examination is to be given.

The only way to be sure which National Teacher Examinations you should take is to get this information from the state department of education, the school system, the graduate school, or the college to which you plan to have your scores sent.

D. DESCRIPTION OF THE EXAMINATIONS

The following are brief descriptions of the individual Core Battery and Specialty Examinations as drawn from the official bulletin of information for candidates.

CORE BATTERY EXAMINATIONS

The Core Battery Examinations are designed to appraise your general preparation for teaching. Tests are offered in (1) Professional Knowledge (including questions in Psychological Foundations of Education, Societal Foundations of Education, and Teaching Principles and Practices), in (2) General Knowledge (including Social Studies, Literature, and Fine Arts; and Science and Mathematics), and in (3) Communication Skills (Written English Expression). The General Knowledge and Professional Knowledge tests each include four 30-minute sections containing multiple-choice questions or problems. The Test of Communication Skills consists of three 30-minute multiple-choice sections and a 30-minute essay. Course work beyond what is required by teacher-preparation programs generally is not essential for the General Knowledge tests. Core Battery Examinations are described in some detail below.

1. PROFESSIONAL KNOWLEDGE (EDUCATION)

The Professional Knowledge test is designed to provide an indication of the candidate's knowledge and understanding of professional educational matters. It contains questions on general principles and methods of teaching, educational psychology and child development, guidance and personnel services, evaluation, principles of curriculum development, and significant research findings in education and related fields.

The Professional Knowledge test consists of four 30-minute sections, one of which is a pretest section. Each section contains 35 questions. The questions in the pretest section are administered solely for developmental purposes and do not contribute to examinees' scores.

This test assesses examinees' understanding of the knowledge and skills that a beginning teacher uses in decision making, with emphasis on the context and process of teaching. Questions concerning the process of teaching assess knowledge of appropriate techniques or means of instructional planning, implementation, and evaluation, as well as knowledge of what constitutes acceptable professional behavior. Questions concerning the context of teaching assess examinees' ability to recognize constitutional rights of students and implications for classroom practice; the implications of state, federal, and judicial policy; and forces outside the classroom that influence teachers and students. Some questions also assess examinees' knowledge of activities and functions of professional organizations and of teachers' rights and responsibilities.

2. GENERAL KNOWLEDGE (EDUCATION)

The General Knowledge test assesses examinees' knowledge and understanding of various disciplines and their interrelationships. The test consists of four separately timed 30-minute sections: Literature and Fine Arts, Mathematics, Science, and Social Studies.

SOCIAL STUDIES, LITERATURE AND FINE ARTS. In the modern classroom, the demands made upon the teacher's cultural background extend far beyond any one field of specialization. It is generally agreed that persons entrusted with the education of children need to have a broad perspective on significant factors in contemporary life. The Social Studies, Literature, and Fine Arts test is designed to furnish an estimate of the breadth of the candidate's cultural background in these areas rather than his mastery of any special subject.

The 30 questions in the Social Studies section of the test assess (1) an understanding of major United States historical and cultural events and movements, political institutions, and political values; (2) an understanding of prominent characteristics of societies and cultures; (3) an understanding of relationships between culture and individuals; (4) an understanding of economic concepts and processes; (5) knowledge and understanding of geographical features and characteristics of human settlement and culture; and (6) an understanding of social science methodologies, methodological tools, and data resources.

The 35 questions in the Literature and Fine Arts section of the test are based on passages from literature, photographic reproductions of art works, film stills, and photographs of theater or dance performances. The questions using these kinds of materials are designed to assess examinees' skills in analysis and interpretation.

The SCIENCE AND MATHEMATICS test is designed to furnish an estimate of the candidate's knowledge of important concepts in the fields of science and mathematics, including contemporary developments in these areas.

The 30 questions in the Science section of the test are designed to measure knowledge and understanding of certain themes that are major areas of scientific interest and current concern. Questions selected emphasize important principles, theories, concepts, and facts of science; applications of these theories and facts; and the methods of science. The science questions are based on important themes from the biological, physical, and earth sciences.

The 25 questions in the Mathematics section of the test are intended to assess examinees' cumulative knowledge of mathematics. Questions are selected from such topics as comparing and ordering numbers; estimation; interpreting graphs, charts, and diagrams; use of ratio, proportion, and percent; reading scales; measurement; interpreting formulas and other expressions written in symbols; logical reasoning; and recognition of more than one way to solve a problem.

3. COMMUNICATION SKILLS (WRITTEN ENGLISH EXPRESSION)

The Communications Skills test is designed to measure two factors judged to be of particular significance for teachers: general verbal ability and skill in the correct use of the English language. The test contains questions on grammatical usage, punctuation, capitalization, spelling, sentence structure and organization, reading skills, and an essay.

The Communications Skills test assesses examinees' knowledge and skills in the areas of listening, reading, and writing.

The Listening section consists of 40 questions that assess the examinee's ability to retain and interpret spoken messages. The questions and the information on which they are based are tape-recorded; they do not appear in the test book. Only the directions and answer choices are printed. Directions are also presented on the tape.

The Listening section is divided into three parts, each with a different question format. In Part A, examinees listen to short statements or questions, then select either the best answer to a question or a sentence that is best supported by the statement. In Part B, examinees listen to short dialogs between two speakers, then answer multiple-choice questions. In Part C, examinees listen to several short talks, each followed by multiple-choice questions.

The Reading section consists of 30 multiple-choice questions that assess the examinee's ability to read for literal content and to analyze and evaluate prose selections. The reading material varies in difficulty and is drawn from a variety of subject areas and real-life situations. The section contains long passages of approximately 250 words, shorter passages of approximately 100 words, and short statements of fewer than 50 words.

The multiple-choice Writing section consists of 45 multiple-choice questions that assess the examinee's ability to use standard written English correctly and effectively and to select and order materials appropriately in sentences or short paragraphs. Examinees are not required to have knowledge of formal grammatical terminology, but rather are asked to detect errors, choose the best way to rewrite certain phrases or sentences, and evaluate strategies for developing ideas.

For the essay component of the Writing section, examinees are asked to write for 30 minutes on an assigned topic. The essays are scored holistically (that is, with a single score for overall quality). Scores are based on such things as the development of the central idea; evidence that the writer understands why the piece is being written and for whom; consistency of point of view; cohesiveness; strength and logic of supporting information; rhetorical force; appropriateness of diction and syntax; and correctness of mechanics and usage.

PRAXIS II: Subject Assessments and NTE Programs Specialty Area Tests
             (continued)

Area	NLC Book Catalog No.
Education of Students with Mental Retardation	NT-24
Educational Leadership: Administration and Supervision	NT-15
Elementary Education: Curriculum, Instruction, and Assessment	NT-1
Elementary Education: Content Area Exercises	
English Language and Literature	NT-4
English Language, Literature, and Composition: Content Knowledge	NT-4
English Language, Literature, and Composition: Essays	
English Language, Literature, and Composition: Pedagogy	NT-4
Environmental Education	NT-54
Foreign Language Pedagogy	NT-55
French	NT-19
French: Linguistic, Literary, and Cultural Analysis	NT-19
French: Productive Language Skills	
General Science	NT-48
General Science: Content Essays	
General Science: Content Knowledge, Part 1	NT-48
General Science: Content Knowledge, Part 2	NT-48
Geography	NT-56
German	NT-32
Government/Political Science	NT-57
Health and Physical Education	NT-38
Health Education	NT-38
Home Economics Education	NT-12
Introduction to the Teaching of Reading	NT-39
Italian	NT-50
Japanese	
Latin	NT-18
Library Media Specialist	NT-29, 17
Marketing Education	NT-46
Marketing	NT-46
Mathematics	NT-6
Mathematics: Content Knowledge	NT-6
Mathematics: Pedagogy	NT-6
Mathematics: Proofs, Models, and Problems, Part 1	
Mathematics: Proofs, Models, and Problems, Part 2	
Music: Analysis	NT-11

PRAXIS II: Subject Assessment and NTE Programs Specialty Area Tests
             (continued)

Area	NLC Book Catalog No.
Music: Concepts and Processes	NT-11
Music Education	NT-11
Office Technology	NT-58
Physical Education	NT-9, 36, 37
Physical Education: Content Knowledge	NT-9, 36, 37
Physical Education: Movement Forms - Analysis and Design	
Physical Education: Movement Forms - Video Evaluation	
Physical Education: Pedagogy	NT-9
Physical Science: Content Essays	
Physical Science: Content Knowledge	NT-7, 7B
Physical Science: Pedagogy	NT-7, 7B
Physics	NT-7B
Physics: Content Essays	
Physics: Content Knowledge	NT-7B
Pre-Kindergarten Education	NT-2
Psychology	NT-42
Reading Specialist	NT-30
Russian	
Safety/Driver Education	NT-59
School Food Service Supervisor	NT-60
School Guidance and Counseling	NT-16, 16a, 16b, 16c
School Psychologist	NT-40
School Social Worker	NT-65
Secretarial	NT-58
Social Studies	NT-8
Social Studies: Analytical Essays	
Social Studies: Content Knowledge	NT-8
Social Studies: Interpretation of Materials	NT-8
Social Studies: Pedagogy	NT-8
Sociology	NT-61
Spanish	NT-14
Spanish: Content Knowledge	NT-14
Spanish: Linguistic, Literary, and Cultural Analysis	NT-14
Spanish: Pedagogy	NT-55
Spanish: Productive Language Skills	NT-14
Special Education	NT-41
Special Education: Preschool/Early Childhood	NT-41,2
Speech Communication	NT-35
Speech-Language Pathology	NT-33
Teaching Deaf and Hard of Hearing Students	NT-28
Teaching English as a Second Language	NT-47

PRAXIS II: Subject Assessments and NTE Programs Specialty Area Tests
             (continued)

Area	NLC Book Catalog No.
Teaching Speech to Students with Language Impairments	NT-26
Teaching Students with Emotional Disturbance	NT-43
Teaching Students with Learning Disabilities	NT-44
Teaching Students with Mild Mental Disabilities	NT-24,43,44
Teaching Students with Orthopedic Impairments	NT-25
Teaching Students with Physical and Mental Disabilities	NT-23, 25
Teaching Students with Visual Impairments	NT-27
Technology Education	NT-5
Theatre	UPFT-5
U.S. History	NT-62
Vocational General Knowledge	NT-64
World and U.S. History	NT-62
World Civilization	NT-63

III.   WHAT IS THE PRAXIS III EXAMINATION?

The Praxis III Examination evaluates the candidate's performance in the complex environment of the modern classroom, using the licensing criteria of the state in which the examination is administered.

As the practical section of the Praxis Series, the Praxis III Examination analyzes the candidate's ability to implement his/her ideas in the classroom. This examination includes a training program that utilizes the most recent materials and teaching techniques. The teacher's knowledge of the diverse requirements for different subjects is assessed, as is the candidate's ability to employ the teaching method that is particularly appropriate to the subject being taught.

Trained local observers constitute a qualified committee that examines the teaching applicant's understanding of the specific needs of individual students. Finally, the Praxis III Examination evaluates the candidate's awareness of multi-cultural issues, an important criterion in today's classroom environment.

———

HOW TO TAKE A TEST

You have studied hard, long, and conscientiously.

With your official admission card in hand, and your heart pounding, you have been admitted to the examination room.

You note that there are several hundred other applicants in the examination room waiting to take the same test.

They all appear to be equally well prepared.

You know that nothing but your best effort will suffice. The "moment of truth" is at hand: you now have to demonstrate objectively, in writing, your knowledge of content and your understanding of subject matter.

You are fighting the most important battle of your life — to pass and/or score high on an examination which will determine your career and provide the economic basis for your livelihood.

What extra, special things should you know and should you do in taking the examination?

BEFORE THE TEST

YOUR PHYSICAL CONDITION IS IMPORTANT

If you are not well, you can't do your best work on tests. If you are half asleep, you can't do your best either. Here are some tips:

1. Get about the same amount of sleep you usually get. Don't stay up all night before the test, either partying or worrying — DON'T DO IT.

2. If you wear glasses, be sure to wear them when you go to take the test. This goes for hearing aids, too.

3. If you have any physical problems that may keep you from doing your best, be sure to tell the person giving the test. If you are sick or in poor health, you really cannot do your best on any test. You can always come back and take the test some other time.

AT THE TEST

EXAMINATION TECHNIQUES

1. Read the *general* instructions carefully. These are usually printed on the first page of the examination booklet. As a rule, these instructions refer to the timing of the examination; the fact that you should not start work until the signal and must stop work at a signal, etc. If there are any *special* instructions, such as a choice of questions to be answered, make sure that you note this instruction carefully.

2. When you are ready to start work on the examination, that is as soon as the signal has been given, read the instructions to each question booklet, underline any key words or phrases, such as *least, best, outline, describe,* and the like. In this way you will tend to answer as requested rather than discover on reviewing your paper that you *listed without describing,* that you selected the *worst* choice rather than the *best* choice, etc.

3. If the examination is of the objective or so-called multiple-choice type, that is, each question will also give a series of possible answers: A, B, C, or D, and you are called upon to select the best answer and write the letter next to that answer on your answer paper, it is advisable to start answering each question in turn. There may be anywhere from 50 to 100 such questions in the three or four hours allotted and you can see how much time would be taken if you read through all the questions before beginning to answer any. Furthermore, if you come across a question or a group of questions which you know would be difficult to answer, it would undoubtedly affect your handling of all the other questions.

4. If the examination is of the essay-type and contains but a few questions, it is a moot point as to whether you should read all the questions before starting to answer any one. Of course if you are given a choice, say five out of seven and the like, then it is essential to read all the questions so you can eliminate the two which are most difficult. If, however, you are asked to answer all the questions, there may be danger in trying to answer the easiest one first because you may find that you will spend too much time on it. The best technique is to answer the first question, then proceed to the second, etc.

5. Time your answers. Before the examination begins, write down the time it started, then add the time allowed for the examination and write down the time it must be completed, then divide the time available somewhat as follows:

    a. If 3½ hours are allowed, that would be 210 minutes. If you have 80 objective-type questions, that would be an average of about 2½ minutes per question. Allow yourself no more than 2 minutes per question, or a total of 160 minutes, which will permit about 50 minutes to review.

    b. If for the time allotment of 210 minutes, there are 7 essay questions to answer, that would average about 30 minutes a question. Give yourself only 25 minutes per question so that you have about 35 minutes to review.

6. The most important instruction is *to read each question* and make sure you know what is wanted. The second most important instruction is to *time yourself properly* so that you answer every question. The third most important instruction is to *answer every question.* Guess if you have to but include something for each question, Remember that you will receive no credit for a blank and will probably receive some credit if you write something in answer to an essay question. If you guess a letter, say "B" for a multiple-choice question, you may have guessed right. If you leave a blank as the answer to a multiple-choice question, the examiners may respect your feelings but it will not add a point to your score. Some exams may penalize you for wrong answers, so in such cases *only*, you may not want to guess unless you have some basis for your answer.

7. Suggestions

    a. Objective-Type Questions

        (1) Examine the question booklet for proper sequence of pages and questions.

        (2) Read all instructions carefully.

        (3) Skip any question which seems too difficult; return to it after all other questions have been answered.

        (4) Apportion your time properly; do not spend too much time on any single question or group of questions.

        (5) Note and underline key words — *all*, *most*, *fewest*, *least*, *best*, *worst*, *same*, *opposite*.

        (6) Pay particular attention to negatives.

        (7) Note unusual option, e.g., unduly long, short, complex, different or similar in content to the body of the question.

        (8) Observe the use of "hedging" words — *probably*, *may*, *most likely*, *etc.*

        (9) Make sure that your answer is put next to the same number as the question.

        (10) Do not second guess unless you have good reason to believe the second answer is definitely more correct.

        (11) Cross out original answer if you decide another answer is more accurate; do not erase, *until* you are ready to hand your paper in.

        (12) Answer all questions; guess unless instructed otherwise.

        (13) Leave time for review.

b. Essay-Type Questions

    (1) Read each question carefully.

    (2) Determine exactly what is wanted. Underline key words or phrases.

    (3) Decide on outline or paragraph answer.

    (4) Include many different points and elements unless asked to develop any one or two points or elements.

    (5) Show impartiality by giving pros and cons unless directed to select one side only.

    (6) Make and write down any assumptions you find necessary to answer the question.

    (7) Watch your English, grammar, punctuation, choice of words.

    (8) Time your answers; don't crowd material.

8. Answering the Essay Question

Most essay questions can be answered by framing the specific response around several key words or ideas. Here are a few such key words or ideas:

    M's: manpower, materials, methods, money, management

    P's: purpose, program, policy, plan, procedure, practice, problems, pitfalls, personnel, public relations

a. Six basic steps in handling problems:

    (1) preliminary plan and background development

    (2) collect information, data and facts

    (3) analyze and interpret information, data and facts

    (4) analyze and develop solutions as well as make recommendations

    (5) prepare report and sell recommendations

    (6) install recommendations and follow up effectiveness

b. Pitfalls to Avoid

    (1) *Taking Things for Granted*
    A statement of the situation does not necessarily imply that each of the elements is necessarily true; for example, a complaint may be invalid and biased so that all that can be taken for granted is that a complaint has been registered

    (2) *Considering only one side of a situation*
    Wherever possible, indicate several alternatives and then point out the reasons you selected the best one.

    (3) *Failing to indicate follow up*
    Whenever your answer indicates action on your part, make certain that you will take proper follow-up action to see how successful your recommendations, procedures, or actions turn out to be.

    (4) *Taking too long in answering any single question*
    Remember to time your answers properly.

EXAMINATION SECTION

PROFESSIONAL EDUCATION

EXAMINATION SECTION

DIRECTIONS FOR THIS SECTION:
Each question or incomplete statement is followed by several sug·
gested answers or completions. Select the one that BEST answers the
question or completes the statement. *PRINT THE LETTER OF THE CORRECT
ANSWER IN THE SPACE AT THE RIGHT*.

TEST 1

1. The objective of *all* art experiences in the elementary   1. ...
   grades is to
   A. develop the ability to draw realistically
   B. keep children busy with motor activity
   C. secure a uniform standard and type of expression
   D. promote emotional stability, uscular coordination, and
      originality of expression

2. An attractive and orderly classroom   2. ...
   A. exerts a silent influence on children and helps them
      to improve their sense of order and taste
   B. is unnoticed by children but good when parents visit
      the school
   C. can be enhanced with crepe paper curtains and color
      transparencies on windows or doors
   D. is possible in new buildings but completely out of the
      question in old buildings

3. The arts are included in the program of the elementary   3. ...
   school CHIEFLY because they
   A. provide an opportunity to discover artistic talent
   B. provide rest and relaxation from studies which involve
      mental activity
   C. provide emotional release, motor coordination, and
      another means of communication
   D. make it possible to illustrate and add color and
      interest to units of study

4. Children will become sensitive to color variations and   4. ...
   better able to use color for personal expression *if* they
   A. learn to identify primary and secondary colors and
      if they make color wheels using those colors
   B. have many opportunities to choose, use and judge
      colors in many materials and for many uses
   C. make many designs using analogous and complementary
      color harmonics
   D. copy color reproductions of paintings by the old
      masters

5. Art and craft activities should be emphasized for low IQ   5. ...
   pupils because
   A. art activities do not require ability to think or to
      judge
   B. they can be furnished with patterns to follow
   C. art gives them another and practical way of learning
      from doing
   D. they will have articles and gifts to take home

6. When a fourth-grade boy says, "I want to draw my street,   6. ...
   but I can't make it look right," the teacher should aid him
   by
   A. giving him a book of perspective to study and copy

1

    B. having him observe carefully similar forms from the classroom window, the corridor or his own street

    C. having him learn the rules of perspective and then make diagrams of blocks above and below eye level in parallel and angular perspective

    D. suggesting that he draw something else which does not involve perspective

7. Of the following, the approach *usually* MOST effective in developing an efficient,happy classroom is   7. ...

    A. promptly and appropriately punishing every infraction of class rules

    B. developing the habit of automatic obedience in the children

    C. keeping parents constantly informed of their children's level of behavior

    D. planning interesting and appropriate activities to meet the needs of the individual children

8. Among the contributions made by the "Gestalt" psychologists 8. ...
is the idea that

    A. the individual reacts to a total environment

    B. a particular isolated stimulus will lead to a specific response

    C. the best method of learning is through "conditioning"

    D. each "faculty" of the brain must be provided with appropriate exercise

9. The development of the contemporary curricular program in   9. ...
elementary education is PRIMARILY associated with the/ideas of

    A. Henry Barnard   B. John Dewey

    C. Horace Mann   D. Edward Thorndike

10. Public schools in the United States receive from the   10. ...
Federal Government

    A. the major part of their financial support, amounting to more than 75% of the total

    B. half of their financial support, the Government matching combined state and local amounts

    C. a small proportion of their total financial support

    D. no financial support

11. The term *correlation* differs from the term *integration*   11. ...
in that the former

    A. is narrower in meaning   B. is broader in meaning

    C. has no relationship to integration

    D. is opposite in meaning to integration

12. In current educational philosophy and practice, guidance   12. ...
is considered to be

    A. the province of the trained practitioner exclusively

    B. a matter of relatively minor importance

    C. the concern of all teachers

    D. a matter for agencies other than the school

13. The PRINCIPAL use of a diagnostic test is to   13. ...

    A. measure achievement

    B. determine weaknesses as a basis for remedial instruction

    C. discover aptitudes

    D. evaluate previous teaching procedures

14. The MOST important purpose for using achievement tests is 14. ...
to measure

    A. capacity for future learning
    B. quality and quantity of previous learning
    C. vocational or educational aptitude
    D. quality and quantity of previous teaching

15. Of the following, the phrase which has been MOST widely   15. ...
used to describe contemporary developments in American
secondary education is:
    A. Activity program
    B. Education for life adjustment
    C. Return to fundamentals
    D. Education for defense of democracy

16. The one of the following which is NOT a book-list for   16. ...
secondary schools is
    A. Reader's Digest of Books
    B. Reading Ladders for Human Relations
    C. Books for You   D. Your Reading

17. The one of the following which is a device to be used in   17. ...
group dynamics is a(n)
    A. metronoscope   B. opaque projector
    C. diorama   D. sociogram

18. The one of the following persons who is NOT a leader in   18. ...
the field of English education is
    A. Angela M. Broening   B. Channing Pollack
    C. Lou La Brant   D. Robert C. Pooley

19. A teacher, in assigning an essay to be read, tells the   19. ...
class that there will be a special test on this assignment and that the mark on the test will count for a large
proportion of the next report-card grade.
This is considered *poor* motivation CHIEFLY because it
    A. is likely to discourage poor readers
    B. gives the better readers an unfair advantage
    C. is not easily understood by pupils
    D. is extrinsic and places undue emphasis on marks

20. In planning a lesson in which a film is to be shown to   20. ...
the class, it is *advisable*
    A. not to tell the class anything about it in advance
       in order that interest may be high
    B. to tell the class to pay close attention to what
       they are going to see because a quiz will follow the
       showing
    C. to assume that the film need not be related to the
       work of the class as long as they enjoy seeing it
    D. to conduct a preparatory discussion and a follow-up
       in which the relationship of the film to the work of
       the class is established

21. Teaching grammar *functionally* means   21. ...
    A. teaching only what you are sure pupils will need
       and use in later life
    B. teaching the functions of parts of speech and parts
       of the sentence
    C. using diagrams, charts, and stick figures
    D. emphasizing usage skills and the relationship between
       grammar and meaning

22. In a distribution of test scores, the BEST measure, among   22. ...
the following, of central tendency is the

A. average deviation B. mode
C. median D. standard-deviation

23. *All* of the following publications are intended particular- 23. ...
ly for teachers EXCEPT
   A. THE ENGLISH JOURNAL B. ELEMENTARY ENGLISH
   C. HIGH POINTS D. PRACTICAL ENGLISH

24. When grading pupil compositions, the BEST method of 24. ...
correction is to
   A. underline the error and indicate the nature of it in the margin by using a correction symbol
   B. assign a general comment to encourage the pupil
   C. correct the errors he has made by writing in the proper form yourself
   D. underline the error without indicating the nature of it

25. As a means of cultivating literary appreciation, oral 25. ...
reading is
   A. superior to silent reading B. the only method to use
   C. inferior to silent reading
   D. ineffective because it is slower than silent reading

TEST 2

1. The norms accompanying a standardized test should be 1. ...
looked upon as scores that
   A. pupils of a given age or grade should make
   B. the teacher should set as a goal for her class
   C. have been made by a large group of pupils of a given age or grade
   D. the pupils should set as a goal for themselves

2. Of the following types of tests, the one that would *prob-* 2. ...
ably yield the HIGHEST correlation with scholastic achievement is
   A. memory span B. sentence completion
   C. weight discrimination D. arithmetic computation

3. A technique that is NOT used to detect color blindness is 3. ...
   A. Ishihara B. Snellen C. Holmgren D. Farnsworth

4. Of the following expressions, the one which CANNOT *by* 4. ...
itself be used to interpret an individual score on an
intelligence test is
   A. standard deviation B. standard score
   C. percentile D. deviation I. Q.

5. The *original* selection of items for an intelligence test 5. ...
would depend PRIMARILY upon the
   A. discriminative ability of the items
   B. interest value to the group for which the scale was intended
   C. simplicity of the response, which would facilitate scoring
   D. concept of intelligence held by the test constructor

6. Of the following intelligence tests, the one which is NOT 6. ...
a *group* test is the
   A. Pintner-Cunningham B. Pintner-Paterson
   C. Pintner-Durost D. Kuhlmann-Anderson

7. A survey test is *generally* used to
    A. yield a precise measure of individuals
    B. measure group status
    C. locate specific areas of weakness or strength
    D. yield a measure of an individual's ability to learn
       in some particular area

    7. ...

8. A technique using the drawing of a man as a measure of
intelligence was developed by
    A. Raven   B. Pintner   C. Goodenough D. R. B. Cattell

    8. ...

9. In deciding upon the inclusion of a specific item in a
pupil personnel record, the MOST important consideration
is whether the item
    A. represents objective data
    B. has value to the pupil as used by school staff members
    C. has reliability when reported by a number of school
       staff members
    D. may be readily interpreted by guidance staff members
       dealing with the pupil

    9. ...

10. The MOST valid reason for keeping pupil personnel records
is to
    A. form a basis for referral to community agencies and
       for reports to higher institutions
    B. provide a basis for distribution of pupils among
       classes of a grade
    C. provide data for educational research on the basis
       of which educational improvements are planned
    D. improve instruction and guidance for the pupil

    10. ...

11. An ailment which does NOT occur as a functional disorder
is
    A. tuberculosis   B. stomach cramps
    C. hysterical paralysis   D. stammering

    11. ...

12. The mental mechanism of minimizing one's own faults and
deficiencies by criticizing and blaming others is known as
    A. compensation   B. rationalization
    C. transference   D. projection

    12. ...

13. Sibling rivalry is the term used to describe the competitive feeling between two or more individuals who
    A. are in the same school grade
    B. are children of the same parents
    C. have similar goals of achievement
    D. are in the same chronological age group

    13. ...

14. Of the following, the *single* characteristic MOST important
in determining an individual's status in a group of pre-
adolescent boys is
    A. intelligence   B. physical ability
    C. school marks   D. language development

    14. ...

15. Research has shown that neighborhood gangs tend to be
more cohesive than groups of the same age functioning as
clubs in more formal youth agencies. This would suggest that
    A. the club is potentially longer-lived than the gang
    B. young people join clubs only if they are not accepted
       by the gang
    C. clubs will not be able to function adequately in a
       given neighborhood until some way is found to destroy
       gangs already in existence

    15. ...

D. the activities of the gang meet the needs of its members better than those of the club program do

16. The individual who emerges as the leader of a group is *usually*
    16. ...
    A. the person who, in the judgment of the group, can best meet the demands of the particular problem
    B. superior to the other members of the group in a wide variety of abilities
    C. chosen on the basis of personal qualities rather than ability
    D. the same person, no matter in what activities the group participates

17. The status of an individual in a group is determined, *for the most part,* by
    17. ...
    A. the possession of those qualities the group deems important
    B. his socio-economic level
    C. his status in other groups of which he is a member
    D. the amount of time and energy he is willing to devote to the purposes of the group

18. Experiments using arithmetic as the subject under consideration have shown that pupils make more progress when they work for themselves than when they work for the progress of the group. This finding *probably* means that
    18. ...
    A. group work does not provide an adequate incentive for maximum achievement
    B. pupils are generally self-centered and selfish
    C. the subject of arithmetic was not important enough to the pupils
    D. the pupils did not consider the group of significance to them

19. Of the following, the BEST way to deal with a 12-year-old boy who feels inferior to his peers is to
    19. ...
    A. provide tasks which he can master with little difficulty
    B. show him how irrational his feelings are
    C. accept his declarations of lack of confidence sympathetically
    D. carefully arrange situations in which he will be obliged to show leadership

20. The professional educator should know that Social Security or Old Age and Survivors Insurance is paid for by
    20. ...
    A. taxes deducted from the employee's salary only
    B. funds set aside by the federal government from income taxes
    C. the state in which the worker lives at the time of his retirement or death
    D. taxes deducted from the employee's salary plus an equal amount paid by the employer

21. Studies involving the relative mental abilities of delinquent and non-delinquent children have *generally*
    21. ...
    A. shown that there are no significant differences between them
    B. shown that delinquent children are slightly but significantly brighter than non-delinquents
    C. shown that non-delinquent children are somewhat brighter than delinquent children

D. been about evenly divided- some finding the delinquent children brighter, others finding mental superiority for non-delinquents

22. Current evidence and thinking on the causative factors in juvenile delinquency support the view that   22. ...
    A. social factors are more basic than psychological factors
    B. psychological factors are more basic than social factors
    C. psychological factors and social factors are of about equal importance
    D. physiological factors are more important than either social or psychological factors

23. Of the following, the behavior which would be considered MOST indicative of potential or actual maladjustment in a junior high school boy is   23. ...
    A. treating his classmates to sodas in an attempt to buy their votes in a school election
    B. spending his entire allowance each week on science fiction paperbacks
    C. finding fault with the work of his classmates
    D. failing to take care of school property

24. Of the following teachers, the one MOST liked by the largest number of junior high school pupils is the one who   24. ...
    A. sets easily attainable standards
    B. demonstrates a high level of intellectual competence
    C. maintains an impersonal objective attitude
    D. is sympathetic

25. Of the following characteristics, the one MOST generally found among children just entering the junior high school is   25. ...
    A. a tendency of boys and girls to seek each other's company
    B. the acceptance of parent and teacher opinion with little question
    C. the popularity of guessing games, puzzles, and games of chance
    D. a preference for highly organized competitive team play

---

TEST 3

1. Starch's study of school ratings showed that the correlation in ratings received in any elementary subject with other elementary subjects was   1. ...
    A. high   B. low but positive   C. negligible   D. negative

2. According to Thorndike, negative correlations between different efficiencies are   2. ...
    A. rare   B. common
    C. found only in bright pupils   D. found only in adults

3. In the formation of habitual reactions, there is a transference of regulative function from the brain to subcortical levels   3. ...
    A. finally   B. sometimes   C. usually   D. never

4. The plateau phenomenon, often found in human learning, does   4. ...
   NOT exist in animal learning experiments because
   - A. animals are unable to spurt in learning
   - B. animals are unable to profit by errors
   - C. the incentive in animal learning is constant
   - D. animals have weak incentives in learning

5. The typical learning curve rises rapidly *at first* usually   5. ...
   because the
   - A. learner is enthusiastic
   - B. measurement of initial response is exaggerated
   - C. beginning is always made easy
   - D. abscissa is arranged to that end

6. All learning is bond connecting; this principle does NOT   6. ...
   apply to
   - A. habits   B. reflexes   C. skills   D. attitudes

7. On the basis of mental age, MOST bright children in the   7. ...
   average school are, as concerns grading,
   - A. accelerated   B. retarded   C. normal   D. much accelerated

8. Studies show that children who make exceptionally good   8. ...
   records in elementary grades
   - A. also make superior records in high school
   - B. do only normal work in high school
   - C. do poor work in high school
   - D. do superior work in only one or two high school sub-
     jects

9. Terman's studies of superior children show that in moral   9. ...
   and personal traits
   - A. they are below normal
   - B. they are evenly distributed about the norm
   - C. the superiority is especially marked
   - D. the superiority is marked except in social adaptability

10. Terman's studies of superior children indicate that their   10. ...
    school work is such in most cases as to warrant promotion
    to a grade closely corresponding to the mental age in
    - A. a few cases   B. most cases
    - C. no case   D. all cases

11. "Transfer of training" occurs MORE fully *among*   11. ...
    - A. morons   B. dull individuals
    - C. bright individuals   D. normal individuals

12. The penalty imposed on an offending pupil by the class   12. ...
    teacher should be
    - A. administered immediately
    - B. primarily retributive and based solely upon the
      damage done
    - C. punitive   D. adjusted to the motive behind the offense

13. Problems of class management and of discipline should be   13. ...
    considered in the light of the principle that the
    - A. interests of the school and of the individual pupil
      are identical
    - B. school is nothing; the child is all
    - C. interests of any individual must always give way before
      those of the group of which he is a member
    - D. interests of the school are supreme and must be main-
      tained

14. Probably the MOST potent cause of nervous breakdown is   14. ...

         A. mental fatigue   B. physical fatigue
         C. ennui   D. emotional stress

15. The MOST effective preventive and remedy for fear is   15. ...
    A. coordinated motor activity of any kind
    B. inhibition of mental activity
    C. transfer of training   D. sudden change of stimuli

16. Delusions of grandeur or persecution are *typical* of   16. ...
    A. paranoia B. hysteria C. dementia praecox D. chorea

17. Plasticity or modifiability of the nervous system is   17. ...
    GREATEST
         A. at birth   B. between the ages of 6 and 12
         C. between the ages of 13 and 18   D. in adult life

18. The sympathetic division of the autonomic nervous system   18. ...
    is connected with the
    A. lower part of the spinal cord
    B. upper part of the cord and the midbrain
    C. intermediate part of the cord   D. upper part

19. In psychology, the term *reaction* refers to   19. ...
    A. all kinds of responses that the organism makes to
       stimuli
    B. muscular responses   C. cortical changes only
    D. reflexes and instincts

20. A synpase is   20. ...
    A. a tree-like cell body with its nucleus and branches
    B. a glia cell
    C. any place where the nerve impulse from one neuron
       may be passed on to another neuron
    D. the sending end of a neuron

21. In all trial and error reaction, improvement is NOT apt   21. ...
    to come *if* the response is
    A. annoying to the individual
    B. entirely satisfactory to the individual
    C. repeated once   D. repeated often

22. Education must *always* start with   22. ...
    A. habits   B. attitudes
    C. instinctive tendencies   D. inhibitions

23. "Reciprocal modification" is a technical term in psychol-   23. ...
    ogy that refers to
    A. forgetting   B. transfer of training
    C. conditioned reflex   D. physiological limit

24. It has been fairly well demonstrated that the ability to   24. ...
    speak or write words depends upon connections established
    in the
    A. reflex level route   B. cortical level
    C. midbrain and adjoining part of central nervous system
    D. sensory neurons

25. The motor area of a man's brain was destroyed in an ac-   25. ...
    cident. It is NOT true that because of this he *cannot*
    A. walk   B. run his typewriter
    C. use a knife and fork   D. sing a song

_____

TEST 4

1. Standardized group tests are used MORE frequently than   1. ...
   individual tests, because

A. the same amount of time is needed to test a whole
   class by a group approach as a single pupil by an
   individual approach
B. group tests give better results than individual tests
C. group tests have primary, intermediate and advanced
   forms whereas individual tests have only one form
D. no training is needed to administer a group test

2. Of the following statements about marks, the one which is   2. ...
   NOT correct is:
   A. Excessive emphasis on marks may cause the pupil to
      consider the mark more important than the material
      to be learned.
   B. The pupil may rely too heavily on mere memory in order
      to get high marks.
   C. Occasionally, overemphasis on marks may lead to cheat-
      ing.
   D. Marks based solely on written tests give a valid
      measure of a pupil's achievement because they are
      always objective.

3. Standardized achievement tests are characterized by *all*   3. ...
   of the following principles EXCEPT they
   A. often show differing results, depending upon the
      particular form of the test used
   B. are administered in accordance with uniform procedures
      indicated in the manual of instructions
   C. have norms for grade or age
   D. are scored in accordance with standard procedures
      indicated in the manual of instructions

4. Of the following, the PRIME purpose of grouping pupils in   4. ...
   a mathematics class is to
   A. develop social attitudes B. separate unruly pupils
   C. provide the teacher with a smaller range of pupil
      ability or disability
   D. help solve book shortages

5. Of these statements concerning grouping, select the one   5. ...
   which is CONTRARY to present-day thinking:
   A. In a math class, grouping enables the teacher to meet
      individual differences.
   B. Results of inventory tests may be used as one of the
      bases for forming groups.
   C. Teachers should avoid attaching any status value to
      groups.
   D. Once in a group, a pupil should be kept there for the
      rest of the year.

6. Of the following statements about slow pupils, the one   6. ...
   which is *most nearly* CORRECT is that they
   A. are always unruly
   B. should be given plenty of busy work
   C. usually have a short attention span
   D. should seldom be given homework

7. Of these statements concerning the use of the overhead   7. ...
   projector, which one is NOT true? It
   A. may not be used with a page of the textbook
   B. enables the teacher to observe the class reaction
   C. may be used with transparencies and with overlays
   D. requires an additional person to operate it

8. Of these statements concerning the use of audio-visual   8. ...
aids, which one is NOT true?
   A. Students are helped to learn faster.
   B. They help students to gain more accurate information.
   C. They help students to perceive and understand meanings.
   D. They substitute for, rather than supplement, instructional techniques.

9. Homework should be assigned regularly in the junior high   9. ...
school, because, among other values,
   A. doing homework aids in the development of more independent study habits
   B. survey results indicate that pupil progress is proportional to the amount of homework assigned
   C. homework keeps pupils out of mischief at home
   D. it is traditional to assign homework, and parents demand it

10. In planning a homework assignment, the teacher should ob-   10. ...
serve which one of the following principles? The assignment should
   A. review material previously taught as well as material taught on the day that the assignment was given
   B. be limited to material taught on the day that the assignment was given
   C. not include any material taught on the day the assignment was given
   D. be done only by those pupils who have not fallen so far behind that they cannot profit from doing the assignment

11. The BEST homework assignment to assist junior high school   11. ...
pupils to prepare for a test is which one of the following?
To
   A. tell them to study for a test
   B. give them a set of problems identical to those that will appear on the test
   C. tell them to prepare a set of questions they think should appear on the test
   D. tell them the scope of the test and to assign specific study references and specific practice material covering the scope

12. Which one of the following statements is CONTRARY to   12. ...
present thinking?
   A. Most teachers regard homework as important.
   B. Experimental evidence is not clearly convincing that homework is truly important.
   C. The voluntary type of assignment in which the pupil does whatever he thinks is necessary is the solution to the homework dilemma.
   D. Many parents think homework is helpful.

13. Which of the following is the BEST approach to the use of   13. ...
the text book by a teacher of mathematics?
   A. Only as a source of practice exercises
   B. Primarily as a source of problems to be placed on tests
   C. To assist pupils in learning how to read explanations of new concepts and techniques
   D. Primarily for review

14. Of the following, the LEAST proper use of the textbook
is as
    A. a quick view of things to be learned
    B. a minimum for which pupils may be held responsible
    C. the course of study
    D. a reference for pictures, maps, graphs, tables

15. Of the following statements concerning questioning, which
one is NOT consistent with current thinking?
    A. Some questions, though perfect in form, may challenge
       only a limited number of pupils.
    B. Vague and incomplete questions tend to confuse pupils.
    C. "Chorus" answers do not afford all pupils an opportu-
       nity to think.
    D. Questions starting with "why" and "how" should general-
       ly be avoided.

16. Of the following, the problems which are of LEAST value
in stimulating real thinking are those
    A. which pupils solve in many ways
    B. which pupils solve in one way which has been thoroughly
       practiced
    C. in which pupils encounter extraneous data
    D. which pupils cannot solve because of insufficient data

17. Of the following, select the suggestion LEAST likely to
help a pupil having difficulty in finding the solutions
to a verbal problem.
    A. Generalize the problem by using letters instead of
       numbers
    B. Estimate the answer   C. Use round numbers
    D. Use diagrams or representations

18. In order to implement the aims and objectives of the
junior high school, the mathematics teacher should NOT
    A. make certain to study each child as an individual and
       provide for the normal, bright, and slow learners
    B. encourage and help pupils to explore and sample the
       fields of algebra, geometry, and trigonometry
    C. assist all pupils in acquiring competence in inde-
       pendent study through effective study habits
    D. encourage all pupils to go on to college

19. Of the following, the one that LEAST describes a principle
of classroom motivation is that
    A. the motivation should be brief
    B. the motivation should be related to the new work being
       introduced
    C. the motivation should be related to the experiences of
       the pupils
    D. interest in the subject for its own sake is always an
       adequate motivation

20. The CORRECT order of teaching-learning pattern, which involves the following processes:
    I. Application of problems II. Computations
III. Experiences   IV. Thinking though
is in the sequence:
    A. I, II, III, IV   B. III, IV, II, I
    C. II, III, IV, I   D. IV, I, II, III

21. Select the one of the following principles of learning
mathematics which is NOT correct:

14. ...
15. ...
16. ...
17. ...
18. ...
19. ...
20. ...
21. ...

12

    A. Pupils learn as individuals even though they are taught in groups.
    B. It should be expected that all pupils can master all elements of mathematics at the same grade and age.
    C. Individual instruction in mathematics is occasionally or even often necessary.
    D. Each pupil tends to learn only in terms of his active interest and participation.

22. When teaching a new topic, the teacher should   22. ...
    A. make sure that all homework difficulties have been corrected before teaching the new material
    B. allow sufficient time for a full presentation of the new material
    C. teach the new material before any discussion of the homework
    D. warn pupils that they will be tested on the new material the next day

23. In a comparison of the developmental and lecture methods   23. ...
    of teaching, which one of the following statements is *most nearly* CORRECT?
    A. In the lecture method, the teacher readily checks the progress of learning.
    B. There is greater pupil participation in the developmental method.
    C. Greater pupil attention is insured in the lecture method.
    D. There is less need for review at the beginning of a developmental lesson.

24. A benefit resulting from the introduction of numbers in   24. ...
    other bases than 10 into the curriculum of junior high school mathematics is that
    A. this results in better understanding of the number system in base 10
    B. there is a better basis for problem solving
    C. computation is simpler with numbers in bases other than 10
    D. fewer digits are required for numbers in bases other than 10

25. Of the following, the statement concerning deductive   25. ...
    proofs which is CORRECT is that they
    A. have no place in the junior high school mathematics curriculum
    B. help junior high school pupils to understand and to appreciate the sequential nature of mathematics
    C. can be used only in geometry
    D. should not be used before a pupil reaches the 9th grade

TEST 5

DIRECTIONS: In each of the following questions there is a pair of numbered sentences. Each pair is followed by four lettered choices. Select the choice which indicates your judgment concerning the accuracy of the information contained in each of the pairs.

1. I. One important aspect of good mental health is free-   1. ...
      dom from anxiety and tension.
   II. Intelligence test ratings are not an indication of
       the person's full potential for solving life's problems.
       A. Both I and II are correct   --
       B. Both I and II are incorrect
       C. I is correct; II is incorrect
       D. I is incorrect; II is correct

2. I. A valid and reliable group test, if well administered, 2. ...
      may still result in some individual scores which are
      misleading.
   II. Gestalt psychology maintains that context plays an
       important part in determining what we perceive.
       A. Both I and II are correct
       B. Both I and II are incorrect
       C. I is correct; II is incorrect
       D. I is incorrect; II is correct

3. I. A longitudinal study is one in which the same children 3. ...
      are measured or evaluated over a period of years.
   II. THE JOURNAL OF THE NEA and SEVENTEEN are both periodi-
       cals dealing with educational matters for the most part.
       A. Both I and II are correct
       B. Both I and II are incorrect
       C. I is correct; II is incorrect
       D. I is incorrect; II is correct

4. I. Children should never leave their seats without the   4. ...
      permission of the teacher.
   II. It is often advisable for the teacher to repeat a
       correct answer so that the entire class will hear
       it clearly.
       A. Both I and II are correct
       B. Both I and II are incorrect
       C. I is correct; II is incorrect
       D. I is incorrect; II is correct

5. I. Children's experiences outside of the school become   5. ...
      part of the curriculum if they are used by the school
      to further the aims of its program.
   II. If the teacher plans carefully and effectively at home,
       the necessity for pupil-teacher planning in the class-
       room is considerably lessened.
       A. Both I and II are correct
       B. Both I and II are incorrect
       C. I is correct; II is incorrect
       D. I is incorrect; II is correct

6. I. It is wise for a teacher to let no act of misbehavior   6. ...
      go unpunished.
   II. A teacher can help reduce juvenile delinquency by hold-
       ing all her pupils to rigid standards of achievement.
       A. Both I and II are correct
       B. Both I and II are incorrect
       C. I is correct; II is incorrect
       D. I is incorrect; II is correct

7. I. There are times when a teacher should deal with behav- 7. ...
      ior itself rather than with the causes of that behavior.
   II. A normal child is made to feel more secure by the
       knowledge that there are limits to what he is permitted

14

to do, and that his parents and teachers will consistently hold to these limits.
   A. Both I and II are correct
   B. Both I and II are incorrect
   C. I is correct; II is incorrect
   D. I is incorrect; II is correct

8. I. Prejudices and antagonistic attitudes toward groups other than one's own are the results of learning experiences.
   II. It is wise to deliberately expose a child to frustrations early in life, to enable him to learn by experience how to cope with frustrations.
   A. Both I and II are correct
   B. Both I and II are incorrect
   C. I is correct; II is incorrect
   D. I is incorrect; II is correct

   8. ...

9. I. A teacher tends to lose standing in the eyes of pupils if she admits not knowing an answer to a question asked by them.
   II. A friendly, personal relationship between pupil and teacher is essential for some important learning outcomes.
   A. Both I and II are correct
   B. Both I and II are incorrect
   C. I is correct; II is incorrect
   D. I is incorrect; II is correct

   9. ...

10. I. A teacher who genuinely loves her pupils and who shows this love to them will, therefore, rarely have discipline problems.
   II. A teacher can develop good relationships with the children in her class if she leads the children to look upon her as their "pal."
   A. Both I and II are correct
   B. Both I and II are incorrect
   C. I is correct; II is incorrect
   D. I is incorrect; II is correct

   10. ...

11. I. The current major function of evaluation by a teacher is to determine which children should repeat a grade, which should be normally promoted, and which accelerated.
   II. Evaluation by children should be encouraged but limited to their own work and to the work of their classmates.
   A. Both I and II are correct
   B. Both I and II are incorrect
   C. I is correct; II is incorrect
   D. I is incorrect; II is correct

   11. ...

12. I. The setting up of classroom routines should be initiated by a teacher on the first day of the term even though she does not yet know her children.
   II. A school system may actually contribute to social-class differences in the community by virtue of the fact that it often groups together children of similar social status.
   A. Both I and II are correct
   B. Both I and II are incorrect
   C. I is correct; II is incorrect
   D. I is incorrect; II is correct

   12. ...

13.   I. Some skills taught in elementary school mathematics   13. ...
             are so difficult that it is best to teach them by
             rote drill, avoiding the time-consuming attempt to
             rationalize them.
    II. Highly organized athletic competitions, such as inter-
             scholastic tournaments and little league games, are
             appropriate sports activities for children of elemen-
             tary school age.
     A. Both I and II are correct
     B. Both I and II are incorrect
     C. I is correct; II is incorrect
     D. I is incorrect; II is correct

14.   I. Children should be permitted to experiment with   14. ...
             various art media without step-by-step direction by
             adults.
    II. Having the children in a class take turns at being
             committee chairmen in connection with social studies
             units is very useful in promoting democratic living.
     A. Both I and II are correct
     B. Both I and II are incorrect
     C. I is correct; II is incorrect
     D. I is incorrect; II is correct

15.   I. If the parents of a maladjusted child refuse to co-   15. ...
             operate with the teacher, there is relatively little
             the teacher can do to help the child adjust.
    II. A knowledge of the goals and objectives of the public
             school system, as a whole, are of little use to a
             teacher in that system, concerned with planning her
             daily teaching activities.
     A. Both I and II are correct
     B. Both I and II are incorrect
     C. I is correct; II is incorrect
     D. I is incorrect; II is correct

KEYS (CORRECT ANSWERS)

TEST 1				TEST 2				TEST 3				TEST 4				TEST 5	
1.	D	11.	A	1.	C	11.	A	1.	A	11.	C	1.	A	11.	D	1.	D
2.	A	12.	C	2.	B	12.	D	2.	A	12.	D	2.	D	12.	C	2.	A
3.	C	13.	B	3.	B	13.	B	3.	A	13.	C	3.	A	13.	C	3.	C
4.	B	14.	B	4.	A	14.	B	4.	A	14.	D	4.	C	14.	C	4.	B
5.	C	15.	B	5.	D	15.	D	5.	A	15.	D	5.	D	15.	D	5.	C
6.	B	16.	A	6.	B	16.	A	6.	B	16.	A	6.	C	16.	B	6.	B
7.	D	17.	D	7.	B	17.	A	7.	B	17.	A	7.	D	17.	A	7.	A
8.	A	18.	B	8.	C	18.	D	8.	A	18.	C	8.	D	18.	D	8.	C
9.	B	19.	D	9.	B	19.	A	9.	C	19.	A	9.	A	19.	D	9.	D
10.	C	20.	D	10.	D	20.	D	10.	B	20.	C	10.	A	20.	B	10.	B
	21.	D			21.	C			21.	B			21.	B		11.	B
	22.	C			22.	B			22.	C			22.	B		12.	A
	23.	D			23.	C			23.	B			23.	B		13.	B
	24.	D			24.	D			24.	B			24.	A		14.	C
	25.	A			25.	C			25.	D			25.	B		15.	B

EXAMINATION SECTION

TEST 1

1. The degree to which a test measures what it is supposed to measure is called its   1.___
   A. validity
   B. coefficient of correlation
   C. objectivity
   D. reliability

2. Of the following audio-visual aids, the one that represents a *MOST* recent innovation in teaching is   2.___
   A. single topic films
   B. film strips
   C. 2 x 2 inch colored slides
   D. 16 mm sound films

3. Of the following reasons for using charts as a teaching device in the classroom, the *MOST* desirable one is the   3.___
   A. ease with which large numbers of charts can be stored
   B. ability to use color for both functional and decorative effect
   C. ability to include many details about a topic on one chart
   D. ease with which they can be followed in a class discussion

4. Of the following techniques employed in questioning, the one that probably has the *LEAST* value for conceptual learning would be questions of a type that are   4.___
   A. varied in difficulty and directed to appropriate pupils
   B. rapid-fire and call for monosyllabic responses
   C. pivotal in nature and call for analysis
   D. questions of pupils that are directed back to other pupils by the teacher

5. Of the following reasons for including essay questions in an examination, the one that is probably *MOST* important is that this type of question   5.___
   A. provides greater coverage of material than other test items
   B. is easier to formulate than good objective type questions
   C. provides opportunities for subjective evaluation of answers
   D. provides for pupil expression in an organized manner and in depth

6. Of the following practices for helping a beginning teacher   6.___
in the classroom, the *BEST* would probably be to
   A. have informal discussions with colleagues at
     opportune times
   B. continue taking courses at the local colleges
   C. follow a planned program of intervisitation
   D. attend departmental conferences devoted to pedagogy

7. Of the following reasons for using, at times, a laser disc   7.___
movie projector rather than a 16 mm movie projector, the one
reason that is *INCORRECT* is that it(s)
   A. is faster to load and unload film
   B. can be used in a more flexible manner
   C. can be used without darkening the room
   D. sound track can produce sound of higher fidelity

8. Of the following practices for training students to give   8.___
reports in class, the one that is *LEAST* recommended is to
   A. insist that they read them
   B. limit their reports to a stated time
   C. encourage them to use simple illustrations
   D. permit reference to notes during a presentation

9. Of the following reasons for experimenting with team teaching   9.___
methods, the one that is probably *MOST* valid from an
educational point of view is that it
   A. would help meet the problem of teacher shortages
   B. would provide overburdened teachers with more free
     time
   C. makes provision for flexible scheduling and independent
     study by pupils
   D. can easily be incorporated into old as well as new
     school plants

10. In considering the roles of a home room teacher, the one of   10.___
the following which would probably be considered *LEAST* important
from an educational viewpoint is to
   A. give guidance since the school has licensed guidance
     counselors
   B. keep accurate and up-to-date school records for students
   C. provide a program of tutorial assistance for students
     that need help
   D. maintain firm discipline while routine school matters
     are being handled

11. Of the following practices followed by teachers in doing pro-   11.___
ject work, the one that probably has the *LEAST* merit is to
   A. require that every student submit an individual project
   B. display class projects in a science fair held in the
     school
   C. encourage students to work in committees on group
     projects
   D. provide opportunity for pupils to discuss their work on
     school time

12. If a teacher wanted to prepare seventy copies of a five   12.___
    page test for two of his classes, he would probably find
    that the machine which was *MOST* practical for this purpose
    is a(n)
    A. polygraph   B. offset   C. web press   D. xerox

13. Of the following, the one who is a Harvard psychologist   13.___
    and author of THE PROCESS OF EDUCATION and TOWARD A THEORY
    OF INSTRUCTION is
    A. James Conant   B. Jerome S. Bruner
    C. John H. Fischer   D. H. Bentley Glass

14. Of the following types of objective questions, the one that 14.___
    is considered *MOST* flexible and statistically reliable is
    the
    A. modified true-false   B. matching
    B. completion   D. multiple choice

15. Of the following, probably the *LEAST* valuable way to begin 15.___
    a new topic or lesson is for the teacher to
    A. distribute a step-by-step outline of the topics
       or lesson
    B. explore some interest already possessed by the subject
    C. elicit an explanation of the importance of the subject
    D. develop an overview of the subject

16. Motivation for a lesson is *BEST* when it   16.___
    A. makes a sharp transition from the previous lesson
    B. is dramatic
    C. raises a question that poses a problem for the
       class
    D. is succinct

17. In administering the IOWA TESTS OF EDUCATIONAL DEVELOPMENT,   17.___
    the one factor among the following that is *NOT* a primary
    aim is to·
    A. identify the intellectually gifted
    B. show parents the fixed limitations of their children
    C. serve as backgrounds for conferences between parents
       and counselors
    D. select students for remedial classes

18. The teacher might curtail continued and disturbing conversa- 18.___
    tions during a recitation by doing all of the following
    EXCEPT
    A. walking around the room, making it a point to stand
       near potential talkers
    B. separating friends who encourage misbehavior in one
       another
    C. singling out the talkers and publicly admonishing and
       embarrassing them
    D. drawing the talkers into the group activity without a
       special reprimand

19. Of the following, the *BEST* reason for the assignment of suitable homework is that it provides

    A. each parent with an opportunity to learn what her child is learning

    B. all the necessary follow-up drill for teaching

    C. practice in reading skills

    D. further opportunities for application of skills or concepts taught

19.___

20. Of the following, the one statement that is *GENERALLY* true of the bright pupil is that he

    A. works up to his capacity

    B. is generally better in reading than in mathematics

    C. is more likely to succeed in his social relationships

    D. is quick to form associations between words and ideas

20.___

———

KEY (CORRECT ANSWERS)

1.	A	11.	A
2.	A	12.	D
3.	D	13.	B
4.	B	14.	D
5.	D	15.	A
6.	C	16.	C
7.	C	17.	B
8.	A	18.	C
9.	C	19.	D
10.	D	20.	D

———

TEST 2

DIRECTIONS: Each question or incomplete statement is followed by several suggested answers or completions. Select the one that *BEST* answers the question or completes the statement. *PRINT THE LETTER OF THE CORRECT ANSWER IN THE SPACE AT THE RIGHT.*

1. Which one of the following questions asked by a teacher is *MOST* acceptable?
   A. "The answer to question 5 is what?"
   B. "Mary, is her answer to question 5 right?"
   C. "What is your answer to question 5, George?"
   D. "Class, tell George the answer to question 5!"

   1.___

2. The technique of using a team teaching design which includes a master teacher, regular teachers and teacher-aides is based *MOST* directly upon which one of the following concepts?
   A. Teachers who have served faithfully deserve master teacher status.
   B. Teaching is a complex art requiring different levels of competence and training.
   C. The conservation of public funds is a moral obligation.
   D. Teacher-aides are often more knowledgeable and skillful than teachers.

   2.___

3. In conducting a developmental lesson, the usually *MOST* desirable way, among the following, of responding to a student's correct answer to your question is to
   A. enter a grade in your record book
   B. Call on another pupil to answer the same question
   C. follow up with another question
   D. elaborate on the pupil answer

   3.___

4. Which one of the following procedures is *MOST* acceptable to use in class when several pupils make flagrant errors in grammar and usage?
   A. Correct the students unobtrusively and proceed with your lesson.
   B. Take a few minutes to explain since every teacher is a teacher of English.
   C. Ignore the errors since such deviations are time-consuming and interfere with covering the required course of study.
   D. Write a note to each pupil's English teacher to inform him of the errors.

   4.___

5. When a parent complains to you that you are underrating her
   son, the *BEST* procedure, among the following, for you to
   follow is to
   A. tell the parent that you alone have the moral and legal
      responsibility for assigning the marks
   B. refer the parent to the principal
   C. agree to raise the grades in the future
   D. explain the grading system and review the pupil's
      grades with the parent

5.___

6. Which one of the following statements would *BEST* describe
   procedures of note-taking in a class of slow learners?
   A. They should have few or no notes at all, since they
      have limited verbal ability.
   B. Mimeographed notes should be given to them, since note-taking
      is frustrating for them.
   C. Notes, of a simple kind, should be developed cooperatively
      by pupils and teacher
   D. A few short notes should be copied directly from the
      text-book to insure accuracy and reinforce reading skills.

6.___

7. In the AMERICAN HIGH SCHOOL TODAY, James B. Conant proposes
   that
   A. the four-year high school should be a comprehensive high
      school
   B. the present curriculum in the fourth year of high school
      is more appropriate for a *community junior college*
   C. *social living* courses should be added in all high
      schools to provide better life adjustment in our atomic
      era
   D. standardized achievement tests, such as state Regents,
      have outlived their usefulness

7.___

8. The *SIMPLEST* way, among the following, to exhibit a newspaper
   clipping to an entire class at one time is to
   A. make a slide for a slide projector
   B. make a highly enlarged photostat
   C. use the overhead projector
   D. use an opaque projector

8.___

9. Of the following, which combination of activities is *LEAST*
   suitable as a homework assignment in preparation for a full-
   period test?
   A. "Study and review all work since (date)."
   B. "Skim through chapters 16 and 17. Study your class
      notes since (date). Review your homework since (date)."
   C. Re-read chapters 16 and 17. Look over the questions at
      the end of each chapter."
   D. "Review all class notes and homework since (date). Do the
      practice mimeo test distributed today."

9.___

10. In selecting the aim for a developmental lesson, the   10.___
    MOST important among the following considerations is the
    A. content of the previous day's lesson
    B. motivation to be used
    C. decision as to which knowledges, attitudes, or skills
       should be taught next
    D. content of the syllabus

11. The validity of intelligence tests as instruments for   11.___
    evaluating native ability has been questioned because
    these tests tend to
    A. lack reliability, especially for gifted children
    B. lack reliability, especially for pupils of low
       motor coordination who consequently have a poor
       sense of spatial relations
    C. place too much emphasis on mathematical and
       scientific aptitude
    D. have an experiential base which is foreign to
       culturally different children in poverty areas

12. Of the following, the major aim for giving a standardized   12.___
    test to classes at the beginning of a new course is
    PROBABLY to
    A. discover weaknesses of previous teaching
    B. discover interests, aptitudes and previous
       learnings in this area
    C. give teachers and supervisors a basis for deciding
       upon the regrouping of classes in terms of ability
    D. arouse pupil curiosity and provide a base for
       motivation

13. Of the following terms, the one *MOST* closely associated   13.___
    with the sum-total of response patterns and abilities
    possessed by the learner at any given time is
    A. adaptation   B. readiness   C. reinforcement   D. response

14. If 48% of your class failed a Unit test, the *BEST* procedure   14.___
    to follow is to
    A. develop a normal curve on a graph and adjust the grades
    B. ask your Chairman to evaluate your test; if he agrees
       it is fair, re-teach parts of the unit, then review and
       give a new test
    C. chastise the failing pupils sternly and write notes to
       the parents, if your Chairman agrees your test is fair
    D. give an *extra-credit* test to the failing pupils to
       raise their grades

15. Of the following reasons for giving homework, the *LEAST*   15.___
    acceptable reason is that it
    A. extends the learning process beyond the classroom
    B. provides practice in the art of self-study
    C. increases the chances of retentivity
    D. trains the pupils in habits of doing hard work

16. Which one of the following sets of statements *BEST*   16.___
    explains the occurrence of disciplinary infractions among
    adolescents in secondary schools?
    A. Adolescents tend to resist authority; they seek
       the admiration of their peers; they are not convinced
       that poor self-control is necessarily harmful to
       future success.
    B. Syllabi are teacher-imposed; rules of conduct in
       secondary schools are unrealistic.
    C. Adolescents undergo rapid physical growth; their
       span of attention is short; they are incapable of
       abstract thoughts.
    D. Adolescence has been extended by modern society;
       there is a widespread lack of pre-vocational
       meaningful study.

17. If you are appointed in mid-year and are assigned a class   17.___
    which has fallen hopelessly behind the time schedule for
    the course of study in your department, which one of the
    following procedures would probably be *MOST* acceptable?
    A. With the aid of your Chairman, re-plan the balance
       of the schedule to include the most vital topics.
    B. Speed up your teaching each period; double the
       assignments; omit audio-visual aids; reduce the
       number of tests.
    C. With the aid of your Chairman, develop copious mimeo-
       graphed notes for pupils to study at home; test pupils;
       catch up as you go.
    D. Proceed at your usual pace; inform your Chairman;
       explain that these pupils are getting excellent training
       on fewer topics and will fare better even though you
       will not be able to go through the whole course of
       study.

18. Of the following, the main reasons why psychologists warn   18.___
    against over-emphasis of the *rewards and punishment*
    motivation in teaching is that this type of motivation
    A. ignores the more effective stimulus of inner
       satisfaction
    B. inevitably leads to a listless class atmosphere
    C. has little or no influence with the bright child
    D. often leads by easy stages to corporal punishment

19. Pragmatism as an educational philosophy was stressed by   19.___
    A. Dewey   B. Terman   C. Binet   D. Pestalozzi

20. A boy has scored 57% on a test in a modified (slow) class.   20.___
    Which one of the following comments by the teacher is *MOST*
    likely to stimulate him towards sustained scholastic improve-
    ment?
    A. Why didn't you study harder?
    B. Some of your answers showed very good understanding.
    C. You will have to work much harder to get out of the
       slow class.
    D. I had hoped that you would prove that we had been
       wrong in putting you into the slow class.

21. Of the following, the *MOST* acceptable measure for encouraging students to speak loudly enough for the class to hear is to
    A. call only upon those students who speak loudly enough to be heard
    B. have students stand up and face the class whenever they are called upon for an answer
    C. use a demerit system for prodding all students to talk in audible tones
    D. stop any student who is speaking too quietly and have him begin again but in a louder voice.

21.___

22. Of the following, the *BEST* way to start a class promptly is to
    A. have one row put the homework on the board
    B. put a class problem on the board
    C. have a monitor put the homework assignment for the next day on the board, while the rest of the class copies it
    D. take class attendance

22.___

23. Which one of the following statements concerning the aim of a lesson is *MOST* valid?
    A. The teacher should write the aim on the blackboard at the beginning of each lesson.
    B. The aim should be an outgrowth of and developed from the motivation.
    C. Each child should write the aim of each lesson in his notebook each day.
    D. The teacher should announce the aim of the lesson to the class at the beginning of each period.

23.___

24. If the class you inherit from another teacher is poorly motivated, and many of the students talk to one another during lessons, you should *NOT*
    A. teach carefully planned lessons daily for those who listen and try to ignore the others
    B. look up records of each member of the class and consult the guidance counselor where appropriate
    C. plan lessons in which students change activity every 15 minutes from written work to oral work to reading, etc.
    D. reaarange the seating, so that groups who talk to one another are separated as far as possible

24.___

25. Among the following, the *MOST* obvious fact that faces the teacher of a 9th grade class is that
    A. the future doctors, chemists, engineers and nurses can be accurately identified
    B. the boys are generally more talented in science and math than the girls
    C. the girls are generally more mature than the boys
    D. the girls prefer the biological aspects of science, while the boys prefer the physical aspects of science and mathematics

25.___

———

KEY (CORRECT ANSWERS)

1. C		11. D
2. B		12. B
3. C		13. B
4. A		14. B
5. D		15. D
6. C		16. A
7. A		17. A
8. D		18. A
9. A		19. A
10. C		20. B

21. D
22. B
23. B
24. A
25. C

———

TEST 3

DIRECTIONS: Each question or incomplete statement is followed by several suggested answers or completions. Select the one that *BEST* answers the question or completes the statement. *PRINT THE LETTER OF THE CORRECT ANSWER IN THE SPACE AT THE RIGHT.*

1. Of the following, the one statement that is *GENERALLY* true of the slow learner is that he is
   A. slow in forming associations between words and ideas
   B. poor in reading but good in arithmetic
   C. more likely to develop into a delinquent
   D. in respect to the general population, at or about the 90th percentile in mechanical ability

   1.___

2. In day to day practice, the *BEST* procedure for handling medial summaries of a lesson is that they be
   A. stated briefly by the teacher
   B. developed into blackboard outlines
   C. elicited from students
   D. be given at the middle of the lesson

   2.___

3. Of the following, probably the *BEST* way for the teacher to determine the true ability of a student is to
   A. consult frankly with his parents
   B. use a carefully standardized group intelligence test with age-grade equivalents
   C. review his records, observe him very carefully and analyze his performance
   D. gain the confidence of a physician who has served the family for years

   3.___

4. Of the following, the *BEST* basis for determining students' grades is usually
   A. tests only
   B. tests, homework, and class participation
   C. tests, homework, class participation, and conduct
   D. tests and class participation

   4.___

5. Of the following, the one *MOST* characteristic of the normally developing adolescent is
   A. continuous need for parental support
   B. development of emotional maturity
   C. desire for constant approval by siblings
   D. freedom from peer group identification

   5.___

6. Assuming that a student asks a question which the
teacher cannot immediately answer, the *BEST* way, among
the following, for the teacher to handle the situation is
to
   A. attempt to answer the question anyway
   B. admit he does not know and have the answer looked up
      and reported to the class at the same or next lesson
   C. state that the question will be answered at a future
      time
   D. accept the answer of a student who seems to know

7. Of the following, the *LEAST* effective method for obtaining
pupil participation is to
   A. permit pupils to answer in concert
   B. permit pupils to evaluate each other's answers
   C. permit pupils to help develop the wording of the aim
      of the lesson
   D. use the experiences of pupils in the lesson development

8. Of the following, the record data *MOST* likely to indicate a
slow learner would show that the pupil has
   A. repeated failure in mathematics
   B. a mental age considerably higher than the chronological
      age
   C. reading achievement at the 20th percentile
   D. been an only child of divorced parents

9. Group morale will be higher, as a rule, in classes that
are run in which one of the following patterns?
   A. Democratic   B. Laissez-faire
   C. Authoritarian   D. Individual

10. Of the following, the *LEAST* desirable procedure for the assign-
ment of project work is that it should
   A. be requested by the student
   B. provide for teacher conferences with pupils
   C. be given only to superior or gifted students
   D. be a substitute for the daily requirements of the
      course

11. The *LEAST* acceptable of the following procedures for using
test scores on teacher-made periodic tests is to
   A. prepare a chart or graph so that each pupil's marks are
      posted on the bulletin board
   B. train each pupil to keep an individual test score graph
      in his own notebook
   C. mount only perfect papers on the bulletin boards
   D. train each pupil to keep a folder of his own corrected
      test papers

6.   7.   8.   9.   10.   11.

12. Of the following, the *BEST* reason for parent-teacher   12.___
    interviews is so that the teacher
    A. is enabled to communicate the importance of homework
    B. and the parent share the task of motivating the student
    C. is enabled to advise the parent about the child's needs
    D. is enabled to tell the parent about the child's strength

13. A good motivation for a class in junior high school is   13.___
    always intended to accomplish all of the following *EXCEPT*
    A. develop a sustained drive
    B. create the feeling of an unsolved problem
    C. communicate the information basic to the lesson
       to be taught
    D. develop around needs of the adolescent

14. Which one of the following approaches to the teaching of   14.___
    democratic attitudes is the *LEAST* effective?
    A. Attitudes should be caught rather than taught
    B. The learner should identify himself with outstanding
       democratic leaders
    C. Direct teaching of moral values will be most productive
    D. Experiences in democratic living will develop proper
       democratic attitudes

15. Which one of the following basic suggestions should one   15.___
    carry out first to establish good class management?
    A. Train the class in distribution of material
    B. Discuss the aims of the year's work
    C. Take out a seating plan
    D. Discuss the required rules for proper class behavior

    ____

KEY (CORRECT ANSWERS)

1. A	6. B	11. A
2. C	7. A	12. B
3. C	8. C	13. C
4. B	9. A	14. C
5. B	10. C	15. D

____

TEST 4

DIRECTIONS: Each question or incomplete statement is followed by several suggested answers or completions. Select the one that *BEST* answers the question or completes the statement. *PRINT THE LETTER OF THE CORRECT ANSWER IN THE SPACE AT THE RIGHT*

1. Of the following, the *MOST* important element in a problem   1.___
   situation, in terms of the pupil's learning, is that
   A. the pupil must feel a need or desire to find a solution
   B. the problem situation must come from the experiences
      of the pupil
   C. there should not be a barrier between the pupil and
      the solution
   D. the problem should be clear cut and be solvable in
      only one way

2. Which one of the following is generally a sound principle of   2.___
   questioning for the teacher to follow?
   A. Speak very loudly to make sure all the pupils hear you,
      especially those who are inattentive.
   B. Repeat pupils' answers to make sure all pupils have heard
      them.
   C. Distribute questions widely so that all or nearly all
      pupils have a chance to participate.
   D. Encourage chorus responses so that the teacher will know
      how many pupils know the answer.

3. A good junior high school lesson will frequently employ   3.___
   which one of the following as its initial phase?
   A. Detailed correction of all parts of the previous night's
      homework.
   B. Explanation of a new kind of problem by the teacher
   C. Warm-up drill for pupils
   D. Discussing problems

4. Which one of the following descriptions of routines is   4.___
   LEAST indicative of good classroom management?
   A. Initiating distribution of paper by pupil monitor's
      placing a pile on first desk of each row.
   B. Adjusting of windows and shades by a pupil monitor.
   C. Placing a sampling of homework examples on chalk board
      for correction and discussion.
   D. Having students choose seats and then preparing a seating
      plan for each class.

5. Which one of the following is a *CORRECT* statement concerning   5.___
   the administration of a pre-test? It
   A. unnecessarily consumes time to acquire information more
      readily discovered by the teacher by informal means
   B. should be confined to the beginning of the school year
      for the entire grade
   C. dispenses with the need for review
   D. serves in part as a survey of individual and class
      background and readiness

6. Which one of the following is an *INCORRECT* procedure in con-   6.___
   structing a multiple-choice, short-answer test for a junior
   high school class?
   A. Providing a separate answer sheet, particularly for a
      long test
   B. Placing a number of easy questions at the beginning of
      the test
   C. Insuring that correct choices are not obvious
   D. Arranging correct answers according to a pattern

7. Which one of the following is generally the *LEAST* effective   7.___
   method of informing pupils of homework assignments?
   A. Dictation of assignments by teacher
   B. Distribution of duplicated assignment sheets
   C. Recording on chalk board by the teacher before period
      begins
   D. Recording on chalk board by pupil secretary at the
      beginning of lesson

8. Of the following, the *BEST* technique in following up homework   8.___
   is:
   A. The homework should be marked as a test daily
   B. Several students should place their homework on the chalk
      board daily
   C. Very little, if any, class time should be consumed in
      going over homework
   D. Only those exercises and problems with which pupils have
      difficulty should normally be explained

9. Which one of the following is the *LEAST* valid method of   9.___
   evaluating a pupil's understanding and readiness for advanced
   work?
   A. Asking the parent how long the pupil takes to do homework
      assignments
   B. Observing the pupil as he works on practice material in
      class
   C. Listening to the pupil's explanation of how he arrived at
      an answer
   D. Analyzing the pupil's test papers

10. When a parent keeps an appointment to visit a teacher to   10.
complain about the progress of her child, the teacher may
properly do which one of the following?
    A. Tell the parent that many children in the class are
failing
    B. Ask the parent whether she has carefully supervised
her child's homework
    C. Be fully prepared for the interview by carefully studying
the pupil's complete school record
    D. Point out that the pupil was probably not held to a high
standard in previous grades

11. Which one of the following is usually a pedagogically *UNSOUND*   11.
procedure in utilizing a filmstrip with a junior high school
class?
    A. Including a follow-up related to the filmstrip in the
home study assignment
    B. Employing the filmstrip as a review device
    C. Having pupils read and explain the captions
    D. Showing a complete filmstrip of 47 frames in one
period

12. Of the following possible techniques for use in connection with   12.
audio-visual aids, the *BEST* is for the
    A. students to take notes during the showing of a film
    B. teacher to explain the film during its showing
    C. teacher to make auxiliary use of the chalk board during
the showing of the film
    D. class to observe the film without interruption and be
questioned about it thereafter

13. Of the following, which one represents the *LEAST* effective   13.
disciplinary technique?
    A. Compelling pupils under threat of punishment to observe
class rules
    B. Helping pupils to enjoy classwork through the use of
meaningful activities
    C. Providing wide participation for all pupils in the work
and administration of the class
    D. Discouraging lateness to class by starting each period
with an interesting activity

14. Which one of the following is a good practical procedure for a   14.
teacher to utilize in maintaining discipline?
    A. Learn names of all pupils as quickly as possible at
beginning of year
    B. Disregard most minor infractions to avoid magnifying
their importance
    C. Prepare a list designating punishments for various in-
fractions and enforce it rigidly
    D. Avoid displaying a sense of humor during the first few
weeks of the term

15. The ratio between the measure of the pupil's actual mental
    maturity and that which is normal for one of his chronological
    age is known as the pupil's
    A. E.Q.   B. I.Q.   C. A.Q.   D. M.A.

15.___

KEY (CORRECT ANSWERS)

1. A	6. D	11. D
2. C	7. A	12. D
3. C	8. D	13. A
4. B	9. A	14. A
5. D	10. C	15. B

TEST 5

DIRECTIONS: Each question or incomplete statement is followed
              by several suggested answers or completions.   Select
              the one that *BEST* answers the question or completes
              the statement. *PRINT THE LETTER OF THE CORRECT
              ANSWER IN THE SPACE AT THE RIGHT.*

1. Maintenance drills should be given   1.___
       A. to all pupils
       B. only to pupils studying algebra
       C. only to pupils who need remedial arithmetic
       D. only to pupils in the general mathematics classes

2. Which one of the following statements concerning skills   2.___
    and drills is *NOT* true?
       A. To maintain skills in mathematics, it is necessary
          to provide distributed practice of a variety of
          processes.
       B. Traditionally, *drill* has meant the routine application
          of the law of *exercise*, whereas *practice* involves
          repetition in a variety of situations.
       C. Suitable provision must be made for helping the learner
          to be aware of his own progress.
       D. All pupils in a class should be given the same drill
          in a given skill.

3. Of the following, the statement which is *NOT* descriptive of a 3.___
    characteristic of a good drill is that
       A. the exercises are graded
       B. understanding precedes the drill
       C. complex processes are emphasized
       D. the drill is addressed to pupil weaknesses

4. Tests should be given   4.___
       A. daily   B. at the completion of a unit
       C. without previous notice D. weekly

5. Of the following procedures, select the one which teachers   5.___
    should *NOT* use after having given the class a test in 9th
    year general mathematics:
       A. Return the marked test papers to all pupils
       B. Allow pupils to check and to discuss the test
       C. Note common errors which will be the basis of future
          lessons
       D. Drill the entire class on every error made by any student

6. Standardized group tests are used more frequently than   6.___
   individual tests because
       A. the same amount of time is needed to test a whole class by a
          grouped approach as a single pupil by an individual approach
       B. group tests give better results than individual tests
       C. group tests have primary, intermediate and advanced
          forms whereas individual tests have only one form
       D. no training is needed to administer a group test

7. Of the following statements about marks, the one which is   7.___
   NOT correct is:
       A. Excessive emphasis on marks may cause the pupil
          to consider the mark more important than the material
          to be learned.
       B. The pupil may rely too heavily on mere memory in
          order to get high marks.
       C. Occasionally, overemphasis on marks may lead to cheating.
       D. Marks based solely on written tests give a valid
          measure of a pupil's achievement, because they are always
          objective.

8. Standardized achievement tests are characterized by all of the   8.___
   following principles *EXCEPT* they
       A. often show differing results, depending upon the
          particular from of the test used
       B. are administered in accordance with uniform pro-
          cedures indicated in the manual of instructions
       C. have norms for grade or age
       D. are scored in accordance with standard procedures
          indicated in the manual of instructions

9. Of the following, the *PRIME* purpose of grouping pupils   9.___
   in a mathematics class is to
       A. develop social attitudes
       B. separate unruly pupils
       C. provide the teacher with a smaller range of pupil
          ability or disability
       D. help solve book shortages

10. Of these statements concerning grouping, select the one which   10.___
    is *CONTRARY* to present day thinking:
       A. In a math class, grouping enables the teacher to meet
          individual differences.
       B. Results of inventory tests may be used as one of
          the bases for forming groups.
       C. Teachers should avoid attaching any status value to
          groups.
       D. Once in a group, a pupil should be kept there for the
          rest of the year.

11. Of the following statements about slow pupils, the one which   11.___
    is *MOST NEARLY CORRECT* is that they
    A. are always unruly
    B. should be given plenty of busy work
    C. usually have a short attention span
    D. should seldom be given homework

12. Of these statements concerning the use of the overhead   12.___
    projector, which one is *NOT* true? It
    A. may not be used with a page of the textbook
    B. enables the teacher to observe the class reaction
    C. may be used with transparencies and with overlays
    D. requires an additional person to operate it

13. Of these statements concerning the use of audio-visual aids,   13.___
    which one is *NOT* true?
    A. Students are helped to learn faster.
    B. They help students to gain more accurate information.
    C. They help students to perceive and understand
       meanings.
    D. They substitute for, rather than supplement, instruc-
       tional techniques.

14. Homework should be assigned regularly in the junior high   14.___
    school because, among other values,
    A. doing homework aids in the development of more independent
       study habits
    B. survey results indicate that pupil progress is propor-
       tional to the amount of homework assigned
    C. homework keeps pupils out of mischief at home
    D. it is traditional to assign homework, and parents
       demand it

15. In planning a homework assignment, the teacher should observe   15.___
    which one of the following principles?
    The assignment should
    A. review material previously taught as well as material
       taught on the day that the assignment was given
    B. be limited to material taught on the day that the
       assignment was given
    C. not include any material taught on the day the assignment
       was given
    D. be done only by those pupils who have not fallen so far
       behind that they cannot profit from doing the assignment

16. The *BEST* homework assignment to assist junior high school   16.___
    pupils to prepare for a test is which one of the following?
    To
    A. tell them to study for a test
    B. give them a set of problems identical to those that will
       appear on the test
    C. tell them to prepare a set of questions they think should
       appear on the test
    D. tell them the scope of the test and to assign specific
       study references and specific practice material covering
       the scope

17. Which one of the following statements is *CONTRARY* to present thinking?   17.___
    A. Most teachers regard homework as important
    B. Experimental evidence is not clearly convincing that homework is truly important .
    C. The voluntary type of assignment in which the pupil does whatever he thinks is necessary is the solution to the homework dilemma
    D. Many parents think homework is helpful.

18. Which of the following is the *BEST* approach to the use of the textbook by a teacher?   18.___
    A. Only as a source of practice exercises
    B. Primarily as a source of problems to be placed on tests
    C. To assist pupils in learning how to read explanations of new concepts and techniques.
    D. Primarily for review

19. Of the following, the *LEAST* proper use of the textbook is as   19.___
    A. a quick view of things to be learned
    B. a minimum for which pupils may be held responsible
    C. the course of study
    D. a reference for pictures, maps, graphs, tables

20. Of the following statements concerning questioning, which one is *NOT* consistent with current thinking?   20.___
    A. Some questions, though perfect in form, may challenge only a limited number of pupils
    B. Vague and incomplete questions tend to confuse pupils
    C. *Chorus* answers do not afford all pupils an opportunity to think
    D. Questions starting with *why* and *how* should generally be avoided.

_____

KEY (CORRECT ANSWERS)

1.	A	11.	C
2.	D	12.	D
3.	C	13.	D
4.	B	14.	A
5.	D	15.	A
6.	A	16.	D
7.	D	17.	C
8.	A	18.	C
9.	C	19.	C
10.	D	20.	D

_____

EXAMINATION SECTION
TEST 1

DIRECTIONS: Each question or incomplete statement is followed by several suggested answers or completions. Select the one that BEST answers the question or completes the statement. *PRINT THE LETTER OF THE CORRECT ANSWER IN THE SPACE AT THE RIGHT.*

1. Which one of the following statements BEST describes the purposes of questioning?
    A. Questions should be challenging, arouse attention, stimulate thinking, and encourage good expression in the answers given.
    B. Simple factual questions should be asked often, to serve as the teacher's best evaluative device.
    C. Questions should be repeated to make sure that every student understands them.
    D. Multiple questions should be asked occasionally to encourage clear thinking in complex situations.
    E. At times, the whip-lash type of question should be used in getting slow learners to respond.

1.___

2. Of the following, the one which may BEST be achieved through a system of programmed instruction is:
    A. Allowing a student to proceed at his own pace
    B. Reducing the number of teaching positions
    C. Providing study materials for homebound students
    D. Providing practice materials for students of low mental and/or reading ability
    .E. Completing coverage of the course of study

2.___

3. To clarify course objectives and daily aims for the students, the BEST procedure is for these objectives and aims to be
    A. clearly stated by the teacher
    B. raised by the students, discussed, and accepted by them
    C. written on the blackboard before they are discussed
    D. written on the blackboard after explanation by the teacher and then copied into notebooks by the students
    E. elicited from the faculty and the PTA and transmitted to the students

3.___

4. Which one of the following methods for getting a lesson started promptly is LEAST sound pedagogically?
    A. Have a challenging motivating question on the blackboard at the beginning of the period
    B. Stand near the door with the marking book and give a zero to any student who does not sit down and take out his work at once
    C. Give a quiz on the previous lesson at the beginning of the period
    D. Stand quietly, yet firmly, in front of the room and wait for attention
    E. Refer to a current event or happening at the start of the class

4.___

5. Many authorities maintain that the teacher, in his role as teacher,   5.___
    A. should engage in counseling relationships with his students provided no medical factors are involved
    B. should keep aloof from his students so as not to encourage them to seek therapeutic aid from him
    C. should engage in counseling relationships with his students but control the amount of transference in the therapeutic contacts
    D. should engage in counseling relationships with his students but only in the form of group therapy wherein the entire class can participate
    E. should not engage in counseling relationships with his students

6. In the teaching of reading, silent reading should be introduced   6.___
    A. after the children have acquired a sufficient experiential background
    B. after good oral reading has been established
    C. after the pupils are able to read primers
    D. after the children can read first readers
    E. from the beginning of book reading

7. Studies in which authoritarian and democratic methods of leadership were compared suggest that authoritarian leadership in the classroom is MOST likely to   7.___
    A. be less effective in developing responsibility in the students
    B. be more effective in developing self-discipline in the students
    C. result in a greater amount of aggressiveness of the students to one another
    D. be accompanied by a more apathetic attitude toward their work on the part of students
    E. be more effective in preparing the students for coping with new situations

Questions 8-10.
Questions 8 to 10 are based on the following class incident:

The teacher of a fifth grade class has left his class at handwork for a few minutes to go to the neighboring supply room for more materials. When he returns, John and Edward, two of the bigger boys, are engaged in a fight.

8. The FIRST thing the teacher should do is to   8.___
    A. shout to John and Edward to stop fighting immediately
    B. ignore the interruption
    C. walk quickly to the combatants and separate them
    D. send one of the larger boys to stop the belligerents
    E. have one of the children go for the principal

9. In order to prevent a recurrence of such fighting between these two boys, the teacher should   9.___
    A. send for the principal immediately since such behavior is very serious

B. take their handwork away and deprive them of the privilege of doing handwork for one week
C. send for their parents
D. hold a conference with the boys later in the day or after school, listen to their grievances, and try to resolve their differences
E. plan a lesson on "cooperation and self-control"

10. John claims that Edward started the fight by pushing him. 10.___
Edward says he bumped into John by accident, and John immediately punched him. The teacher knows that John gets into fights more frequently than does Edward. The boys' statements suggest that
A. one of the boys must be intentionally lying
B. it was John's fault, and he should be punished
C. Edward is overly sensitive
D. each boy was equally responsible for the fight
E. each boy may be giving an account of the situation as he understands it

11. The stimulus-response theory of learning explains 11.___
behavior in terms of
A. sub-liminal motivational cues
B. sociological and psychological process
C. physiological processes
D. causation and insight
E. massive retaliation

12. In the elementary school, the classroom teacher's 12.___
responsibility for imparting occupational information includes
A. awarding positive social recognition to all occupations
B. using career information as an instrument in educational motivation
C. helping students understand the occupational implications of a particular subject
D. demonstrating the relationship between school work and career work
E. all of these

13. Generally, a program of occupational information in the 13.___
elementary school can be set up within the framework of the regular curriculum. The part of the curriculum BEST suited to such a program is
A. arts and crafts
B. social studies
C. language arts
D. health and physical education
E. science

14. Which of the following is BEST known for his preparation 14.___
of a list of educational outcomes as abilities to be acquired?
A. Charters   B. Spaulding
C. Thorndike   D. Bobbitt
E. Lorge

15. Which of the following educators is BEST known for his   15.___
    activity analyses as a basis for curriculum development?
    A. Kilpatrick   B. Charters
    C. Nelson   D. Melvin
    E. Arthur

16. Which of the following educators has been an outstanding   16.___
    proponent of the social bases of the curriculum?
    A. Caswell   B. Nystrom
    C. Rugg   D. Mearns
    E. Durrell

17. The author of "The Foundations of Curriculum Building" is   17.___
    A. Norton   B. Caswell
    C. Bruner   D. Harap
    E. Van Wagenen

18. Which of the following educators is BEST known for his   18.___
    work in the field of spelling?
    A. Briggs   B. Judd
    C. Terman   D. Horn
    E. Finch

Questions 19-25.
Questions 19 to 25 refer to Helen, a ten-year-old pupil who has
just been admitted into a class for slow learners. Her former
teacher reports that Helen's attendance and punctuality record
is good and that her paintings show she is much better than most
children of her age. Her reading ability is reported as being
relatively good, but she has a strong distaste for arithmetic.
Her former teacher indicates further that Helen is weak in the
practice of social amenities and seems to have little awareness
of the concept of democratic behavior.

19. The teacher's FIRST step in planning for Helen's develop-   19.___
    ment should be to help her to
    A. bring her arithmetic level up to her reading age
    B. use her ability in painting to explore her interests
       and capacities in other areas
    C. try to help Helen succeed in her social relations
       with other members of the class group
    D. develop the appreciational aspect of her education to
       insure a well-balanced personality
    E. become a member of the school monitorial squad,
       building on her strengths in attendance and punctuality

20. Helen's dislike for arithmetic can BEST be replaced with   20.___
    a more positive attitude by
    A. citing cases of adults who, in later life, regretted
       they had not learned arithmetic
    B. creating situations in which she has to use simple
       arithmetic
    C. continued drill in basic computations she has not
       mastered
    D. the use of number tricks and puzzle devices
    E. giving her special attention during arithmetic lessons

21. In the light of Helen's ability in painting, the teacher   21.___
    should
    A. introduce the girl to varied art media
    B. launch an art appreciation unit that would benefit
       the whole class
    C. suggest that Helen study techniques of famous artists
       to improve her work
    D. discuss with her parents the possibility of a career
       in art
    E. encourage her to take art lessons at an independent
       art school

22. One morning, Helen arrives just after the bell has rung   22.___
    and unobtrusively slips into her seat. Wise class
    management indicates that
    A. the teacher should say nothing about the incident
    B. the girl needs a reminder of the importance of the
       habit of punctuality
    C. a comment on Helen's sneaking to her seat is in order
    D. Helen be questioned to prevent a recurrence of the
       tardiness
    E. Helen should apologize in front of the class for her
       lateness

23. During a recreation period, Helen's teacher notes that   23.___
    Helen is jumping rope with a group of girls from a class
    for intellectually gifted pupils at the school. The
    teacher should
    A. ask Helen to play with the girls of her own class
    B. caution Helen not to pay attention to remarks about
       the fact that she is in a slow class
    C. take Helen aside and warn her of the possible dangers
       of playing with these children, e.g., she may acquire
       an inferiority complex
    D. compliment the girls for their acceptance of Helen
       in their group
    E. make no comment at all and allow Helen to continue
       playing with the group

24. Helen fails to follow one of the rules for the proper   24.___
    handling of tools, although her attention has been called
    to the rule once before. The teacher should
    A. have the girl write the rules a number of times
       until she can repeat it verbatim
    B. stop the girl's work and remind her never to violate
       the rule again
    C. warn Helen that the next time she violates the rules,
       she will be barred from arts and crafts work
    D. re-explain and demonstrate the correct use of the tools
    E. punish Helen by having her stop her art work for the
       day

25. As applied to Helen, the teacher's acceptance of the   25.___
    principle of "equal opportunity for all" would be evidenced
    by

A. teaching Helen the minimum essentials of the common
   school curriculum through the sixth grade
B. arranging Helen's daily program so that the amount
   of time available for arts and crafts is the same as
   that for normal children
C. advising the parents that the opportunity for a free
   education for all children to the age of seventeen is
   a right and obligation that should not be denied
D. exploring Helen's interests and capacities and providing
   suitable experience for their development
E. treating Helen in the same manner as the other children
   in her class

_____

KEY (CORRECT ANSWERS)

1. A		11. C	
2. A		12. E	
3. B		13. B	
4. B		14. D	
5. E		15. B	
6. E		16. C	
7. A		17. A	
8. C		18. D	
9. D		19. C	
10. E		20. B	

21. A
22. A
23. E
24. D
25. D

_____

TEST 2

DIRECTIONS: Each question or incomplete statement is followed by several suggested answers or completions. Select the one that BEST answers the question or completes the statement. *PRINT THE LETTER OF THE CORRECT ANSWER IN THE SPACE AT THE RIGHT.*

1. Which one of the following is usually MOST basic in determining the effectiveness of a given lesson having an appropriate aim? The
   A. logical organization of the subject matter
   B. adequacy of the teacher's presentation of the aim of the lesson
   C. absence of classroom misbehavior on the part of the pupils
   D. relationship of the lesson to the felt needs and interests of the teacher
   E. degree of pupil involvement in the learning activity

1.___

2. Of the following, probably the BEST method for a teacher to use in helping students retain the material learned in class is to
   A. insist on note-taking
   B. encourage memorization
   C. use and re-use the material in various meaningful situations
   D. encourage cramming for quizzes
   E. give frequent tests which cover "back" material, as well as the present unit

2.___

3. The stimulus-response aspects of programmed instruction are *most closely* associated with the precepts advanced by which one of the following authors?
   A. James Conant   B. B. F. Skinner
   C. Martin Mayer   D. Jacques Barzun
   E. John Kenneth Galbraith

3.___

4. Which one of the following statements concerning the aim of a lesson is MOST valid?
   A. The teacher should write the aim on the blackboard at the beginning of each lesson.
   B. The aim should be an outgrowth of, and developed from, the motivation.
   C. Each child should write the aim of each lesson in his notebook each day.
   D. The teacher should announce the aim of the lesson to the class at the beginning of each period.
   E. Students should be called on, one by one, to state the aim of the lesson until common agreement is reached.

4.___

5. The MOST important value of a teacher's lesson plan is to   5.___
   A. enable the chairman to determine whether the teacher
   is to follow the syllabus
   B. enable the teacher to evaluate the teaching he has
   done
   C. ensure continuity of instruction in the event of the
   teacher's absence
   D. provide an opportunity for the teacher to give
   organized thought to work that will be carried on
   by the class
   E. provide for the many varied abilities and interests
   present in the classroom

6. Which of the following philosophies of education played   6.___
   the LEAST important role in the early development of the
   movement commonly referred to as Progressive Education?
   A. Essentialism   B. Experimentalism
   C. Instrumentalism   D. Pragmatism
   E. Realism

7. Under a progressive philosophy of education as practiced   7.___
   in the classroom of an experienced and competent teacher,
   the children's first-hand experiences SHOULD BE
   A. supplemented and reinforced by organized instruction
   and purposeful drill
   B. so rich and significant that there is no necessity
   for organized instruction or drill periods
   C. supplemented occasionally by organized instruction
   without the necessity of having purposeful drill
   D. sufficient if supplemented by occasional purposeful
   drills
   E. so strongly reinforced as to make home assignments
   unnecessary

8. Pragmatism as an educational philosophy was stressed by   8.___
   A. Dewey   B. Terman
   C. Binet   D. Pestalozzi
   E. Cubberley

9. When a student answers a question so that most of the   9.___
   class cannot hear him, the LEAST effective of the
   following practices is for the teacher to
   A. repeat the answer
   B. require the student to stand and face the class
   C. ask another student to repeat the answer
   D. have the student repeat his answer
   E. ask the class how many heard him

10. The developmental lesson is LEAST characterized by which   10.___
    one of the following?
    A. Medial and final summaries
    B. Lecture and demonstration
    C. The eliciting of factual information through questioning
    D. The eliciting and clarification of an aim with the
    help of a motivating technique
    E. The movement of the recitation arrow from pupil pupil,
    pupil teacher, teacher pupil

11. Of the following reasons for experimenting with team   11.___
    teaching methods, the one that is probably MOST valid
    from an educational point of view is that it
    A. would help meet the problem of teacher shortage
    B. would provide overburdened teachers with more free
       time
    C. makes provision for flexible scheduling and
       independent study by pupils
    D. can easily be incorporated into old, as well as
       new, school plants
    E. would provide more highly skilled teachers

12. If a teacher is unsuccessful in eliciting the aim of a   12.___
    lesson through questioning in a few minutes, the MOST
    acceptable procedure, of the following, would be for
    the teacher to
    A. abandon the day's plan and reteach the previous
       day's work
    B. continue to rephrase pivotal questions to try to
       elicit the aim for as long as necessary
    C. state the aim and continue with the planned lesson
    D. give a homework assignment designed so as to help
       elicit the aim the next day
    E. lay this aside and take up the content of the lesson,
       knowing that the aim will be elicited from the
       students at an appropriate place in the lesson

13. Of the following, probably the LEAST valuable way to   13.___
    begin a new topic or lesson is for the teacher to
    A. distribute a step-by-step outline of the topics
       or lesson
    B. explore some interest already possessed by the student
    C. elicit an explanation of the importance of the subject
    D. develop an overview of the subject
    E. refer to some current event

14. Of the following criteria for determining the quality of 14.___
    a classroom discussion, the one which is LEAST important
    is whether or not it
    A. serves to identify and refine the problem under
       discussion
    B. provides for a useful exchange of ideas
    C. consists of a series of questions and answers
    D. helps to interpret information and draw conclusions
    E. produces meaningful effects on the content, objectives,
       materials, methods, and evaluation of instruction

15. Gestalt psychologists state as one of their more   15.___
    important concepts that learning takes place MOST
    effectively when the material
    A. is rehearsed mentally as often as possible
    B. is put into a meaningful context
    C. does not elicit interfering, repressing associations
    D. is associated with something pleasant
    E. relates to the needs and interests of the community

16. Of the following, the one which would BEST provide for
    effective, creative teaching is
    A. emphasizing student memorization of the important
       sets of facts
    B. following a carefully developed uniform methodology
       to improve efficiency of teaching and learning
    C. permitting students to decide all important classroom
       management problems in order to encourage initiative
    D. leading students to feel the need for learning the
       various topics in the course of study
    E. affording maximum opportunity for disagreement and
       alternatives in the classroom

16.___

17. Which one of the following is the BEST statement about
    a teacher's technique of questioning?
    A. No question should be so difficult that even the
       slowest pupil couldn't answer it.
    B. Each lesson should have at least one question which
       would require the pupils to do critical thinking.
    C. There should be a series of pivotal questions, to
       highlight the chief learnings.
    D. Each question should be simple and short.
    E. At times, use the "whip-lash" or "tugging" types
       with slow learners.

17.___

18. Of the following, the BEST statement concerning skill
    in questioning is:
    A. To make sure all students hear, the teacher should
       often repeat her question
    B. Answers should be repeated because some children sit
       far away from the pupil who is answering
    C. Each question should be addressed to a particular
       pupil by giving his name before asking the question
    D. To vary the kinds of questions, include the double
       question, particularly for bright students
    E. A question should be addressed to the entire class

18.___

19. Of the following, the LEAST effective method for
    obtaining pupil participation is to
    A. give a warm-up drill to the entire class
    B. group the class and give different assignments to
       each group
    C. have pupils answer in concert
    D. use experiences of pupils in the lesson development
    E. ask thought-provoking pivotal questions

19.___

20. Of the following, which one is usually LEAST effective
    as a means of dealing with individual differences in the
    classroom?
    A. Heterogeneous grouping
    B. The lecture method
    C. Differential assignments
    D. The "unit" method of teaching-learning organization
    E. Committee assignments and reports

20.___

21. A *primary* purpose of homogeneous grouping is to 21.___
  A. cut down class size
  B. prevent conflict between ethnic groups
  C. decrease the teacher's work
  D. enable a maximum number of students to achieve optimally
  E. simplify pupil personnel accounting

22. Of the following, the MOST significant criticism of the 22.___
lecture method is that it fails adequately to
  A. develop content and present concepts
  B. stimulate scientific research
  C. meet adolescents' social and personal needs
  D. develop self-discipline and self-interest
  E. involve teacher participation and preparation

23. Which one of the following statements about lesson plans 23.___
is LEAST acceptable? They
  A. should be done anew each year even if the same subjects are to be taught
  B. should deal with a variety of lesson types and techniques
  C. should include the actual phraseology of pivotal questions to be asked
  D. may be prepared weekly but be flexible enough to permit daily additions and corrections
  E. continue to become less necessary as the teacher's years of experience increase

24. Which one of the following types of lessons will MOST 24.___
likely enable a teacher to help children to learn by themselves?
  A. Supervised study and research
  B. Lecture-demonstration
  C. Developmental
  D. Laboratory-demonstration
  E. Unit

25. Summaries of learnings elicited during and at the end of 25.___
a lesson are, usually
  A. unproductive educationally
  B. useful only to slow learners
  C. important in focusing attention on the concepts considered and developed
  D. not so good as summaries dictated by the teacher for copying into the students' notebooks
  E. springboards of motivation for the home assignment

KEY (CORRECT ANSWERS)

1. E	6. A	11. C	16. D	21. D
2. C	7. A	12. C	17. C	22. C
3. B	8. A	13. A	18. E	23. E
4. B	9. A	14. C	19. C	24. A
5. D	10. B	15. B	20. B	25. C

EXAMINATION SECTION
TEST 1

DIRECTIONS: Each question or incomplete statement is followed by several suggested answers or completions. Select the one that BEST answers the question or completes the statement. *PRINT THE LETTER OF THE CORRECT ANSWER IN THE SPACE AT THE RIGHT.*

1. The factors in the presentation to which the teacher should give the GREATEST weight are
   A. stage presence, style, and personal appearance
   B. audibility, dramatic expression, and the progress of the student
   C. selection of the tourist attraction, number of points made, and number of errors in French
   D. level of memorization, quality of the written notes, and willingness to stand in front of the room

   1.____

2. How can students BEST be encouraged to listen to classmates as they make their presentations?
   A. Have the creators of the dialogue write key questions on the board for classmates to answer.
   B. Indicate that you will lower the grade of anyone who cannot behave courteously.
   C. Announce that you will ask questions about the attraction based on the previous lessons.
   D. Indicate that you will be in back of the room watching the audience.

   2.____

3. A slowing of the pace of a lesson is an indication that the
   A. students have not had ample time to assimilate the new material
   B. students are bored and are reticent to participate
   C. energy level of the teacher has decreased
   D. teacher has exerted pressure on the students to respond quickly

   3.____

4. Discipline problems can BEST be minimized and/or avoided if the teacher
   A. engages the students in a lot of busy work
   B. plans effectively and provides variety in each lesson
   C. maintains high expectations for all students
   D. penalizes the entire class for the infraction of one

   4.____

5. When teaching a new topic, the teacher should
   A. make sure that all homework difficulties have been corrected before teaching the new material
   B. allow sufficient time for a full presentation of the new material
   C. teach the new material before any discussion of the homework
   D. warn pupils that they will be tested on the new material the next day

   5.____

6. In a comparison of the developmental and lecture method   6.___
   of teaching, which one of the following statements is
   MOST NEARLY CORRECT?
   A. In the lecture method, the teacher readily checks
      the progress of learning.
   B. There is greater pupil participation in the
      developmental method.
   C. Greater pupil attention is insured in the lecture
      method.
   D. There is less need for review at the beginning of a
      developmental lesson.

7. When classroom teachers attempt to deal with children's   7.___
   emotional difficulties which are at the basis of much
   serious misconduct, they are inclined to
   A. plan treatment programs which cover too long a
      period of time
   B. stress the removal of the cause rather than the
      elimination of annoying symptoms
   C. deal with immediate rather than basic causes of
      misconduct
   D. spend too much time assembling unnecessary data
      before they initiate their treatment program

8. In teaching that 12 inches equal 1 foot, 3 feet a yard,   8.___
   and 36 inches a yard, a teacher is MOST justified in
   A. providing experience for discovering these facts
      before helping the children to relate one fact to
      another
   B. having the children learn the three facts at one
      time in order to have them see the relationship of
      one fact to another
   C. not aiming at complete mastery of these facts since
      they are readily available, when needed, in reference
      books accessible to children and adults
   D. having the children first memorize the facts and
      then give them problems to solve in which the facts
      are applied

9. If a student in one of your subject classes has not done   9.___
   any homework for two weeks, which one of the following
   would be the BEST procedure to follow as an initial measure?
   A. Send him to your chairman with a note explaining
      the situation.
   B. Keep him after school while he makes up the homework.
   C. Discuss with him privately the reasons for his failure
      to do the homework.
   D. Give him a failing rating on the first report,
      regardless of his test average.

10. In seating your classes, it is USUALLY wisest to do which 10.___
    one of the following?
    A. Rearrange their seats according to marks on tests.
    B. Seat them so that the better students can assist
       poorer students easily.
    C. Seat them in strict alphabetical order.
    D. Let them sit wherever they wish.

11. Which one of the following is LEAST likely to succeed in sustaining the attention of slow learners?   11.___
    - A. A 30-minute film
    - B. A 30-minute lecture
    - C. A change in activity every 10 minutes
    - D. A 20-minute laboratory exercise

12. That "practice makes perfect" is USUALLY more acceptable   12.___
    - A. for slow learners than it is for rapid learners
    - B. for average learners than it is for slow learners
    - C. for rapid learners than it is for slow learners
    - D. for superior students than it is for average learners

13. Through which one of the following types of lessons will a teacher be MOST likely to succeed in helping children become able to learn by themselves?   13.___
    - A. Supervised study
    - B. Lecture-demonstration
    - C. Note-giving
    - D. Laboratory-demonstration

14. Of the following, which man has written a series of books on American education?   14.___
    - A. Jansen   B. Pauling   C. Conant   D. Acheson

15. In connection with teaching a technical term, it is usually BEST to   15.___
    - A. develop the concept before giving the term its technical name
    - B. introduce the technical term and then develop the concept
    - C. give the technical term and define it without follow-up discussion
    - D. give the technical term, define it, and then explain the concept to the class

16. Of the following possible justifications for surprise quizzes, the BEST one is that   16.___
    - A. they are periodically necessary to deflate the sense of superiority of the students who ordinarily get high marks
    - B. it is best to punish a class for poor discipline with these quizzes
    - C. they encourage the students to study regularly
    - D. they cause the students to have more respect for the teacher

17. Assume that you have just met a class for the first time and that soon after the lesson begins a boy makes a loud noise. Usually the BEST of the following suggestions for the immediate handling of this situation is to   17.___
    - A. send him to the dean at once
    - B. assign him the task of writing "I must be a gentleman at all times" 200 times for homework
    - C. warn him about the possibility of expulsion from the school
    - D. tell him to see you after class; then proceed with the lesson

18. Which one of the following statements concerning the   18.___
    purposes of questioning is MOST reasonable?
    A. Questions should be challenging, arouse attention,
       stimulate thinking, and encourage good expression
       in the answers given.
    B. Simple, factual questions should be asked often to
       serve as the teacher's best evaluative device.
    C. Questions should be repeated to make sure that every
       student understands them.
    D. Multiple questions should be asked occasionally to
       encourage clear thinking in complicated situations.

19. Of the following, the one which may BEST be achieved by   19.___
    programmed instruction is
    A. allowing a student to proceed at his own pace
    B. reducing the number of teaching positions
    C. providing study materials for homebound students
    D. providing practice materials for students of low
       reading ability

20. Of the following procedures for the handling of the   20.___
    clarification of course objectives and daily aims to the
    students, the BEST one is for these objectives and aims
    to be
    A. clearly stated by the teacher
    B. raised by the students, discussed, and accepted by them
    C. written on the blackboard before they are discussed
    D. written on the blackboard after explanation by the
       teacher and then copied into notebooks by the students

21. Summaries of learnings elicited during and at the end of   21.___
    a lesson are USUALLY
    A. a waste of time
    B. useful only to slow learners
    C. important in focusing attention on the concepts
       developed
    D. not as good as summaries dictated by the teacher for
       copying into pupils' notebooks

22. When there is some unnecessary commotion in the hallway   22.___
    during a lesson, a teacher should FIRST
    A. shut the door and continue with the lesson
    B. send one of the students to the administrative
       assistant's office and alert him
    C. step to the door to see what is the cause of the
       commotion so that he may take appropriate action
    D. send the students involved to the dean's office

23. Which one of the following statements about lesson plans   23.___
    is LEAST acceptable?
    A. They should be done anew each year even if the same
       subjects are to be taught.
    B. They continue to become less and less necessary as
       your years of experience increase.
    C. They should include the actual phraseology of pivotal
       questions to be asked.
    D. They should be prepared weekly but be flexible enough
       to permit daily additions and corrections.

24. Of the following, the BEST approach to use in connection with the reporting of subject-class absentees who are not on the daily official class absentee list is to   24.___
    A. be very certain to send in a "cutting" slip for each missing student not on the absentee list, no matter what his record is in the subject-class
    B. select those in whom you have least faith, and send in "cutting" slips for them
    C. wait a week or so before sending in any "cutting" slips and try to use your personal influence on the students as you meet them later
    D. send in one "cutting" slip each day as an example to the others

25. When the common element in a number of experiences has been recognized and extracted by a student, then the student has MOST likely formed a(n)   25.___
    A. percept   B. concept
    C. objective   D. hypothesis

26. Which one of the following is NOT the responsibility of the homeroom teacher?   26.___
    A. Encourage average students who are doing poorly in school to drop out of school and go to work
    B. Discuss with students the possible courses they may request for next term
    C. Assist students to get help in handling homework difficulties in various subjects
    D. Encourage students to join school clubs and organizations which will meet their needs

27. Of the following, the BEST course of action for a new teacher who is having difficulty in presenting a particular type of lesson to take is to   27.___
    A. make an arrangement with an experienced teacher to observe his classes
    B. consult the chairman and request an opportunity for intervisitation
    C. try to adjust without outside help to avoid demonstrating weakness to colleagues
    D. discuss the problem frankly with the class and ask for suggestions from the class

28. Of the following, the BEST situation for using essay questions is where   28.___
    A. it is desired to test the ability of a pupil to organize his answers
    B. the class is made up chiefly of slow pupils
    C. "single shot" questions are needed to complete an examination
    D. it is desired to sample a large area of subject matter

29. In a lesson in which a new topic is to be taught, which one of the following is the MOST desirable principle to follow?   29.___
    A. Make certain that all difficulties encountered by pupils in doing the previous homework assignment have been corrected before beginning the new topic

B. Allow sufficient time to include a suitable motivation of the new material, a development, and independent pupil practice
C. Introduce the new topic, but require pupils to study the textbook for a complete explanation
D. Insist that no questions be asked by pupils until the development is completed

30. A test may be said to be reliable when   30.___
    A. it consistently measures what it attempts to measure
    B. it adequately deals with the types of educational outcomes to be measured at proper levels of difficulty for pupils
    C. there is a high correlation between test scores and criterion measures
    D. it can be obtained on time from publishers

31. Of the following, the one which does NOT measure the   31.___
    concentration of scores in any set of scores or group of data is the
    A. mode   B. modulus   C. mean   D. median

32. Of the following, the GREATEST advantage of short-answer   32.___
    tests is the
    A. ease with which the test items can be constructed
    B. ease with which such tests can be standardized
    C. wide sampling of the subject matter of the course
    D. ease with which the test results can be interpreted

33. The MOST effective use of the talents and abilities of   33.___
    the able pupils in your subject area would be gained by
    which one of the following procedures?
    A. Give them extra homework assignments in order to earn better marks.
    B. Give them the responsibility of tutoring disadvantaged pupils.
    C. Give them monitorial duties, such as marking test papers.
    D. Excuse them from class work which they grasp easily so they do enrichment work in other subject areas.

34. The MAIN advantage of standardized tests is   34.___
    A. objectivity
    B. ease of marking for teachers
    C. marks may be compared with other groups
    D. it provides greater motivation for students

35. A percentile score of 55 is   35.___
    A. a score equivalent to the arithmetic median of the scores
    B. equaled or exceeded by 45% of the scores in the distribution
    C. equivalent to a score of 55 out of 100
    D. the accepted norm

36. The process of reviewing homework daily is time-consuming.   36.___
    Of the following suggestions made by a group of teachers,
    which one is MOST sound pedagogically?
    A. Do not go over the homework at all.
    B. Go over in class only the problems with which pupils
       had trouble.
    C. Collect the homework of only one row at a time and
       return it corrected the next day.
    D. Collect the homework of the whole class once a week
       on a specific day.

37. Which one of the following is the BEST statement about a   37.___
    teacher's technique of questioning?
    A. No question should be so difficult that even the
       slowest pupil couldn't answer it.
    B. Each lesson should have at least one question which
       would require the pupils to do critical thinking.
    C. There should be a series of pivotal questions to
       highlight the chief learning.
    D. Each question should be simple and short.

38. Of the following, the BEST statement concerning skill in   38.___
    questioning is that
    A. to make sure all students hear, the teacher should
       often repeat her question
    B. answers should be repeated because some children sit
       far away from the pupil who is answering
    C. each question should be addressed to a particular
       pupil by giving his name before asking the question
    D. a question should be addressed to the entire class

39. When a parent complains to you that you are underrating   39.___
    her son, the BEST procedure, among the following, for you
    to follow is to
    A. tell the parent that you alone have the moral and
       legal responsibility for assigning the marks
    B. refer the parent to the principal
    C. agree to raise the grades in the future
    D. explain the grading system and review the pupil's
       grades with the parent

40. Which one of the following statements would BEST describe   40.___
    procedures of note-taking in a class of slow learners?
    A. They should have few or no notes at all since they
       have limited verbal ability.
    B. Mimeographed notes should be given to them since
       note-taking is frustrating for them.
    C. Notes, of a simple kind, should be developed coopera-
       tively by pupils and teacher.
    D. A few short notes should be copied directly from the
       textbook to insure accuracy and reinforce reading
       skills.

41. In THE AMERICAN HIGH SCHOOL TODAY, James B. Conant proposes 41.___
    that

A. the four-year high school should be a comprehensive high school
B. the present curriculum in the fourth year of high school is more appropriate for a "community junior college"
C. "social living" courses should be added in all high schools to provide better life adjustment in our atomic era
D. standardized achievement tests, such as State Regents, have outlived their usefulness

42. The SIMPLEST way, among the following, to exhibit a newspaper clipping to an entire class at one time is to   42.___
    A. make a slide for a slide projector
    B. make a highly enlarged photostat
    C. use the overhead projector
    D. use an opaque projector

43. Of the following, which combination of activities is LEAST suitable as a homework assignment in preparation for a full-period test?   43.___
    A. "Study and review all work since (date)."
    B. "Skim through chapters 16 and 17. Study your class notes since (date). Review your homework since (date)."
    C. "Re-read chapters 16 and 17. Look over the questions at the end of each chapter."
    D. "Review all class notes and homework since (date). Do the practice mimeo test distributed today."

44. In selecting the aim for a developmental lesson, the MOST important among the following considerations is the   44.___
    A. content of the previous day's lesson
    B. motivation to be used
    C. decision as to which knowledges, attitudes, or skills should be taught next
    D. content of the syllabus

45. The validity of intelligence tests as instruments for evaluating native ability has been questioned because these tests tend to   45.___
    A. lack reliability, especially for gifted children
    B. lack reliability, especially for pupils of low motor coordination who consequently have a poor sense of spatial relations
    C. place too much emphasis on mathematical and scientific aptitude
    D. have an experiential base which is foreign to culturally different children in poverty areas

46. Of the following, the MAJOR aim for giving a standardized test to classes at the beginning of a new course is probably to   46.___
    A. discover weaknesses of previous teaching
    B. discover interests, aptitudes and previous learnings in this area
    C. give teachers and supervisors a basis for deciding upon the regrouping of classes in terms of ability
    D. arouse pupil curiosity and provide a base for motivation

47. Of the following terms, the one MOST closely associated   47.___
    with the sum total of response patterns and abilities
    possessed by the learner at any given time is
    A. adaptation   B. readiness
    C. reinforcement   D. response

48. If 48% of your class failed a unit test, the BEST   48.___
    procedure to follow is to
    A. develop a normal curve on a graph and adjust the grades
    B. ask your chairman to evaluate your test; if he agrees
       it is fair, re-teach parts of the unit, then review
       and give a new test
    C. chastise the failing pupils sternly and write notes
       to the parents, if your chairman agrees your test
       is fair
    D. give an "extra credit" test to the failing pupils
       to raise their grades

49. Of the following reasons for giving homework, the LEAST   49.___
    acceptable reason is that it
    A. extends the learning process beyond the classroom
    B. provides practice in the art of self-study
    C. increases the chances of retentivity
    D. trains the pupils in habits of doing hard work

50. Which one of the following sets of statements BEST   50.___
    explains the occurrence of disciplinary infractions
    among adolescents in secondary schools?
    A. Adolescents tend to resist authority; they seek the
       admiration of their peers; they are not convinced that
       poor self-control is necessarily harmful to future
       success.
    B. Syllabi are teacher-imposed; rules of conduct in
       secondary schools are unrealistic.
    C. Adolescents undergo rapid physical growth; their span
       of attention is short; they are incapable of abstract
       thoughts.
    D. Adolescence has been extended by modern society; rules
       of conduct do not parallel chronological age; there is
       a widespread lack of pre-vocational meaningful study.

KEY (CORRECT ANSWERS)

1. B	11. B	21. C	31. B	41. A
2. A	12. A	22. C	32. C	42. D
3. A	13. A	23. B	33. B	43. A
4. B	14. C	24. A	34. C	44. C
5. B	15. A	25. B	35. B	45. D
6. B	16. C	26. A	36. B	46. B
7. C	17. D	27. B	37. C	47. B
8. A	18. A	28. A	38. D	48. B
9. C	19. A	29. B	39. D	49. D
10. B	20. B	30. A	40. C	50. A

TEST 2

DIRECTIONS: Each question or incomplete statement is followed by several suggested answers or completions. Select the one that BEST answers the question or completes the statement. *PRINT THE LETTER OF THE CORRECT ANSWER IN THE SPACE AT THE RIGHT.*

1. Of the following, the generally LEAST acceptable type of short-answer question is
   A. multiple choice
   B. completion
   C. true-false
   D. matching

   1.___

2. Pupils who seem sensitive, timid, and/or immature USUALLY respond most favorably to a teacher's efforts when the teacher uses which one of the following methods?
   A. Reproves them frequently
   B. Punishes even minor infractions
   C. Urges them to enter competitions
   D. Praises even minor progress

   2.___

3. Which one of the following is the MOST efficient way to distribute duplicated sheets to a class?
   A. The teacher individually hands each pupil a sheet.
   B. A monitor hands each pupil a sheet.
   C. The teacher counts off a set of papers for each column and asks the first pupil in each column to take one and pass the rest back.
   D. A monitor counts off a set of papers for each row and asks the first pupil in each row to take one and pass the rest to the side.

   3.___

4. Intervisitation among teachers in a department is
   A. unwise, because teachers should be creative, not imitative
   B. wise, because teachers can gain a great deal from sharing methods and techniques
   C. unwise, because teachers do not like to be observed by their colleagues
   D. wise, because only the few "master teachers" have ideas which are good enough for the others to use

   4.___

5. The BEST discipline in a classroom is that which is
   A. instilled by a system of severe penalties
   B. learned by the lecture method
   C. self-imposed by the students
   D. obtained through using interesting visual aids

   5.___

6. Homework assignments are MOST effective when they are
   A. used to introduce new concepts to a class
   B. used to provide practice for a skill taught that day
   C. given to the class as a whole without differentiation
   D. used in a punitive fashion

   6.___

7. Of the following devices, the one that is LEAST likely to   7.___
   motivate a skills lesson is
   A. the teacher's announcement that the skill is necessary
      for success in the course
   B. award of extra credit for quick mastery of the skill
   C. demonstration of pupil weakness and consequent need
      for the skill
   D. announcement of a test to cover that particular skill

8. In making up a lesson plan, the new teacher should attach   8.___
   MOST significance to
   A. what students are expected to achieve by the end of
      the lesson
   B. preparation for uniform examinations
   C. textual explanations
   D. medial and final summaries

9. In setting up classroom routines, the teacher is well   9.___
   advised to
   A. be consistent in the application of these routines
   B. allow for variation for individual students
   C. ensure student understanding of the reasons for the
      routines
   D. consider all of these

10. The MOST effective way to review after a test is to   10.___
    A. make a frequency distribution of student errors and
       reteach areas of demonstrated weakness
    B. review each test question and give students the
       correct answer
    C. review each test question and have students give the
       correct answers
    D. ask individual students why they had difficulty with
       particular questions

11. The BEST way for a teacher to determine how well a lesson   11.___
    has succeeded is to
    A. provide time at the end of the period for immediate
       application of the new learnings
    B. give a test on the new learnings at the end of the
       week
    C. review carefully the homework handed in the next day
    D. provide for a brief review of the new learnings at
       the beginning of the next day's lesson

12. Of the following statements regarding the role of the   12.___
    teacher, the one that does NOT belong is to
    A. develop a consistent and reasonable relationship
       with students
    B. create a meaningful and motivated instructional
       program
    C. accept responsibility for helping to maintain school
       tone
    D. concentrate on covering as much material as possible

13. An effective technique of questioning is to   13.___
    - A. fix one's vision on a particular student while
      presenting the stimulus
    - B. identify the student to respond before presenting
      the stimulus
    - C. present the stimulus before indicating who is to
      respond
    - D. present the stimulus and permit students to call
      out their responses

14. In an oversized class, MAXIMUM oral participation is BEST   14.___
    achieved through
    - A. students' interaction with their neighbor
    - B. choral repetition
    - C. the use of a tape as a stimulus
    - D. group work

15. Which one of the following procedures would be of MOST   15.___
    value in helping the pupil who has unusually severe
    difficulty with spelling?
    - A. Saying each word distinctly before and after writing it
    - B. Tracing the words written in large letters with his
      finger
    - C. Copying a word many times till it becomes automatic
    - D. Stressing oral rather than written spelling

16. "Teachers contribute to good discipline by seating   16.___
    children appropriately." In practice, appropriate seating
    means that pupils
    - A. of different ability levels will be intermingled
    - B. of different ability levels will be separated into
      distinct groups
    - C. will be seated according to their reading groups
    - D. will be allowed to choose their own seats in class

17. In a fire drill, the teacher should   17.___
    - A. walk at the front of the line
    - B. walk at the rear of the line
    - C. walk in the middle of the line, keeping the head
      and rear of the line under observation
    - D. start at the front of the line, and then send the
      class on ahead as she waits for the last child

18. It is generally accepted that one of the MOST frequent   18.___
    errors made by teachers in teaching reading is
    - A. failure to use workbooks to supplement basic readers
    - B. failure to have books for recreational reading on
      more than one level in the classroom
    - C. assigning children books that are too difficult for
      them
    - D. over-stress on developing critical thinking in
      reading activities

19. Current evaluation of curriculum materials indicates that   19.___
    large courses of study are being replaced by
    - A. brief pamphlets emphasizing "character education"
    - B. joint planning conferences by parents and teachers

C. reports of pupil-teacher cooperative planning
D. special bulletins on aspects of teaching and learning

20. In the teaching of arithmetic, it is *generally* believed   20.___
that drill should
    A. either precede or follow understanding
    B. not be used
    C. follow the development of understanding
    D. precede the development of understanding

21. In surveys of the junior high school, the curriculum   21.___
organization is moving *increasingly* toward
    A. reemphasizing the unity of specific subjects
    B. requiring mathematics of all pupils
    C. combining certain subjects with English or the
       social studies
    D. requiring science as a three-year sequence

22. Which one of the following persons has written important   22.___
books and articles on the teaching of reading?
    A. E. F. Lindquist   B. Laura Eads
    C. Raymond B. Cattell   D. Nila B. Smith

23. Drill in mathematics is MOST effective when the teacher   23.___
    A. devotes five or ten minutes of each lesson to drill
    B. plans for specific lessons devoted entirely to drill
    C. plans for drill lessons only when the need arises
    D. provides for drill through homework assignments

24. Pupils should be taught to write mathematical symbols   24.___
    A. at the same time as these symbols are presented for
       their recognition
    B. at the same time as they are introduced to cursive
       writing
    C. after they understand and can recognize them
    D. at the same time as they are introduced to manuscript
       writing

25. In selecting poems for presentation to children in the   25.___
intermediate grades, the teacher should realize that children
at this level are MOST likely to enjoy
    A. poems written in blank verse
    B. lyrics
    C. ballads
    D. sonnets

26. Of the following, which type of sound is the easiest for   26.___
beginning readers to discriminate?
    A. Final consonant sounds
    B. Initial consonant sounds
    C. Short vowel sounds
    D. Initial digraph sounds

27. Dave, a sixth-grader who reads on a second-grade level, 27.____
rejects the books in the classroom that are of appropriate
difficulty on the basis that they are "baby stuff." The
BEST way of solving this problem is to
   A. delay book reading and confine instruction for a while
      to word-recognition techniques
   B. use interesting word games such as "Wordo," "Anagrams,"
      "Go Fish," etc., until his confidence in his teacher
      has increased
   C. use a book that, while difficult for him, is better
      suited to his interest and enjoyment until his
      confidence is gained
   D. use an experience-story approach based on Dave's own
      stories until he is reading on a higher level

28. In the teaching of phonics, instruction should start with 28.____
   A. seeing differences in printed symbols
   B. learning the sound of various letters
   C. using picture clues
   D. hearing sounds in spoken words

29. The teacher who strives to be impersonal in her relation- 29.____
ship to her pupils is generally LEAST effective with
those pupils who
   A. do excellent work   B. are discouraged
   C. seek to win approbation D. are independent and mature

30. The BEST time for systematic teaching of phonics is 30.____
   A. at the very beginning of instruction in reading in
      the first grade
   B. after the child has learned a basic sight vocabulary
      of more than fifty words
   C. in the fourth grade after the child has learned the
      alphabet
   D. as soon as the child has attained a mental age of
      six years

31. Although teacher domination of a classroom is looked upon 31.____
with disfavor by educational theorists, classes characterized
by such firm teacher control generally
   A. spend more time in actual work
   B. afford greater satisfaction to the pupil
   C. increase pupil motivation to obtain high grades
   D. enlist faster pupil cooperation

32. Of the following statements concerning the inclusion of 32.____
individual and group activities in a playground program,
the one MOST sound educationally is:
   A. Group activities should be used exclusively so as to
      give stress to social values and outcomes
   B. Individual and group activities should be included
      and equal emphasis given to each
   C. Individual activities should be included only when
      children request them
   D. Individual activities should be included but greater
      emphasis should be placed on group activities

33. Of the following procedures, on the part of the teacher, the one which is MOST likely to cause poor discipline is
    A. punishing infractions too severely
    B. threatening disciplinary action and failing to carry out the punishment
    C. failing to identify the true peer leadership among students
    D. being impatient with children

33.___

34. In teaching skills in physical education, the BEST order of techniques essential to learning is
    A. participation, demonstration, analysis
    B. demonstration, analysis, participation
    C. analysis, participation, demonstration
    D. discussion, participation, analysis, correction

34.___

35. An effective teacher in a playground does all of the following EXCEPT:
    A. Allows for program changes when circumstances make these desirable
    B. Consults parents to learn more about individual children
    C. Comments regularly on the lapses and mistakes that a child makes
    D. Notes the peer judgments of children

35.___

36. In the teaching of sports skills, it is recommended that the playground teacher do all of the following EXCEPT:
    A. Analyze the component parts of the skill clearly
    B. Explain the reasons for performing the skill in a specific way
    C. Pick a participant at random to demonstrate
    D. Provide sufficient opportunity for practicing the skill

36.___

37. For the purpose of providing instruction for small groups that require explanation and demonstration, it is generally BEST to arrange the learners in
    A. a circle formation   B. a semi-circle
    C. any random position   D. line formation

37.___

38. Of the following, the LEAST important consideration in planning the athletic program of the playground is
    A. the facilities that are available
    B. the age groups of the participants
    C. seasonal interests
    D. the skill and ability of the teacher in the activities selected

38.___

39. Of the following responsibilities of the playground teacher, the one which is FIRST in importance is to
    A. provide activities for the participation of the maximum number
    B. emphasize big muscle activity
    C. give individual instruction
    D. introduce new activities

39.___

40. Studies comparing the forgetting of completed and incomplete tasks tend to show that
    A. completed tasks tend to be forgotten more rapidly than incompleted ones
    B. incompleted tasks tend to be forgotten more rapidly than completed ones
    C. there is no difference in retention of the two types of tasks
    D. the inconclusive results that have been obtained make it impossible to generalize

40.___

41. Of the following, which is generally MOST conducive to the mastery of a skill?
    A. The practice of the skill in a daily routine
    B. Emphasis on speed rather than accuracy in early practice
    C. Overlearning
    D. Lack of emotion and pressure during practice

41.___

42. Degree of maturity, amount of previous experience, and motivation are all factors affecting the degree of
    A. intelligent activity shown by a learner
    B. transfer of skills shown by a learner
    C. readiness shown by a learner
    D. retention shown by a learner

42.___

43. Of the following, which one is of relatively minor effectiveness in determining the amount of transfer of learning from one subject to another?
    A. The degree of relationship between the two subjects involved
    B. The methods used by the teacher to establish a relationship between the subjects involved
    C. The amount of study time put in by the learner on the material
    D. The ability of the learner to make generalizations

43.___

44. Which of the following processes is basic to all learning?
    A. Verbalization   B. Insight
    C. Trial and error   D. Discrimination

44.___

45. Modern psychological theory suggests that the success of a classroom learning experience will depend primarily upon the
    A. motivation of the learner
    B. climate of the classroom
    C. readiness of the learner
    D. personality of the teacher

45.___

46. Research has demonstrated that the MOST efficient way of distributing one's effort in learning
    A. entails scheduling long units of practice with short intervals between units
    B. involves scheduling short units of practice with long intervals between units
    C. calls for units of practice and intervals of approximately equal duration
    D. depends on the material to be learned and the individual learner

46.___

47. As defined by the Gestalt psychologist, "insight" should   47.___
    be looked upon as
    A. a subconscious solution of a problem
    B. a sudden reorganization of experience
    C. a form of creative inspiration
    D. orientation of the learner toward the solution of a
       problem

48. The use of rewards and punishments to stimulate learning   48.___
    involves the psychological principle known as the law of
    A. effect   B. elimination
    C. disinhibition   D. behavioral facilitation

49. Which of the following generalizations concerning transfer   49.___
    of training would be accepted by MOST present day
    psychologists?
    A. Positive transfer is widespread, but it is more
       specific than general.
    B. Little transfer occurs, but when it does, it is more
       or less general.
    C. There is practically no transfer from school subjects
       to daily living.
    D. The humanities contribute more to general improvement
       of thinking than mathematics or science.

50. Usually, the rate of forgetting material learned in the   50.___
    classroom
    A. is slow for a short time and then increases rapidly
    B. increases gradually from the time learning occurs
    C. is rapid immediately after learning occurs and then
       tends to level off
    D. varies depending upon the nature of the material
       learned

    ____

KEY (CORRECT ANSWERS)

1. C	11. A	21. C	31. A	41. C
2. D	12. C	22. D	32. D	42. C
3. D	13. D	23. A	33. B	43. C
4. B	14. B	24. C	34. B	44. D
5. C	15. B	25. C	35. C	45. C
6. B	16. A	26. B	36. C	46. D
7. C	17. A	27. D	37. B	47. B
8. A	18. C	28. D	38. D	48. A
9. D	19. D	29. B	39. A	49. A
10. A	20. C	30. B	40. A	50. C

EXAMINATION SECTION

TEST 1

DIRECTIONS: Each question or incomplete statement is followed by several suggested answers or completions. Select the one that BEST answers the question or completes the statement. *PRINT THE LETTER OF THE CORRECT ANSWER IN THE SPACE AT THE RIGHT.*

1. The statement among the following which is NOT appropriately applied to the modern concept of individualized education is:
   A. Growth and learning are almost synonymous.
   B. Readiness for learning is determined by the individual's intellectual acumen.
   C. Standardized teaching methods may run counter to the individual's optimum learning methods.
   D. The good life is not fully realized unless maximum individual and social growth is taking place.

   1.___

2. The description among the following which is NOT properly associated with core curriculum is:
   A. Units which cut across subject fields and which may be taught by one or more teachers are used.
   B. Learning is centered on large topics around which activities are organized.
   C. Pupils play a major part in planning, launching, and developing the work of the group.
   D. Activities, excursions, and community resources are utilized instead of textbooks and research.

   2.___

3. In which one of the following areas does conditioning play a major role?
   A. Development of motor skills
   B. Acquisition of facts
   C. Development of attitudes
   D. Formation of concepts

   3.___

4. Most present-day psychologists accept the principle that drill should be used in the modern classroom only when
   A. reviewing material that has already been covered
   B. it is necessary to clarify pupil understanding of a concept
   C. test results reveal poor mastery of factual material
   D. an automatic response is considered desirable

   4.___

5. Of the following, which would ordinarily be the LEAST effective means of modifying an attitude?
   A. Listening to a lecture
   B. Role playing
   C. A panel discussion following a film
   D. Group discussion

   5.___

6. In the guidance of pupil learning, research has indicated   6.___
   that
   A. emphasis on correct responses is more effective than
      emphasis on errors
   B. demonstration is more effective than practice
   C. massed practice is more effective than distributed
      practice
   D. verbal guidance is more effective than demonstration

7. In grades kindergarten through 2, mathematics is taught   7.___
   by the teacher
   A. in a definite sequence, beginning in first grade
   B. in a definite sequence, beginning in the kindergarten
   C. in a definite sequence, beginning in the second grade
   D. as the topics arise naturally from projects in other
      areas or from real experiences

8. Which one of the following procedures is of MOST value in   8.___
   developing problem-solving ability in grades 1-4?
   A. Children should be encouraged to solve problems in
      a variety of ways.
   B. Children should represent problems symbolically before
      attempting to solve them.
   C. Most problems should be presented to children in
      written form.
   D. Problems presented in written form should be discussed
      before children attempt to solve them.

9. Which one of the following incentives should be stressed   9.___
   by the teacher in promoting learning of a given skill by
   her pupils?
   A. Need to use the skill
   B. Desire to please the teacher
   C. Fear of low grades or failure
   D. Desire for good grades

10. The rate of forgetting of information acquired by rote   10.___
    memorization is
    A. gradually accelerating
    B. gradually decelerating
    C. slow at first, and then more rapid
    D. rapid at first, and then slower

11. Questioning is one of the most valuable devices of the   11.___
    teacher. Of the following, which statement is the LEAST
    valid?
    A. A good question provides for reflective or critical
       thinking.
    B. Teachers' questions can directly affect the develop-
       ment of children's thinking skills.
    C. Questions are useful in diagnosing an individual
       child's progress.
    D. Effective questions result from the innate talents of
       teachers.

12. Each of the following principles is valid in daily   12.___
    planning EXCEPT that it
    A. includes specific time allotments to the topics to
       be taught
    B. reflects the needs, interests, and abilities of the
       children
    C. provides sufficient time for all subject areas
    D. is flexible to allow for unexpected occurrences

13. Of the following classroom practices, the one which is   13.___
    generally UNDESIRABLE is:
    A. Whenever possible, classroom bulletin boards and
       charts should be placed at children's eye level.
    B. Windows in the classroom should be covered with crepe
       paper to make the room attractive
    C. Classroom "centers of interest" should vary from grade
       to grade in accordance with children's learning needs
    D. A room indicator card should be used to indicate the
       whereabouts of the class when it is not in the
       classroom

14. The MOST effective method of helping children to develop 14.___
    the concept of cooperation is to provide
    A. opportunities for listening to stories about
       children cooperating with each other
    B. speakers to tell about how they cooperated with people
       of various ethnic groups
    C. audio-visual materials which illustrate the concept
       of cooperation among ethnic groups
    D. many experiences that will involve them in cooperating
       with children of different ethnic groups

15. The LEAST effective strategy in stimulating children to   15.___
    express themselves orally in social studies lessons would
    be for the teacher to
    A. direct questions to specific children and get a
       response
    B. encourage children to talk with classmates and to give
       guidance when needed
    C. accept contributions from all the children
    D. help shy children express their ideas

16. Of the following statements regarding pupil discussion,   16.___
    the LEAST valid is:
    A. Use of the amenities helps to move a discussion
       forward
    B. Discussion of a topic or problem leads to a solution
       or an agreement
    C. A discussion period allows for an honest interchange
       of comments among pupils
    D. Discussion by pupils is more or less organized talking
       directed to a matter of common concern

17. Of the following, the MOST valid reason for using mimeo-   17.___
    graphed sheets for homework assignments for pupils is that
    A. the chance of pupil error in copying the assignment
       from the blackboard is reduced
    B. they make possible more interesting, varied assignments
    C. if a pupil is absent, there is no problem about
       getting the assignment
    D. it saves the teacher a good deal of time

18. The FIRST and MOST important step in planning a test is to   18.___
    A. decide what kinds of questions are to be used
    B. define the objectives of instruction
    C. determine how much time is to be allocated for testing
    D. determine the ability levels of the students

19. If, as the lesson progresses, the teacher feels that he   19.___
    will NOT be able to cover all of the content included in
    his lesson plan, he should
    A. eliminate a final summary
    B. halt discussion and write the important notes on
       the blackboard
    C. conclude the lesson on the following day
    D. discontinue questioning and complete the lesson by
       lecturing

20. The MAJOR difference between the developmental lesson and   20.___
    the unit organization is that the unit plan
    A. usually lasts from one week to two months
    B. falls entirely within one subject field
    C. is motivated by some item of current events and is
       introduced by the teacher
    D. is logically organized around a small subdivision of
       subject matter

21. During a lesson, a student who is not paying attention does   21.___
    not hear the teacher's question. The BEST procedure for
    the teacher to follow is to
    A. repeat the question for the student
    B. have another student repeat the question
    C. elicit the answer from another student
    D. reprimand the student and repeat the question

22. Good class discussion is LEAST encouraged if   22.___
    A. it is guided by questions presented by the teacher
    B. a give-and-take procedure is employed in evaluating
       the points introduced by the pupils
    C. the slower as well as the better student presents
       his idea even if it may be of little value
    D. the teacher at the start of the discussion presents
       his point of view

23. If a student's answer to a question is so important that   23.___
    it calls for further stress, it is POOR teaching for the
    teacher to
    A. ask various members in the class to comment on the answer
    B. repeat it for its proper emphasis
    C. follow it with subsidiary queries
    D. use this answer as the basis for his next question

24. The MOST worthwhile technique for the teacher to check on whether and how well homework assignments are being done is to
    A. collect the assignments daily and return them the next day
    B. walk around the room and examine each student's homework
    C. have appropriate answers read aloud
    D. have the first student in each row examine the assignments

24.____

25. The BEST procedure is to have the aim of a lesson
    A. stated clearly by the teacher at the outset of the lesson
    B. contain more than is achievable during the lesson
    C. erased from the board after it has been accepted and understood by the class
    D. grow out of the motivation

25.____

26. Of the following, the MOST appropriate summary for a lesson is the one in which the
    A. teacher briefly reviews the highlights of the lesson
    B. students briefly review the highlights of the lesson
    C. students apply to a situation the information learned in the lesson
    D. teacher quizzes the students at the end of the lesson on the information taught in the lesson

26.____

27. For an effective final summary, the teacher should
    A. have the pupils repeat the facts learned during the lesson
    B. point out the significant facts himself
    C. determine a summary question as the lesson progresses, rather than in advance of the lesson
    D. seek a recapitulation of the material presented during the lesson

27.____

28. In teaching, rapid questioning BEST serves the purpose of
    A. recalling essential facts learned earlier
    B. developing judgment
    C. evaluating viewpoints
    D. recalling concrete experiences

28.____

29. An organized discussion of a definite problem by a selected group of pupils in a class is called a
    A. forum   B. symposium
    C. sociodrama   D. debate

29.____

30. The BEST method of evaluating the affective outcomes of education is to utilize
    A. anecdotal records kept by pupils
    B. frequent short unannounced quizzes
    C. reports to the class by pupils
    D. standardized tests with national norms

30.____

31. The BEST approach for the teacher to use in an effort to
    enhance pupil participation and the quality of discussion
    is to
        A. allow volunteers to carry the discussion
        B. restrict the slow or shy pupil who may stall the
           discussion
        C. discourage the evaluation of student responses
        D. provide an answer himself rather than continually
           rephrase a question

   31.___

32. All of the following are examples of behavioral objectives
    EXCEPT:
        A. "The student can list six links of the infectious
           disease process."
        B. "Under supervision, the student can safely apply a
           triangular bandage."
        C. "The student chooses food in the cafeteria that
           comprises a well-balanced diet."
        D. "The student knows that communicable diseases are
           caused by microorganisms."

   32.___

33. An auto-instructional approach to teaching relying on the
    psychological principles of reinforcement and associative
    learning is called
        A. programmed instruction   B. problem solving
        C. socio-dramatization   D. role playing

   33.___

34. If a student's answer to a key question posed by the
    teacher is correct but ungrammatically expressed, of the
    following, it is WISEST for the teacher to
        A. interrupt the pupil's answer in order to correct the
           error
        B. ignore the error since the content of the answer is
           more important
        C. accept it and have the answer rephrased by another
           student
        D. ask the class what was wrong with the answer

   34.___

35. In the use of a blackboard, all of the following are
    desirable practices EXCEPT the one in which the teacher
        A. provides sketches large enough so that they are
           visible to all pupils in the room
        B. places complex drawings on the blackboard in advance
           of the lesson to aid in pupils' understanding
        C. keeps all information on the blackboard to assist in
           the final summarization of the lesson
        D. stands to one side as he sketches a diagram or writes
           information

   35.___

36. Of the following, the MOST desirable use of questioning
    during a lesson is the one which
        A. provides discovery of pupils' inadequate preparation
           of homework
        B. allows for the learning of the answers the teacher
           considers important enough to be remembered
        C. checks on pupil inattention during the development
           of the lesson
        D. focuses pupil attention on important aspects of the topic

   36.___

37. During a lesson, it is LEAST advisable to use audio-visual   37.___
    material
    A. when a new unit of work is being introduced
    B. during the body of the lesson in which these
       materials are the basis for the lesson
    C. as a means of summarizing the lesson
    D. as the means of encouraging spontaneous oral student
       reactions

38. In the planning of developmental lessons, there should be   38.___
    great *similarity* of the
    A. aim and motivation   B. motivation and medial summary
    C. aim and summary   D. pivotal questions and summary

39. Note-taking by pupils should be   39.___
    A. eliminated since it detracts from the pupils' ability
       to listen attentively
    B. limited to the recording of the essentials presented
       during the lesson
    C. used by the teacher as a means of measuring the extent
       to which a pupil uses his notebook
    D. concerned with the copying of all notes from the
       blackboard which were presented during the lesson

40. In order to determine if a test question has the ability   40.___
    to discriminate between better and poorer students, the
    teacher should
    A. compare the results of the better students
    B. compare the results of the poorer students
    C. perform an item analysis
    D. perform a validity and reliability analysis

41. The BEST method of appraising the understandings of   41.___
    students with language difficulties is the use of ____
    tests.
    A. essay   B. oral
    C. objective   D. standardized achievement

42. If a teacher wanted to elicit from students spontaneous   42.___
    responses regarding any topic, the method she would have
    the MOST success with is called
    A. role playing   B. problem solving
    C. brainstorming   D. self-appraisal

43. The MAIN purpose of a pivotal question is to   43.___
    A. direct thought from one aspect of a topic to another
       aspect of the same topic
    B. have students recall facts related to the topic
       being discussed
    C. drill students in specific knowledge previously learned
    D. encourage students to come up with a variety of answers

44. In providing for individual differences, of the following, 44.___
    the one that represents the MOST advisable plan for the
    teacher to adopt is to
    A. allow each child in the class complete freedom of
       choice in pursuing his projects

B. have each student apprised of his specific weakness
   and to work toward correcting it
C. arrange the students into small groups and plan his
   work so that the needs of each group are provided for
D. provide short, frequent tests to determine variations
   in individual differences and to provide drill to
   reduce the variations

45. In dealing with slow learners in a heterogeneous class,
    the teacher should
    A. exempt them from any special reports
    B. spread them throughout the classroom
    C. call upon them only if they volunteer
    D. require them to do the exact same homework assignments
       as others in the class

45.___

46. Of the following, the one which is a disadvantage of
    grouping bright students together is that
    A. the standard high school curriculum will be covered
       too quickly
    B. in being with other bright students, these talented
       pupils become too humble
    C. the teachers with special talents have to be assigned
       to the bright group at the expense of the rest of the
       students
    D. it tends to deprive them of leadership opportunities

46.___

47. If a class as a whole does very poorly on a full-period
    unit test, the MOST effective of the following procedures
    is to
    A. return the papers and warn the pupils they must
       improve
    B. give another test on the same unit after clarifying
       the main concepts with which the students had had
       difficulty and providing remedial instruction
    C. go over the test and then have each pupil bring in two
       copies of the correct solution of every problem he
       failed to work correctly
    D. discard the test papers and proceed to the next topic,
       resolving to deal with it more effectively

47.___

48. Of the following, the one which is usually the LEAST
    important purpose for giving a quiz is that it
    A. is often part of the learning process
    B. often provides a basis for remedial work
    C. gives an opportunity for additional review and drill
    D. provides objective evidence on which to base marks

48.___

49. Which one of the following principles of learning is the
    LEAST acceptable?
    A. Concepts and processes should be developed from
       concrete and familiar situations in the life of the
       pupil.
    B. The pupils should always understand the reason for a
       process.

49.___

     C. Drill may occasionally be conducted effectively in preparation for understanding.

     D. When a rule is developed, it should be, as far as possible, the pupil's own generalization on the way he solves a problem.

50. Of the following, the LEAST desirable function of a school club is to   50.___

     A. promote interest in a subject and develop a broader understanding of its nature

     B. select bright pupils for a subject team, thus providing opportunities to coach them

     C. discuss with interested students the many applications of the subject

     D. foster special interests and talents along subject lines

____

KEY (CORRECT ANSWERS)

1. B	11. D	21. A	31. A	41. B
2. D	12. C	22. D	32. D	42. C
3. C	13. B	23. A	33. A	43. A
4. D	14. D	24. A	34. B	44. A
5. A	15. A	25. A	35. D	45. C
6. A	16. B	26. C	36. D	46. D
7. A	17. A	27. C	37. D	47. B
8. A	18. D	28. A	38. C	48. D
9. A	19. C	29. A	39. B	49. C
10. D	20. D	30. C	40. D	50. B

____

TEST 2

DIRECTIONS: Each question or incomplete statement is followed by
              several suggested answers or completions. Select the
              one that BEST answers the question or completes the
              statement. *PRINT THE LETTER OF THE CORRECT ANSWER IN
              THE SPACE AT THE RIGHT.*

1. Which one of the following questions asked by a teacher   1.___
    is MOST acceptable?
        A. "The answer to question 5 is what?"
        B. "Mary, is her answer to question 5 right?"
        C. "What is your answer to question 5, George?"
        D. "Class, tell George the answer to question 5!"

2. The technique of using a team teaching design which   2.___
    includes a master teacher, regular teachers and teacher-
    aides is based MOST directly upon which one of the
    following concepts?
        A. Teachers who have served faithfully deserve master
           teacher status.
        B. Teaching is a complex art requiring different levels
           of competence and training.
        C. The conservation of public funds is a moral obligation.
        D. Teacher-aides are often more knowledgeable and skillful
           than teachers.

3. In conducting a developmental lesson, the usually MOST   3.___
    desirable way, among the following, of responding to a
    student's correct answer to your question is to
        A. enter a grade in your record book
        B. call on another pupil to answer the same question
        C. follow up with another question
        D. elaborate on the pupil's answer

4. Which one of the following procedures is MOST acceptable   4.___
    to use in class when several pupils make flagrant errors
    in grammar and usage?
        A. Correct the students unobtrusively and proceed with
           your lesson.
        B. Take a few minutes to explain since every teacher is
           a teacher of English.
        C. Ignore the errors since such deviations are time-consuming.
        D. Write a note to each pupil's English teacher to inform
           him of the errors.

5. A technique which permits students to talk about their   5.___
    own impressions, opinions, and feelings is called
        A. a learning activities packet
        B. values clarification
        C. team teaching
        D. individualized instruction

6. Good questioning technique involves all of the following   6.___
   objectives EXCEPT the one in which questions
   A. are multiple in type in order to satisfy the varying
      abilities of the pupils in the class
   B. are limited to one or two points in the chain of
      reasoning
   C. follow a predetermined order which develops the train
      of thought in logical sequence
   D. place the burden of thinking upon the student

7. The MOST desirable type of classroom discipline is BEST   7.___
   attained through which one of the following practices?
   A. encouraging traits of self-discipline
   B. including class behavior in the final rating
   C. establishing the idea that rules and regulations will
      be strictly enforced
   D. anticipating difficulty and sending the first few
      minor cases of breach of discipline to the chairman
      or dean

8. If you find a student in one of your classes doing very   8.___
   poorly despite an obviously high potential, the MOST
   desirable procedure among the following to take is to
   A. refer the student to the guidance counselor
   B. ask the student to bring his parents to school to
      see you
   C. write a letter to his parents asking them to come to
      school to see you
   D. interview the student yourself before making any
      referrals or calling his parents

9. The procedure of requiring students to stand and face the   9.___
   class, when responding, is
   A. advisable because it discourages calling out of answers
   B. inadvisable because it creates an ordeal for the shy
      student
   C. advisable because it increases audibility of answers
   D. inadvisable because a recalcitrant student would
      dispute the rule

10. Of the following, the BEST procedure for obtaining the aim 10.___
    of a specific lesson is
    A. for the teacher to state the aim of the lesson and
       write it on the blackboard so that all will be sure
       to have it
    B. to elicit the aim from the class and have it written
       on the board
    C. for the teacher to dictate the aim of the lesson so
       that all students can get it in their notebooks
    D. to give the aim the previous day so that the students
       can prepare for the lesson

11. To obtain better results, when a problem has arisen, a   11.___
    teacher should
    A. ignore the problem and not become picayune over
       every little detail
    B. reprimand the group, knowing that their pride will
       cause them to work harder

C. reprimand specific students who have caused the problem in class
D. learn the positive effects of praise and optimism on his students

12. One method of creating an atmosphere for successful learning is to
    A. compare students with one another
    B. indiscriminately criticize students' abilities
    C. treat students with respect
    D. single out students who are not performing up to standards set by class
        12.___

13. The prescribed procedure for recording the attendance in the official class is that it
    A. may be recorded in the roll book by a reliable pupil, with the clear understanding that the teacher assume full responsibility for the accuracy of the report
    B. may be recorded in the roll book by a pupil, provided the teacher checks daily
    C. must be recorded in the roll book by the teacher daily, since it is a legal document, the accuracy of which is imperative
    D. may be kept on a card and, in a day or so, be recorded in the roll book after errors have been corrected, excuse passes obtained, etc., to avoid having corrections frequently made in the roll book itself
        13.___

14. Which one of the following would be the LEAST effective procedure for insuring a prompt start of a lesson?
    A. Give a quiz as the initial step in the lesson.
    B. Assign pupils to blackboard work while others copy the next assignment.
    C. Take attendance and call for attention.
    D. Have pupils copy the new assignment and start on a "warm-up" exercise.
        14.___

15. During a supervised study period on an assignment, the teacher should NOT
    A. grade test papers and prepare reports
    B. confer quietly with individual pupils about proper study habits
    C. note the common errors made and the difficulties encountered by several pupils and conduct a quiet discussion with these pupils
    D. note the general quality and quantity of the pupils' work and modify plans for subsequent lessons, if necessary
        15.___

16. A curriculum guide *usually* contains
    A. specific techniques which the teacher must follow
    B. a file of tests that the teacher can duplicate
    C. a list of cultural and linguistic items which should be covered
    D. the daily lesson plans for the topics to be taught at each level
        16.___

17. A student should be removed from class   17.___
 A. if he habitually fails to hand in completed assignments
 B. when the positive benefits to the student are out-
 weighed by his negative influence on the group
 C. if he continually falls asleep in class
 D. if he comes late constantly and wears his hat during
 class

18. A KEY element in developing classroom discipline is   18.___
 A. the socio-economic background of the students
 B. behavior modification
 C. a big, husky male teacher
 D. a strong administration

19. Teachers who assign reference tasks must be sure that 19.___
 children are capable of performing them. Of the following,
 the task that is LEAST significant is
 A. the assignment should consist of finding answers to
 fairly specific questions
 B. children should know how to locate printed information
 in reference books
 C. children are to know that they are to copy word-for-
 word from the reference book
 D. the information should be available and locatable in
 the classroom or the school library

20. All of the following are criteria for worth-while homework 20.___
 assignments EXCEPT:
 A. All homework assignments should be written assignments
 B. Homework assignments should serve a valid educational
 purpose
 C. They should extend the pupil's fund of information or
 give practice that he needs
 D. Homework assignments should be specific and completely
 understood

21. The LEAST effective method for dealing with discipline 21.___
 problems in the classroom is to
 A. keep students busy with appropriate assignments
 B. single out difficult children for reprimand before
 the whole class
 C. make sure children understand what is expected of them
 D. keep expectations within the ability level of children

22. Which one of the following types of learning is stressed 22.___
 in the gestalt psychologists' explanation of how the
 individual learns?
 A. Classical conditioning   B. Instrumental learning
 C. Perceptual learning   D. Programmed learning

23. The concept that one can train school children to be neat 23.___
 in their appearance and in the care of their belongings by
 teaching them to be neat in their arithmetic and spelling
 papers
 A. is a characteristic tenet of the advocates of
 behavioristic psychology
 B. has been proved by recent experimental studies

C. has been virtually abandoned by educators today
D. is of central importance in the development of programs of "life adjustment education"

24. Of the following, the MOST important purpose served by teaching machines is
   A. updating curriculum material presented to the children
   B. eliminating the need for drill work
   C. providing the learner with continuous knowledge of results
   D. teaching the learner systematic study technique

25. Of the following, which one constitutes the GREATEST stumbling block faced by the teacher in helping a pupil learn how to study effectively?
   A. Identifying good methods of study
   B. Teaching pupils how to organize a study routine
   C. Developing motivation to study
   D. Teaching pupils how to pace themselves

26. If the goal of a composition is self-expression, the teacher should base the grade *primarily* on
   A. content and secondarily on form
   B. content and secondarily on appearance
   C. form and secondarily on content
   D. appearance and secondarily on content

27. A printed statement which describes a desired performance by a student is called a
   A. student program   B. lesson contract
   C. study module   D. behavioral objective

28. One of the teacher's MOST important tasks is to
   A. provide a variety of purposeful listening activities
   B. repeat students' questions and answers
   C. remain totally silent to students' utterances
   D. give detailed instructions

29. Maximizing class time and maintaining discipline are two categories of
   A. lesson planning   B. reading exercises
   C. classroom management   D. group work

30. The BEST way to make classroom dialogue more meaningful to the student is to
   A. personalize questions
   B. use the same techniques consistently
   C. call on students who know the answers
   D. let the student read out of the book

31. Of the following, the LEAST effective method for obtaining pupil participation is to
   A. give a warm-up drill to the entire class
   B. group the class and give different assignments to each group
   C. have pupils answer in concert
   D. use experiences of pupils in the lesson development

32. A test which is too difficult will USUALLY yield scores
    that fall into a
    A. bell-shaped distribution
    B. negatively skewed distribution
    C. positively skewed distribution
    D. bimodal distribution

32.___

33. The MOST desirable routine procedure for going over home-
    work is to
    A. compare answers orally with the class
    B. have students put their work on the board and explain
       it to the rest of the class
    C. have the teacher do each example together with the class
    D. collect it and mark it outside of class, returning it
       within a week

33.___

34. Of the following characteristics of a good lesson plan,
    the one which applies LEAST is that it
    A. forms part of a larger unit
    B. helps give direction to the lesson
    C. be adhered to even if vital side issues appear
    D. focuses on a meaningful problem

34.___

35. Which one of the following statements concerning the aim
    of a lesson is MOST valid?
    A. The teacher should write the aim on the blackboard
       at the beginning of each lesson.
    B. The aim should be an outgrowth of and developed from
       the motivation.
    C. Each child should write the aim of each lesson in
       his notebook each day.
    D. The teacher should announce the aim of the lesson to
       the class at the beginning of each period.

35.___

36. If a class you inherit from another teacher is poorly
    motivated and many of the students talk to one another
    during lessons, you should NOT
    A. teach carefully planned lessons daily for those who
       listen and try to ignore the others
    B. look up records of each member of the class and
       consult the guidance counselor where appropriate
    C. plan lessons in which students change activity every
       15 minutes from written work to oral work to reading,
       etc.
    D. rearrange the seating so that groups who talk to one
       another are separated as far as possible

36.___

37. Among the following, the MOST obvious fact that faces the
    teacher of a ninth grade class is that
    A. the future doctors, chemists, engineers, and nurses
       can be accurately identified
    B. the boys are generally more talented in science and
       math than are the girls
    C. the girls are generally more mature than the boys
    D. the girls prefer the biological aspects of science,
       while the boys prefer the physical aspects of science
       and mathematics

37.___

38. Which one of the following methods for getting a lesson   38.___
    started promptly is LEAST sound pedagogically?
    A. Have a challenging motivating question on the
       blackboard at the beginning of the period.
    B. Stand near the door with the marking book and give
       a demerit to any student who does not sit down and
       take out his work at once.
    C. Give a quiz on the previous lesson at the beginning
       of the period.
    D. Stand quietly in front of the room and wait for
       attention.

39. Of the following, experience with various kinds of tests   39.___
    and measurements utilized for predicting academic success
    of pupils in advanced high school courses and honor
    classes in a given subject has shown that
    A. an aptitude test is the most satisfactory single
       instrument
    B. previous achievement represented by pupil's grades
       in that subject is best
    C. all other factors should be subordinated to the I.Q.
    D. the child's motivation is the paramount factor

40. It has been found that "learning by wholes," i.e., being   40.___
    challenged by a total situation, is usually BEST achieved
    by which one of the following groups?
    A. Dull-normal pupils
    B. Girls
    C. Pupils whose attention span is small
    D. The brighter pupils

41. MOST psychologists would agree that knowledge of results   41.___
    facilitates learning because it
    A. makes the learner more cautious
    B. leads to correction of erroneous responses
    C. stresses competition within a peer group
    D. provides the learner with social recognition when
       results are good

42. Of the following, the factor that has the GREATEST effect   42.___
    in contributing to the quality of pupil learning in the
    classroom is the
    A. personality of the teacher
    B. structure of the group
    C. characteristics of the learner
    D. physical aspects of the setting in which learning takes
       place

43. Of the following, research in the field of learning has   43.___
    MOST closely established the efficacy of
    A. whole rather than part learning
    B. reward rather than punishment as a stimulus for learning
    C. distributed rather than massed practice
    D. the Law of Exercised advanced by Thorndike

44. Of the following, it is MOST essential that an anecdotal   44.___
    record include
    A. verbatim quotations by witnesses
    B. a thoughtful interpretation of the child's behavior
    C. an objective description of what the child said
       and did
    D. a daily log of the problems the child presents

45. Which one of the following is the MOST desirable way of   45.___
    economizing on time during a subject-class period?
    A. Review the homework only occasionally.
    B. Establish definite routines for the pupils.
    C. Use the blackboard sparingly.
    D. Discourage the asking of questions by students.

46. If, soon after the start of a new term, a pupil in one of   46.___
    your academic classes should refuse to do the class work,
    which one of the following procedures would, as a general
    rule, be the BEST one to follow in such a case?
    A. Send the pupil to your chairman immediately.
    B. Assert your authority at once and let him know who
       is "boss".
    C. Speak to him after class to ascertain the cause of
       his behavior.
    D. Ignore the pupil but give him a failing mark at the
       end of the term.

47. Of the following possible criteria for evaluating the   47.___
    success of the teaching of reluctant learners in "second
    track" courses, the LEAST significant is
    A. achievement on standardized tests
    B. improvement in social behavior
    C. improvement in work habits
    D. improvement over past performance

48. Which one of the following statements about lesson plans   48.___
    is pedagogically sound?
    A. They should be made up at least a month in advance
       and adhered to strictly so that nothing is neglected.
    B. They are not needed by the experienced teacher.
    C. They should be made up week by week, according to
       the special needs of each class, and be used flexibly.
    D. They need not include pivotal questions.

49. The PRIMARY aim of assigning homework should generally be   49.___
    to
    A. review for class and term tests
    B. drill
    C. develop habits of working hard
    D. instill concepts

50. The daily homework assignment should USUALLY   50.___
    A. not include exercises on the new work if the class
       understands it
    B. have part devoted to review and part based on the
       new lesson
    C. consist, at least in part, of reading ahead in the
       new work to be taught

D. be patterned after Regents-type questions

————

KEY (CORRECT ANSWERS)

1. C	11. C	21. B	31. C	41. B
2. B	12. C	22. C	32. C	42. C
3. C	13. C	23. C	33. B	43. C
4. A	14. C	24. C	34. C	44. C
5. B	15. A	25. C	35. B	45. B
6. A	16. C	26. A	36. A	46. C
7. A	17. B	27. D	37. C	47. A
8. D	18. A	28. A	38. B	48. C
9. C	19. C	29. C	39. B	49. D
10. B	20. A	30. A	40. D	50. B

————

EXAMINATION SECTION

DIRECTIONS: Each question or incomplete statement is followed by several suggested answers or completions. Select the one that BEST answers the question or completes the statement. *PRINT THE LETTER OF THE CORRECT ANSWER IN THE SPACE AT THE RIGHT.*

1. Studies have shown that children from different social classes learn prejudices at different stages in their development.
   Compared with the other social classes, the lower-class children GENERALLY develop biases
   A. earlier than the other classes
   B. later than the other classes
   C. at about the same time as middle-class children but later than upper-class children
   D. at about the same stage of development as other classes
   E. unpredictably, depending on the area in which the bias was first encountered

   1.___

2. Studies dealing with stability of I.Q.'s of culturally deprived children who stay in underprivileged environments show
   A. a steady increase in median score with age
   B. a stable I.Q. although below the national average
   C. an unpredictable direction of average I.Q. score due to individual differences
   D. slight increase in I.Q. score due to exposure to TV, radio, etc.
   E. a steady decline in median score with age

   2.___

3. Recent disclosures of the use of narcotics by adolescents have caused great concern among educators.
   Studies have revealed that
   A. there is a low correlation between the intelligence of the children involved
   B. the majority of school-age addicts are mental retardates
   C. mental retardates in low socio-economic areas comprise more than 50 percent of adolescent narcotic users
   D. use of narcotics is more prevalent among Spanish-speaking than other ethnic groups
   E. approximately 50% of adolescent narcotics users have parents who are also narcotics users

   3.___

4. For satisfactory functioning in the community, the following MINIMUM reading level is generally necessary: _____ year.
   A. third   B. fourth   C. fifth
   D. sixth   E. seventh

   4.___

5. Of the following, a technique that is especially useful   5.___
   for the study of inter-pupil relationships in a group or
   classroom situation is the
   A. anecdotal record
   B. sociogram
   C. Rorschach Test
   D. Thematic Apperception Test
   E. Vineland Social Maturity Scale

6. Generally speaking, the FIRST source, chronologically,   6.___
   of racial biases is
   A. the peer group   B. teachers   C. parents
   D. siblings   E. the community

7. All of the following statements concerning social rela-   7.___
   tionships in the early school years are usually true
   EXCEPT:
   A. Groups are small and shift rapidly
   B. Friends are selected because of propinquity and the
      accident of sharing objects
   C. Children play and work with others to satisfy
      personal rather than social desires
   D. Friends are selected on the basis of belonging to
      the same sex
   E. Sometimes friendships may result from a chance
      meeting in which similarity in interests or attitudes
      is discovered

8. Sex differences in interests are influenced MAINLY by   8.___
   which one of the following?
   A. Heredity   B. Instincts
   C. Physiological factors   D. Cultural experiences
   E. Emotional factors

9. Of the following concepts, the one LEAST consonant with   9.___
   John Dewey's philosophy of education is
   A. learning through experience
   B. extrinsic motivation
   C. emphasis on the learner rather than on the subject
   D. democracy and pragmatism
   E. authority is vested in the situation

10. Dr. James Bryant Conant wrote all of the following   10.___
    EXCEPT
    A. THE SCHOOLS
    B. SLUMS AND SUBURBS
    C. MODERN SCIENCE AND MODERN MAN
    D. EDUCATION IN A DIVIDED WORLD
    E. GENERAL EDUCATION IN A FREE SOCIETY

11. Which of the following statements is LEAST likely to be   11.___
    true of first grade children as compared with fifth
    graders?
    A. There is much concern for group welfare and group
       approval.
    B. There is little concern for order and neatness.
    C. Some regular routines give security to children of
       this age.
    D. There is little intermingling of boys and girls in
       their play activities.
    E. There is a dislike for oral reading.

12. In order to secure good group play activities in her   12.___
    class, the teacher of a class should plan
    A. classroom procedures with a view to minimizing
       individual play activities on the part of her
       children
    B. for personal participation in every group play
       activity which is organized
    C. to play with small groups several times before the
       children play without her
    D. to set aside one day a week for independent group
       play activity
    E. play activities in which she can provide all needed
       assistance to each of her children

13. Of the following statements regarding juvenile delin-   13.___
    quency, the one that is MOST NEARLY true is:
    They
    A. almost invariably come from families of low economic
       level
    B. are almost invariably of a low intellectual level
    C. are usually more mature socially and physically than
       other children
    D. are fast learners when properly motivated and are
       especially good in manual work
    E. often suffer from a combination of emotional illness
       and lack of conscience

14. Given only the information that most *juvenile delinquents*   14.___
    come from low socio-economic neighborhoods, the conclusion
    that such neighborhoods cause the delinquency is logically
    based on all of the following assumptions EXCEPT:
    A. No other more basic factors cause both the juvenile
       delinquency and the poor neighborhoods
    B. The higher incidence of such delinquency in low
       socio-economic areas is not due to chance
    C. Juvenile delinquency is more serious when it occurs
       in poor neighborhoods
    D. The same definition of delinquent behavior has been
       applied to all socio-economic levels of juveniles
    E. Some factors present in low socio-economic neighbor-
       hoods which cause delinquent behavior are apparently
       not present at all, or at least to the same degree,
       as in other neighborhoods

15. A sociogram is a device utilized to represent relation-   15.___
    ships among the
    A. data obtained by the social worker associated with
       a guidance clinic
    B. major institutions characterizing our contemporary
       society
    C. different socio-economic classes usually found in
       a school
    D. members of a group in respect to social acceptance
    E. members of a group in respect to decision-making

16. Susan doesn't have any friends in the classroom. So far,   16.___
    she hasn't won the group's approval.
    The MOST effective of the following means for helping
    Susan is to
    A. have her be class messenger with the privilege of
       going into other classrooms
    B. plan a class play and select Susan for the leading
       role
    C. appoint her class president
    D. find out the pupils with whom Susan would like to be
       friendly and give her a chance to work with them
    E. ask the children how they would feel if they were in
       Susan's place

17. Sociometric testing provides a technique for   17.___
    A. analyzing each person's position and status within
       the group with respect to a particular criterion
    B. revealing the prejudices of each individual
    C. obtaining a picture of boy-girl relationship
    D. analyzing the pupil's understanding of the problems
       faced by society and encouraging efforts to solve
       them
    E. revealing data obtained by the social worker asso-
       ciated with a guidance clinic

18. Most differences in play activities and interests between   18.___
    boys and girls in the elementary school years can PROBABLY
    be attributed to
    A. inherent biological differences
    B. inherent emotional differences
    C. instinctual influences
    D. cultural influences
    E. inherent intellectual differences

19. Personal and social adjustment schedules, inventories,   19.___
    and checklists are especially valuable
    A. in identifying pupils who cannot answer personal
       questions frankly
    B. in effecting the readjustment of mildly neurotic
       individuals
    C. as a crude means of locating pupils who need help
       in adjustment
    D. in helping students plan their study time
    E. in ascertaining whether the teaching methods used
       are reaching all of the children in the class

20. If some children of very slow learning parents were reared in a very stimulating cultural environment, the PROBABLE result would be
    A. some but relatively small increase in the test I.Q.
    B. a slight decrease in I.Q.
    C. no change in I.Q.
    D. giftedness
    E. academic success

20.____

21. Studies of the intelligence of delinquents compared with normal children indicate that
    A. delinquents are superior to normal children
    B. conclusions on inferiority of normals or delinquents cannot be drawn
    C. delinquents are equal to normal children
    D. delinquents are inferior to normal children
    E. delinquents are more creative but slightly less intelligent than normal children

21.____

22. Studies of the relation of body build to social class level in the United States have shown that
    A. no significant differences in body build apparently exist between children of different social class levels
    B. upper-class children are shorter and broader than lower-class children
    C. upper-class children are taller and thinner than lower-class children
    D. middle-class children are both taller and broader than either upper-class or lower-class children
    E. lower-class children are short and broad while upper- and middle-class children are tall and thin

22.____

23. One of the effects of automation and productivity has been to
    A. increase the education and training requirements of jobs
    B. eliminate many middlemen in trade and service fields
    C. decrease the number of semi-professional jobs
    D. lower the level of earnings in service jobs
    E. raise the level of earnings for semi-skilled workers

23.____

24. As part of the socialization process, the phenomenon of ambivalence is at its HIGHEST intensity during the _____ years.
    A. toddler   B. preschool
    C. early school   D. intermediate school
    E. high school

24.____

25. The psychological climate of the home which influences adjustment of the child is MOST closely related to the
    A. number of children in the home
    B. educational level of the parents
    C. occupational level of the father
    D. attitudes of the parents
    E. socio-economic status of the family

25.____

26. Of the following characteristics, the one MOST generally   26.____
    found among children just entering the junior high
    school is
    A. a tendency of boys and girls to seek each other's
       company
    B. the acceptance of parent and teacher opinion with
       little question
    C. the popularity of guessing games, puzzles, and games
       of chance
    D. a preference for highly organized competitive team
       play
    E. a conscientious and ardent effort to achieve
       academic success

27. Of the following teachers, the one MOST liked by the   27.____
    largest number of pupils is the one who
    A. sets easily attainable standards
    B. demonstrates a high level of intellectual competence
    C. maintains an impersonal objective attitude
    D. demonstrates great athletic ability
    E. is sympathetic

28. The MOST valid reason for keeping pupil personnel records   28.____
    is to
    A. form a basis for referral to community agencies and
       for reports to higher institutions
    B. provide a basis for distribution of pupils among
       classes of a grade
    C. provide data for educational research on the basis
       of which educational improvements are planned
    D. improve instruction and guidance for the pupil
    E. facilitate school groupings, either homogeneous or
       heterogeneous

29. *It is imperative for a school system to force periodic*   29.____
    reconsideration of its specific objectives.
    The MOST important of the following reasons for this
    dictum is that some objectives may
    A. have lost their usefulness
    B. have been overlooked
    C. not be easily attainable
    D. no longer be accepted by the teaching staff
    E. be unrealizable under the present administrative
       structure

30. The MOST important of the following elements of a plan   30.____
    for an educational program is
    A. definition of the goals
    B. assignment of resources
    C. setting up the time schedule
    D. provision for evaluation
    E. organizing a cadre

31. One of the CHIEF aims of the junior high school which differentiates it from the senior high school is that the junior high school
    A. makes provision for pre-vocational training
    B. emphasizes an exploratory program through curricular and extra-curricular activities
    C. seeks to meet individual differences through individual pupil programs
    D. has a larger number of extra-curricular activities
    E. encourages the enrichment and expansion of pupils' social contacts

31.____

32. In order to maintain healthy emotional growth in children, there should be
    A. a laissez-faire classroom atmosphere
    B. strict control by the teacher at all times
    C. continuous and unhampered expression by the children
    D. opportunities for internalizing all tensions
    E. a judicious combination of free expression and control

32.____

33. Of the following, the MOST important thing for a teacher in a bilingual community to do is to
    A. teach as though all of the children in her group understand English
    B. avoid referring to anything foreign in order to encourage the children to adopt American ways
    C. learn about the culture of the non-English-speaking children in order to understand their feelings and behavior
    D. give the non-English speaking a feeling of security and identification by separating them from the English-speaking children at first
    E. help the non-English-speaking children gain a sense of *belonging* by giving them extra attention at all times

33.____

34. *Constrain neither child nor culture* is typical of a philosophy of education which could properly be called
    A. progressive   B. authoritarian   C. laissez-faire
    D. developmental   E. maturational

34.____

35. In an ideal class, the social climate would indicate that
    A. the teacher is in complete control of the situation
    B. every pupil knows his limits
    C. ideas flow freely
    D. the desires of the pupils are paramount
    E. an almost equal combination of the desires of the teacher and the desires of the pupils pervades

35.____

36. In home-school relations, the teacher is the key, and so she should
    A. work on problems alone
    B. seek the help of other informed people
    C. tell the parents what to do

36.____

D. consider the school more important than the home
E. help the parents understand their child as well as she does

37. Studies of child growth indicate that

37.___

    A. the onset of puberty adversely effects the child's motor coordination
    B. mentally retarded children are usually above norms in physical growth
    C. each child has his own growth pattern
    D. mental growth and physical growth are highly correlated
    E. physical growth and emotional stability are highly correlated

38. A teacher is practicing the BEST of the following devices for personal guidance when she

38.___

    A. keeps her class in perfect order by regular lectures on good manners and obedience
    B. lets her pupils know that lack of consideration for others is a personal affront to her
    C. provides an atmosphere in which each pupil is made to feel conscious of his own worth
    D. keeps her pupils busy at their work all through the period
    E. provides time to hold personal discussions with each of her pupils once a week

39. The GREATEST value in an extensive program of class trips and excursions is that they

39.___

    A. break the monotony of the daily school routine
    B. develop an appreciation of the many points of interest available
    C. provide training in proper behavior in public places
    D. provide enrichment and experiences related to class studies
    E. encourage the pupils to visit these places on their own

40. The core curriculum is in harmony with that tenet of modern psychology which holds that the MOST important factor in the learning process is the

40.___

    A. integration of the trial and error method into creative effort
    B. repetition of facts or skills until they are mastered
    C. training of the mind through mental discipline
    D. law of satisfactions
    E. feeling of a need or purpose

41. If a controversial issue is raised in class, the teacher should

41.___

    A. tell the children that there is no value in discussing it because there is no correct answer
    B. give the children the best available answer to the issue

C. permit the children to form their own conclusions after all the facts are presented
D. obtain the sanction of the principal before discussing it
E. permit the children to discuss the issue but she should not express her own viewpoint

42. More than three centuries ago, Comenius enunciated the principle of *Things-Ideas-Words*.
This principle is MOST clearly explained by the statement that
A. essay themes should deal with concrete ideas
B. the sequence of learning proceeds from experiencing to conceiving to defining
C. all learning requires manipulation of things
D. abstract ideas grow out of concrete concepts
E. knowledge falls into one or more of these categories

42.___

43. Parents of physically handicapped youngsters often tend to overprotect their children.
In MOST instances, this overprotection may be attributed to the parents'
A. recognition of the child's greater need for protection
B. projection of his own dependency needs on to the child
C. unrecognized feelings of hostility and guilt toward the child
D. wealth of affection which has too few outlets
E. reinforced understanding of the emotional trauma often caused by physical defects

43.___

44. MOST studies of children showing physical defects indicate that the incidence of defects is
A. greater among mentally retarded children than among normal children
B. smaller among mentally retarded children than among normal children
C. about the same among mentally retarded and normal children
D. sometimes greater among mentally retarded children and sometimes greater among normal children, depending upon the specific defect under study
E. without pattern

44.___

45. Of the following, the MOST important determinant of a favorable learning environment is the
A. physical setting of the classroom
B. course of study used
C. interpersonal relationships in the classroom
D. age range of the children
E. students' respect for the teacher

45.___

46. In order to employ mental hygiene problems effectively,   46.___
    parents of school children need MOST of all
    A. an understanding of the meaning, purpose, and goals
       of mental hygiene
    B. appropriate specialized courses in psychology
    C. membership in an organization for retarded children
    D. a well-organized set of rules to guide them
    E. an insight into their child's problems

47. The MAJOR barrier in the way of successful conferences   47.___
    between the teacher and parents is the
    A. hostile attitude of most of the parents
    B. lack of training on the part of the teacher in how
       to conduct an interview
    C. overzealousness on the part of the teacher to help
       her children
    D. problem of getting the parents to verbalize at such
       conferences
    E. lack of objectivity on the part of both the parents
       and the teacher

48. In our present economy, other workers tend to   48.___
    A. reject mental retardates because they have a low
       level of productivity
    B. accept mental retardates because they do not con-
       stitute an economic threat
    C. accept some mental retardates and reject others,
       depending upon the personalities involved
    D. reject mental retardates because they work for less
       money
    E. accept mental retardates because they feel sorry
       for them

49. Many schools organize separate discussion groups for   49.___
    parents of children in special education classes.
    Of the following, the MOST valid objection to this
    procedure is
    A. children in special education classes do not have
       unique problems
    B. parents of children in special education classes
       generally have lower mentality themselves
    C. parents of children in special education classes
       tend to be stigmatized by this arrangement
    D. it creates an artificial division between parent
       groups
    E. it leads to hostility between the various groups of
       parents

50. Early in the school year, you learn that many parents   50.___
    refuse to allow their children to play with the children
    in your special class.
    Of the following, the BEST procedure you can adopt is to
        A. arrange activities for the children in your class
           which will be carried on after school hours
        B. reassure the parents of your exceptional children
           that the problem is not serious and will resolve
           itself in time
        C. confer with local community agencies about the
           problem and possible solutions
        D. ask teachers of other classes to make a special effort
           to change attitudes of parents of their children
        E. reassure the parents that the disabilities of
           exceptional youngsters do not affect their normal
           capacity for playing with other children

           _____

KEY (CORRECT ANSWERS)

1. A	11. A	21. D	31. B	41. C
2. E	12. B	22. C	32. E	42. B
3. A	13. E	23. A	33. C	43. C
4. B	14. C	24. B	34. C	44. A
5. B	15. D	25. D	35. C	45. C
6. C	16. D	26. C	36. B	46. E
7. D	17. A	27. E	37. C	47. B
8. D	18. D	28. C	38. C	48. C
9. B	19. C	29. A	39. D	49. D
10. C	20. A	30. A	40. E	50. C

           _____

GENERAL INFORMATION AND BACKGROUND
EXAMINATION SECTION

DIRECTIONS FOR THIS SECTION:
   Each question or incomplete statement is followed by several suggested answers or completions. Select the one that *BEST* answers the question or completes the statement. *PRINT THE LETTER OF THE CORRECT ANSWER IN THE SPACE AT THE RIGHT.*

TEST 1

1. Written by one who is often called the greatest story-
   teller of all literature, this masterpiece deserves
   praise for its narrative interest and its vivid and
   realistic pictures of life and people. It contains a
   wide diversity of types of story, including romances,
   adventure stories, stories of illicit love, satiric
   stories directed against the clergy, and comic anec-
   dotes. The stories are told during a period of 10 successive days by a group of people gathered in the
   country to escape the Great Plague.
   The work referred to in this passage was written by
      A. Marco Polo   B. Rabelais   C. Castiglione
      D. Boccaccio   E. Cervantes
                                                                    1. ...

2. In the United States, in the 1920's, the trend toward
   uniformity was hastened by *which* of the following?
      I. An increase in the number of independent newspapers
     II. The development of national advertising media
    III. The radio
     IV. The movies
   The *CORRECT* combination is:
      A. I and II   B. III and IV   C. I, II, and IV
      D. II, III, and IV E. I, II, III, and IV
                                                                    2. ...

3. *Which* of the following is the *MOST IMPORTANT* argument
   for laws stringently controlling the use of DDT?
      A. It is responsible for the near extinction of the
         whooping crane.
      B. Its use has resulted in the extermination of some
         insect species.
      C. It becomes concentrated in certain body tissues of
         organisms high in food chains.
      D. It has resulted in the starvation of the songbirds
         that commonly winter in the northern states.
      E. Chemically it has a long half-life.
                                                                    3. ...

4. The figures in the graph on the following page pertain to
   the United States. They are figures for the number of
      A. cities   B. counties   C. towns
      D. school districts   E. townships
                                                                    4. ...

1

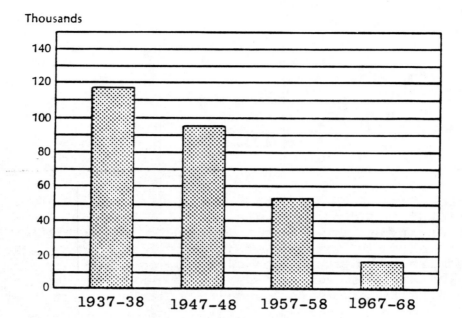

Thousands

| | 1937–38 | 1947–48 | 1957–58 | 1967–68 |

5. An increase in *which* of the following was a *NECESSARY*   5. ...
   condition for the development of the earliest urban areas?
      A. Agricultural productivity   B. Immigration
      C. Contact with other cultures D. Birth rate
      E. Mechanization

6. A classicist in literature, royalist in politics, and   6. ...
   Anglo-Catholic in religion is the description of *himself*
   given by
      A. T. S. Eliot   B. Stephen Spender
      C. W. H. Auden   D. Archibald MacLeish
      E. John Masefield

7. *Which* of the following has had the *GREATEST* effect on   7. ...
   the rate of population change in the less developed of
   the developing nations?
      A. Increases in the average age at marriage
      B. Modern medicine and pesticides
      C. Rises in the net reproduction rate
      D. Improvements in birth-control techniques
      E. Sterilization and abortion programs

8. *Which* of the following *BEST* characterizes the situation   8. ...
   of the European powers during the 10 years before the
   First World War?
      A. Relations were fluid, with few indications of final
         alignments.
      B. Major alignments were maintained without change as
         crises decreased in number and intensity.
      C. The status quo was maintained in a period of relative
         calm.
      D. The absence of serious clashes facilitated the formula-
         tion of new alignments.
      E. Major alignments were completed while crises accelerated.

9. He sees the drama in functional terms as a social instru-   9. ...
   ment to help organize and motivate black communities. He
   wants the black theatre not only to be entertaining and

artful, but also to reflect, inerpret, teach, chronicle, take part in, and, in a sense, lead a black revolution. The dramatist described above is

   A. Marc Connelly   B. LeRoi Jones   C. Edward Albee
   D. Arthur Miller   E. Tennessee Williams

10. The explanation for the red appearance of the setting sun   10. ...
also explains why

   A. a red barn looks redder at sunset than at noon
   B. red is a better color than blue for the navigation lights on top of radio transmission towers
   C. a blue object looks black in red light
   D. the flame from burning calcium is red
   E. blood looks red under white light

11.   11. ...

The *structural system* used in this building is

   A. load-bearing masonry   B. prestressed concrete
   C. cast-iron panels   D. steel frame
   E. thin-shell concrete

12. Cities often grow up in locations near bulky raw materi-   12. ...
als, if power and markets are fairly accessible.
The factors above influenced the development of *all* of the following cities *EXCEPT*

   A. Birmingham, Alabama   B. Wilmington, Delaware
   C. Duluth, Minnesota   D. Des Moines, Iowa
   E. Oklahoma City, Oklahoma

13. *Which* of the following has had the effect of *STRENGTHEN-*   13. ...
ING the system of checks and balances in the national government?

   A. National political parties
   B. The power of judicial review
   C. The popular election of United States senators
   D. Federal grants-in-aid
   E. The trend toward bipartisanship in foreign affairs

14. A musical program devoted solely to major compositions   14. ...
by Mahler, Beethoven, and Shostakovich would, *most likely*, be a(n)

   A. piano recital   B. symphony orchestra concert

C. string quartet recital   D. organ recital
E. song recital

15. *Which* of the following is the *BEST* criterion for objec-   15. ...
    tively determining an individual's social class in the
    United States?
    A. Income   B. Ancestry   C. Religious belief
    D. Political belief   E. Interests

16. If Country I can produce Commodity A with 1 unit of in-   16. ...
    put and Commodity B with 3 units of input and if Country
    II can produce Commodity A with 5 units of input and Com-
    modity B with 10 units of input, it would be *most likely*
    that
    A. Country I would produce both commodities and that
       Country II would produce neither
    B. no trade would take place between the two countries
    C. Country II would gain from trade but that Country I
       would not
    D. Country I would gain from trade but that Country II
       would not
    E. each country would gain by trading with the other

17. *Which* of the following statements concerning executives   17. ...
    in the Federal Government of the United States is *CORRECT?*
    A. Political executives, appointed by the President or
       by heads of agencies, tend to have a common background
       and work experience.
    B. While the President has had little success in co-
       ordinating and directing the work of the executive
       branch, the department heads have successfully over-
       come the preference of their bureaus and divisions for
       operating autonomy.
    C. Salaries of executives compare favorably with salaries
       of business executives.
    D. Normally, Congress has clearly defined the objectives
       of various administrative programs and so has reduced
       the range and degree of discretion exercised by execu-
       tives.
    E. Heads of agencies and their political assistants rare-
       ly have complete control over their programs partly
       because other agencies with related and perhaps con-
       flicting interests must be consulted.

18. The artist *most closely* associated with works such as the 18. ...
    one following is
    A. Picasso   B. Calder
    C. Braque   D. Dali
    E. Brancusi

19. The Emancipation Proclamation, January 1, 1863, granted   19. ...
    freedom *to*
    A. all slaves   B. slaves in the border states
    C. slaves in the North
    D. slaves in areas occupied by the Union Army
    E. slaves in areas still in rebellion

20. What was thy pity's recompense?   20. ...
    A silent suffering, and intense;
    The rock, the vulture, and the chain.
    All that the proud can feel of pain.

    These lines *probably* refer to the fate of
    A. Laocoön   B. Cassandra   C. Tantalus
    D. Prometheus   E. Atlas

21. The number of voters participating in the *1920* United   21. ...
    States presidential election increased relatively more
    than the total population increased from *1916-1920 PRIMARILY*
    because
    A. the increase in the urban population made it relatively
       easy for a larger percent to vote
    B. improvements in educational methods increased popular
       interest. in politics
    C. the Nineteenth Amendment was ratified in 1920

      D. voters turned out in large numbers to vote against
         the League of Nations
      E. Harding waged a vigorous campaign for the presidency

22. *Which* of the following statements is *typically* associated   22. ...
with Hobbes?
      A. Men require government for civil peace.
      B. Government should be limited by certain constitution-
         al safeguards.
      C. The best protection for individual liberty is freedom
         of private associations.
      D. Government is a trust that may be revoked by the
         governed whenever those who govern violate it.
      E. Political conflict results from competition among
         economic forces in society.

23. Political boundaries in Africa at the *mid-twentieth*   23. ...
century were determined *PRIMARILY* by
      A. geographic realities   B. economic factors
      C. tribal organization
      D. nineteenth-century European power politics
      E. nationalist sentiments

24. During the 1930's, an *important* reason for friction be-   24. ...
tween the United States and Mexico was Mexico's
      A. alignment with Germany   B. support for neutralism
      C. expropriation of foreign mineral concessions
      D. trade expansion in South America
      E. opposition to reciprocal trade agreements

25. *Which* of the following has contributed *MOST* to the in-   25. ...
crease in real wages in the United States since 1900?
      A. Rising prices   B. Increasing productivity
      C. Increasing strength of labor unions
      D. Increasing use of the corporate form of business
         organization
      E. Increasing legislation favorable to labor

TEST 2

1. The present international political system is *MOST*   1. ...
ACCURATELY characterized as a
      A. loose concert of power tending toward a world empire
      B. unit-veto system tending toward a balance of power
      C. tight bipolar system tending toward a universal
         system
      D. balance of power system tending toward a loose bi-
         polar system
      E. loose bipolar system tending toward a multi-polar or
         unit-veto system

2. W. E. B. Du Bois led the early twentieth-century reaction   2. ...
against the doctrines of Booker T. Washington on the ground
that blacks should
      A. repatriate themselves to Africa
      B. demand their full constitutional rights
      C. work through the Republican party rather than the
         Colored Farmers' Alliance

    D. seek to win a place in American society through
       vocational training

    E. remain in rural areas rather than be encouraged to
       migrate to cities

3. *Which* of the following are *CHANGES* in the pattern of   3. ...
   economic behavior in the United States that have oc-
   curred during the past 50 years? A(n)
      I. decrease in the proportion of farm workers
    II. decrease in the hours worked per week
  III. decrease in the proportion of service workers
   IV. increase in productivity per hours worked
   The *CORRECT* combination is:
    A. I and II   B. III and IV   C. I, II, and III
    D. I, II, and IV   E. II, III, and IV

4. With two films, Z and STATE OF SEIGE, he has emerged as   4. ...
   the contemporary director who has best mastered the technique of transforming odious political situations into
   tension-filled feature films, and he has moved the political film from a genre with sectarian appeal to one with a
   mass audience.
   The film director described above is
    A. Costa Gavras   B. Jean-Luc Godard
    C. Michelangelo Antonioni   D. Luis Bunuel
    E. Ingmar Bergman

5. An *essential* feature of French economic planning is   5. ...
    A. close regulation of foreign trade
    B. close collaboration of business in the planning process
    C. close collaboration of labor in the planning process
    D. the wide use of formal mathematical planning models
    E. the close coordination of short-term stabilization
       policies with medium-term plans

6. *Which* of the following are *TRUE* of the *majority* of im-   6. ...
   migrants who came to the United States between 1880 and
   1920? They
      I. came under contract and worked primarily as domestics
    II. arrived able to speak and write the English language
  III. were from Southern and Eastern Europe
   IV. settled in large cities
    V. settled in large cities
   The *CORRECT* combination is:
    A. I and II   B. I and V   C. II and IV
    D. III and IV   E. III and V

7.   7. ...

The painting reproduced above is *characteristic* of the work of

7

A. Andrew Wyeth   B. Gilbert Stuart   C. Norman Rockwell
D. William Harnett E. Grant Wood

8. Although their objectives are frequently similar, business
and public administration differ *MOST* in *which* of the following respects?

   A. Public administration is more interested in research
and development than is business administration.
   B. As a measure of performance, profit is often lacking
in public administration.
   C. Business is concerned primarily with production whereas government is concerned primarily with long-range
planning activities.
   D. Business furnishes goods to the public whereas government furnishes services.
   E. Unlike the situation in business administration, there
are no measurable units of output in the provision of
public goods and services.

8. ...

9. *Which* of the following contributed *MOST* to increasing the
yield of rice in Asian countries in the 1960's?

   A. Use of fertilizers   B. Use of insecticides
   C. Increased use of irrigation
   D. Rotation of crops
   E. Development of new strains

9. ...

10.

10. ...

Which of the following statements about the building
shown above is *CORRECT?*

   A. The use of flying buttresses to support the roof
indicates that it is a Gothic cathedral.
   B. Although the structure of the nave and transept is
basically Romanesque, eclectic additions have been
made to the cathedral.
   C. The minarets interspersed among the domes indicate
a Chinese influence.
   D. The several domes indicate that it was originally
a Roman temple, later converted into a Christian
church.
   E. Although at first glance the building seems to be
High Renaissance, the rose window in the facade
identifies it as Gothic.

11. In recent decades the composition of the population of
Japan has been changed *PRIMARILY* by *which* of the following?

11. ...

    A. Emigration planned and directed by the government
    B. The accelerated rate of industrialization since the Second World War
    C. An increase in life expectancy
    D. The restriction of immigration
    E. The drastic reduction of the birthrate

12. The reply was to the effect that the *Creative Power,* when he made the earth, made no marks, no lines of division or separation upon it, and that it should be allowed to remain as then made. The earth was his mother. He was made of the earth and grew up on its bosom. The earth, as his mother and nurse, was sacred to his affections, too sacred to be valued by or sold for silver and gold. He could not consent to sever his affections from the land that bore him. He was content to live upon such fruits as the *Creative Power* placed within and upon it, and unwilling to barter these and his free habits away for the new modes of life proposed by us.

    This reply was *most likely* made by a(n)

    A. Massachusetts Puritan to the English Privy Council
    B. American Indian to a United States Government commission
    C. Mormon leader to the governor of the Utah Territory
    D. Mexican official to American settlers in Texas
    E. New England transcendentalist to a local tax assessor

13.

PERCENT OF FEMALE-HEADED FAMILIES IN THE UNITED STATES IN 1960 BY INCOME, RACE, AND PLACE OF RESIDENCE

	Rural Percent	Urban Percent	Total Percent
Black			
Under $3,000	18	47	36
$3,000 and over	5	8	7
Total	14	23	21
White			
Under $3,000	12	18	22
$3,000 and over	2	4	3
Total	4	7	6

The data in the table above indicate that in the United States in 1960 female-headed families were *more common*

    A. in rural areas than in urban areas
    B. among whites than among blacks at the same income level
    C. among poor whites than among nonpoor blacks
    D. among the poor than the nonpoor only in urban areas
    E. among blacks than whites in urban areas but not in rural areas

14. If each of the following groups of artists could collaborate on a work, *which group* would *most probably* create an American folk opera based upon themes drawn from the early history of the nation?

    A. Leonard Bernstein, Jack Kerouac, and Pearl Primus
    B. Aaron Copland, Carl Sandburg, and Agnes de Mille
    C. Lukas Foss, Ernest Hemingway, and George Balanchine
    D. Paul Hindemith, Henry Miller, and Anthony Tudor
    E. Gian-Carlo Menotti, Tennessee Williams, and Martha Graham

15. Assume that in a United States presidential election,   15. ...
    salient campaign issues favored the Republican party
    and the Republican presidential nominee was very popular
    but not highly partisan. In these circumstances, a post-
    election analysis would be *most likely* to show that
    A. voters who considered themselves strong Democrats
       supported the Democratic candidate almost without
       defection
    B. the independent vote split giving a slight advantage
       to the Republican party
    C. voters who considered themselves Democrats defected
       in large numbers and voted for the Republican nominee
    D. voters who classified themselves as strong Republicans
       tended not to vote if they thought the Republican
       nominee was too liberal
    E. the independent vote split in roughly the same pro-
       portions as party affiliations in the United States

16. The Nazi-Soviet Nonaggression Pact in 1939 was followed   16. ...
    almost immediately by
    A. Germany's attack on Poland
    B. Germany's attack on the Soviet Union
    C. United States entry into the Second World War
    D. the Munich Agreement   E. the Atlantic Charter

17. Studies of social class in the United States show that   17. ...
    the *overwhelming majority* of Americans
    A. conceptualize themselves as middle-class
    B. refer to themselves as working-class people
    C. believe that there are no social classes in the
       United States
    D. resent the dominance of middle-class values
    E. believe that education is no longer essential for
       social mobility

18. Easy access to raw materials, the availability of a large 18. ...
    and efficient labor supply, well established railway facili-
    ties, proximity to a large steel market, and a stimulating
    climate due to the moderating influence of the lake were
    factors in the establishment of major iron and steel manu-
    facturing plants in this area.
    Which of the following areas is described in the passage
    above?
    A. Pittsburgh   B. Birmingham   C. Duluth
    D. Chicago-Gary   E. Los Angeles-Fontana

19. *All* of the following statements express policies of the   19. ...
    United States government during the Cold War *EXCEPT:*
    A. Our policy with regard to Europe was not to interfere
       with her internal concerns but to consider each
       European government de facto as the legitimate govern-
       ment and to cultivate friendly relations with it.
    B. Even though Soviet leaders professed to believe that the
       conflict between capitalism and communism was irrecon-
       cilable and must eventually be resolved by the triumph
       of the latter, was our hope that a fair and equitable
       settlement would be reached when they realize that we
       were too strong to be beaten and too determined to be
       frightened.

C. If we find it impossible to enlist Soviet cooperation
in the solution of world problems, we should be prepared to join with the British and other Western
countries in an attempt to build up a world of our own.
D. The role of this country should consist of friendly aid
in the drafting of a European economic program to get
Europe on its feet and to provide financial support for
such a program so far as it may be practical for us to
do so.
E. The United States seeks no territorial expansion or
selfish advantage and has no plans for aggression
against any other state, large or small, but is committed to the mutual security of non-Communist nations
in Europe.

20. A high level of industrialization has *generally* been accompanied by   20. ...
    A. greater interdependence of various sectors of the
society
    B. a rigidity in the class structure
    C. lessening of competition for scarce commodities and
resources
    D. increased demands for animate sources of power
    E. increased importance of the family as an agency of
socialization

21. *Which* of the following has the *GREATEST* proportion of   21. ...
its foreign trade with the United States?
    A. Australia   B. West Germany   C. Japan
    D. Great Britain   E. Canada

22. The question of the rights of neutrals on the high seas   22. ...
was a major issue in the involvement of the United States
in *which* of the following wars?
    I. The War of 1812   II. The Spanish-American War
    III. The First World War   IV. The Second World War
    The *CORRECT* answer is:
    A. I *only*   B. IV *only*   C. I and III
    D. III and IV   E. I, II, III, and IV

23. *Which* of the following is the *MAJOR* significance of the   23. ...
Wagner Act? It
    A. provided federal recognition for labor organization
and collective bargaining
    B. established procedures for compulsory arbitration
of labor-management disputes
    C. defined unfair labor practices on the part of unions
    D. established a cooperative federal-state system of
unemployment compensation
    E. marked the beginning of government regulation of
labor unions

24. The *MOST EFFECTIVE* power of the United States Congress   24. ...
in influencing executive action in foreign policy making
is its
    A. role in the treaty-making process
    B. exclusive authority to declare war
    C. control over the appropriations process
    D. role in confirming presidential appointments
    E. authority to regulate the nation's armed forces

25. Prior to the nineteenth century, state formation in the interior of East Africa was stimulated by all of the following *EXCEPT*

    A. the growth of long-distance trade
    B. increases in population
    C. the development of an economy based on fixed cultivation
    D. a need to control conquered territory
    E. introduction of European forms of political organization

25. ...

KEYS (CORRECT ANSWERS)

TEST 1		TEST 2	
1.	D	1.	E
2.	D	2.	B
3.	C	3.	D
4.	D	4.	A
5.	A	5.	B
6.	A	6.	E
7.	B	7.	E
8.	E	8.	B
9.	B	9.	E
10.	B	10.	B
11.	D	11.	E
12.	B	12.	B
13.	B	13.	C
14.	B	14.	B
15.	A	15.	C
16.	E	16.	A
17.	E	17.	A
18.	B	18.	D
19.	E	19.	A
20.	D	20.	A
21.	C	21.	E
22.	A	22.	C
23.	D	23.	A
24.	C	24.	C
25.	B	25.	E

GENERAL INFORMATION AND BACKGROUND
EXAMINATION SECTION

DIRECTIONS FOR THIS SECTION:
Each question or incomplete statement is followed by several suggested answers or completions. Select the one that *BEST* answers the question or completes the statement. *PRINT THE LETTER OF THE CORRECT ANSWER IN THE SPACE AT THE RIGHT.*

TEST 1

1. Which of the following statements concerning executives   1. ...
in the Federal Government of the United States is correct?
    A. Political executives, appointed by the President or
       by heads of agencies, tend to have common backgrounds
       and work experiences.
    B. While the President has had little success in coordinat-
       ing and directing the work of the executive branch, the
       department heads have successfully overcome the preference
       of their bureaus and divisions for operating autonomy.
    C. Salaries of executives compare favorably with salaries
       of business executives.
    D. Normally, Congress has clearly defined the objectives
       of various administrative programs and so has reduced
       the range and degree of discretion exercised by executives.
    E. Heads of agencies and their political assistants rarely
       have complete control over their programs partly because
       other agencies with related and perhaps conflicting inter-
       ests must be consulted.
2. The first Hoover Commission (1949), in a list of the prin-   2. ...
cipal shortcomings of the independent regulatory commissions
of the United States, included *all* of the following *EXCEPT:*
    A. Appointments of commissioners are sometimes below de-
       sirable standards because of inadequate salaries or
       the failure of the President to appreciate the impor-
       tance of the positions.
    B. Commissions have to undertake administrative duties
       which interfere with the performance of their regu-
       latory functions.
    C. The internal organization of the commissions is un-
       satisfactory because responsibility for planning and
       guiding the general program of commission activity is
       not fixed.
    D. Unnecessarily involved procedures result in increased
       delay and expense.
    E. Commissioners are too deferential to presidential
       authority.
3. The nature and limitations of the President's power have   3. ...
been a *major* concern of
    A. Jean Gottmann   B. George R. Terry
    C. Richard E. Neustadt   D. A. T. Mason
    E. James Bryce
4. *Which* of the following officers in a department of the   4. ...
United States Government is *MOST GENERALLY* considered a
line officer? A
    A. director of research   B. budget officer
    C. general counsel   D. bureau chief
    E. personnel director

1

5. The function of "settling the accounts" of each of the administrative agencies of the U. S. Government is part of the work of the
    A. Department of the Treasury   B. General Accounting Office
    C. Office of Management and Budget
    D. Internal Revenue Service   E. Congress

          5. ...

6. In contrast to the AFL, the CIO was a federation of
    A. industrial unions   B. craft unions
    C. company unions   D. independent unions
    E. national unions

          6. ...

7. Its object is to abolish tariffs between its members in ten to fifteen years, to establish a common tariff with the outside world, and to promote a close association in economic and social matters.
This statement describes the
    A. European Free Trade Association
    B. General Agreement on Tariffs and Trade
    C. Organization for European Cooperation and Development
    D. International Trade Organization
    E. European Economic Community

          7. ...

8. In the United States, in the 1920's, the trend toward uniformity was *HASTENED* by *which* of the following?
    I. An increase in the number of independent newspapers
   II. The development of national advertising media
  III. The radio
   IV. The movies
The *CORRECT* combination is:
    A. I and II   B. III and IV
    C. I, II, and IV   D. II, III, and IV
    E. I, II, III, and IV

          8. ...

9. When the German colonies in central Africa were mandated to Great Britain and France following the First World War, the mandatories assumed all of the following obligations *EXCEPT* to
    A. deny themselves special economic advantages
    B. prepare the colonies for immediate self-government
    C. guarantee freedom of conscience and religion
    D. prevent the establishment of military bases
    E. prohibit the slave trade

          9. ...

10. *Which* of the following is *CHARACTERISTIC* of the governments of West Germany, Canada, and the United States?
A(n)
    A. system of checks and balances
    B. independently elected executive
    C. established two-party system   D. federal system
    E. republican form of government

         10. ...

11. Up to our own day American history has been in a large degree the history of the colonization of the Great West. The existence of an area of free land, its continuous recession, and the advance of American settlement westward, explain American development.
The views expressed in this statement are those of
    A. Henry Adams   B. George Bancroft
    C. Francis Parkman   D. Charles A. Beard
    E. Frederick J. Turner

         11. ...

12. The political instability of France in the first half   12. ...
    of the 20th century is often explained in part as a re-
    sult of an anti-republican heritage from the past. In
    citing evidences of this heritage, one would mention *all*
    of the following *EXCEPT*
        A. anticlericalism   B. the Dreyfus affair
        C. President MacMahon   D. the Vichy regime
        E. the Stavisky affair

13. Almost two centuries of experience in England and the   13. ...
    colonies, rather than political theory, accounted for the
    provisions of the Constitution as framed in 1787.
    Which of the following provisions of the Constitution de-
    rives *PRIMARILY* from the theoretical source mentioned above?
        A. "The House of Representatives shall choose their
           speaker...."
        B. "Each house shall be the judge of the elections, re-
           turns, and qualifications of its own members...."
        C. "All bills for raising revenue shall originate in
           the House of Representatives...."
        D. "This Congress shall have the power to lay and col-
           lect taxes...."
        E. "He (the President) shall have power, by and with
           the consent of the Senate, to make treaties,...."

14. The *number of voters* participating in the 1920 United   14. ...
    States presidential election increased *relatively more*
    than the *total population* increased from 1916 to 1920
    PRIMARILY because:
        A. The increase in the urban population made it rela-
           tively easy for a larger percent to vote.
        B. Improvements in educational methods increased popular
           interest in politics.
        C. The Nineteenth Amendment was ratified in 1920.
        D. Voters turned out in large numbers to vote against
           the League of Nations.
        E. Harding waged a vigorous campaign for the Presidency.

15. In *which* of the following lists did the events occur   15. ...
    within the *SAME* 5-year period?
        A. Morrill Tariff, Homestead Act, Chinese Exclusion Act
        B. Root-Takahira Agreement, first Immigration Restriction
           Act, outbreak of the Russo-Japanese War
        C. Pope Leo XIII's *RERUM NOVARUM*, Haymarket Incident,
           organization of the American Federation of Labor
        D. Memorial Day Massacre, bombing of the gunboat *PANAY*.
           Dumbarton Oaks Conference
        E. Wilson-Gorman Tariff, Franco-Prussian War, Federal
           Reserve Act

16. In the second half of the 19th century, significant   16. ...
    changes in India resulted from *all* of the following
    EXCEPT the
        A. formation of the Congress party
        B. extension of the railways
        C. opening of the Suez Canal
        D. expansion of secondary and collegiate education
        E. suppression of the East India Company

17.　　　　　　　　　　　　　　　　　　　　　　　　　　　　17. ...

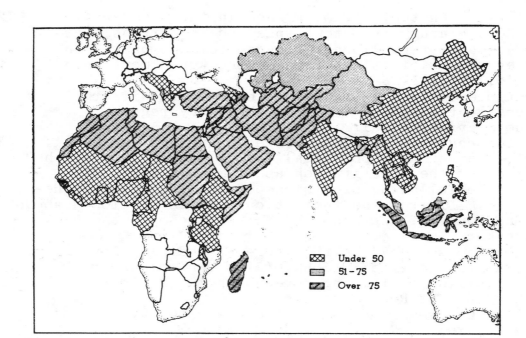

The above map was drawn to indicate
　A. population density per square mile
　B. percent of Muslims in total population
　C. annual mean temperature D. annual mean rainfall
　E. percent of arable land under cultivation

18. Open as it is, on theoretical democratic grounds, to 　　18. ...
serious objection, this arrangement rests on two basic
assumptions. The *FIRST* is that, in any enforcement action,
the great powers must necessarily bear the predominant
burden. The *SECOND* is that the organization must depend
for its strength upon the essential solidarity of the
great powers. If this solidarity fails, then the security
of enforcement arrangements will as surely fail.
The arrangement referred to above is the
　A. provision for collective action in the United Nations
　　General Assembly's Uniting for Peace Resolution
　B. voting formula adopted for the Security Council of
　　the United Nations
　C. alliance system which emerged from the Congress of
　　Vienna
　D. system of economic sanctions provided for in the
　　Covenant of the League of Nations
　E. "most-favored-nation" treatment required of signatories
　　of the General Agreement on Tariffs and Trade

19. The enlightened despots of the 18th century were so styled 19. ...
because they
　A. attempted to disguise their autocratic rule by giving
　　petty concessions to the common people
　B. were able to maintain the monarchical form of govern-
　　ment in an age when the people increasingly demanded
　　representation
　C. professed to believe in a liberalism which their ac-
　　tions belied

D. possessed a high degree of learning
E. possessed a high sense of responsibility and a desire to improve the lot of their subjects

20. All of the following statements concerning mass transportation in the United States are *correct EXCEPT*:   20. ...
    A. Rail and bus services for commuters have continued to shrink and become increasingly inadequate.
    B. The Federal Government has proposed taking responsibility for running commuter lines.
    C. Piecemeal attempts by local governments to plan, coordinate, and finance new systems of mass transportation have not been adequate to meet the transit crisis.
    D. The growing use of private cars for traveling to work and for other downtown trips has had a strangling effect on cities.
    E. Since the end of the Second World War, many cities, towns, and villages have lost all their mass transit facilities.

21. A modern political principle which can be traced to feudal law is the concept that   21. ...
    A. church and state should be separate
    B. the political ruler should be bound by law
    C. there should be a political party in opposition to the party in power
    D. there should be no taxation without representation
    E. government should be based on the separation of powers

22. The interest which Russia has historically manifested in the Dardanelles arises from a desire to have an outlet to the   22. ...
    A. Black Sea   B. Adriatic Sea   C. North Sea
    D. Mediterranean Sea   E. Caspian Sea

23. With respect to *which* of the following is there the *GREATEST* similarity between the countries of the Middle East and those of Latin America?   23. ...
    A. The traditional lack of a middle class
    B. The lack of economic viability
    C. Dependence on agricultural products for export earnings
    D. Type of government organization
    E. Topography

24. Voting studies have been based *LARGELY* on   24. ...
    A. extended interviews with samples of less than 2,500 voters
    B. brief interviews with samples of more than 50,000 voters
    C. questionnaires mailed to election officials, party leaders, and political scientists
    D. close observation, by trained observers, of what happens on election day
    E. quantitative analysis of published election returns

25. *All* of the following are *CHARACTERISTIC* of the Russian economy *EXCEPT* the use of   25. ...
    A. differential wage rates
    B. prices to allocate consumer goods
    C. the turnover tax as a main source of revenue
    D. planning to determine the composition of output
    E. the interest rate to determine the rate of growth

TEST 2

1. From *which* of the following countries will the United States *probably* have the *GREATEST* number of tourists during the 1990's?
   A. Pakistan   B. Argentina   C. Japan
   D. Sweden   E. Greece

2. Current studies in social change indicate that
   A. most social groups anticipate change and have accommodative machinery to make the adjustment
   B. all aspects of society change at a similar rate
   C. social progress and social change are synonymous
   D. social change in one part of the social structure often disrupts the equilibrium in other parts
   E. ideological change is more easily diffused into the culture than is technological change

3. *Which* of the following influenced the introduction of general numerical controls on immigration into the United States with the First Quota Act of 1921?
   I. Racial-ethnic reactions generated by earlier immigration patterns
   II. Isolationist reaction within the United States resulting from the First World War
   III. Growth and development of the labor-union movement
   IV. Extension of the vote to women with the passage of the Nineteenth Amendment
   V. Unsettled economic and political conditions in Europe after the First World War
   The *CORRECT* combination is:
   A. I and II only   B. II and III only
   C. III, IV, and V only   D. I, II, III, and V only
   E. I, II, III, IV, and V

4. The *LARGEST NUMBER* of United States immigrant visas are presently issued to residents of
   A. Latin America   B. Australia   C. Asia
   D. Canada   E. Africa

5. The total of the entries on the credit side of a nation's balance of payments must equal the total of those on the debit side. Yet, one often hears of a nation's deficit or surplus in the balance of payments.
   The apparent paradox is resolved when one realizes that
   A. not all international transactions are reported to the authorites responsible for collecting balance-of-payments statistics
   B. balance-of-payments statistics are notoriously inaccurate
   C. all the foreign-aid receipts or payments are not included when measuring payments imbalances
   D. entries, such as changes in monetary reserves, considered as compensatory transactions are not included when measuring payments imbalances
   E. the terms "deficit" and "surplus" are actually totally unrelated to the balance of payments

6. Under the United States judicial system, the accused is   6. ...
   entitled to *all* of the following *EXCEPT*
      A. access to counsel before making a statement
      B. refusal to give self-incriminating testimony during
         a trial
      C. trial by a jury
      D. cross-examination of persons testifying against him
      E. trial within a period of 90 days of the formal filing
         of criminal charges by the prosecution

7. *Which* of the following *ACCURATELY* describes the principal   7. ...
   responsibilities of the Central Intelligence Agency?
      A. Direction of United States "cloak and dagger" opera-
         tions at home and abroad
      B. Coordination of the foreign intelligence activities
         of the federal government in order to provide estimates
         of threats to American security
      C. Responsibility for identifying military threats to
         national security and advising the Secretary of De-
         fense on strategic plans to meet the threats
      D. Conduct of surveillance over persons suspected of
         disloyalty to the United States
      E. Gathering of intelligence information about suspected
         illegal aliens in the United States

8. In the context of international relations, the term "good   8. ...
   offices" is used in connection with the
      A. priority system for assigning floor space to delega-
         tions at the United Nations
      B. selective system for assigning locations to foreign
         embassies in Washington
      C. practice of diplomatic immunity
      D. procedure for mediation of disputes between nations
      E. maintenance of liaison between the United States and
         the Soviet Union

9. Students active in reform movements on United States   9. ...
   college campuses *tend to be*
      A. from conservative families
      B. better than average academically
      C. relatively unconcerned about issues beyond the campus
      D. working for degrees in the physical sciences rather
         than the humanities
      E. commuting students at residential colleges

10. *Which* of the following has *NOT* been a major cause of   10. ...
    large-scale immigration to the United States?
       A. Religious persecution
       B. Marriages of United States servicemen abroad to
          foreign nationals
       C. War and civil disorders   D. Famine
       E. Economic opportunity in this country

11. *Which* of the following would probably *NOT* be considered   11. ...
    for inclusion in a fiscal program designed to combat a
    recession in the United States economy?
       A. The reduction or elimination of federal excise taxes
       B. An increase in the level of spending for public works
       C. A reduction in corporation and personal income tax
          rates

D. A gradual reduction of the national debt

E. An extension of the term or enlargement of the benefits of unemployment compensation

12. The *PRIMARY* function of legal reserve requirements of the Federal Reserve Board today is to   12. ...

A. protect depositors from asset depreciation

B. provide commercial banks with liquidity

C. force commercial banks to lend money to the Federal Reserve System

D. encourage commercial banks to save part of their deposits

E. allow the central bank to control the creation of money

13. *Which* of the following *BEST* describes the relationship   13. ...
between the United States balance-of-payments deficit and the persistence of relatively high unemployment levels in the United States?

A. The balance-of-payments deficit caused the unemployment.

B. The low level of employment caused the deficit.

C. The excess of imports over exports caused the deficit and the low level of economic activity.

D. The tools which the United States could use to mitigate unemployment might aggravate the deficit.

E. Inflation in the United States caused both the deficit and the unemployment.

14. Historically, patterns of population change during the   14. ...
process of industrialization *generally* have shown that

A. the birth rate drops markedly and is followed by decreases in the death rate

B. the birth and death rates show marked and simultaneous reductions

C. the death rate falls initially and is followed by reductions in the birth rate

D. both birth and death rates remain fairly constant until very high levels of material prosperity are achieved

E. the death rate falls and is followed by a rise in the birth rate

15. *Which* of the following statements *BEST* expresses the mean- 15. ...
ing of the adjectives "republican" and "democratic" as used in describing the American political experience? The

A. "democratic" perspective emphasizes the primacy of the mass of voters in political decision-making, whereas the "republican" would leave such decision-making to a natural elite

B. "democratic" movement aspires to change the American political system fundamentally, even radically, whereas the "republican" one seeks a reaffirmation of traditional American social values

C. "democratic" movement originated among poorer farmers of the South and West as an expression of their opposition to the "republicanism" of the eastern establishment

D. term "democratic" refers to an alliance of ethnic minorities and city dwellers opposed to a "republican" alliance of upper classes, businessmen, and farmers

    E. "democratic" ethos stresses the sovereignity of the
       popular will, and the "republican" ethos defines that
       sovereignty in terms of individual participation and
       effective representation

16. Unites States citizens have tended to regard *all* the fol-   16. ...
    lowing propositions as true of the role of cities in their
    culture *EXCEPT:*
    A. Cities are necessary as centers of economic and com-
       mercial activity and as homes for the arts.
    B. Cities are useful places for receiving new immigrants
       and teaching them American values and ideals.
    C. Although cities are valuable for the typically urban
       amenities they offer, they are not the best places to
       live.
    D. Cities are expressions of essentially American social
       values, and so of our best political ideals.
    E. The dirt, noise, and crime cities create makes them at
       best necessary evils, rather than distinct social assets.

17. *Which* of the following statements about the General Ac-   17. ...
    counting Office is *CORRECT?* It is
    A. part of the Office of Management and Budget
    B. part of the office of the President
    C. part of the legislative branch
    D. an independent agency
    E. attached to the Treasury Department

18. *Which* of the following countries have a *federal,* as opposed 18. ...
    to a *unitary,* system of government?
    I. India   II. West Germany   III. Canada
   IV. The Soviet Union   V. Switzerland
    The *CORRECT* combination is:
    A. I and III only   B. II and V only
    C. I, II, and IV only   D. III, IV, and V only
    E. I, II, III, IV, and V

19. *Which* of the following *ACCURATELY* describes the Peronist   19. ...
    movement in Argentina?
    A. Christian Democratic   B. Marxist working class
    C. Social Democratic   D. Trotskyist
    E. Personalist-populist

20. Rank the following countries according to the size of   20. ...
    their 1990 per capita GNP (from *largest* to *smallest).*
    I. Israel   II. Great Britain   III. Mexico
   IV. Sweden   V. Egypt
    The *CORRECT* order is:
    A. I, II, IV, V, III   B. I, IV, II, III, V
    C. II, IV, III, I, V   D. IV, I, II, V, III
    E. IV, II, I, III, V

21. *All* of the following are characteristics of an authori-   21. ...
    tarian personality *EXCEPT:*
    A. Disrespect toward superiors in the ingroup
    B. Extreme hostility toward outgroups
    C. A vision of the world as a realm of conflict
    D. A repugnance for the expression of affection toward
       others
    E. Disdain for purely theoretical contemplative activi-
       ties

22. The process is one of thesis, antithesis, and synthesis. 22. ...
The thesis affirms a proposition. The antithesis denies
or "negates" it. The synthesis embraces what is true in
both the thesis and the antithesis, and thus brings us
one step nearer to realtiy.
Which of the following philosophers advocated this method
of thought?
    A. Kant   B. Hegel   C. Aristotle
    D. Plato   E. Rousseau

23. *Which* of the following aspects of the Soviet Union's 23. ...
economic system is *MOST* criticized by Western observers?
    A. Inadequate pricing mechanism
    B. Uneven income distribution   C. Overproduction
    D. Inadequate specialization of labor
    E. Industrial pollution

24. *All* of the following are examples of regional economic 24. ...
integrative organizations *EXCEPT* the
    A. Central American Common Market
    B. Caribbean Free Trade Association
    C. Andean Group
    D. Organization of American States
    E. European Free Trade Association

25.   25. ...

The setting in the painting above is *characteristic* of
that in the literary works of
    A. William Dean Howells   B. James T. Farrell
    C. Willa Cather   D. Ernest Hemingway
    E. F. Scott Fitzergald

10

TEST 3

1. *Which* of the following represents an *important* group of   1. ...
   writers in American literature in the period 1950-1973?
   - A. The Lost Generation   B. The Transcendentalists
   - C. The Ashcan School   D. The Harlem Renaissance
   - E. The Black Mountain School

2. *Which* of the following is *most* closely identified with   2. ...
   the thesis that increased educational input does *little*
   to eliminate economic inequality?
   - A. Ivan Illich   B. Christopher Jencks
   - C. Charles Silberman   D. Alvin Toffler
   - E. Charles Reich

3. Which American newspaper is generally credited with open-   3. ...
   ing the way to mass circulation with its "penny paper"?
   - A. The New York Times   B. Philadelphia Bulletin
   - C. Atlanta Constitution   D. Chicago Tribune
   - E. New York Sun

4. Columbia and Reston are examples of *which* of the follow-   4. ...
   ing?
   - A. Urban sprawl at its worst
   - B. Inner-city areas that have been redeveloped successfully
   - C. Satellite cities with a full range of community services
   - D. Plans of future towns to be built in the 1990's
   - E. Scandinavian efforts at solving urban problems

5. *Which* of the following playwrights is (are) known for plays   5. ...
   about lives and problems of black Americans?
   - I. Maxwell Anderson   II. Lorraine Hansberry
   - III. Melvin Van Peebles   IV. Ed Bullins   V. William Inge

   The *CORRECT* combination is:
   - A. I only   B. II and III   C. II,III, IV
   - D. III,IV,V   E. I,II,III,IV,V

6. All of the following innovations in higher education in   6. ...
   the United States are of recent origin EXCEPT the
   - A. introduction of open admissions policies
   - B. inclusion of Black Studies programs
   - C. accreditation of programs by regional accrediting
     agencies
   - D. increase in the number of community colleges
   - E. formation of consortiums

7. Country Y is isolated, with few links of trade or communi-   7. ...
   cation with the outside world. Its economy is overwhelmingly
   agricultural and its social structure is traditional, i.e.,
   patriarchal and based on the extended family. Social relations are differential and conducted according to an elaborate
   code of etiquette characterized by extreme politeness. The
   mythic literature of the society is dominated by stories of
   knightly heroes.
   As an information officer stationed in Country Y, during a
   first visit to an important newspaper editor, your most ad-
   vantageous approach would be *which* of the following?
   - A. After a word of praise for the editor's newspaper, state
     your business quickly so as not to waste his time.
   - B. After a word of praise for the editor's newspaper, make
     discreet inquiries about the well-being of his family.
   - C. After a forthright description of your duties, modestly
     state your journalistic credentials.

11

D. After a forthright description of your duties, impress on him the very real services you could perform for him.

E. After a forthright description of your duties, make a few graceful allusions to your record in military service.

8. Since the line between commercial and fine arts has never   8. ...
been finely drawn in this country, _____ is unusual in
the context of American art only in that it self-consciously,
with an eye to parody,appropriates the techniques and images
of commercial illustration and advertising,but it uses them
with the sophistication of the fine arts instead of the Buckeye
painter.
Which of the following BEST completes the passage above?

   A. Surrealistic art   B. Impressionist art
   C. Expressionistic art   D. Pop art
   E. Neorealist art

9. *Which* of the following is a *cloister*?   9. ...
   A. Any building designed for religious services
   B. The central hall of a building
   C. The upper part of a bell tower
   D. A sacristy
   E. A covered passage on the side of a court

10. *Which* of the following measures would have the MOST bene-   10. ...
ficial,long-term effects in a country where there is a high
incidence of intestinal diseases?
   A. The installation of modern sewage disposal systems
   B. A program of insect eradication
   C. Increase of modern hospital facilities
   D. The quarantine of infected people
   E. The hygienic handling and preparation of food

KEYS (CORRECT ANSWERS)

TEST 1				TEST 2				TEST 3	
1.	E	11.	E	1.	C	11.	D	1.	E
2.	E	12.	A	2.	D	12.	E	2.	B
3.	C	13.	E	3.	D	13.	D	3.	E
4.	D	14.	C	4.	A	14.	C	4.	C
5.	B	15.	C	5.	D	15.	E	5.	C
6.	A	16.	A	6.	E	16.	D	6.	C
7.	E	17.	B	7.	B	17.	C	7.	B
8.	D	18.	B	8.	D	18.	E	8.	D
9.	B	19.	E	9.	B	19.	E	9.	E
10.	D	20.	B	10.	B	20.	E	10.	E
	21.	B			21.	A			
	22.	D			22.	B			
	23.	A			23.	A			
	24.	A			24.	D			
	25.	E			25.	B			

SOCIAL SCIENCES - HISTORY
EXAMINATION SECTION

DIRECTIONS FOR THIS SECTION:
  Each question or incomplete statement is followed by several suggested answers or completions. Select the one that BEST answers the question or completes the statement. *PRINT THE LETTER OF THE CORRECT ANSWER IN THE SPACE AT THE RIGHT.*

TEST 1

1. In 1823 an IMPORTANT reason why the British government favored the Monroe Doctrine was that   1. ...
    A. Great Britain feared the Quadruple Alliance would annex her colonies in the West Indies
    B. British merchants had a profitable trade with the colonies of South America
    C. Great Britain feared that Napoleon III might gain a foothold in Mexico
    D. Great Britain had recognized the independence of Texas
    E. the British government had aided the revolutionists in Spanish America
2. The so-called "Roosevelt corollary" to the Monroe Doctrine 2. ...
resulted from
    A. financial crises in Santo Domingo
    B. obligations under the Platt Amendment
    C. the need to stimulate trade by reciprocal tariff reductions
    D. unrest in Nicaragua
    E. a boundary dispute between Venezuela and British Guiana
3. An IMPORTANT reason why the United States repudiated the   3. ...
Roosevelt corollary was the
    A. trend toward isolation immediately after World War I
    B. increasing military strength of the Caribbean nations
    C. policy established by the Johnson Act
    D. recognition of the principle of the multilateral interpretation of the Monroe Doctrine
    E. opposition of the United States taxpayers to the cost of intervention
4. Imports of Philippine products into the United States are   4. ...
now
    A. dutiable at the same rate as goods from other countries
    B. taxed on a sliding scale
    C. tax-exempt for the next several years
    D. taxed as Congress determines
    E. taxed at ad valorem rates
5. The government of Canada resembles that of the United   5. ...
States in which of the following respects?
    A. The head of the government is elected directly by the people.
    B. It has the federal form of government.
    C. It is a republic.
    D. Elections are held at specified intervals.
    E. Members of the cabinet are also members of the legislative branch of the government.
6. United States-Canadian relations during the past have been   6. ...
marked by all of the following EXCEPT
    A. resentment toward Canada during the Civil War

1

B. an agreement to establish a Permanent Joint Committee on Defense
C. reciprocal trade agreements
D. establishment of an International Joint Commission
E. limitation of migration from one country to the other

7. "The most favored nation" clause in the reciprocal trade agreement with Great Britain meant that the United States would
    A. receive special privileges in Canada
    B. receive all the privileges granted to any other country by Great Britain
    C. grant special privileges to all the members of the British Empire
    D. make separate treaties with the British Dominions
    E. establish air bases in Bermuda
        7. ...

8. Our CHIEF interest in preventing the partitioning of China about 1900 was that
    A. we feared Chinese markets might be closed to our trade
    B. China might be used as a base of military operations against our Pacific islands
    C. the United States needed Chinese tin, tungsten and manganese
    D. the Washington Nine Power Pact guaranteed the territorial integrity of China
    E. the United States would receive special privileges from China
        8. ...

9. The Boxer rebellion was an uprising against
    A. Chinese immigration restrictions
    B. Chinese imperialistic aims
    C. commercial concessions to foreigners in China
    D. economic isolation of China
    E. importation of opium into China
        9. ...

10. The CHIEF purpose of the neutrality legislation of the 1930's was to
    A. deprive munition makers of the chance to make excessive war profits
    B. prevent war trade from drawing the United States into war
    C. prevent the spread of fascism in our country
    D. safeguard our traditional claim to freedom of the seas
    E. prevent government loans to European belligerents
        10. ...

11. All of the following were problems at the end of *both* World War I and World War II EXCEPT
    A. civil war in China   B. the status of Trieste
    C. independence of Korea   D. the boundaries of Poland
    E. Zionist demands concerning Palestine
        11. ...

12. The first Bank of the United States *differed* from the Federal Reserve System in that
    A. the United States Government was part owner of the Bank of the United States
    B. it was authorized by law to issue paper currency
    C. the United States Government had a voice in the management
    D. it was a stabilizing influence on private financial dealings
    E. it held Government funds and assisted in floating Government loans
        12. ...

2

13. In his "war" on the second Bank of the United States,   13. ...
Jackson was motivated by all of the following beliefs
about the bank EXCEPT that it
    A. was tending toward dangerous inflation
    B. was unconstitutional
    C. was an unfair private monopoly
    D. was playing politics
    E. discriminated against the West

14. Although not primarily intended for that purpose, a meas-   14. ...
ure that was *frequently* used by the courts to protect big
business is the
    A. sixteenth amendment
    B. Federal Trade Commission Act
    C. National Industrial Recovery Act
    D. fourteenth amendment
    E. Sherman Anti-Trust Act

15. The Wheeler-Rayburn "death sentence" law for public util-   15. ...
ity holding companies was enacted because
    A. none of the antitrust laws had made it possible for
       the government to dissolve holding companies
    B. it was believed that the restoration of competition
       would lower prices to the consumer
    C. certain public utility holding companies were not con-
       sidered justifiable on the grounds of efficiency of
       operation of the business
    D. the elimination of public utility holding companies
       would insure the financial success of the TVA
    E. the holding company form of organization had become
       obsolete

16. All of the following are functions of the Securities and   16. ...
Exchange Commission EXCEPT
    A. regulation of the marginal requirements for purchases
       of securities
    B. establishment of rules for the conduct of business on
       the security exchanges
    C. supervision of the financial practices of public-
       utility holding companies
    D. authorization of the issuance of new securities
    E. approval of statements made in companies' prospectuses

17. All of the following changes in our currency and banking   17. ...
systems were made as a result of the banking crisis of
1933 EXCEPT
    A. establishment of insurance of bank deposits
    B. separation of security affiliates from commercial
       banks
    C. retirement from circulation of the notes of state
       banks
    D. separation of investment and commercial banking
    E. reorganization of the Federal Reserve System

18. The TVA project provides all of the following EXCEPT   18. ...
    A. hydroelectric power   B. flood control
    C. reduction of soil erosion
    D. water for irrigation of cotton and tobacco lands
    E. navigation on inland waterways

3

19. In dealing with the railroads since 1920, the United   19. ...
    States government has *generally*
    A. encouraged the railroads to charge what the traffic
       will bear
    B. encouraged competition among the railroads
    C. established rates to prevent excessive charges
    D. failed to regulate competing means of transportation,
       while regulating railroads strictly
    E. taken over the railroads in wartime to insure more
       efficient operation
20. The strikes in the steel and automobile industries that   20. ...
    broke the "little steel formula" were
    A. condemned by the leaders of the C. I. O.
    B. the basis for pay increases of 18-1/2 cents per hour
    C. accompanied by sympathetic railroad strikes
    D. the reason for the seizure of those industries by
       the United States government
    E. called primarily because organized labor was dis-
       satisfied with the decisions of the presidential
       fact-finding board
21. The major function of the National Labor Relations Board   21. ...
    is to
    A. act as the final arbitration board in labor contro-
       versies
    B. protect the workers' right to organize
    C. act as a fact-finding board for the President
    D. recommend wage increases
    E. administer welfare funds
22. In a period of rising prices, the interests of farm owners 22. ...
    are MOST similar to those of
    A. bankers   B. manufacturers
    C. organized laborers   D. salaried employees
    E. holders of savings bank accounts
23. Adam Smith in THE WEALTH OF NATIONS advocates that nations 23. ...
    should
    A. try to accumulate gold and silver
    B. follow a policy of free trade
    C. practise the mercantile theory of trade
    D. build up colonial empires
    E. increase government regulation of industry and trade
24. Which of the following statements about the immigration   24. ...
    policy of the United States was *true* after World War II?
    A. We have allowed Chinese immigrants to come here free-
       ly since World War II.
    B. Jewish refugees may enter the United States without
       regard to quotas
    C. The quota provisions do not apply to nations of the
       Western Hemisphere.
    D. Under our quota system Russia may send a larger
       number of immigrants than Germany.
    E. Applicants for citizenship must have the approval of
       their country of origin.
25. During the 20 years before the Civil War, which of the   25. ...
    following groups sent the LARGEST number of immigrants
    to the United States?
    A. Scotch and French   B. French and Irish

4

C. Irish and German   D. Germans and Scandinavians
E. Italians and Russians
26. In the United States, which type of community has shown   26. ...
the MOST rapid rate of population growth since 1930?
  A. Cities of 100,000 to 250,000 population
  B. Rural farming areas
  C. Villages and towns near large cities
  D. County seat towns
  E. Cities of 1,000,000 or more population
27. Before the Civil War New Orleans had distinguished itself   27. ...
as a center of
  A. opera and music   B. finance
  C. manufacturing   D. public education
  E. railroads
28. Which of the following social experiments originated in   28. ...
the 20th century?
  A. New Harmony   B. Brook Farm
  C. Oneida Community   D. Tuskegee Institute
  E. The Matanuska Valley Project
29. All of the following were *closely* identified with social   29. ...
reforms EXCEPT
  A. William Wilberforce   B. Friedrich Engels
  C. Count Leo Tolstoy   D. Robert Owen
  E. Ferdinand de Lesseps
30. Which of the following magazines is considered to present   30. ...
the point of view of a group of liberals?
  A. TIME   B. READER'S DIGEST   C. NEWSWEEK
  D. NEW REPUBLIC   E. THE NATIONAL GEOGRAPHIC MAGAZINE

TEST 2

1. The breakdown of feudalism commenced FIRST in   1. ...
  A. France   B. Hungary   C. England
  D. Prussia   E. Russia
2. The Industrial Revolution in England caused   2. ...
  A. a decline in the desire for colonies
  B. closer relations between employer and employees
  C. dislocations in the system of representative govern-
     ment in England
  D. an increase in the powers of kings
  E. an increase in the influence of the landed aristocracy
3. The English Reform Bill of 1832 was an *advance* in democracy 3. ...
because it aimed to
  A. restrict greatly the power of the king
  B. eliminate the veto power of the House of Lords
  C. improve the system of representation in the House of
     Commons
  D. give the right to vote to all men over twenty-one
  E. establish the cabinet system of government
4. The act which greatly limited the power of the English   4. ...
king by giving Parliament control over the levying of
taxes, was the
  A. Bill of Rights of 1689   B. Magna Carta
  C. Statute of Westminster   D. Reform Act of 1884
  E. Parliament Act of 1911

5. The Labor government in England in the 1950's 5. ...
    A. nationalized the textile and automobile industries
    B. opposes extension of the social security program
    C. placed the Bank of England under national control
    D. upholds Russia's policy in Eastern Europe
    E. favors internationalization of Gibraltar and the Suez Canal

6. A MAJOR test of the power of the League of Nations to 6. ...
prevent aggression came in 1931 at the time of the
    A. border dispute between Russia and Poland
    B. occupation of Manchuria by Japan
    C. German recovery of the Saar
    D. invasion of Ethiopia by Italy
    E. bombardment of Corfu

7. Of the following regions, the one with the GREATEST density 7. ...
of population is
    A. Greece   B. Belgium   C. England
    D. Italy   E. Kazak Republic

8. A *result* of the Franco-Prussian War was 8. ...
    A. the establishment of the Third French Republic
    B. a setback to Italian unification
    C. the union of Austria and Prussia in the new German Empire
    D. a war between France and Russia
    E. an increase in democracy in Prussia

9. All of the following policies were used by the Congress 9. ...
of Vienna in 1815 EXCEPT
    A. suppression of revolutions
    B. restoration of monarchs
    C. preservation of the peace in Europe
    D. self-determination of nations
    E. balance of power in Europe

10. All of the following men were leaders in the democratic 10. ...
movement in the 19th century EXCEPT
    A. Lord John Russell   B. Joseph Mazzini
    C. John Bright   D. William Gladstone
    E. the Duke of Wellington

11. All of the following statements are *descriptive* of Den- 11. ...
mark's government EXCEPT that it
    A. is a monarchy   B. is a democracy
    C. has a parliamentary government
    D. promotes cooperatives
    E. supports collective farms

12. All of the following men were *prominently* identified with 12. ...
the history of South Africa EXCEPT
    A. Cecil Rhodes   B. Warren Hastings C. Ian Smuts
    D. Louis Botha   E. Lord Milner

13. The civilization of the Incas of Peru was characterized by 13. ...
    A. extreme of wealth and poverty
    B. wide explorations of the islands of the Pacific
    C. extensive road building
    D. distinguished literature
    E. trade with Mexico and the West Indies

14. All of the following statements about culture in Latin   14. ...
America are *true* EXCEPT:
   A. Within the last 20 years, the power of the landed
      aristocracy has been replaced by that of the middle
      classes.
   B. The purchasing power of a majority of the population
      is low.
   C. European culture has had a strong influence on Latin-
      American thought.
   D. Latin-American universities exert considerable influ-
      ence on politics.
   E. Racial barriers do not constitute a major social prob-
      lem in Brazil.

15. None of the following is *true* of present-day life in post- 15. ...
Soviet Russia EXCEPT
   A. government censorship of the arts
   B. an increase in literacy
   C. a ban on the services of the Eastern Orthodox Church
   D. the encouragement of cooperatives
   E. the right to own personal property

16. The U.S.S.R. had attempted to secure control or gain   16. ...
rights in all of the following ports EXCEPT
   A. Petsamo   B. Dairen   C. Bergen
   D. Vladiovostok   E. Port Arthur

17. For nearly 400 years before 1830, the Balkans were domi- 17. ...
nated by
   A. Russia   B. Italy   C. Turkey
   D. Germany   E. Austria

18. When World War I began, all of the following were heads   18. ...
of governments EXCEPT
   A. President Sun Yat-sen   B. President Woodrow Wilson
   C. Kaiser Wilhelm II   D. Queen Victoria
   E. Czar Nicholas II

19. Which of the following is a FUNDAMENTAL requirement for   19. ...
the realization of a workable system of World Government?
   A. Agreement on a method of atomic control
   B. Resettlement of displaced persons
   C. Reduction of armaments
   D. Limitation of national sovereignty in certain fields
   E. International control of waterways

20. Of the following contributory causes of business panics   20. ...
in the United States, the one which did NOT figure prom-
inently in the panic of 1929 was
   A. the overproduction or underconsumption of consumer goods
   B. excessive security speculation
   C. overexpansion of credit
   D. excessive government lending to railroads
   E. lack of balance between spending and investment

21. All of the following are arguments for reciprocal trade   21. ...
agreements EXCEPT the argument that they
   A. encourage economic nationalism
   B. foster economic peace and stability
   C. promote scientific methods of dealing with trade problems
   D. make countries interdependent
   E. tend to encourage countries to produce goods for which
      they are best adapted

Questions 22-30.
DIRECTIONS: Questions 22-30 are based on the hypothetical map to the right.

22. The latitudinal location of this island group is
    A. N   B. S
    C. E   D. W
    E. indeterminate

22. ...

23. The longitudinal location of this island group is
    A. N   B. S
    C. E   D. W
    E. indeterminate

23. ...

24. The ocean in which this island group would be located is the
    A. Indian   B. Arctic
    C. Antarctic D. Atlantic
    E. Pacific

24. ...

25. The group spreads over a north-south distance of about
    A. 300 mi.   B. 690 mi.
    C. 1300 mi. D. 2000 mi.
    E. 18 mi.

26. The approximate area of Island II is *most nearly*
    A. 5,000 sq. mi.   B. 15,000 sq. mi.   C. 25,000 sq. mi.
    D. 100,000 sq. mi. E. 150,000 sq. mi.

26. ...

27. If the prevailing winds are from the southeast, which of the following places probably has the LEAST rainfall?
    A. B   B. E   C. J   D. N   E. L

27. ...

28. On Island I, the steepest slope on the hill is along path
    A. a   B. b   C. c   D. d   E. e

28. ...

29. Places that would experience the overhead sun at some time during the year are
    A. L, Q   B. R, S   C. E, D   D, A, B   E, A, S

29. ...

30. All of the following products might be grown on Island I EXCEPT
    A. cotton   B. corn   C. sugar cane
    D. rubber   E. wheat

30. ...

TEST 3

Questions 1-30.
DIRECTIONS: In Questions 1-30, the possible answers are numbered I, II, III, IV, V, VI. *Any, all or none* of these answers may be right. In each case choose from the alternatives lettered A to E the one that includes the numbers preceding *all* the right answers. *PRINT THE LETTER OF THE CORRECT ANSWER IN THE SPACE AT THE RIGHT.*

1. Factors that contributed to the early development of sailing among people living along the shores of the Mediterranean were:
    I. High visibility of stars and landmarks in the dry summer air
   II. Long periods of stormless weather

1. ...

8

   III. Many navigable rivers on which to gain experience
    IV. Islands and peninsulas that provided easy stages for
       a journey
The CORRECT combination is:
   A. I, II, III   B. I, II, IV   C. I, IV
   D. II, III, IV   E. III, IV

2. Which of the following statements are *true* of the develop-   2. ...
ment of Arabian civilization?
   I. The Arabs became a great world power in the seventh
     century.
   II. The Moslem Empire included western Asia, northern
     Africa and Spain.
  III. Arab literature was preserved on clay tablets in
     temples throughout the empire.
   IV. Arab unity was promoted by a common language, litera-
     ture and religion.
   V. The Arabs believed in only one God.
  VI. The Arabs were famous for statues of great men.
The CORRECT combination is:
   A. I, II, III, IV B. I, II, IV, V   C. I, III, IV, V
   D. I, III, V, VI E. III, IV, V, VI

3. Which of the following were *true* of navigation in Columbus' 3. ...
time?
   I. Ptolemy's GEOGRAPHY gave Europeans their first accurate
     information about the East.
   II. Navigators had to sail without benefit of instruments
     to give them direction.
  III. The discoveries of Galileo and Kepler convinced most
     navigators that the world was a sphere.
The CORRECT combination is:
   A. *None* of them B. I *only*   C. I, II
   D. II, III   E. III *only*

4. Which of the following were *generally* characteristic of   4. ...
education in the English colonies in North America?
   I. Universal elementary education
   II. Higher education for leaders
  III. Special emphasis on teaching the "three R's"
   IV. Education for religious reasons
The CORRECT combination is:
   A. I, II, III   B. I, III, IV   C. I, IV
   D. II, III, IV   E. III, IV

5. Which of the following colleges were founded during *coloni-* 5. ...
al times?
   I. Colgate   II. Cornell   III. Harvard
  IV. Wellesley   V. William and Mary
The CORRECT combination is:
   A. I, II, V   B. I, III, IV   C. II, III, V
   D. III, IV, V   E. III, V

6. Which of these statements are *true* of the system of checks 6. ...
and balances in our federal government?
   I. The Congress may override a Presidential veto by a
     two-thirds vote of both houses.
   II. Appointments made by the President must be approved
     by both houses of Congress.

III. The President chooses justices of the federal courts with the approval of the Supreme Court.

IV. A two-thirds vote of the Supreme Court is required to declare a law *unconstitutional*.

The CORRECT combination is:

A. I *only*   B. I, II, IV   C. I, III
D. II, III   E. II, IV

7. Which of these statements are *true* of the governments of both Great Britain and the United States?

   7. ...

I. Members of the lower house of the legislative body are elected by universal suffrage.

II. The recognized procedure for removing the chief executive from office is impeachment.

III. The chief executive and members of the cabinet may introduce bills in the legislature.

IV. Constitutionality of any law passed by the national legislature may be tested in court.

The CORRECT combination is:

A. I *only*   B. I, II   C. I, II, IV
D. I, III   E. III, IV

8. For which of the following does the Constitution of the United States provide *by name?*

   8. ...

I. Supreme Court   II. District Courts
III. A Customs Court   IV. A Court of Claims
V. Circuit Courts of Appeals

The CORRECT combination is:

A. *None* of them   B. I   C. I, II, V
D. I, III, IV   E. *All* of them

9. For which of the following has the original method of selection been *changed* by constitutional amendment?

   9. ...

I. Members of the House of Representatives
II. United States Senators
III. Federal judges
IV. Cabinet members
V. Vice-President of the United States

The CORRECT combination is:

A. I, III, IV   B. II *only*   C. II, III, V
D. II, V   E. III, V

10. Which of the following would be considered *original* sources of information concerning the founding of the University of Virginia?

   10. ...

I. Thomas Jefferson's letters to a friend explaining his plans for the University
II. A high school textbook account
III. A college textbook account
IV. The charter of the University
V. A history of the University published on the hundredth anniversary of its founding

The CORRECT combination is:

A. I, III, IV, V   B. I, IV   C. I, IV, V
D. II, III, IV   E. III, V

11. Which of the following were characteristic of farm life in the United States a hundred years ago?

   11. ...

I. Farms were usually self-sufficient.

II. Most farms were operated as family enterprises.

III. Farm products were protected from foreign competition by tariff laws.

IV. Most farms were operated by tenants.

The CORRECT combination is:

A. I, II
B. I, II, III
C. I, III, IV
D. II, III
E. III, IV

12. Which of the following acts of the federal government pro-   12. ...
vided for aid to education?

I. Morrill Act (1862)
II. Hepburn Act (1906)
III. Clayton Act (1914)
IV. Smith-Hughes Act (1917)
V. Glass-Steagall Act (1932)

The CORRECT combination is:

A. I, II, III
B. I, II, IV
C. I, II, V
D. I, IV
E. III, V

13. Which of these persons are or were eligible to hold the   13. ...
office of President of the United States?

I. Susan B. Anthony
II. Robert F. Wagner
III. Henry Ford 2d
IV. Alexander Hamilton
V. George Washington Carver

The CORRECT combination is:

A. *None* of them
B. I, IV, V
C. I, V
D. II, III
E. II, III, IV

14. Which of the following have been *increasing* tendencies   14. ...
in 20th-century American art?

I. The use of the American scene as a subject
II. Imitation of the Italian Renaissance painters
III. Some support of art by the federal government
IV. The use of romantic rather than realistic subjects
V. A greater opportunity for the people to enjoy art

The CORRECT combination is:

A. I, II
B. I, III
C. I, III, V
D. II, IV, V
E. III, IV, V

15. On several occasions the United States has gone to war to   15. ...
preserve the freedom of the seas. In which of the following wars was this an *important* factor?

I. War with Tripoli (1801-5)
II. War of 1812
III. Spanish-American War
IV. World War I

The CORRECT combination is:

A. I, II, III
B. I, II, IV
C. I, III, IV
D. II, III, IV
E. *All* of them

16. A *good* natural harbor is characterized by:

I. Space for anchorage of vessels
II. Warehouses and storage facilities
III. Sufficient depth for large vessels
IV. Dredging equipment and dry docks
V. Protection from winds and storms

The CORRECT combination is:

A. I, II, III
B. I, III, V
C. I, III
D. II, V
E. III, IV

17. Use of the southern pine forests in the United States has   17. ...
certain advantages in paper-pulp production over use of
the northern spruce forests because

I. the long, moist open season favors growth
II. softwoods grow faster than hardwoods

III. the southern forests are nearer the market
IV. pulp can be made more easily by mechanical means in
the South
The CORRECT combination is:
A. I *only* B. I, II   C. I, IV   D. II, IV E. III, IV

18. Which of the following statements are *true* regarding   18. ...
American political parties?
I. The Democrats consider George Washington the founder
of their party.
II. The Republican party of 1860 opposed a strong central
government.
III. The Populist party of the late 19th century represented
business and financial interests.
IV. A split in the Republican party contributed to the
election of Wilson in 1912.
V. Third parties seldom win elections but exert consider-
able influence on major parties.
The CORRECT combination is:
A. I, III B. I, V   C. II, IV D. II, V   E. IV, V

19. Which of the following were proposed at the Bretton Woods   19. ...
Conference of 1944?
I. A security council
II. The "five freedoms of aviation"
III. A world bank
IV. An international court
V. A currency stabilization fund
The CORRECT combination is:
A. I *only*   B. I, III   C. II, IV
D. III *only*   E. III, V

20. Which of the following functions of the United Nations   20. ...
are delegated to the Security Council?
I. To judge disputes between nations in terms of inter-
national law
II. To deal with such world problems as trade, health,
education and labor
III. To use force to prevent war
IV. To supervise the governments of backward colonial
areas
The CORRECT combination is:
A. I *only*   B. I, III, IV   C. III *only*
D. III, IV   E. *All* of them

21. The position of Great Britain as a commercial nation has   21. ...
been aided by:
I. Large supplies of petroleum within the British Isles
II. Large supplies of coal within Great Britain
III. A large home iron and steel industry
IV. A surplus of agricultural products for export
The CORRECT combination is:
A. I, III   B. I, III, IV   C. I, IV
D. II, III   E. II, III, IV

22. Factors that helped make the Ruhr one of the MAJOR in-   22. ...
dustrial regions of the world are:
I. Rich iron ore deposits near by
II. Large supplies of high quality coal within the region

12

    III. Convenient inland water transportation
     IV. Markets in western Europe
      V. Hydroelectric power from the Alps
  The CORRECT combination is:
    A. I, II, III, IV B. I, II, V   C. I, III, IV
    D. II, III, IV   E. II, III, IV, V

23. Which of the following states appeared on the map of   23. ...
Europe for the FIRST time after World War I?
    I. Bulgaria   II. Czechoslovakia   III. Poland
   IV. Romania   V. Yugoslavia
  The CORRECT combination is:
    A. I, II, IV, V   B. II, III, IV   C. II, III, V
    D. II, V   E. III, V

24. Which of the following have caused interal disturbances   24. ...
in the Balkans?
    I. Minority populations   II. Political boundaries
  III. Economic rivalries   IV. National sentiment
    V. Racial and religious differences
  The CORRECT combination is:
    A. I, II, III, IV B. II, III, V   C. II, IV
    D. III, IV   E. *All* of them

25. Which of the following statements about the Balkan penin- 25. ...
sula are *true?*
    I. The Balkan countries are largely agricultural.
   II. Bulgaria sided with Germany in both World Wars.
  III. In World War II, the Balkan countries solidly sup-
      ported the Axis powers.
   IV. Greece has a longer coastline than Albania.
  The CORRECT combination is:
    A. I, II, III   B. I, II, IV   C. I, III
    D. II, III, IV   E. *All* of them

26. Which of the following statements about Russia   26. ...
are *true?*
    I. Murmansk may be reached via the Arctic Ocean.
   II. There are more good river ports than seaports.
  III. The Donets Basin is important as a grazing region.
  The CORRECT combination is:
    A. I *only*   B. I, II   C. I, III
    D. II, III   E. *All* of them

27. Which of these statements about India are *true?*   27. ...
    I. India has been the home of civilized peoples for
      almost 5000 years.
   II. About one fifth of the people in the world live there.
  III. The All-India National Congress is a political party.
   IV. Tagore has received the Nobel Prize for literature.
  The CORRECT combination is:
    A. I, II   B. I, II, III   C. I, II, IV
    D. II, III, IV   E. *All* of them

28. Which of the following statements about the economic   28. ...
geography of the Far East are *true?*
    I. The chief source of tin in that region is the
      Philippine Islands.
   II. New Zealand was our principal source of quinine
      before World War II.

III. Petroleum refining in the Far East is concentrated
in the Dutch East Indies.

IV. Before this war, the Dutch East Indies produced about
half the world's coffee supply.

The CORRECT combination is:

A. *None* of them   B. I, II, IV   C. II *only*

D. II, III   E. III *only*

29. Which of these statements about Brazil are *true*?   29. ...

I. Brazil borders every South American country except
Chile and Ecuador.

II. It is the northernmost country of South America.

III. Brazil is the only Portuguese-speaking country in
South America.

IV. Brazil is the world's chief source of rubber.

The CORRECT combination is:

A. I, II, III   B. I, II, IV   C. I, III

D. II, IV   E. *All* of them

30. Which of the following statements about Latin America are   30. ...
true?

I. Brazil is larger than continental United States.

II. Buenos Aires is farther from New York than is any
European capital.

III. The Pan-American highway has been completed as far
south as Panama.

IV. Bolivia and Paraguay have no seaports.

The CORRECT combination is:

A. I, II, IV   B. I, III   C. I, III, IV

D. II, IV   E. *All* of them

TEST 4

1. According to the census, in 1990, the population of the   1. ...
United States and all her territories and overseas possessions was, *approximately*,

A. 210,000,000   B. 230,000,000   C. 250,000,000

D. 280,000,000   E. 310,000,000

2. All of the following have written significant works on   2. ...
economic problems in the United States EXCEPT

A. Edward Bellamy   B. Stuart Chase   C. Henry George

D. Upton Sinclair   E. Lorado Taft

3. A PRIMARY function of the National Labor Relations Board   3. ...
is to

A. enforce the closed shop

B. determine the wages industry can pay without raising
prices

C. conduct elections to determine bargaining representatives for the workers in a plant

D. operate plants taken over by the Government because
of labor troubles

E. arbitrate wage disputes

4. Organized labor has *generally* favored all of the following   4. ...
EXCEPT

A. collective bargaining   B. compulsory free education

C. immigration restriction   D. social security

E. compulsory arbitration of industrial disputes

5. Of the following, the result MOST likely to be produced   5. ...
   by international cartels is
   A. more competition among small businesses
   B. better trade opportunities for all business
   C. more employment
   D. higher prices for consumer goods
   E. fairer sharing of world trade and profits

6. Which of the following events occurred LAST?   6. ...
   A. Stalin succeeded Lenin as titular head of the Com-
      munist party in the U. S. S. R.
   B. Churchill succeeded Chamberlain as Prime Minister
      of Great Britain.
   C. Mussolini assumed power as dictator of Italy.
   D. Franklin D. Roosevelt was elected President of the
      United States for the first time.
   E. Chiang Kai-shek assumed leadership of the Nationalist
      movement in China.

7. *Immediately* before World War II, the governmental status   7. ...
   of the Philippines was that of a(n)
   A. mandate of the United States
   B. colony under the control of the United States
   C. territory of the United States
   D. independent republic with an elective Filipino president
   E. commonwealth practicing self-government under the
      guidance of the United States

8. During World War II, the straits at the entrance to the   8. ...
   Black Sea were controlled by
   A. Bulgaria   B. Germany   C. Great Britain
   D. Russia   E. Turkey

9. All of the following countries have experienced the polit-   9. ...
   ical effects of having petroleum deposits within their
   borders EXCEPT
   A. Iraq   B. Iran   C. Israel
   D. Rumania   E. Saudi Arabia

10. In a treaty with China in 1943, the United States *gave up*   10. ...
    the right to
    A. maintain treaty ports in China after the war
    B. control China's post offices
    C. impose tariff duties against Chintse goods
    D. try American citizens in China in American courts
    E. restrict Chinese immigration

11. The Potsdam Conference (1945) occurred   11. ...
    A. *before* the death of President Roosevelt
    B. *between* the death of Roosevelt and V-E Day
    C. *between* V-E Day and the atomic bombing of Hiroshima
    D. *between* the bombing of Hiroshima and V-J Day
    E. *after* V-J Day

12. The UNRRA was organized to   12. ...
    A. provide for the rehabilitation of soldiers and
       sailors of World War II
    B. conduct elections in liberated countries
    C. provide for the welfare of civilians in countries
       devastated by war
    D. restore foreign nations to economic solvency
    E. administer local government in occupied areas

15

13. Many of the Asiatic characteristics of eastern European   13. ...
    culture may be traced to the influence of the
        A. explorations of Bering
        B. reforms of Mustapha Kemal
        C. period of Mongol rule
        D. invasion of the Moors
        E. conquests of Ivan the Terrible
14. Pravda was the name of a Russian   14. ...
        A. censor   B. editorial writer   C. newspaper
        D. radio network   E. war reporter
15. The country with the LARGEST population in the world is   15. ...
        A. Brazil   B. China   C. India
        D. Soviet Russia   E. the United States

KEYS (CORRECT ANSWERS)

TEST 1		TEST 2		TEST 3		TEST 4	
1.	B	1.	C	1.	C	1.	C
2.	A	2.	C	2.	B	2.	E
3.	D	3.	C	3.	A	3.	C
4.	C	4.	A	4.	E	4.	E
5.	B	5.	C	5.	E	5.	D
6.	E	6.	B	6.	A	6.	B
7.	B	7.	B	7.	A	7.	E
8.	A	8.	A	8.	B	8.	E
9.	C	9.	D	9.	D	9.	C
10.	B	10.	E	10.	B	10.	D
11.	C	11.	E	11.	A	11.	C
12.	A	12.	B	12.	D	12.	C
13.	A	13.	C	13.	A	13.	C
14.	D	14.	A	14.	C	14.	C
15.	C	15.	E	15.	B	15.	B
16.	A	16.	C	16.	B		
17.	C	17.	C	17.	A		
18.	D	18.	D	18.	E		
19.	C	19.	D	19.	E		
20.	B	20.	D	20.	C		
21.	B	21.	A	21.	D		
22.	B	22.	B	22.	A		
23.	B	23.	D	23.	D		
24.	B	24.	E	24.	E		
25.	C	25.	C	25.	B		
26.	C	26.	E	26.	B		
27.	A	27.	D	27.	E		
28.	E	28.	A	28.	E		
29.	E	29.	C	29.	C		
30.	D	30.	D	30.	A		

EXAMINATION SECTION

TEST 1

PASSAGE

By far, the best-known industry in Steuben County is the manufacture of glass. Just after the Civil War, the Flint Glass Company moved from Brooklyn to Corning. One reason why the company chose to settle in Corning was that the railroad from Pennsylvania to Corning brought coal for fuel at a low cost. In the early days, the company made lantern chimneys, bottles, and such familiar products. Later, it began making electric light bulbs. Now it manufactures all kinds of glass products. It makes Pyrex, a kind of glass that resists heat so well that it is used for cooking and baking. The company also makes glass wool, which is used for insulation and other purposes, and glass bricks, out of which the walls of some modern buildings are built.

1. The Flint Glass Company moved to Corning because it
   A. would be exempt from local taxes
   B. had been promised free land for its buildings
   C. could obtain coal cheaply
   D. could make glass bricks there

2. Glass wool, made in Corning, is used for
   A. insulation
   B. low cost fuel
   C. manufacturing lantern chimneys
   D. making electric blankets

3. Since its early days in Corning, the number and variety of the products of the glass industry have
   A. decreased   B. remained about the same
   C. increased slightly   D. increased greatly

4. The county in which Corning is located is
   A. Chautauqua   B. Cortland   C. Seneca   D. Steuben

5. Pyrex is used for
   A. antifreeze   B. cooking utensils
   C. curtain material   D. refrigeration

TEST 2

PASSAGE

While Admiral Dewey was waiting in Manila Bay, exciting events were happening in the Atlantic. Soon after the start of the war, a Spanish fleet under Admiral Pascual Cervera set sail from the coast of Spain. An American fleet under Admiral William T. Sampson set out to give battle to Cervera's fleet. On May 19, Cervera's fleet came to anchor in the Cuban harbor of Santiago. Sampson's fleet quickly took up its position just outside the channel in order to blockade the *harbor, which was too well defended by forts for the Americans to sail in. An American army was landed on the coast a few miles south of Santiago. On July 1-2, this force captured the outer defenses of the city at San Juan Hill and began a siege of Santiago. One of the regiments of volunteers that took part in the charge at San Juan Hill had been recruited by Theodore Roosevelt, who was second in command. The victory of the American army caused the Spaniards to give up hop The Spanish commander in Cuba ordered Admiral Cervera to put to sea and save his fleet if he could. On July 3, Cervera, with his ships under full steam, started out of Santiago Harbor.*

1. The paragraph describes a campaign in the   1.
    A. War of 1812   B. Mexican War
    C. Civil War   D. Spanish-American War

2. At the time of the Cuban campaign, a new regiment was   2.
    recruited by
    A. Cervera   B. Dewey   C. Roosevelt   D. Sampson

3. The American victory at San Juan Hill caused the enemy to   3.
    A. lose confidence   B. surrender unconditionally
    C. retreat to San Juan Hill   D. enter Santiago

4. The war was fought   4.
    A. only in the Atlantic Ocean
    B. only in the Pacific Ocean
    C. on both land and sea
    D. off the coast of Tripoli

5. Sampson's fleet tried to   5.
    A. keep Cervera's fleet from entering the harbor
    B. blockade Santiago Harbor
    C. attack San Juan Hill
    D. prevent the United States regiment from entering the battle

---

TEST 3

PASSAGE

In the generation after Appomattox, the pattern of our present society and economy took shape. Growth - in area, numbers, wealth, power, social complexity, and economic maturity - was the one most arresting fact. The political divisions of the republic were drawn in their final form, a dozen new states were admitted to the Union, and an American empire was established. In a space of forty years, population increased from thirty-one to seventy-six million, fifteen million immigrants - an ever-increasing proportion of them from southern and eastern Europe - poured into the Promised Land, and grea cities like New York, Chicago, Pittsburgh, Cleveland, and Detroit doubled and redoubled their size. In swift succession, the Indians were harried out of their ancient haunts on the high plains and in the mountains and valleys beyond and herded into reservations, the

mining and cattle kingdoms rose and fell; the West was peopled and
farmed, and by the end of the century, the frontier was no more.
Vast new finds of iron ore, copper, and oil created scores of great
industries; small business grew into big business.

1. Which one of the following terms BEST describes the   1.___
   period discussed?
       A. Expansion   B. Conservation   C. Regulation   D. Isolation

2. The policy of the Federal government toward the Indians   2.___
   was to
       A. break up the tribal governments
       B. disenfranchise the Indians
       C. educate all Indian children in public schools
       D. remove them to reservations

3. An IMPORTANT factor in the industrial development that   3.___
   followed the Civil War was the
       A. diversification of agriculture
       B. development of new mineral resources
       C. rapid transformation of farmers into industrial workers
       D. development of a colonial empire

4. The last stage in the development of the West was   4.___
   accomplished by
       A. Indians   B. farmers   C. ranchers   D. miners

5. Which one of the following statements is made concerning   5.___
   the United States during the period described in the paragraph? The United States
       A. established an empire
       B. secured special interests in the oil wells and copper
          mines of Mexico
       C. developed a policy of dollar diplomacy
       D. advocated the open-door policy

6. Which one of the following statements concerning the   6.___
   frontier is made in the paragraph?
       A. After the admission of twelve states, expansion ceased.
       B. An outstanding characteristic of the frontier people
          was their intense nationalism.
       C. At the end of the 19th century, the frontier came to
          an end.
       D. The frontier was most important in shaping our present
          society.

———

TEST 4

PASSAGE

If George Washington could have visited the United States in
the 1840's, his thoughts might have run somewhat like this:

"I find it hard to believe that over 20,000,000 people now live
in the United States, and that towns have been built beyond the

Mississippi River. In my day, there were only 4,000,000 people, and most of these lived along the Atlantic Coast. Can this great city be New York, where I took the oath of office as President? The city I knew had 60,000 inhabitants; today, they tell me, it is the largest city in the New World and has a population of 500,000. What is this engine belching smoke and sparks which carries people across the countryside? When I traveled from Mount Vernon to New York in 1789, I depended on horses. I see factories where machines spin thread to weave it into cloth. Who ever heard in my day of a machine that could spin eighty threads at one time? Here is a boat run by steam which travels against the current of a river! In my time, we depended on the wind to drive our boats. Who would have believed that this country could change so greatly in fifty years!"

1. How much GREATER was the population of the United States in 1840 than in 1789?
   A. Twice as great
   B. Five times as great
   C. Twelve times as great
   D. Twenty times as great

   1.___

2. George Washington was inaugurated in
   A. Boston
   B. Mount Vernon
   C. New York
   D. Philadelphia

   2.___

3. A method of transportation used in the 1840's but not in Washington's time was the
   A. airplane   B. automobile   C. sailboat   D. railroad

   3.___

4. The changes described in the paragraph took place within a period of about ____ years.
   A. 10   B. 20   C. 50   D. 70

   4.___

5. In Washington's time, MOST of the people in the United States lived
   A. beyond the Mississippi
   B. along the eastern seaboard
   C. in the deep South
   D. in the Northwest

   5.___

TEST 5

PASSAGE

In philosophy, the New Deal was democratic, in method evolutionar Because for fifteen years legislative reforms had been dammed up, the now burst upon the country with what seemed like violence but when the waters subsided, it was clear that they ran in familiar channels. The conservation policy of the New Deal had been inaugurated by Theodore Roosevelt; railroad and trust regulation went back to the eighties; banking and currency reforms had been advocated by Bryan and partially achieved by Wilson; the farm-relief program borrowed much from the Populists, labor legislation from the practices of such states as Wisconsin and Oregon. Even judicial reform, which caused such a mighty stir, had been anticipated by Lincoln and Theodore Roosevelt. And in the realm of international relations, the policies of the New Deal were clearly continuations of the traditional policies of strengthening national security, maintaining freedom of the seas, supporting law and peace, and championing democracy in the Western wor

4

1. All of the following are suitable titles for the selection   1.___
   EXCEPT
   A. The New Deal - an Evolution
   B. The Radical Program of the New Deal
   C. Precedents for the New Deal
   D. Conservatism in the New Deal

2. Many students of history do not agree that legislative   2.___
   reforms had been *dammed up* during the fifteen-year period
   preceding the New Deal.
   All of the following legislative measures were passed
   during this fifteen-year period EXCEPT the ____ Act.
   A. Norris-LaGuardia
   B. Reconstruction Finance Corporation
   C. Sherman Antitrust
   D. Agricultural Marketing

3. This selection traces the origin of many of the policies   3.___
   of the New Deal to all of the following EXCEPT
   A. former Presidents
   B. legislation of the Western states
   C. minority parties
   D. the Supreme Court

4. All of the following were indications of isolationism in   4.___
   the New Deal period EXCEPT the
   A. *cash-and-carry* policy   B. Johnson Debt-Default Act
   C. Lima Conference   D. *America First* organization

5. Abraham Lincoln, Theodore Roosevelt, and Franklin   5.___
   Roosevelt had all of the following policies in common EXCEPT
   A. trust regulation
   B. expansion of executive powers
   C. land reforms
   D. economic betterment of the common man

6. According to the selection legislative reforms of the   6.___
   New Deal are characterized by all of the following adjectives
   EXCEPT
   A. democratic   B. evolutionary
   C. reactionary   D. traditional

7. All of the following Presidents were associated with   7.___
   banking reforms EXCEPT
   A. Warren Harding   B. Andrew Jackson
   C. Abraham Lincoln   D. Woodrow Wilson

8. According to the selection, some legislative precedents   8.___
   for the New Deal were furthered in the United States by
   all of the following Presidents EXCEPT
   A. Abraham Lincoln   B. Theodore Roosevelt
   C. Calvin Coolidge   D. Woodrow Wilson

9. The student seeking primary source material on the New
   Deal farm program should consult
   A. THE WORLD ALMANAC
   B. the CONGRESSIONAL RECORD
   C. an encyclopedia of the social studies
   D. WHO'S WHO IN AMERICA ___

TEST 6

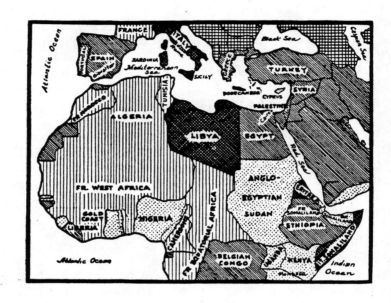

PASSAGE

London, August 14, 1948. A bankrupt empire was put for disposal
in London this week. Although the empire, once the property of Italy
has few assets, bidding for the properties was spirited. Italy,
despite her present domestic problems, was bidding strongly. Only
Italy seemed to want the whole lot; others were angling for bits and
pieces and odd parcels of the colonies. On the other hand, Great
Britain, which wants the properties almost as badly as Italy, was
bidding timidly as if she were afraid of running up the price too fas
and too far.

The international auction sale was arranged last year when the
winning powers in the recent war settled accounts with Italy. In the
Italian peace treaty, Italy renounced all rights to her colonies. Th
Dodecanese promptly were ceded to Greece. In an annex to the treaty,
the Big Four agreed that their Foreign Ministers should decide on the
disposal of the other three colonies - Eritrea and Italian Somaliland
on the east coast of Africa and Libya in North Africa. Failing a
decision within one year, that is, by September 15, 1948, the Big Four
agreed that they would hand over the problem to the United Nations
General Assembly and abide by its verdict.

That year was nearly out when the deputies of the Big Four
Foreign Ministers met, not to decide finally the future of the coloni
but merely to pass on recommendations to the Council of Foreign Minis

ters. When these deputies met last October, they sent out a four-power commission to investigate the situation in the colonies and the wishes of the inhabitants. Reports of that commission were in the hands of the deputies when they met this week.

1. The writer believes that the former Italian colonies   1.____
   A. have many fine resources
   B. are desired by some of the great powers
   C. are financially sound
   D. are strategically important to Russia

2. The Italian colonies in Africa include   2.____
   A. Ethiopia, Eritrea, Libya
   B. Italian Somaliland, Eritrea, Libya
   C. Eritrea, Libya, and the Dodecanese
   D. Ethiopia, Tripoli, and the Dodecanese

3. Italy's African colonies bordered on the   3.____
   A. Mediterranean Sea
   B. Indian Ocean
   C. Atlantic Ocean and Red Sea
   D. Red Sea, Mediterranean Sea, and Indian Ocean

4. The MOST appropriate title for the article would be   4.____
   A. PROBLEMS OF WORLD EMPIRES
   B. FATE OF ITALY'S AFRICAN EMPIRE UNDECIDED
   C. FOUR POWERS INVESTIGATE ITALY'S COLONIES
   D. ITALY'S WEALTH IN AFRICA

5. Libya lies   5.____
   A. east of Algeria   B. east of Egypt
   C. north of Egypt   D. west of Tunisia

6. The author of the article   6.____
   A. thinks that the colonies will be restored to the
      natives
   B. says the colonies will be given to the Arabs
   C. predicts that the colonies will be returned to Italy
   D. makes no prediction as to the action of the United
      Nations Assembly

7. MOST of Libya's boundaries bordered on   7.____
   A. possessions of the French Empire
   B. possessions of the British Empire
   C. the sea
   D. independent countries

8. If the Big Four cannot agree upon the disposition of the   8.____
   Italian colonies, they will refer the problem to the
   A. International Court of Justice
   B. Trusteeship Council
   C. General Assembly of the United Nations
   D. Security Council of the United Nations

7

9. The author of the article states that
   A. the colonies were disposed of in the Italian peace treaty
   B. Greece received all the Italian colonies
   C. the Big Four were first assigned disposal of the colonies
   D. the United Nations Assembly would have to approve the disposal of the colonies

9.

10. The author names the following countries as bidders in the disposal of the remaining colonies
   A. France and the Netherlands
   B. Great Britain and France
   C. Italy and Portugal
   D. Great Britain and Italy

10.

11. By a study of this map, a student could determine the
   A. number of air miles from Rome to Cairo
   B. most densely populated areas
   C. notable topographic features of Ethiopia
   D. boundaries and comparative areas

11.

12. Of the following statements selected from the article, the one that is CLEARLY a statement of opinion is that
   A. the Dodecanese were ceded to Greece
   B. the Big Four agreed to hand over the problem to the United Nations under certain conditions
   C. the deputies met in October, 1947
   D. Great Britain was afraid of running the price up too fast and too far

12.

TEST 7

PASSAGE

"We hold these truths to be self-evident: that all men and women are created equal; that they are endowed by their Creator with certain inalienable rights; that among these are life, liberty, and the pursuit of happiness...

"The history of mankind is a history of repeated injuries and usurpations on the part of man toward woman, having in direct object the establishment of an absolute tyranny over her. To prove this, let facts be submitted to a candid world.

"He has never permitted her to exercise her inalienable right to the elective franchise.

"He has compelled her to submit to laws, in the formation of which she had no voice...

"He has so framed the laws of divorce, as to what shall be the proper causes, and in case of separation, to whom the guardianship of the children shall be given, as to be wholly regardless of the

happiness of women - the law, in all cases, going upon a false supposition of the supremacy of man, and giving all power into his hands...

"He has monopolized nearly all the profitable employments, and from those she is permitted to follow, she receives but a scanty remuneration. He closes against her all the avenues to wealth and distinction which he considers most honorable to himself. As a teacher of theology, medicine, or law, she is not known.

"He has denied her the facilities for obtaining a thorough education, all colleges being closed against her..."

RESOLUTIONS ADOPTED AT THE SENECA FALLS CONVENTION, 1848

1. This selection appeals for support of the movement for   1.____
   A. temperance   B. women's rights
   C. social security   D. child labor legislation

2. Which served as a model for this selection?   2.____
   A. Federal Bill of Rights   B. Emancipation Proclamation
   C. Mayflower Compact   D. Declaration of Independence

3. An *inalienable right* is BEST defined as a right that   3.____
   A. cannot be taken away
   B. is granted to women only
   C. is granted to all except aliens
   D. is guaranteed by the preamble to the Federal Constitution

4. Which right did women enjoy at the time of the Seneca Falls 4.____
   Convention?
   A. The right to serve on juries
   B. The right of assembly
   C. Equal vocational opportunities
   D. Equal rights before the law

5. Which problem of the Seneca Falls Convention remains a   5.____
   legal issue in the United States today?
   A. A voice in making laws
   B. College admission
   C. Equal pay for equal work in industry
   D. Exclusion from the practice of medicine

6. About how long after the Seneca Falls Convention was the   6.____
   right to the elective franchise (referred to in the selection) achieved by a constitutional amendment?   ____ years.
   A. 5   B. 50   C. 75   D. 100
                                                    ____

9

TEST 8

FROM THE FOUR CORNERS OF THE COUNTRY

1. The cartoon suggests that in the 82nd Congress   1.__
    A. harmony **prevailed**
    B. more agreement **existed** on domestic issues than on
       foreign policy
    C. only the reactionary Democrats **opposed** Truman's foreign
       policy
    D. there **was** disagreement within both the Democratic and
       the Republican parties

2. The cartoon specifically refers to division within the   2.__
    Republican party over
    A. foreign policy   B. inflation
    C. civil rights   D. taxation

3. Which of the following are leaders of the two Republican   3.__
    groups represented in the cartoon?
    A. Taft and Acheson   B. Dewey and Hoover
    C. Austin and Dulles   D. Stassen and Lehman

4. We can conclude from the cartoon that in the 82nd Congress, 4.__
    there **was**
    A. little prospect that either group in the Democratic
       party will take a world-minded view
    B. no possibility of any important legislation
    C. no possibility that the President's recommendations
       will receive favorable consideration
    D. little likelihood of settling significant foreign
       policy issues on strict party lines

5. Which of the following conclusions drawn from the cartoon   5.___
   can be readily proved?
   A. There was a reaction group in the Democratic party.
   B. All isolationists came from the same part of the
      country.
   C. The 82nd Congress was evenly divided between Republicans
      and Democrats.
   D. The Republicans were more interested in foreign policy
      than in domestic issues.

   ────

TEST 9

FAMILY INCOME BEFORE TAXES
United States,   1946 and 1953

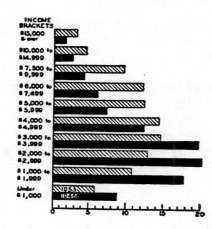

PERCENT OF FAMILIES

1. In 1953, the percent of families with incomes between   1.___
   $3000 and $3,999 was APPROXIMATELY
   A. 5%   B. 10%   C. 15%   D. 20%

2. In 1946, which income bracket included the largest   2.___
   percentage of families?
   A. $1,000 to $1,999   B. $2,000 to $2,999
   C. $3,000 to $3,999   D. $4,000 to $4,999

3. Which of these income brackets included a larger   3.___
   percentage of families in 1953 than in 1946?
   A. $1,000 to $1,999   B. $2,000 to $2,999
   C. $3,000 to $3,999   D. $4,000 to $4,999

4. In 1953, the percent of families with incomes less than   4.___
   $3,000 was about
   A. 30   B. 45   C. 60   D. 75

5. The average family income in 1953 was CLOSEST TO   5.___
   A. $1,500   B. $2,500   C. $4,500   D. $6,000

   ────

TEST 10

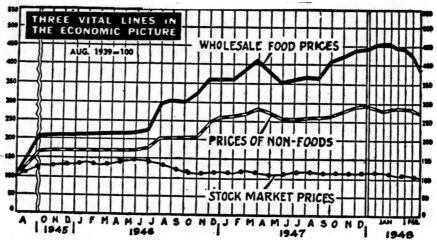

1. For the year 1948, the chart shows a _____ period.   1.__
    A. two-month   B. six-week   C. seven-week   D. eight-week

2. Throughout the period from October 1945 to February 1948,   2.__
    stock market prices
    A. rose sharply
    B. declined sharply
    C. remained comparatively steady
    D. fluctuated greatly

3. A comparison of wholesale food prices at the end of the   3.__
    second week in February 1948 with wholesale food prices
    in October 1945 shows an increase of APPROXIMATELY ____
    points.
    A. 50   B. 100   C. 200   D. 300

4. In the period covered by the graph, wholesale food prices   4.__
    declined sharply
    A. once   B. twice   C. three times D. four times

5. The prices of non-food items reached their highest peak   5.__
    in
    A. March 1946   B. December 1946
    C. March 1947   D. December 1947

6. For the period shown in 1948, all items   6.__
    A. rose   B. remained the same
    C. declined   D. fluctuated greatly

7. The month in which the GREATEST increase in wholesale   7.__
    food prices occurred was
    A. July 1946   B. October 1946
    C. September 1947   D. December 1947

8. The same wholesale order of groceries that cost $100 in   8.__
    August 1939 cost approximately $450 in
    A. November 1946   B. March 1947
    C. December 1947   D. January 1948

———

12

KEYS (CORRECT ANSWERS)

<table>
<tr><td>

TEST 1

1. C
2. A
3. D
4. D
5. B

</td><td>

TEST 2

1. D
2. C
3. A
4. C
5. B

</td><td>

TEST 3

1. A
2. D
3. B
4. B
5. A
6. C

</td><td>

TEST 4

1. B
2. C
3. D
4. C
5. B

</td><td>

TEST 5

1. B
2. C
3. D
4. C
5. A
6. C
7. A
8. C
9. B

</td></tr>
</table>

<table>
<tr><td>

TEST 6

1. B
2. B
3. D
4. B
5. A
6. D
7. A
8. C
9. C
10. D
11. D
12. D

</td><td>

TEST 7

1. B
2. D
3. A
4. B
5. C
6. C

</td><td>

TEST 8

1. D
2. A
3. B
4. D
5. A

</td><td>

TEST 9

1. C
2. B
3. D
4. A
5. C

</td><td>

TEST 10

1. C
2. C
3. C
4. B
5. D
6. C
7. A
8. D

</td></tr>
</table>

EXAMINATION SECTION
TEST 1

Questions 1-8.

Whenever micro-organisms have successfully invaded the body and are growing at the expense of the tissues, the process is called an infection. The term *infection* should always imply the existence of an abnormal state or unnatural condition resulting from the harmful action of micro-organisms. In other words, the simple presence of an organism is not sufficient to cause disease.

Infection may arise from the admission of microorganisms to the tissues through the gastrointestinal tract, through the upper air passages, through wounds made by contaminated teeth or claws of animals or by contaminated weapons, and by the bite of suctorial insects. Another type of infection sometimes occurs when for some reason the body has become vulnerable to the pathogenic action of bacteria whose normal habitat is the body.

The reaction of the body to the attack of an invading organism results in the formation of substances of a specific nature. Those reaction bodies which circulate mainly in the blood serum are known as antibodies and are classified according to their activity. Some known as antitoxins, neutralize poisonous substances produced by the infecting organism. Others, called bacteriolysins, destroy bacteria by dissolving them. Opsonins or bacteriotropins prepare the bacteria for destruction by phagocytes, while precipitins and agglutinins have the property of grouping the invading agents into small clumps or precipitates. The formation of defensive substances is specific for each organism.

1. The passage states "the formation of defensive substances is specific for each organism." This implies that
   A. organisms inherit the ability to produce antibodies
   B. only specific organisms can produce antibodies
   C. the same organism cannot cause the production of two kinds of antibodies
   D. diphtheria antitoxin will not neutralize tetanus toxin
   E. only specific microorganisms can cause the production of antibodies in the human body

1. _____

2. The passage you have read defines the term *infection*. In the light of what it says, which of the following conditions

2. _____

would illustrate an infection?
   A. A guinea pig is injected with diphtheria toxin. It be-
      comes very ill and dies.
   B. A nurse taking care of a tubercular patient inhales
      some tuberculosis bacilli.
   C. A man cuts his finger with a dirty knife. He uses no
      antiseptic.
   D. A student examines his saliva with a microscope. Under
      high power he observes some streptococci.
   E. An anopheles mosquito bites a healthy soldier. Some
      time thereafter, the soldier experiences alternate
      periods of chill and fever.

3. Phagocytes are mentioned in the last paragraph of the pas-   3. ___
   sage. Of the following, the statement that is TRUE of
   phagocytes is:
   A. All white corpuscles are phagocytes.
   B. Some white corpuscles are phagocytes.
   C. Phagocytes are always red corpuscles.
   D. Phagocytes are usually platelets.
   E. Parasitic amebas are phagocytes.

4. In their control of infection the phagocytes are aided by   4. ___
   A. enzymes   B. insulin   C. fibrinogen   D. lipids
   E. lymph glands

5. The passage mentions several ways in which germs may enter   5. ___
   the body. One of those mentioned is by way of the gastrointestinal tract. A disease that enters in this way is
   A. beriberi   B. typhoid   C. typhus
   D. yellow fever E. cancer of the stomach

6. With which of the following statements would the author   6. ___
   of the passage agree?
   A. The white blood corpuscles help ward off infection by
      distributing antibodies to all parts of the body.
   B. A disease organism may live in the body of a person with-
      out having any bad effect on the person.
   C. Antibodies are classified according to the type of or-
      ganism they attack.
   D. Infection is usually accompanied by swelling and the for-
      mation of pus.
   E. Antitoxins are formed against every organism which enters
      the body.

7. A child comes down with diphtheria. His brother, who has   7. ___
   never had diphtheria and has never been immunized against
   it, should receive
   A. the Shick test
   B. injections of diphtheria toxin
   C. injections of diphtheria antitoxin
   D. injections of diphtheria toxoid
   E. nothing, as any treatment would be ineffective

8. Not long ago a child in a large city died of diphtheria.   8. ___
   The following opinions were expressed by different people
   when they read about this. Which opinion is in best keep-
   ing with modern medical knowledge and practice?
   A. In the struggle for existence the weak die off. There-
      fore, the death of this child is of advantage to so-
      ciety because the child was probably a weakling.
   B. Diphtheria is a disease of childhood and some children
      must die of it.
   C. In a large city some deaths from diphtheria must be
      expected despite all precautions.
   D. This death was unnecessary. The child could have been
      saved if the proper medical care had been provided while
      the child was ill.
   E. No child should sicken with diphtheria, much less die of
      it. Where children still die of diphtheria, either the
      parents are ignorant of the fact that it is preventable
      or they are negligent of the welfare of their children.

9. Accidents in the home occur MOST frequently from   9. ___
   A. burns   B. falls   C. firearms   D. poisons
   E. suffocation

10. When a motor car is going 20 miles per hour, its brakes   10. ___
    can stop it in 40 feet. When the same car is going 40
    miles per hour, its brakes ought to stop it in about
    A. 40 ft.   B. 80 ft.   C. 160 ft.   D. 200 ft.
    E. 240 ft.

11. Emotional stability is a characteristic of mental health 11. ___
    that is MOST important to
    A. clearness of complexion   B. digestion
    C. muscle tone
    D. resistance to infectious disease
    E. respiration

12. Anne and Margaret went to a restaurant for lunch. Anne   12. ___
    had a cup of consommé, four saltines, a square of butter,
    a serving of plain jello and a gingersnap. Margaret had
    a cup of tomato soup, two slices of buttered toast, a glass
    of milk and a baked apple. Comparison of their lunches in-
    dicated that
    A. Margaret's lunch was a poorer source of calcium than
       Anne's
    B. Margaret's lunch was a poorer source of vitamin C
    C. Anne's lunch was higher in caloric value than Mar-
       garet's
    D. Anne's lunch was a better source of iron than Mar-
       garet's
    E. Anne's lunch was a poorer source of vitamin A

13. A family consists of father, mother and three children   13. ____
    aged fifteen, thirteen and five. The MINIMUM amount of
    milk the family should buy per week is
       A. 7 quarts   B. 14 quarts   C. 21 quarts
       D. 28 quarts   E. 35 quarts

14. In buying citrus fruit for juice it is MOST economical   14. ____
    to select the fruit
       A. with thick skins   B. heavy for their size
       C. extra large in size   D. small in size
       E. with most highly colored skins

15. In selecting eggs for the family, it is BEST to buy   15. ____
    those that
       A. are fertile   B. are whitest in color
       C. seem light in the hand   D. have smooth, shiny shells
       E. have rough, dull shells

16. In caring for plastics (such as bakelite), it is impor-   16. ____
    tant to know that
       A. an abrasive is a good cleanser for them
       B. they can be subjected to high temperatures
       C. they are resistant to water and most chemicals
       D. they are molded
       E. their colors are apt to fade

17. Which of the following circuits could you wire from this 17. ____
    diagram?

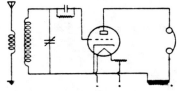

       1. code oscillator   B. doorbell system
       C. electric chime   D. radio receiving set
       E. electric train signal

18. Which process does the illustration represent?   18. ____

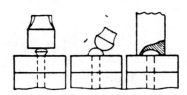

       1. heading a rivet   B. flattening a bolt
       C. setting a nail   D. clinching a nail
       E. forming the head of a screw

4

19. Which drawing illustrates a wired edge in sheet metal work?   19. ___

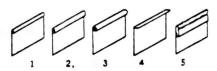

20. Which symbol represents an electrical ground connection?   20. ___

21. With what kind of saw should the type of curve illustrated below be cut?   21. ___

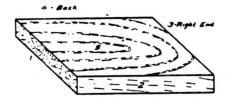

   1. back saw   B. coping saw   C. dovetail saw
   D. key-hole saw D. rip saw

22. In squaring up a piece of rough lumber, which of the surfaces indicated would you plane first?   22. ___

23. Which diagram illustrates the CORRECT method of determining the position of a circle?   23. ___

5

24. All of the following are drawing instruments EXCEPT   24. ___
    A. T-square   B. compass   C. triangle
    D. scale rule   E. plumb bob

25. The instrument used to regulate the temperature of a   25. ___
    refrigerator is a
    A. thermocouple   B. thermograph
    C. thermometer   D. thermoscope
    E. thermostat

26. The source from which MOST electromagnetic waves ra-   26. ___
    diate is
    A. electromagnets   B. power plants   C. the spectrum
    D. the sun   E. uranium 235

27. If the bulb of a glass thermometer is plunged into hot   27. ___
    water, the mercury first falls before rising because the
    A. air above the mercury expands
    B. mercury contracts from the shock
    C. glass expands faster than the mercury
    D. mercury has a negative coefficient of expansion
    E. expanding glass absorbs heat from the mercury

28. A Diesel engine operates without   28. ___
    A. a crankshaft   B. a cooling system
    C. an ignition coil   D. a flywheel
    E. pistons

29. Electric clocks commonly used in homes rarely need set-   29. ___
    ting because they
    A. are well regulated at the factory
    B. keep in step with carefully regulated generators
    C. are manufactured with such fine tolerances
    D. contain ingenious governors
    E. are kept wound by small motors

30. The fuse in a household wiring circuit is a metal with   30. ___
    a high
    A. capacity   B. combustion point
    C. coefficient of expansion D. melting point
    E. resistance

31. The area of a regular-size postage stamp is about   31. ___
    A. 8 square millimeters   B. 1 square centimeter
    C. 5 square centimeters   D. 50 square centimeters
    E. 2.4 square decimeters

32. The spectroscope is used to   32. ___
    A. calibrate periscopes
    B. study the interior of the lungs
    C. magnify small objects enormously
    D. analyze the composition of hot materials
    E. discover the defects in large castings

6

33. The Beaufort scale is used in the measurement of   33. ___
    A. wind velocity
    B. very low temperatures
    C. earthquake intensities
    D. light intensity
    E. small changes in gravitational forces

34. Electrons are   34. ___
    A. neutral particles   B. the nuclei of atoms
    C. negative particles   D. neutralized protons
    E. positive particles

35. The differential in an automobile is a device that al-   35. ___
    lows
    A. a continuous change of gear ratio
    B. the rear wheels to turn independently of each other
    C. a variable battery-charging voltage
    D. traction for one rear wheel when the other is on a
       slippery surface
    E. compensation for gasolines of various octane ratings

36. A railroad locomotive stopped with a crankshaft on dead 36. ___
    center is started forward by
    A. an auxiliary engine
    B. the stored inertia from previous motion
    C. the opposite piston
    D. cranking the crankshaft off center
    E. first backing up

37. The exhaust gas of an automobile is mainly carbon, car- 37. ___
    bon dioxide, carbon monoxide, nitrogen, and
    A. hydrogen   B. oxygen   C. steam
    C. gasoline vapor   E. silicon carbide

38. A woman bought a navy blue dress with white polka dots   **38.** ___
    in a store illuminated with a pure yellow light. The
    colors of the dress as they appeared in the store were
    A. blue with yellow polka dots
    B. black with white polka dots
    C. black with yellow polka dots
    D. green with white polka dots
    E. green with yellow polka dots

39. Of the following, the one that weighs MOST is   39. ___
    A. 50 grams of feathers
    B. 1 pound of cotton
    C. 12 ounces of lead
    D. 1 cubic centimeter of mercury
    E. 600,000 milligrams of sulfur

40. Water is obtained from an artesian well   40. ___
    A. with a shallow lift pump B. with a shallow force pump

C. with a deep lift pump   D. with a deep force pump
E. without a pump

41. Which one of the following items would NOT have to be   41. ___
seriously considered by a group of scientists exploring
on the moon?
    A. Effects of insolation
    B. Effects of gravity
    C. Temperature changes after nightfall
    D. Changing weather conditions
    E. Communication with the earth

42. Each day between March 21 and June 21, the sun appears   42. ___
to set a tiny bit farther north of west than it rose
north of east because the
    A. days are getting longer
    B. earth has moved on its orbit during the day
    C. earth's axis tilts a little more each day
    D. earth rotates on its axis
    E. earth is coming closer to the sun

43. The twinkling of a star is caused by   43. ___
    A. the star itself
    B. interplanetary dust
    C. defects in the structure of the human eye
    D. objects passing between the star and our eyes
    E. turbulence within the atmosphere

44. The Aurora borealis and the Aurora australis are indi-   44. ___
cations that
    A. the earth's atmosphere is more than 200 miles in
       depth
    B. large ice sheets reflect considerable light
    C. the earth's orbit and its axis are not mutually
       perpendicular
    D. moonlight is reflected from cirrus clouds

45. A point on the earth's surface diametrically opposite   45. ___
latitude 40°N, longitude 70°W is
    A. 40°N 70°E   B. 40°S 70°E   C. 50°S 110°E
    D. 40°S 110°E   E. 50°S 70°E

46. The BEST estimate of the age of the earth comes from   46. ___
studies of
    A. the total thickness of sedimentary rocks
    B. certain changes in radioactive minerals
    C. the amount of salt in the ocean
    D. the amount of erosion
    E. the mineralization of the lowest fossil-bearing
       rock

47. Which of the following elements related to the process of nuclear fission does NOT occur in nature?   47. ___
    A. barium   B. curium   C. radium   D. thorium
    E. uranium

48. The nucleus of an atom of uranium 235 contains   48. ___
    A. 235 protons
    B. 235 neutrons
    C. 92 protons and 143 neutrons
    D. 90 protons and 146 neutrons
    E. 146 protons and 89 neutrons

49. A mineral mined in large quantities in the East is   49. ___
    A. aluminum   B. coal   C. magnesium   D. salt
    E. sulfur

50. Certain metals are added to increase the hardness and toughness of steel. A group of such metals is   50. ___
    A. magnesium, cadmium, antimony
    B. manganese, chromium, nickel
    C. carbon, tin, copper
    D. zinc, lead, aluminum
    E. nickel, tin, zinc

___

KEY (CORRECT ANSWERS)

1.	D	11.	B	21.	B	31.	C	41.	D
2.	E	12.	E	22.	E	32.	D	42.	B
3.	B	13.	D	23.	A	33.	A	43.	E
4.	E	14.	B	24.	E	34.	C	44.	A
5.	B	15.	E	25.	E	35.	B	45.	D
6.	B	16.	C	26.	D	36.	C	46.	B
7.	C	17.	D	27.	C	37.	C	47.	B
8.	E	18.	A	28.	C	38.	C	48.	C
9.	B	19.	C	29.	B	39.	E	49.	D
10.	C	20.	C	30.	E	40.	E	50.	B

___

TEST 2

DIRECTIONS: Each question or incomplete statement is followed by several suggested answers or completions. Select the one that *BEST* answers the question or completes the statement. *PRINT THE LETTER OF THE CORRECT ANSWER IN THE SPACE AT THE RIGHT.*

1. A relatively inert gas, such as argon, is included in many incandescent electric lamps because the gas
    A. excludes oxygen, which would corrode the filament
    B. glows when electrically excited
    C. reacts with the filament to cause the glow
    D. permits rapid vaporization around the filament
    E. prevents rapid vaporization around the filament

1.___

2. Wet wood will usually burn but does *NOT* make good tinder because
    A. water does not burn
    B. so much heat is needed to evaporate the water
    C. wet wood has a higher kindling temperature than dry wood
    D. the water vapor produced smothers the fire
    E. wet wood has a lower kindling temperature than dry wood

2.___

3. When coal burns in a furnace, the weight of all the substances derived from the burning will be equal to the weight of
    A. the coal
    B. the ashes taken from the furnace
    C. all the air entering the furnace
    D. the air entering the furnace plus the weight of the ashes
    E. the oxygen entering the furnace plus the weight of the coal

3.___

4. Hard coal burns with less smoke than soft coal because hard coal
    A. is more nearly pure carbon
    B. contains more volatile materials
    C. has a lower kindling temperature
    D. undergoes chemical change more readily
    E. contains more smoke-reducing compounds

4.___

5. A metal much used in the construction of permanent magnets is
    A. brass   B. copper
    C. nickel   D. tin
    E. zinc

5.___

6. The frequency of visible light falls between that of   6.____
    A. infrared rays and radio waves
    B. X rays and cosmic rays
    C. ultraviolet rays and X rays
    D. short radio waves and long radio waves
    E. ultraviolet rays and infrared waves

7. In the visible spectrum, yellow is between   7.____
    A. red and orange   B. orange and green
    C. green and blue   D. green and blue
    E. blue and violet

8. The centripetal force that holds the earth in a   8.____
   nearly circular orbit is
    A. the momentum of the earth
    B. the inertia of the earth
    C. the gravitational attraction of the earth and sun
       for each other
    D. the atomic energy of the sun
    E. the electromagnetic attraction of the sun for the
       iron core of the earth

9. A light year is a measure of   9.____
    A. acceleration   B. distance
    C. intensity   D. time
    E. velocity

10. The atmosphere contains about 1%   10.____
    A. argon   B. carbon dioxide
    C. helium   D. hydrogen
    E. krypton

11. Air that has a relative humidity of 50%   11.____
    A. has half as much water vapor as it can hold
    B. is half water vapor and half air
    C. has half its water vapor condensed
    D. has its water vapor half way condensed
    E. has half its water content condensed and half
       evaporated

12. As a mass of air rises   12.____
    A. its temperature increases and its pressure
       increases
    B. its temperature decreases and its pressure
       increases
    C. its temperature decreases and its pressure
       decreases
    D. its temperature increases and its pressure
       decreases
    E. its temperature stays the same and its pressure
       increases

13. The meridian at which the time is 5 hours earlier than the time at Greenwich is
   A. 105° E   B. 105° W
   C. 75° E   D. 75° W
   E. none of these answers

13._____

14. Which of the following will absorb *MOST* water per given volume?
   A. gravel   B. humus
   C. quartz   D. sand
   E. sandy loam

14._____

15. Coal consists of organic matter which, during geologic ages, was
   A. thoroughly decayed   B. unable to oxidize
   C. thoroughly oxidized   D. preserved unchanged
   E. incompletely calcified

15._____

16. The plants of which of the following groups act as hosts to nitrogen-fixing bacteria?
   A. Wheat, oats, rye
   B. Corn, rye, barley
   C. Pumpkins, squash, cucumbers
   D. Beets, carrots, turnips
   E. Clover, alfalfa, soybeans

16._____

17. Of the following deciduous trees, the one that loses its leaves *LAST* after a summer's growing season is the
   A. box elder   B. elm
   C. oak   D. poplar
   E. sumac

17._____

18. Seedless orange trees are produced by
   A. planting oranges that contain no seeds
   B. cross-pollination
   C. careful breeding
   D. budding or grafting
   E. planting an orange segment that has no seeds

18._____

19. The oxygen absorbed from water by aquatic animals is
   A. dissolved in the water
   B. produced by the respiration of plants
   C. produced by the respiration of animals
   D. derived by breaking down water into hydrogen and oxygen
   E. produced by oxidation of decaying materials

19._____

20. Which of the following is the *BEST* definition of
    photosynthesis? The   20.____
      A. action of sunlight on chlorophyl
      B. process by which plants give off oxygen
      C. building of protoplasm by a plant
      D. manufacture of carbohydrate by a green plant
      E. process by which plants use carbon dioxide

21. Muskrats share with beavers the habit of   21.____
      A. cutting down trees
      B. building dams
      C. building lodges
      D. slapping the water with their tails when alarmed
      E. digging canals

22. The primary source of fish food in a pond is   22.____
      A. one-celled animals   B. one-celled plants
      C. crayfish and snails   D. large water plants
      E. insects falling in or washed in from the land

23. The principal food of our larger hawks is   23.____
      A. calves   B. chickens
      C. game birds   D. small rodents
      E. songbirds

24. The young of houseflies are   24.____
      A. caterpillars   B. cocoons
      C. small flies   D. gnats
      E. maggots

25. Of the following, the animal that is *MOST* dangerous
    to man in America is the   25.____
      A. black bear   B. housefly
      C. mountain lion   D. rattlesnake
      E. black widow spider

26. All of the following diseases are spread by animals   26.____
    EXCEPT
      A. bubonic plague   B. malaria
      C. scarlet fever   D. tularemia
      E. yellow fever

27. All of the following are parasitic diseases   27.____
    EXCEPT
      A. diabetes   B. malaria
      C. tuberculosis   D. typhoid fever
      E. streptococcic sore throat

28. A sharp blow in the front of the abdomen just   28.____
    below the ribs may cause a momentary stoppage of
    breathing because
      A. so much air has been knocked from one's lungs
      B. the secretion of adrenalin has been temporarily ended

13

C. the portion of the autonomic nervous system which is centered in the solar plexus is affected
D. the aveoli of the lungs have collapsed
E. the diaphragm muscles are no longer stimulated by the cerebrum

29. In the control of disease, it has been found that   29.____
    A. all diseases can be prevented by vaccines or serums
    B. all communicable diseases can be cured by specific drugs
    C. effective treatment for all diseases is not known at the present time
    D. an individual who follows hygienic practices will avoid illness.
    E. a low-caloric diet should be given to all who are seriously ill

30. Children are **not** being successfully immunized to   30.____
    prevent
        A. chicken pox   B. **measles**
        C. mumps   D. pneumonia
        E. whooping cough

31. A disease that is highly infectious, incurable if not   31.____
    immediately treated and transmissible to unborn chil-
    dren is
        A. cancer   B. measles
        C. syphilis   D. tuberculosis
        E. infantile paralysis

32. The greatest danger from malaria is that it   32.____
        A. produces chills and a high fever
        B. attacks brain cells
        C. causes dysentery
        D. destroys red blood corpuscles
        E. upsets hormone distribution

33. Binocular vision is a type of eye functioning that   33.____
        A. is acquired at birth
        B. results in double vision
        C. is the simultaneous use of both eyes
        D. causes squinting
        E. is the result of discordant movements of the eyes

34. Infantile paralysis often causes immediate damage to   34.____
        A. blood vessels   B. bones
        C. muscles   D. the spinal cord
        E. connective tissues

35. In one type of treatment of hay fever, the patient   35.____
    is given, over a period of a month, increasing doses of

the pollen that causes his allergy. This type of treatment resembles most closely
    A. the injection of antitoxin for curative purposes
    B. the Pasteur treatment for rabies
    C. vaccination against smallpox
    D. the toxoid treatment for tetanus
    E. the use of penicillin

36. When a person is confined to his bed by diphtheria,   36.____
    A. everything should be removed from the sickroom except the bed, table and chair
    B. a window should be kept open
    C. liquids should be given as the best nourishment
    D. anyone entering the room should wear a gown over the regular clothing
    E. the room should be fumigated immediately upon recovery

37. In many states, the health officer should be notified   37.____
when a person has
    A. measles   B. pellagra
    C. mumps   D. scabies
    E. scurvy

38. Depilatories are used to   38.____
    A. relieve pain
    B. overcome constipation
    C. remove hair
    D. check perspiration
    E. remedy skin blemishes

39. The ultraviolet rays of the sun are especially   39.____
beneficial in
    A. eczema   B. measles
    C. rickets   D. scabies
    E. scurvy

40. Safe drinking water in small quantities can be   40.____
obtained quickly and economically
    A. from a spring   B. by chlorination
    C. by distillation   D. by filtration
    E. by exposure to the sun

41. The principal minerals that food should provide for   41.____
building and preserving sound teeth are
    A. iodine and phosphorus
    B. iron and calcium
    C. calcium and phosphorus
    D. magnesium and iron
    E. phosphorus and iron

42. The enamel of one's permanent teeth is   42.____

A. formed entirely before eruption
B. formed entirely after eruption
C. partially formed before eruption and added constantly after eruption
D. entirely formed before eruption and added as needed to replace damage
E. partially formed before eruption and added at certain periods through one's life

43. The vitamin that affects the clotting of the blood is
    A. ascorbic acid
    B. riboflavin
    C. thiamin
    D. vitamin D
    E. vitamin K

43. ____

44. One function of the liver is the
    A. secretion of adrenalin
    B. formation of red blood cells
    C. temporary storage of glycogen
    D. digestion and absorption of starches
    E. absorption of fats from the intestinal tract

44. ____

45. The principal function of red blood cells is to
    A. destroy disease germs
    B. carry oxygen to cells
    C. act as toxins in the blood stream
    D. cause the blood to coagulate
    E. give the blood a red color

45. ____

46. The use of iodine in the body is most closely related to the functioning of the
    A. gall bladder
    B. kidneys
    C. lymph nodes
    D. pancreas
    E. thyroid

46. ____

47. One function of the projections (villi) of the small intestine is to
    A. produce digestive hormones
    B. aid in the grinding of foods
    C. synchronize the peristaltic action of the intestine
    D. increase the absorptive surface of the intestine
    E. reverse peristaltic action

47. ____

48. One function of sweat is to
    A. cleanse the pores
    B. lubricate the skin
    C. nourish the hair
    D. cool the body
    E. produce perspiration

48. ____

49. An example of an enzyme is
    A. adrenalin   B. ptyalin   C. thiamin   D. thyroxine
    E. trichinosis

49. ____

50. The acid found in our stomachs is _____ acid.
    A. acetic B. formic C. hydrochloric   D. nitric
    E. sulfuric

50. ____

16

KEY (CORRECT ANSWERS)

1.	E	11.	A	21.	C	31.	C	41.	C
2.	C	12.	C	22.	B	32.	D	42.	A
3.	E	13.	D	23.	D	33.	C	43.	E
4.	A	14.	B	24.	E	34.	D	44.	C
5.	C	15.	B	25.	B	35.	B	45.	B
6.	E	16.	E	26.	C	36.	D	46.	E
7.	B	17.	C	27.	A	37.	A	47.	D
8.	C	18.	D	28.	C	38.	C	48.	D
9.	B	19.	A	29.	C	39.	C	49.	B
10.	A	20.	D	30.	D	40.	B	50.	C

TEST 3

DIRECTIONS: Each question or incomplete statement is followed by several suggested answers or completions. Select the one that BEST answers the question or completes the statement.

1. Petroleum consists MAINLY of   1. ___
   A. carbon and hydrogen   B. hydrogen and oxygen
   C. oxygen and nitrogen   D. nitrogen and carbon
   E. carbon and oxygen

2. If a strong solution of table salt is poured on the soil   2. ___
   of a potted plant,
   A. much salt will diffuse into the juices of the plant
   B. the plant will be unaffected
   C. minerals dissolved in the plant juices will diffuse
      into the salt solution
   D. the plant will lose water through its roots
   E. root pressure will be increased and the plant will
      become turgid

3. The MAIN function of humus in soil is to   3. ___
   A. keep the soil "sweet"
   B. provide carbon dioxide for photosynthesis in the
      roots
   C. conserve moisture
   D. absorb nitrogen from the air
   E. live symbiotically with the plants

4. Fungi procure their food   4. ___
   A. by photosynthesis
   B. from the air
   C. from materials produced by other organisms
   D. from soil minerals
   E. by combining inorganic materials

5. A grain of wheat is PRIMARILY   5. ___
   A. a fertilized plant egg
   B. an embryo plant plus a food supply
   C. a developed pollen grain
   D. a miniature of the adult plant
   E. a food supply for the unfertilized plant egg

6. An oak tree increases in diameter because of the growth   6. ___
   that takes place
   A. in the bark
   B. just under the bark
   C. in the center of the trunk
   D. uniformly throughout the trunk
   E. in the size of each cell in the tree

18

7. Grapefruit are so named because they   7. ___
   A. are closely related to a species of tropical grapes
   B. grow in clusters
   C. are mutants of a domestic grape
   D. grow on trees whose leaves are almost indistinguish-
      able from grape leaves
   E. are produced on vines

8. Of the following, the plant that requires two growing   8. ___
   seasons to complete its life cycle is the
   A. bean   B. cabbage   C. corn   D. tomato
   E. watermelon

9. The flounder   9. ___
   A. swims in its unique manner from birth
   B. has a symmetrical head
   C. has one eye that migrates to the opposite side of
      its head
   D. is a surface feeder
   E. is the main enemy of the oyster

10. One can drink water from a brook with his head lower than 10. ___
    his feet because of the
    A. peristaltic action of the esophagus
    B. capillary action in the throat
    C. difference in pressure between the stomach and the
       atmosphere
    D. pumping action of the diaphragm
    E. valvular action of the larynx

11. Radioactive isotopes have been used in medicine to   11. ___
    A. trace the course of certain compounds through the
       body
    B. cure anema
    C. determine the amount of phosphorus in the body
    D. supplement the bactericidal action of streptomycin
    E. make vaccines for the treatment of cancer

12. The effect of a specific antibody in the blood is to   12. ___
    cause
    A. disintegration of white blood corpuscles
    B. destruction of all disease-producing bacteria
    C. disintegration of most bacteria
    D. destruction of specific bacteria
    E. rapid blood-clotting in wounds

13. Expressed in the centigrade scale, the average normal   13. ___
    temperature of the human body is
    A. 37°C   B. 55°C   C. 68°C   D. 98°C   E. 212°C

14. The incubation period of a disease is the   14. ___
    A. time required for the bacterium to hatch

B. time from infection until the appearance of symptoms
C. length of the life cycle of the infecting organism
D. period during which the patient should be confined to bed
E. length of exposure necessary to acquire a disease

15. As individual may do much to protect himself against hook-
worm in an infected area by
    A. being vaccinated against hookworm
    B. taking preventive medicine
    C. avoiding all pork
    D. eating only food that has been cooked under pressure
    E. wearing shoes

16. The iron lung is a device that
    A. replaces one lobe of the lungs
    B. blows air into the lungs
    C. raises and lowers the pressure on the outside of the body
    D. supplies pure oxygen to invalids
    E. increases peristaltic action

17. Sir Alexander Fleming is BEST known for his work in connection with the
    A. discovery of insulin
    B. development of the iron lung
    C. use of X-rays in the treatment of cancer
    D. prevention of yellow fever
    E. discovery of penicillin

18. Radioactive isotopes produced by atomic energy have already been used successfully in the
    A. removal of superfluous hair
    B. treatment of certain types of goiter
    C. prevention of tooth decay
    D. treatment of certain forms of mental disease
    E. treatment of water supplies to kill dangerous bacteria

19. When caring for an invalid in the home, one should remember that
    A. unless a person is ill, the body temperature is always 98.6°F.
    B. the red arrow point on a clinical thermometer is at 100°F.
    C. the normal body temperature may vary as much as one and one-half degrees during the day
    D. a rectal temperature of 98°F. is considered normal
    E. the body temperature is usually lowest at about 4 p.m. and highest at about 3 a.m.

20. Which of the following statements is TRUE?   20. ___
    A. Salivation is a sign that a baby is teething.
    B. After a baby has had an accidental fall, the mother
       should try to put it to sleep as soon as possible.
    C. Breast-fed babies usually have greater immunity to
       contagious diseases than bottle-fed babies have.
    D. Thumb sucking is a sign that a baby is not getting
       enough to eat.
    E. Infant mortality is higher in females than in males.

21. A disease to which a person is USUALLY permanently im-   21. ___
    mune after recovering from an attack is
    A. influenza   B. malaria   C. pneumonia
    D. poliomyelitis   E. syphilis

22. Of the following, the BEST treatment for someone who   22. ___
    looks as if he were about to faint is to
    A. have him sit down in a chair and close his eyes
       for a few minutes
    B. have him hold his arms above his head
    C. have someone take hold of him on either side and
       keep him walking
    D. have him sit down on the floor or ground with his
       head between his knees
    E. slap him vigorously on the back several times

23. Of the following, the BEST first-aid treatment for a   23. ___
    person whose eyes have been exposed to irritating fumes
    is to
    A. flush the eyes with water from a drinking fountain
    B. put powdered boracic acid in the eyes
    C. apply cold towels to the eyes
    D. rub the eyes to stimulate the flow of tears
    E. rush the patient to the nearest physician

24. The MOST serious type of fatigue is induced by   24. ___
    A. emotional strain
    B. mental work
    C. physical activity
    D. sedentary occupations
    E. inadequate sleep over several days

25. The BEST body position in going to sleep has been found   25. ___
    to be
    A. on the abdomen   B. on the left side
    C. on the right side   D. flat on one's back
    E. any way that is comfortable

26. The use of a common towel by two or more persons may re-   26. ___
    sult in the spread of
    A. eczema   B. hives   C. impetigo   D. rickets
    E. shingles

27. Legally prohibiting expectoration in public places helps   27. ___
    prevent
      A. cancer   B. pneumonia   C. scabies   D. tetanus
      E. typhoid fever

28. When in need of a stimulant, one may BEST use   28. ___
      A. brandy   B. hot milk   C. orange juice D. tea
      E. bicarbonate of soda in water

29. Toasted bread is more digestible than untoasted bread be- 29. ___
    cause the toasting process changes a part of the carbohy-
    drate into
      A. dextrin   B. heparin   C. melanin   D. opsonin
      E. palmitin

30. Insufficient calcium in the diet of a child may cause   30. ___
      A. bowlegs   B. impaired vision   C. infantile paralysis
      D. wryneck   E. tuberculosis of the bones

31. A generous supply of vitamin C may be included in a day's 31. ___
    diet by using a sufficient quantity of
      A. broiled mackerel   B. stewed prunes
      C. pork chops   D. tomato juice
      E. whole wheat bread or cereals

32. Of the following, the food nutrient that provides energy   32. ___
    in the diet is
      A. cellulose   B. iron   C. protein   D. riboflavin
      E. thiamin

33. Of the foods listed below, the one that will contribute   33. ___
    the GREATEST number of calories to the diet is
      A. one cup of milk
      B. two cups of cabbage
      C. one-half cup of cornstarch pudding
      D. four tablespoonfuls of mayonnaise
      E. two medium-sized white potatoes

34. In case of high price or shortage of meat, other foods   34. ___
    rich in protein may be used. The BEST substitute from
    the following list is
      A. egg plant   B. dark rice   C. spaghetti
      D. string beans E. red kidney beans

35. The BEST of the following lunches for a two-year old   35. ___
    child would be
      A. egg yolk, baked potato, whole wheat toast, chopped
         peas, milk
      B. cream soup, cabbage, graham crackers, custard, milk
      C. meat loaf, cabbage salad, toast, chocolate pudding,
         milk
      D. soft cooked egg, pineapple and raw carrot salad, toast,
         junket, milk

E. creamed corn, toast, weak cocoa, custard

36. Which of the following statements is TRUE?   36. ___
    A. One can become physically ill from ailments that
       are purely imaginary.
    B. A receding chin usually indicates a weak will.
    C. Good and bad personality traits are sometimes in-
       herited.
    D. Believing that a thing is true often makes it true.
    E. A person's intelligence can always be improved
       through education

37. Which of the following would be injured if a baking soda 37. ___
    solution were allowed to stand in it overnight?
    A. An earthenware casserole
    B. An enamel saucepan
    C. A pyrex double boiler
    D. An aluminum saucepan
    E. A stainless steel pressure saucepan

38. The illustration below represents a   38. ___

    A. brad   B. casing nail   C. common nail
    D. cut nail   E. finishing nail

39. A doorbell is USUALLY connected to the household circuit 39. ___
    (A.C.) through a
    A. base plug B. condenser   C. rectifier
    D. resistor   E. transformer

40. An ordinary automobile storage battery consists of   40. ___
    A. one large dry cell   B. several dry cells
    C. one large wet cell   D. several wet cells
    E. a chemical rectifier

41. The tool illustrated below is used MOST often by   41. ___

    A. an electrician   B. a machinist   C. a printer
    D. a plumber   E. a garage mechanic

42. The term "kiln dried" applies to   42. ___
    A. linseed oil   B. lumber   C. plaster
    D. pottery   E. cold-rolled steel

43. A "stud" in a frame building is a part of the   43. ___
    A. ceiling   B. floor   C. foundation
    D. roof   E. side wall

23

44. The joint shown below is a   44. ____

   A. butt   B. dado C. dovetail D. half lap E. rabbet

45. Which of the following prevents a saw from binding?   45. ____
   A. set   B. sharpness   C. curve of back
   D. number of teeth   E. thickness of blade

46. Two men are pulling on ropes attached to a rock. It is   46. ____
   found that their resultant force is less than that used
   by either man. It MUST be that the forces are
   A. acting at less than 90° to each other
   B. acting at more than 90° to each other
   C. acting at 90° to each other
   D. both large
   E. both small

47. An observer is moving away from a vibrating object with   47. ____
   the speed of sound. The observer will
   A. hear a note an octave higher
   B. hear a note an octave lower
   C. hear the same note but more faintly
   D. hear the same note emphasized
   E. not hear the emitted note

48. The extraction of nitrogenous wastes from the blood is   48. ____
   the CHIEF function of the
   A. bladder   B. kidneys   C. large intestine
   D. liver   E. lungs

49. The surface of the earth has been changed the MOST by   49. ____
   A. winds   B. glaciers C. running water
   D. volcanos   E. chemical action of the atmosphere

50. Molds are to spores as green plants are to   50. ____
   A. flowers   B. leaves   C. roots   D. seeds
   E. stems

KEY (CORRECT ANSWERS)

1.	A	11.	A	21.	D	31.	D	41.	D
2.	D	12.	D	22.	D	32.	C	42.	B
3.	C	13.	A	23.	A	33.	D	43.	E
4.	C	14.	B	24.	A	34.	E	44.	B
5.	B	15.	E	25.	E	35.	A	45.	A
6.	B	16.	C	26.	C	36.	A	46.	B
7.	B	17.	E	27.	B	37.	D	47.	E
8.	B	18.	B	28.	D	38.	C	48.	B
9.	C	19.	C	29.	A	39.	E	49.	C
10.	A	20.	C	30.	A	40.	D	50.	D

TEST 4

DIRECTIONS: Each question or incomplete statement is followed by several suggested answers or completions. Select the one that BEST answers the question or completes the statement.

1. The dinosaur was a prehistoric   1. ___
   - A. amphibian
   - B. arthropod
   - C. mammal
   - D. primate
   - E. reptile

2. Evidence indicating that great climatic changes have oc-   2. ___
   curred in the past is found in
   - A. the appearance of mountains
   - B. the delta of the Mississippi
   - C. coal deposits in Alaska
   - D. lava deposits
   - E. the records of the United States Department of Agriculture

3. A structure that helps to keep air pressure in the middle   3. ___
   ear equal to atmospheric pressure is the
   - A. eardrum
   - B. Eustachian tube
   - C. Islands of Langerhans
   - D. nasal passage
   - E. semicircular canal

4. One factor NOT necessary for photosynthesis is   4. ___
   - A. carbon dioxide
   - B. chlorophyll
   - C. free oxygen
   - D. sunlight
   - E. water

5. Carbon grains are an essential part of a   5. ___
   - A. doorbell
   - B. radio loudspeaker
   - C. storage battery
   - D. transformer
   - E. telephone transmitter

6. A container of water is placed on a scale and the scale   6. ___
   reading is 100 pounds. If a block of wood weighing 25 pounds
   is then floated half submerged in the water, the scale will
   read
   - A. 75 pounds
   - B. 87.5 pounds
   - C. 100 pounds
   - D. 112.5 pounds
   - E. 125 pounds

7. Most evidence seems to indicate that the first vertebrate   7. ___
   animal to appear on the earth was the
   - A. amphibian
   - B. bird
   - C. fish
   - D. mammal
   - E. reptile

8. The earth's crust contains about 50% oxygen by weight.   8. ___
   The next MOST abundant element in the earth's crust is
   - A. aluminum
   - B. calcium
   - C. hydrogen
   - D. iron
   - E. silicon

9. A large steel drum containing air at normal atmospheric   9. ___
   pressure is found to float with 40% of its volume under
   water. When compressed air is forced into the drum until its
   pressure is doubled, the drum will
       A. float at the same level
       B. float higher in the water
       C. float lower in the water
       D. sink to a depth between the surface and the bottom
       E. sink to the bottom

10. When a bacterial cell is submerged in a strong salt solu-   10. ___
    tion, the cell shrinks because
        A. minerals enter the cell
        B. the cytoplasm within the cell decomposes
        C. the salt dissolves the cell wall
        D. the salt enters the cell
        E. water leaves the cell

11. Mosaic vision is characteristic of   11. ___
        A. bacteria   B. bees   C. earthworms   D. man   E. robins

12. Ambergris, a substance used to make perfume, comes from   12. ___
        A. an inflammation in the body of the sperm whale
        B. distilled attar of roses
        C. the hardened resin from pine trees
        D. the musk-producing organs of a deer
        E. the nectar-producing organs of the honeysuckle vine

13. Blood plasma consists CHIEFLY of   13. ___
        A. amino acids   B. fats   C. glucose   D. water
        E. urea and uric acids

14. Appendicitis is generally accompanied by   14. ___
        A. daily fluctuation of red cell count
        B. high red cell count
        C. high white cell count
        D. low white cell count
        E. pain in the carotids

15. The dead red corpuscles in the blood stream are removed   15. ___
    and decomposed by the
        A. heart   B. liver   C. lungs   D. small intestine
        E. white corpuscles

16. Auxins are   16. ___
        A. growth hormones   B. insect poisons   C. new plastics
        D. new textiles   E. respiratory enzymes

17. On the desert the Arabs are able to keep water cool in   17. ___
    earthenware jugs because
        A. particles of earthenware dissolve in the water and
           lower its temperature

B. the attraction between the molecules of the jug and
   the water is a cooling process
C. the change of some of the water to a vapor lowers
   the temperature
D. the jug is a good conductor of heat
E. the rough surface of the jug radiates heat more
   rapidly

18. An object weighs 10 pounds in air and floats in water with   18. ___
    one half of its volume above the surface. The MINIMUM force
    that must be added to submerge the object is
    A. 5 pounds   B. 10 pounds   C. 20 pounds   D. 31.25 pounds
    E. 62.5 pounds

19. A hot stove poker is held near the face. The rays of   19. ___
    light chiefly responsible for the sensation felt on the
    cheek are those of
    A. blue light   B. infrared light   C. red light
    D. ultraviolet light   E. white light

20. Plastic-coated screen is often used in place of glass in   20. ___
    chicken coops and barns because
    A. glass filters out most of the infrared rays of sun-
       light
    B. glass filters out most of the ultraviolet rays of sun-
       light
    C. plastic filters out harmful rays of light
    D. plastic is far safer for the cattle or chickens since
       it will not shatter
    E. plastic transmits more of the rays of visible light

21. When smoke from a locomotive tends to settle to the ground,   21. ___
    it may indicate that an area of rainy weather is approach-
    ing because
    A. the air is less dense and will not support the smoke
       particles
    B. the air is rising in a low pressure area
    C. the air is sinking near the low pressure area
    D. the smoke is sucked into the low pressure area
    E. there is less oxygen so that the smoke particles are
       not completely burned and are heavier

22. In order to overcome losses during long-distance trans-   22. ___
    mission of electrical energy, it is common practice to
    A. decrease both the voltage and the current
    B. decrease the voltage and increase the current
    C. increase both the voltage and the current
    D. increase the voltage and keep the current constant
    E. increase the voltage and decrease the current

23. Oil is poured on water to reduce the height of waves be-   23. ___
    cause the
    A. added weight of the oil makes the waves break at a
       lesser height
    B. oil is a lubricant
    C. chemical action between oil and water produces a
       heavier substance
    D. oil fills up the troughs of the waves
    E. surface tension of the water will be weakened

24. The MOST penetrating of the following forms of radiation   24. ___
    is
    A. heat   B. infrared light   C. the cosmic ray
    D. the X-ray   E. ultraviolet light

25. A good index of the health of a community is its death   25. ___
    rate from
       A. arteriosclerosis   B. diphtheria   C. influenza
       D. meningitis   E. typhoid

26. Fehling's solution is added to a test tube containing a   26. ___
    sample of breakfast cereal that has been heated in water.
    If the Fehling's solution turns brick red, the breakfast
    food PROBABLY contains
       A. animal fat   B. grape sugar   C. protein   D. starch
       E. vitamin C

27. The part of the eye that corresponds to the diaphragm of   27. ___
    the camera is the
       A. cornea   B. iris   C. lens   D. pupil   E. retina

28. The pneumothorax treatment is used in cases of   28. ___
       A. cancer   B. heart disease   C. tuberculosis
       D. pneumonia   E. paralysis of the upper thorax

29. In outer space, where there is no atmosphere, a jet-pro-   29. ___
    pelled rocket
       A. cannot be stopped
       B. cannot change its direction
       C. will not operate since there is no air against which
          the expelled gases can push
       D. will not operate since there is no air to supply oxy-
          gen for combustion of the fuel
       E. will operate more efficiently because there is no air
          resistance

30. A man has a cup of hot coffee, a teaspoonful of sugar, an   30. ___
    ounce of cream. He desires to drink the combination at the
    lowest temperature possible at the end of three minutes. He
    should add the
       A. cream at once and the sugar in three minutes
       B. cream at once and the sugar slowly throughout the three-
          minute period

C. sugar and cream at the end of three minutes
D. sugar and cream immediately
E. sugar at once and the cream slowly throughout the three-minute period

31. In one State, the average temperature on August 6 is USUALLY higher than on June 21. This is BEST explained by   31. ___
    A. the fact that August 6 is midway between June 21 and September 21
    B. the fact that the humidity is higher on August 6
    C. the reason that accounts for 2 p.m. usually being warmer than noon
    D. the sun's rays being more vertical on August 6

32. Ordinary photographic film is developed under a ruby-colored light because the film is   32. ___
    A. not sensitive to long wave lengths of visible light
    B. not sensitive to short wave lengths of visible light
    C. not sensitive to ultraviolet light
    D. not sensitive to visible light
    E. sensitive to all wave lengths of visible light

33. In a plant the semipermeable membrane which surrounds the cell is the   33. ___
    A. cell membrane B. cell wall C. vacuole membrane
    D. nuclear membrane   E. cytoplasmic inclusion

34. Tobacco mosaic is due to   34. ___
    A. a bacterium   B. a lack of iron C. too much sun
    D. a virus   E. a lack of magnesium

35. When sheets are washed, bluing is sometimes added to the water because   35. ___
    A. a chemical change called bleaching will occur
    B. it destroys most water-borne bacteria
    C. it is a water softener
    D. its color is complementary to yellow
    E. the soap is made less harsh

36. The HIGHEST clouds are   36. ___
    A. alto-cumulus   B. cirrus   C. cumulus   D. nimbus
    E. stratus

37. Acetylcholine is a substance that controls the   37. ___
    A. absorption of vitamins   B. action of nerves
    C. digestion of food   D. germination of seeds
    E. storage of fat

38. The PRINCIPAL function of the white blood cells is to   38. ___
    A. act as toxins in the blood stream
    B. carry away waste products
    C. carry oxygen to the cells

29

D. destroy disease germs
E. produce antitoxins

39. There are indications that decay is retarded by treating   39. ___
    the teeth of children with a compound of
    A. bromine   B. chlorine   C. fluorine   D. iodine
    E. sulfur

40. Poisons manufactured by bacteria are called   40. ___
    A. molds   B. phagocytes   C. septics   D. toxins
    E. viruses

41. Aero-embolism is a body disturbance commonly known as   41. ___
    A. appendicitis   B. bends   C. infantile paralysis
    D. pneumonia   E. sugar diabetes

42. Diabetes is caused by the improper functioning of the   42. ___
    A. adrenals   B. digestive juices   C. pancreas
    D. parathyroids   E. thyroid

43. The air we exhale, compared to the air we inhale, con-   43. ___
    tains
    A. less carbon dioxide   B. less nitrogen
    C. more nitrogen   D. more oxygen
    E. more water vapor

44. Studies of sleep by psychologists and health specialists   44. ___
    indicate that
    A. a tired, stuporous feeling sometimes following a
       profound sleep is attributed to tossing too much
    B. adults reveal considerable individual differences in
       their need of sleep, but infants and pre-school child-
       ren reveal insignificant differences at a given age
    C. best rest is obtained from sleep when the stomach is
       empty
    D. the typically healthy sleeper usually changes from one
       gross bodily position to another between twenty and
       forty-five times during eight hours of sleep
    E. young children show more movements in sleep than older
       children and adults

45. Edward Jenner perfected a method of making people immune   45. ___
    to
    A. anthrax   B. bubonic plague   C. diphtheria
    D. smallpox   E. yellow fever

46. A file clerk who has the habit of moistening her finger   46. ___
    to facilitate the turning of pages can MOST easily break
    the habit by
    A. applying a bitter but harmless substance to her finger
    B. asking a co-worker to remind her when she puts her
       finger to her tongue

30

    C. making a practice of using the eraser of a pencil to
       turn pages
    D. placing a large sign in a conspicuous place on her
       desk
    E. putting a piece of adhesive plaster on her finger as
       a reminder

47. Ascorbic acid is the scientific name for   47. ____
    A. a narcotic obtained from poppies
    B. a poisonous substance in tobacco
    C. acid in the stomach
    D. digitalis
    E. vitamin C

48. The HIGHEST concentration of oxygen is found in the   48. ____
    A. hepatic vein   B. jugular vein   C. pulmonary artery
    D. pulmonary vein   E. right auricle

49. A workman was injured by a blunt piece of flying steel.   49. ____
   The wound, close to his eye, was dirty and lacerated but
   there was only slight bleeding. In giving first aid, his
   co-worker should
    A. apply a mild tincture of iodine and cover the wound
       with sterile gauze
    B. clean the wound carefully with alcohol and cover with
       sterile gauze
    C. cover the wound with sterile gauze and leave the clean-
       ing to a physician
    D. remove the specks of dirt with a sterile swab before
       covering the wound with sterile gauze
    E. wash the wound carefully with soap and water and cover
       it with sterile gauze

50. Which one of the following statements concerning first   50. ____
   aid is TRUE?
    A. A tourniquet should be loosened every 30 or 40 minutes
       to prevent stoppage of circulation and possible gangrene.
    B. It is essential to wash the hands before applying digital
       pressure to an open wound.
    C. It is useless to continue artificial respiration for more
       than one hour of there is no sign of returning conscious-
       ness.
    D. The pulse of a person suffering from shock is rapid and
       weak.
    E. Whiskey is a good stimulant to give a person bitten by
       a poisonous snake.

KEY (CORRECT ANSWERS)

1.	E	11.	B	21.	A	31.	C	41.	B
2.	C	12.	A	22.	E	32.	A	42.	C
3.	B	13.	D	23.	E	33.	A	43.	E
4.	C	14.	C	24.	C	34.	D	44.	D
5.	E	15.	B	25.	E	35.	D	45.	D
6.	E	16.	A	26.	B	36.	B	46.	C
7.	C	17.	C	27.	B	37.	B	47.	E
8.	E	18.	B	28.	C	38.	D	48.	D
9.	C	19.	B	29.	E	39.	C	49.	C
10.	E	20.	B	30.	C	40.	D	50.	D

———

TEST 5

DIRECTIONS: Each question or incomplete statement is followed by several suggested answers or completions. Select the one that BEST answers the question or completes the statement. *PRINT THE LETTER OF THE CORRECT ANSWER IN THE SPACE AT THE RIGHT.*

1. Of the following, the BEST source of vitamin E is   1. ___
   A. citrus fruits   B. cod liver oil
   C. halibut liver oil   D. wheat germ oil
   E. milk and milk products

2. Which one of the following may be caused by a plant?   2. ___
   A. amoebic dysentery   B. influenza   C. malaria
   D. ringworm   E. yellow fever

3. Which one of the following parts of the circulatory sys-   3. ___
  tem carries digested fats away from the intestines?
   A. arterial capillaries   B. lacteals
   C. pancreatic duct   D. pulmonary artery
   E. venal capillaries

4. At which one of the following points should digital pres-   4. ___
  sure be applied to stop arterial bleeding in the hand or
  forearm?
   A. brachial   B. carotid   C. femoral   D. subclavian
   E. temporal

5. The hormone that regulates the general metabolism of the   5. ___
  body is
   A. adrenalin   B. gastrin   C. insulin   D. pituitrin
   E. thyroxin

6. The small dipper seems to turn about the North Star once   6. ___
  each day because
   A. all stars move in great circles on the celestial sphere
   B. the earth turns on its axis
   C. the North Star is the last star in the handle of the
      dipper
   D. the planets revolve around the sun
   E. the solar system rotates about a fixed star

7. The component of the atmosphere that shows the GREATEST   7. ___
  percentage of variation is
   A. argon   B. carbon dioxide   C. nitrogen   D. oxygen
   E. water vapor

8. Slate is to shale as marble is to
   A. feldspar   B. gneiss   C. limestone   D. mica schist
   E. sandstone

9. A disease caused by the malfunction of the pancreas is   9. ___
    A. coronary thrombosis   B. diabetes   C. gallstones
    D. rickets   E. tuberculosis

10. Respiration is to carbon dioxide as photosynthesis is to 10. ___
    A. carbon dioxide   B. chlorophyll   C. oxygen
    D. starch   E. sunlight

11. When a machine that is 80% efficient does 1000 foot- 11. ___
    pounds of work, the work input MUST be
    A. 80 foot-pounds   B. 800 foot-pounds
    C. 1000 foot-pounds   D. 1250 foot-pounds
    E. 1800 foot-pounds

12. A siphon is NOT used to empty the water out of the hold 12. ___
    of a ship into the ocean because
    A. a siphon does not create a sufficient vacuum
    B. a siphon will not operate at sea level
    C. salt water is heavier than fresh water
    D. the air pressure is less on the ocean's surface
       than it is in the hold
    E. the hold is beneath the ocean's surface

13. A full moon might be seen   .   13. ___
    A. faintly at noon
    B. high in the sky at sunset
    C. low in the east in the evening
    D. low in the east in the morning
    E. low in the west at midnight

14. A kerosene lamp burns with a yellow flame due to the 14. ___
    A. burning of hydrogen
    B. complete burning of the hydrocarbons
    C. heating of the wick
    D. incandescence of unburned carbon particles
    E. natural color of any burning kerosene

15. On which one of the following days will a person's sha- 15. ___
    dow be LONGEST at noon in the East?
    A. Christmas   B. Easter Sunday   C. Fourth of July
    D. Labor Day   E. Thanksgiving

16. Perfume is made by dissolving oils containing the essence 16. ___
    of the desired odor in
    A. alcohol   B. banana oil   C. distilled water
    D. glycerin   E. volatile mineral oil

17. Which one of the following is produced naturally by 17. ___
    living things?
    A. aspirin   B. atabrine   C. lysol   D. quinine
    E. sulfanilamide

18. Which one of the following terms is NOT associated with   18. ___
    the others?
    A. beriberi   B. leukemia   C. rickets   D. scurvy
    E. xerophthalmia

19. Like most great caverns, the Howe Caverns of New York State 19. ___
    A. are made of sandstone   B. are the result of glaciation
    C. occur in limestone rock D. were formed by earthquakes
    E. were formed by wind erosion

20. The unrelated member of the following group is   20. ___
    A. cyclotron   B. deuteron   C. electron   D. neutron
    E. positron

21. Fossils are MOST likely to be found in   21. ___
    A. igneous rocks   B. marble quarries
    C. metamorphic rocks   D. ocean deeps
    E. sedimentary rocks

22. The watershed of a river has reference to   22. ___
    A. its delta
    B. its flood plain
    C. the body of water into which the river drains
    D. the land from which water drains into the river
    E. the river and its tributaries

23. An increase of temperature from 10°C. to 30°C. is equi- 23. ___
    valent to an increase of
    A. 11 1/2°F.   B. 36°F.   C. 43 1/2°F.   D. 68°F.
    E. 86°F.

24. The body proper of all insects consists of three parts, 24. ___
    namely, the head, the abdomen and the
    A. antennae   B. legs   C. shell   D. thorax
    E. wings

25. The rate of sugar storage in the liver may be studied by 25. ___
    using radioactive
    A. calcium   B. carbon   C. carbon dioxide   D. iron
    E. nitrogen

26. A water table is   26. ___
    A. a flat rock mass eroded by waves B. a rain gauge
    C. a river flood stage   D. the sea level
    E. an underground water level

27. We can see only one side of the moon because the period 27. ___
    of the moon's
    A. revolution about the earth equals that of the earth's
       revolution about the sun
    B. rotation is equal to its period of revolution about the
       earth

C. rotation is equal to that of the earth's rotation
D. rotation is half that of the earth's rotation
E. rotation is twice that of the earth's rotation

28. The term that includes all others in the following group 28. ____
    is
    A. absorption   B. assimilation   C. circulation
    D. digestion   E. nutrition

29. The unrelated member of the following group is   29. ____
    A. adrenin   B. amylopsin   C. insulin
    D. parathormone   E. thyroxin

30. An object that weighs 500 pounds in air appears to lose   30. ____
    200 pounds when submerged in water to a depth of 10 feet.
    If the object is then lowered to a depth of 20 feet, its
    apparent weight will be
    A. 100 lb.   B. 200 lb.   C. 300 lb.   D. 400 lb.
    E. 500 lb.

31. The color of the sky is blue because   31. ____
    A. blue light is reflected from the Heaviside layer
    B. cosmic rays transmit blue light
    C. dust particles are blue in color
    D. the short wave lengths of visible light are scattered
       most
    E. there is an excess of ultraviolet rays in the strato-
       sphere

32. If you were placed in the middle of a room where the   32. ____
    floor was perfectly frictionless, the BEST method to use in
    betting to a side wall would be to
    A. crawl over
    B. roll over
    C. throw an object horizontally
    D. walk over
    E. wave your arms violently up and down

33. A disease caused by a protozoan is   33. ____
    A. arteriosclerosis   B. endocarditis   C. malaria
    D. poliomyelitis   E. tuberculosis

34. A one-cubic meter, closed, rigid tank contains air and   34. ____
    11 grams of water vapor at a temperature of 20°C. If the
    temperature of the confined air is raised to 35°C., which
    one of the following will result?
    A. The absolute himidity will rise.
    B. The absolute humidity will fall.
    C. The relative humidity will rise.
    D. The relative humidity will fall.
    E. No change will occur in either absolute or relative
       humidity

35. The use of a soda-acid type fire extinguisher is recommended for putting out fires involving burning
    A. dry chemicals   B. fats or vegetable oils
    C. gasoline   D. painted woodwork
    E. insulation on wires carrying 110-220 volts

35. ___

36. The alloy, alnico, is widely used in making
    A. aluminum utensils   B. cutting tools
    C. permanent magnets   D. springs
    E. thermostats

36. ___

37. A container is filled to the brim with ice water in which is floating an ice cube with 10 cc. of its volume above the surface. The specific gravity of ice is about 0.9. After the ice has completely melted,
    A. about one cc. of water will have overflowed
    B. about nine cc. of water will have overflowed
    C. about ten cc. of water will have overflowed
    D. the water level will have dropped
    E. the water level will have remained constant

37. ___

38. A sextant is an instrument used to determine by a single observation the
    A. direction of true north
    B. elevation of a given place
    C. exact time at a given place
    D. latitude of a given place
    E. longitude of a given place

38. ___

39. A 5-pound pail containing 25 pounds of water stands on a platform scale. A 4-pound piece of cork with a specific gravity of 0.25 is floated on the water. Weights are then placed on the piece of cork until it floats flush with the surface of the water. The platform scale now reads
    A. 30 lb.   B. 34 lb.   C. 37 lb.   D. 46 lb.   E. 50 lb.

39. ___

40. The north pole of a magnet attracted one end of a freely swinging bar of metal marked A. This shows that the bar is
    A. made of a magnetic material
    B. made of iron
    C. made of iron with a south pole at A
    D. magnetized with a north pole at A
    E. unmagnetized

40. ___

41. The corn plant produces its pollen and ovules
    A. at the same node
    B. in different rows
    C. on different plants
    D. on different flowering structures
    E. on the same flowering structure

41. ___

42. Which one of the following prehistoric men appeared the LATEST chronologically?
    A. Cro-Magnon   B. Java   C. Neanderthal   D. Peking   E. Piltdown

42. ___

43. Tissues are to cells as organs are to   43. ____
    A. blood   B. human beings   C. organisms   D. tissues
    E. vessels

44. The number of people who die each year from cancer is in- 44. ____
    creasing because
    A. communicable diseases are better controlled and more
       people live longer
    B. it is a communicable disease
    C. it is an inherited disease
    D. malignant tumors are more prevalent than benign or
       harmless tumors
    E. medical science knows less about the disease than
       about any other disease

45. At noon on shipboard, a chronometer reads 10:00 p.m.,   45. ____
    Greenwich time. The longitude of the ship is
    A. 10° east   B. 150° east   C. 10° west   D. 100° west
    E. 150° west

46. In the East, hailstorms are MOST likely to occur in   46. ____
    A. fall   B. late winter   C. midwinter   D. summer
    E. very early spring

47. An unused electric refrigerator was placed in a room   47. ____
    which was surrounded with a perfect heat insulator. The
    refrigerator was put into opeation by connecting it to an
    external electrical circuit and at the same time its door
    was left open. During the first hour the temperature of
    the room would
    A. fall continuously
    B. fall somewhat and remain at this temperature
    C. fall somewhat and then return to its original tempera-
       ture
    D. remain constant
    E. rise

48. The *Rh* factor is of importance in the study of   48. ____
    A. fingerprinting   B. the acidity of a solution
    C. the blood   D. the determination of sex
    E. the resistance to infection

49. Which one of the following is the GREATEST advantage of 49. ____
    growing up in a large family?
    A. Each member may be able to borrow articles from other
       members.
    B. Each member may be easily provided with recreation with-
       in his family circle.
    C. Each member may be required to give and receive financial
       support.
    D. Each member may have a chance to make adjustments to him-
       self and to other people early in life.
    E. Each member may have fewer responsibilities.

50. Small **arteries** branch to form a network of capillaries. 50. ___
    In turn, the capillaries unite to form
      A. alveoles   B. arteries   C. auricles   D. veins
      E. ventricles

___

KEY (CORRECT ANSWERS)

1.	D	11.	D	21.	E	31.	D	41.	D
2.	D	12.	E	22.	D	32.	C	42.	A
3.	B	13.	C	23.	B	33.	C	43.	D
4.	A	14.	D	24.	D	34.	D	44.	A
5.	E	15.	A	25.	B	35.	D	45.	E
6.	B	16.	A	26.	E	36.	C	46.	D
7.	E	17.	D	27.	B	37.	E	47.	E
8.	C	18.	B	28.	E	38.	D	48.	C
9.	B	19.	C	29.	B	39.	D	49.	D
10.	C	20.	A	30.	C	40.	A	50.	D

___

ANSWER SHEET

TEST NO. _____ PART _____ TITLE OF POSITION _____

(AS GIVEN IN EXAMINATION ANNOUNCEMENT · INCLUDE OPTION, IF ANY)

PLACE OF EXAMINATION _____ DATE _____

(CITY OR TOWN)   (STATE)

RATING

USE THE SPECIAL PENCIL.   MAKE GLOSSY BLACK MARKS.

	A B C D E		A B C D E		A B C D E		A B C D E		A B C D E
1		26		51		76		101	
2		27		52		77		102	
3		28		53		78		103	
4		29		54		79		104	
5		30		55		80		105	
6		31		56		81		106	
7		32		57		82		107	
8		33		58		83		108	
9		34		59		84		109	
10		35		60		85		110	

Make only ONE mark for each answer.   Additional and stray marks may be counted as mistakes.   In making corrections, erase errors COMPLETELY.

	A B C D E		A B C D E		A B C D E		A B C D E		A B C D E
11		36		61		86		111	
12		37		62		87		112	
13		38		63		88		113	
14		39		64		89		114	
15		40		65		90		115	
16		41		66		91		116	
17		42		67		92		117	
18		43		68		93		118	
19		44		69		94		119	
20		45		70		95		120	
21		46		71		96		121	
22		47		72		97		122	
23		48		73		98		123	
24		49		74		99		124	
25		50		75		100		125	

EXAMINATION SECTION
TEST 1

DIRECTIONS: Each question or incomplete statement is followed by several suggested answers or completions. Select the one that BEST answers the question or completes the statement. *PRINT THE LETTER OF THE CORRECT ANSWER IN THE SPACE AT THE RIGHT.*

1. Legend claims that the Argonauts set sail in search of the
   - A. Holy Grail
   - B. Fountain of Youth
   - C. abode of the gods
   - D. Golden Fleece
   - E. river of forgetfulness

   1.___

2. The invulnerability of Achilles was due to his having been dipped into the river
   - A. Lethe
   - B. Styx
   - C. Tiber
   - D. Nile
   - E. Acheron

   2.___

3. In avoiding Scylla, one is likely to run into
   - A. Medusa
   - B. Charybdis
   - C. Cerberus
   - D. Mt Pelion
   - E. Charon

   3.___

4. Naomi was Ruth's
   - A. mother
   - B. mother-in-law
   - C. aunt
   - D. sister
   - E. daughter

   4.___

5. In Norse legends the warlike maidens were known as the
   - A. Amazons
   - B. Harpies
   - C. Lorelei
   - D. Valkyries
   - E. Gorgons

   5.___

6. The country now called Switzerland was known to the Romans as
   - A. Dacia
   - B. Helvetia
   - C. Gallia
   - D. Etruria
   - E. Pannonia

   6.___

7. The Nobel prize winner who was a native of the same country as Nobel is
   - A. Anatole France
   - B. Selma Lagerlof
   - C. Thomas Mann
   - D. Maurice Maeterlinck
   - E. Pearl Buck

   7.___

8. THE DOLL'S HOUSE is a drama that deals with
   - A. the position of women
   - B. neglected children
   - C. the evils of a criminal life
   - D. a domineering woman
   - E. hereditary insanity

   8.___

9. Lin Yutang was the author of   9.
    A. BETWEEN TWO AUTUMNS   B. BETWEEN TEARS AND LAUGHTER
    C. BETWEEN TWO WORLDS   D. BETWEEN THE THUNDER AND THE SUN
    E. BETWEEN THE BOOK ENDS

10. Although he wrote in English, Joseph Conrad was a native of   10.
    A. Albania   B. Bulgaria
    C. Hungary   D. Poland
    E. Russia

11. The setting of THE CHERRY ORCHARD is   11.
    A. the United States   B. Russia
    C. Japan   D. Bavaria
    E. Palestine

12. WAR AND PEACE tells of   12.
    A. the siege of Stalingrad   B. the battle of Tannenberg
    C. the Russian Revolution   D. Napoleon's Russian campaign
    E. the Crimean War

13. Sancho Panza was a   13.
    A. prize rooster   B. knight
    C. bandit   D. squire
    E. artist

14. Rabindranath Tagore was a poet of   14.
    A. Australia   B. China
    C. Egypt   D. India
    E. Ireland

15. Pirandello was awarded the Nobel prize for distinguishing   15.
    himself in the field of
    A. drama   B. poetry
    C. history   D. biography
    E. philosophy

16. The one of the following who was NOT a noted dramatist is   16.
    A. Corneille   B. Molière
    C. Racine   D. Rostand
    E. Rousseau

17. The Shakespearean play in which female characters are LEAST   17.
    prominent is
    A. A MIDSUMMER NIGHT'S DREAM
    B. MACBETH
    C. JULIUS CAESAR
    D. THE MERCHANT OF VENICE
    E. HAMLET

18. One group of names below is made up of three characters   18.___
    from the same Shakespearean play.
    Identify the group.
        A. Claudius, Portia, Snout
        B. Macbeth, Oberon, Ophelia
        C. Polonius, Brutus, Lysander
        D. Rosencranz, Jessica, Laertes
        E. Lorenzo, Antonio, Nerissa

19. The Shakespearean play NOT based on important historical   19.___
    events is
        A. RICHARD III   B. JULIUS CAESAR
        C. HENRY V   D. OTHELLO
        E. ANTONY AND CLEOPATRA

20. THE SCHOOL FOR SCANDAL makes a witty attack on   20.___
        A. rivalry for promotions in the Army
        B. corruption in city politics
        C. hypocrisy in social life
        D. college sororities
        E. newspaper columnists

21. An English playwright whose plays caused much the same kind 21.___
    of controversy as Ibsen's is
        A. J.M. Barrie   B. Noel Coward
        C. A.A. Milne   D. Robert Sherriff
        E. G.B. Shaw

22. A play NOT written by Galsworthy is   22.___
        A. JUSTICE   B. LOYALTIES
        C. NERVES   D. STRIFE
        E. THE SILVER BOX

23. The portion of England called Shropshire has been celebrated 23.___
    in verse by
        A. Robert Bridges   B. Rupert Brooke
        C. A.E. Housman   D. John Masefield
        E. Siegfried Sassoon

24. Stoke Poges churchyard is famous as the setting of a poem   24.___
    containing the lines
        A. *Ill fares the land, to hastening ills a prey,*
           Where wealth accumulates, and men decay
        B. *If I should die, think only this of me:*
           That there's some corner of a foreign field
           That is forever England.
        C. *In his heart is a blind desire,*
           In his eyes foreknowledge of death.
        D. *Some mute inglorious Milton here may rest,*
           Some Cromwell guiltless of his country's blood.
        E. *I have a rendezvous with death*
           When spring brings back blue days and fair.

25.   *If Winter comes, can Spring be far behind?* is the first
      line of
      A. THANATOPSIS   B. THE FOUR SEASONS
      C. TO A SKYLARK   D. THE LAST LEAF
      D. ODE TO THE WEST WIND

25.

KEY (CORRECT ANSWERS)

1. D	6. B	11. B	16. E	21. E
2. B	7. B	12. D	17. C	22. C
3. B	8. A	13. D	18. E	23. C
4. B	9. B	14. D	19. D	24. D
5. D	10. D	15. A	20. C	25. E

TEST 2

DIRECTIONS: Each question or incomplete statement is followed by several suggested answers or completions. Select the one that BEST answers the question or completes the statement. *PRINT THE LETTER OF THE CORRECT ANSWER IN THE SPACE AT THE RIGHT.*

1. The field of the short story was much enriched by the work of
    A. G.B. Stern   B. Katherine Mansfield
    C. Jan Struther   D. Rebecca West
    E. Virginia Wolff

    1.___

2. An English writer famous for social satire was
    A. Sir Walter Scott   B. Rudyard Kipling
    C. George Eliot   D. Charlotte Bronte
    E. William M. Thackeray

    2.___

3. The two central figures in THE OLD WIVES TALE are
    A. school friends   B. enemies
    C. neighbors   D. sisters
    E. mother and daughter

    3.___

4. A novel that is largely autobiographical is
    A. ADAM BEDE   B. MISS LULU BETT
    C. DAVID COOPERFIELD D. HENRY ESMOND
    E. LORD JIM

    4.___

5. A book that deals with World War II is
    A. LONDON PRIDE
    B. GRAPES OF WRATH
    C. HEADHUNTING IN THE SOLOMON ISLANDS
    D. SHAKE HANDS WITH THE DRAGON
    E. THE TREE OF LIBERTY

    5.___

6. HE HEARD AMERICA SING is a biography of
    A. Louis Adamic   B. Stephen Foster
    C. George Gershwin   D. Carl Sandburg
    E. Lauritz Melchior

    6.___

7. The phrase that best expresses the ideals of Emerson is
    A. labor and liberty   B. solitude and sacrifice
    C. reward for merit   D. poverty, chastity, obedience
    E. plain living and high thinking

    7.___

8. *These are the times that try men's souls* is the opening sentence in an essay by
    A. Cotton Mather   B. Thomas Paine
    C. Henry Thoreau   D. Benjamin Franklin
    E. Oliver Wendell Holmes

    8.___

9. There has been no recent outstanding biography written of   9.___
    A. Abraham Lincoln   B. Benjamin Franklin
    C. Paul Revere   D. Theodore Roosevelt
    E. George Washington Carver

10. Lincoln Steffens did NOT   10.___
    A. write the story of his life
    B. expose political graft
    C. become a police reporter
    D. write articles for McClure's
    E. become a radio commentator

11. Thomas Craven was a recognized authority in   11.___
    A. Chinese jade   B. modern art
    C. oriental philosophy   D. English cathedrals
    E. graphology

12. A play NOT written by Eugene O'Neill is   12.___
    A. THE MASQUE OF KINGS   B. THE GREAT GOD BROWN
    C. EMPEROR JONES   D. BEYOND THE HORIZON
    E. THE HAIRY APE

13. *Out of me unworthy and unknown*
   The vibrations of deathless music;   13.___
  are the opening lines of a poem about
    A. Anne Rutledge   B. the man without a country
    C. Clara Barton   D. Nathan Hale
    E. Jenny Lind

14. A long poem published posthumously during World War II is   14.___
    A. WESTERN STAR   B. WHITE CLIFFS OF DOVER
    C. THE PEOPLE, YES   D. MAKE BRIGHT THE ARROWS
    E. WAKE ISLAND

15. A writer who received the Pultizer prize four times is   15.___
    A. Lloyd Douglas   B. Stuart Chase
    C. Robert Frost   D. Maxwell Anderson
    E. Edna St Vincent Millay

16. Walt Whitman, in his poetry as a whole, sought to   16.___
    A. expose the faults of mankind
    B. glorify tradition
    C. express the democratic spirit
    D. be objective in his attitude
    E. return to classical themes

17. The MOST famous books about American boyhood were written by   17.___
    A. R.L. Stevenson   B. Jack London
    C. Herman Melville   D. Samuel L. Clemens
    E. Stephen Crane

18. A contemporary novelist who employed fantasy extensively is 18.___
   A. Sinclair Lewis   B. John Dos Passos
   C. Robert Nathan   D. John P. Marquand
   E. Kenneth Roberts

19. After a fight, the Lenape became a nation of mourning in 19.___
   A. WESTWARD HO   B. CUSTER'S LAST STAND
   C. THE BLOODY GROUND   D. THE LAST OF THE MOHICANS
   E. GIANTS IN THE EARTH

20. Which of the following was a noted newspaper columnist? 20.___
   A. Raymond Gram Swing   B. James Truslow Adams
   C. John Gunther   D. Walter Lippmann
   E. Edmund Wilson

21. Newspapers and magazines carried numerous articles by Hanson 21.___
   Baldwin on
   A. health   B. military tactics
   C. economic trends   D. architecture
   E. postwar planning

22. Semantics relates to 22.___
   A. library research   B. why authors write
   C. poetic forms   D. the meaning of words
   E. grammatical constructions

23. In looking for a nonfiction book in the card catalog of a 23.___
   library, you might expect to find a separate card for it
   under each of the following:
   A. author and title   B. author only
   C. author and subject   D. author, title, and subject
   E. subject and title

24. To find the text of a television speech by President Kennedy, 24.___
   one should first consult the
   A. READERS' GUIDE   B. EDUCATIONAL INDEX
   C. U.S. CATALOG OF BOOKS D. NEW YORK TIMES INDEX
   E. CONGRESSIONAL RECORD

25. To find the titles of several anthologies that contain 25.___
   THE SOLDIER, by Rupert Brooke, one should consult
   A. Stevenson's HOME BOOK OF VERSE
   B. Palgrave's GOLDEN TREASURY
   C. Roget's THESAURUS
   D. Granger's INDEX
   E. Becker's ADVENTURES IN READING

KEY (CORRECT ANSWERS)

1.	B	6.	B	11.	B	16.	C	21.	B
2.	E	7.	E	12.	A	17.	D	22.	D
3.	D	8.	B	13.	A	18.	C	23.	D
4.	C	9.	D	14.	A	19.	D	24.	D
5.	A	10.	E	15.	C	20.	D	25.	D

TEST 3

1. *He prayeth best, who loveth best*
   All things both great and small
   is quoted from
   A. the NEW TESTAMENT   B. Tennyson's HOLY GRAIL
   C. Burn's TO A MOUSE   D. Coleridge's ANCIENT MARINER
   E. Longfellow's BIRDS OF KILLINGWORTH

   1.____

2. The poet whose neighbor insists that good fences make good neighbors is
   A. William C. Bryant   B. Robert P.T. Coffin
   C. Robert Frost   D. John G. Whittier
   E. William Wordsworth

   2.____

3. *More things are wrought by prayer*
   Than this world dreams of
   is a quotation from
   A. PILGRIMS'S PROGRESS   B. THE BOOK OF COMMON PRAYER
   C. PARADISE LOST   D. THE BIBLE
   E. THE PASSING OF ARTHUR

   3.____

4. The poem WHEN LILACS LAST IN THE DOORYARD BLOOM'D (Whitman) has as its theme the
   A. beauty of New England spring
   B. death of a great man
   C. freshness of a city park in spring
   D. varied colors of spring flowers
   E. wickedness of war

   4.____

5. The British Tommy whom Kipling makes speak in his poem GUNGA DIN
   A. pledges loyalty to Queen Victoria
   B. pays tribute to a water carrier
   C. wishes for a handsome uniform
   D. sings a marching song
   E. makes friends with the colonel's son

   5.____

6. In De La Mare's poem THE LISTENERS, the Traveler speaks to
   A. the dead   B. three spies
   C. three small children   D. eavesdropping relatives
   E. an elderly couple

   6.____

7. The poet who says *All I ask is a tall ship and a star to steer her by* is   7.__
    A. Lord Byron   B. Samuel T. Coleridge
    C. John Masefield   D. Robert Louis Stevenson
    E. Alfred Tennyson

8. Carl Sandburg compares fog to   8.__
    A. a cat   B. a veil
    C. moonlight   D. a ghost
    E. a wet blanket

9. GOD'S WORLD is a poem by   9.__
    A. Joyce Kilmer   B. Rudyard Kipling
    C. Vachel Lindsay   D. Edna St Vincent Millay
    E. Alfred Noyes

10. THE GREAT LOVER tells chiefly of Rupert Brooke's love of   10.__
    A. a beautiful English lady
    B. a fascinating gypsy
    C. everyday comforts and pleasures
    D. horses and dogs
    E. the children of London

11. To make ROBINSON CRUSOE seem plausible, Daniel Defoe presented   11.__
    A. 18th-century characters   B. London settings for the action
    C. startling openings   D. minute and realistic details
    E. remote settings for the action

12. The action of THE BLACK ARROW takes place during the   12.__
    A. Mexican War   B. Polish War for Independence
    C. Civil War in Spain   D. War of the Roses
    E. French and Indian War

13. In George Eliot's novels much stress is laid on   13.__
    A. beauty of setting   B. complexity of plot
    C. English history   E. love of nature
    E. portrayal of character

14. Hepzibah Pyncheon supported herself by   14.__
    A. opening a beauty parlor   B. teaching kindergarten
    C. opening a shop   D. writing children's stories
    E. shoplifting

15. Jim Bludso was   15.__
    A. given a medal   B. killed in a trench
    C. blown up in a steamboat   D. scalped by the Indians
    E. cremated

16. Edgar Allan Poe was interested in deciphering   16.___
    A. intricate road maps   B. manuscripts of ancient poetry
    C. charts of the skies   D. cryptograms
    E. the Rosetta Stone

17. The plot of Stephen Vincent Benet's THE DEVIL AND DANIEL   17.___
    WEBSTER has a theme similar to that of
    A. THE PIT AND THE PENDULUM B. DESCENT INTO THE MAELSTROM
    C. MOONFACE   D. FAUST
    E. BLOOD AND SAND

18. The man who was given the job of copying the ENCYCLOPEDIA   18.___
    BRITANNICA because of the color of his hair was
    A. Samuel Johnson   B. Professor Moriarity
    C. Mr. Moto   D. Noah Webster
    E. Jabez Wilson

19. If there was any tar in the neighborhood, *little gentleman*   19.___
    was a dangerous name to call
    A. Huck Finn   B. Tom Sawyer
    C. Penrod   D. Willie Winkle
    E. Little Lord Fauntleroy

20. Jalna was   20.___
    A. a race horse
    B. a collection of poems
    C. a military station in India
    D. an estate in England
    E. the home of the Court family in Ireland

21. CROSS CREEK (Majorie K. Rawlings) acquaints the reader with   21.___
    A. the rural life in Florida
    B. Revolutionary history
    C. the gold rush of 1840
    D. a French settlement in Maine
    E. exploits of pirates in the 17th century

22. FAIR STOOD THE WIND FOR FRANCE (H.E. Bates) gives the   22.___
    experiences of
    A. the crew of a grounded bomber
    B. a girl who was a lone pilot
    C. Lindbergh on his transatlantic flight
    D. men engaged in setting up an artificial harbor
    E. three friends who sailed with the Spanish Armada

23. The fictional detective paired with the wrong creator is   23.___
    A. Sherlock Holmes - A. Conan Doyle
    B. Hercule Poirot - Agatha Christie
    C. Reggie Fortune - Gilbert Chesterton
    D. Lord Peter Wimsey - Dorothy Sayers
    E. Mr. Tutt - Arthur Train

24. Which of the following compilers is best known for collections 2 of short stories?
    A. Helen Louise Cohen   B. Edward J. O'Brien
    C. Louis Untermeyer   D. W.M. Tanner
    E. Jessie B. Rittenhouse

25. An American recognized for skill in staging plays is   25
    A. Walter P. Eaton   B. Susan Glaspell
    C. Helen Hayes   D. Edmond Rostand
    E. Margaret Webster

KEY (CORRECT ANSWERS)

1. D	6. A	11. D	16. D	21. A
2. C	7. C	12. D	17. D	22. A
3. E	8. A	13. E	18. E	23. C
4. B	9. D	14. C	19. C	24. B
5. B	10. C	15. C	20. C	25. E

TEST 4

DIRECTIONS: Each question or incomplete statement is followed by several siggested answers or completions. Select the one that BEST answers the question or completes the statement. *PRINT THE LETTER OF THE CORRECT ANSWER IN THE SPACE AT THE RIGHT.*

1. A biography of Benjamin Franklin was written by   1.___
   A. Carl Van Doren   B. Carl Sandburg
   C. Esther Forbes   D. Emil Ludwig
   E. André Maurois

2. SAWDUST CAESAR discusses   2.___
   A. Hitler   B. Franco
   C. Mussolini   D. Napoleon
   E. Wilhelm II

3. MOTHER AMERICA tells of our relations with the   3.___
   A. Philippines   B. Indians
   C. Canadians   D. Australians
   E. Mexicans

4. At the funeral of Julius Caesar, Mark Antony succeeded in   4.___
   arousing the populace against the conspirators because
   A. he praised Brutus   B. his speech was fair and just
   C. the crowd admired him   D. he appealed to the emotions
   E. he loved Caesar greatly

5. The main reason why Shakespeare's plays are still popular   5.___
   today is that they
   A. are historically accurate
   B. are original in plot
   C. have so much witty dialogue
   D. show wide understanding of human nature
   E. contain valuable moral lessons

6. In HAMLET the ghost serves chiefly as a(n)   6.___
   A. incentive to action
   B. emissary of mercy
   C. reminder of the uncertainty of human life
   D. guardian of Hamlet's welfare
   E. mouthpiece for philosophic remarks

7. A play in which all the characters are given a second chance   7.___
   is
   A. JUSTICE   B. THE GREEN PASTURES
   C. DEAR BRUTUS   D. EVE OF ST MARK
   E. THE PETRIFIED FOREST

8. The slamming of the door in A DOLL'S HOUSE was heard down   8.___
   the ages because it foreshadowed
        A. juvenile delinquency
        B. a new relationship between parents and children
        C. relaxation of censorship of the theatre
        D. the emancipation of women
        E. the First World War

9. The main characters in Chekhov's plays are usually   9.___
        A. heroes   B. villains
        C. common people   D. soldiers
        E. royalty

10. In ancient mythology the Cyclops were   10.___
        A. satyrs   B. elves
        C. one-eyed giants   D. pygmies
        E. gremlins

11. *Crossing the Rubicon* signifies   11.___
        A. an irrevocable decision B. submarine attacks
        C. air raids   D. infantry charges
        E. tank maneuvers

12. Vergil, a great Roman,   12.___
        A. spent some time at Dido's court
        B. was one of the founders of Rome
        C. described the growth of the Roman Empire
        D. died for his country
        E. wrote an epic about the founding of Rome

13. Don Quixote, hero of Cervantes' immortal novel, rode forth   13.___
        A. in quest of the Holy Grail
        B. to serve his king and country
        C. to escape from an ill-tempered wife
        D. to defend the oppressed and right wrongs
        E. to see the world and seek a fortune

14. An epic poem describing the author's imaginary journey   14.___
    through the other world is
        A. PARADISE LOST
        B. THE DIVINE COMEDY
        C. THE ODYSSEY
        D. THE FALL OF THE HOUSE OF USHER
        E. THE SONG OF ROLAND

15. Daudet's THE LAST CLASS shows the teacher explaining the   15.___
    value of
        A. science   B. language
        C. mathematics   D. art
        E. music

16. Francois Villon was a(n)   16.___
    A. vagabond poet   B. country squire
    C. French king   D. knight
    E. itinerant merchant

17. In THE COUNT OF MONTE CRISTO, Edmond Dantes was wrongfully   17.___
    imprisoned on(in)
    A. Devil's Island   B. the Castle of Chillon
    C. the Conciergerie   D. the Bastille
    E. the Chateau D'If

18. Pierre Loti, the French novelist, is noted for his colorful   18.___
    stories of
    A. Paris   B. fishermen
    C. the Renaissance   D. farm life
    E. the French Revolution

19. The name of a German legendary hero was given to the   19.___
    A. Maginot Line   B. Gustav Line
    C. Mareth Line   D. Mannerheim Line
    E. Siegfried Line

20. The chief reason for teaching a student how to find   20.___
    materials in a library is to
    A. save work for the librarians
    B. help the student learn more facts
    C. teach the student something about library work
       as a profession
    D. make the student more independent in using the
       library
    E. help the student use more than one reference in
       in preparing his papers

21. To find a listing by professions of American women who have   21.___
    been in the news recently, one would consult
    A. WHO'S WHO IN AMERICA
    B. CURRENT BIOGRAPHY
    C. THE CENTURY CYCLOPEDIA OF NAMES
    D. WHAT'S THE NAME, PLEASE
    E. THE WORLD BOOK

22. One would find a chronological description of World War II   22.___
    during the year 1944 in
    A. THE WORLD ALMANAC - 1945
    B. the READERS' GUIDE
    C. Shepherd's HISTORICAL ATLAS
    D. the CONGRESSIONAL DIRECTORY
    E. THE STATESMAN'S YEAR-BOOK - 1944

23. For the critical analysis of great books of all times, one   23.___
    should listen to the radio program entitled
        A. INVITATION TO LEARNING
        B. INFORMATION PLEASE
        C. UNIVERSITY OF CHICAGO ROUND TABLE
        D. THE AUTHOR MEETS THE CRITIC
        E. THE AMERICAN SCHOOL OF THE AIR

24. Which of the following was well known as a book reviewer?   24.___
        A. Brooks Atkinson   B. John Chamberlain
        C. Virgil Thomson   D. Burns Mantle
        E. George Fielding Eliot

25. Which of the following was NOT a newspaper correspondent   25.___
    or columnist?
        A. Arthur Krock   B. Sumner Welles
        C. Walter Lippmann   D. Mark Sullivan
        E. Anne O'Hare McCormick

————

KEY (CORRECT ANSWERS)

1. A	6. A	11. A	16. A	21. B
2. C	7. C	12. E	17. E	22. A
3. A	8. D	13. D	18. B	23. A
4. D	9. E	14. B	19. E	24. B
5. D	10. C	15. B	20. D	25. B

————

TEST 5

DIRECTIONS: Each question or incomplete statement is followed by several suggested answers or completions. Select the one that BEST answers the question or completes the statement. *PRINT THE LETTER OF THE CORRECT ANSWER IN THE SPACE AT THE RIGHT.*

1. All of the following pairs of characters occur in Bible stories EXCEPT   1.___
    A. Castor and Pollux   B. David and Jonathan
    C. Eli and Samuel   D. Jacob and Esau
    E. Samson and Delilah

2. *I fear the Greeks even when bearing gifts* is a quotation from   2.___
    A. the AENEID   B. the ILIAD
    C. the ODYSSEY   D. PARADISE LOST
    E. PILGRIM'S PROGRESS

3. The insignia of the Medical Corps of the United States Army is a replica of the magic wand of Mercury, known as the   3.___
    A. aegis   B. trident
    C. lyre   D. arrow
    E. caduceus

4. *All hope abandon, ye who enter here* was the inscription that met the eyes of   4.___
    A. Daniel when he was cast into the lions' den
    B. Aeneas at the entrance to the cave of the Sibyl
    C. Dante and Virgil at the gate of Hell
    D. Parsifal in the magic garden of Klingsor
    E. Edmond Dantes as he entered the dungeon of Chateau d'If

5. In Cervantes' immortal book, DON QUIXOTE, Rosinante is a   5.___
    A. castle in Spain   B. horse
    C. sword   D. squire
    E. town barber

6. The NIBELUNGENLIED is a   6.___
    A. Latin myth   B. Russian folk song
    C. Chinese legend   D. medieval German epic
    E. Shakespearean play

7. As D'Artagnan was setting out for the French court, his mother gave him   7.___
    A. good advice
    B. a horse
    C. an amulet to preserve him from evil
    D. a recipe for an ointment to cure wounds
    E. fifteen crowns

8. In LES MISERABLES, Javert is the symbol of   8.__
    A. the poor man's defender B. petty intrigue
    C. physical vigor   D. generous good will
    E. devotion to duty

9. In THE NECKLACE, a short story by Guy de Maupassant,   9.__
    Julie Loisel
    A. dies in poverty   B. steals a diamond necklace
    C. serves a prison term   D. is declared innocent
    E. loses a borrowed necklace

10. In Edmond Rostand's play, Cyrano de Bergerac is a(n)   10.__
    A. selfish, handsome man with an ugly soul
    B. heroic figure who embarks upon a career of crime
    C. rich peasant who marries a noblemen's daughter
    D. poetic genius who sacrifices his own happiness for the
       sake of the woman he loves
    E. adventurous youth whose daring leads him into a series
       of misadventures

11. In order to save Ali Baba, Morgiana   11.__
    A. married his son   B. danced for his guest
    C. put salt in the food   D. begged for pieces of silver
    E. knocked the dagger from the hand of Hoseyn

12. In a short story by Tolstoy entitled WHERE LOVE IS, THERE   12.__
    GOD IS ALSO, Martin Avdeitch was a
    A. cobbler   B. monk
    C. peddler   D. soldier
    E. thief

13. Which of the following is MOST applicable to Godfrey Cass   13.__
    in SILAS MARNER?
    A. Beware of false friends.
    B. It is sweet to labor for those we love.
    C. The wages of sin is death.
    D. As ye sow, so shall ye reap.
    E. It is more blessed to give than to receive.

14. In the siege of the Castle of Torquilstone by the Saxons in   14.__
    IVANHOE, the turning point was brought about by
    A. Athelstane   B. Cedric
    C. Locksley   D. Rowena
    E. Ulrica

15. Becky Sharp was a(n)   15.__
    A. heroine without brains B. widow without children
    C. spinster without money D. adventuress without a heart
    E. noble lady without a title

16. Madame Defarge's intense hatred of the Evremond family   16.___
    grew out of their
        A. belonging to the aristocracy
        B. ruining her husband's business
        C. treatment of her family
        D. ill-treatment of Dr. Manette
        E. destruction of the Bastille

17. In Macbeth we see a man whose downfall was caused by   17.___
        A. overweening ambition for power
        B. supernatural intervention
        C. an unfair plot against his life
        D. a moving forest
        E. a naturally blood-thirsty disposition

18. Which of the following Shakespearean characters is most   18.___
    philosophic in his outlook on life?
        A. Antony   B. Banquo
        C. Falstaff   D. Horatio
        E. Jaques

19. The chief purpose intended to be served by Caesar's ghost 19.___
    in Shakespeare's JULIUS CAESAR is evidently to
        A. establish belief in the immortality of the soul
        B. show the superstition of the times
        C. provide an agent of retribution
        D. increase the tension of the audience
        E. justify the title of the play

20. *They also serve who only stand and wait,* was written with 20.___
    particular reference to a(the)
        A. blind poet
        B. sentry in World War II
        C. mother waiting for her son to come home from the war
        D. fiancee of a soldier
        E. faithful servant

21. By revealing her past, Tess of the D'Urbervilles   21.___
        A. lost her husband's respect
        B. won Angel's support
        C. found courage to face life
        D. brought her husband material wealth
        E. became a saint to the villagers

22. Lord Jim spent nearly all his life trying to   22.___
        A. find his real name
        B. atone for one act of cowardice
        C. defend his theory of navigation
        D. discover the pirate's gold
        E. become master of a ship

23. The theme of THE ADMIRABLE CRICHTON is
    A. the exploitation of labor
    B. class distinctions
    C. the importance of little things
    D. injustice in the courts
    E. political intrigue

24. All of the following are celebrated authors of children's
    literature EXCEPT
    A. Hans Andersen   B. Lewis Carroll
    C. Wilhelm Grimm   D. Victor Heiser
    E. A.A. Milne

25. *Come down to Kew in lilac time* is the refrain of
    A. THE GARDEN BY MOONLIGHT
    B. THE BALLAD OF EAST AND WEST
    C. THE BARRELL-ORGAN
    D. UNDER THE LILACS
    E. THE PRINCESS

23.

24.

25.

KEY (CORRECT ANSWERS)

1.	A	6.	D	11.	B	16.	C	21.	A
2.	A	7.	D	12.	A	17.	A	22.	B
3.	E	8.	E	13.	D	18.	E	23.	B
4.	C	9.	E	14.	E	19.	C	24.	D
5.	B	10.	D	15.	D	20.	A	25.	C

TESTS IN ART

DIRECTIONS: Each of the questions in this part is followed by several suggested answers or completions. Select the one that BEST answers the question or completes the statement. *PRINT THE LETTER OF THE CORRECT ANSWER IN THE SPACE AT THE RIGHT.*

TEST 1

1. A type of early furniture having cabriole leg; much-carved, 1. ...
   pierced, splat-back chairs; heavy ball-and-claw, bracket
   foot was designed by
   A. Adam   B. Sheraton   C. Hepplewhite   D. Chippendale
   E. Duncan Phyfe
2. A kind of decoration made up of colored enamels separated   2. ...
   by fine metal lines is
   A. chiaroscuro   B. Chinese lacquer   C. cloisonné
   D. bas relief   E. decalcomania
3. Columns decorated with lotus buds and papyrus flowers were 3. ...
   used in the temples of the
   A. Romans   B. Greeks   C. Babylonians   D. Egyptians
   E. Byzantines
4. Gothic architecture is known for its   4. ...
   A. height   B. pointed arches   C. round domes
   D. low ceilings   E. decorated columns
5. American domestic architecture of the late 18th and early 5. ...
   19th centuries was MOST strongly influenced by the architec-
   ture of
   A. Rome   B. Elizabethan England   C. France
   D. Greece   E. Victorian England
6. The architects of today build skyward for   6. ...
   A. safety   B. economy   C. fresh air   D. light   E. beauty
7. The distinguished American architect who designed the Im- 7. ...
   perial Hotel in Tokyo is
   A. Charles Bullfinch   B. George Gray Barnard
   C. Ralph Adams Cram   D. Frank Lloyd Wright
   E. Cass Gilbert
8. A great artist who was an inventor and engineer as well as 8. ...
   an artist and architect was
   A. Titian   B. Tintoretto   C. Correggio   D. da Vinci
   E. Corot
9. A famous American political cartoonist of the late 19th cen-9. ...
   tury was
   A. Charles Dana Gibson   B. James McNeill Whistler
   C. Stanford White   D. Thomas Nast
   E. Frank Currier
10. A contemporary artist who specialized in woodcuts is   10. ...
    A. Arthur William Brown   B. Rockwell Kent
    C. James Montgomery Flagg   D. Gordon Grant
    E. Thomas Hart Benton
11. An artist who painted many portraits of George Washington 11. ...
    and left his last one unfinished was
    A. Sargent   B. Homer   C. Stuart   D. Bellows   D. Inness

12. The decorations in the Sistine Chapel of the Vatican are   12. ..
    the work of
    A. Giotto   B. Michelangelo   C. Raphael   D. Botticelli
    E. del Sarto
13. The famous statue of which the head is lost is   13. ..
    A. Athena Parthenos   B. Diana of Versailles
    C. Hermes of Praxiteles   D. Venus de Milo
    E. Victory of Samothrace
14. A famous artist who proved that many shades of blue could 14. ..
    be used together harmoniously was
    A. Reynolds   B. Gainsborough   C. Turner   D. Burne-Jones
    E. Romney
15. Show card colors belong to the class of painting materials 15. ..
    called
    A. tempera   B. oils   C. pastels   D. lacquers
    E. transparent water colors
16. The color harmony formed by adjacent colors in the color   16. ..
    wheel is known as
    A. complementary   B. triadic   C. analogous
    D. monochromatic   E. sliding
17. For GREATEST effectiveness, the letters on a two-color   17. ..
    sign at a street intersection should be
    A. green against a red background
    B. yellow against a blue background
    C. orange against a blue background
    D. black against a yellow background
    E. red against a black background
18. Mountains in a water color can MOST effectively be made to 18. ..
    appear farther away by
    A. making them bluer
    B. making them smaller
    C. painting snow on the top
    D. painting a large hill in the foreground
    E. placing the horizon high on the painting
19. The BEST color for the walls of a kitchen with a northern   19. ..
    exposure is
    A. blue   B. green   C. violet   D. rose   E. yellow
20. A color to be avoided in summer clothes because it absorbs 20. ..
    the sun's rays is
    A. black   B. blue   C. green   D. white   E. yellow
21. A thin girl with a long neck should avoid   21. ..
    A. a crew neckline   B. a round neckline
    C. collars   D. a V neckline
    E. frills at the neck
22. Of the following, the one that is NOT a kind of glass is   22. ..
    A. Stiegel   B. Sandwich   C. Fostoria   D. Heisey
    E. Jensen
23. In mixing colors, which of the following will NOT make   23. ..
    orange more gray?
    A. Adding a small amount of gray
    B. Adding a small amount of blue
    C. Adding a darker shade of orange
    D. Adding small amounts of black and white
    E. Adding small amounts of red and yellow

2

24. A name that does NOT belong to a kind of china is   24. ...
    A. Haviland   B. Royal Worcester   C. Candlewick
    D. Wedgwood   E. Spode
25. An artist who did NOT belong to the Dutch school was   25. ...
    A. Van Gogh   B. Rubens   C. Rembrandt   D. Hobbema   E. Hals

TEST 2

1. The front elevation of a building is known as the   1. ...
    A. architrave   B. cornice   C. facade   D. piazza
    E. parapet
2. The ornamental pinnacle of a spire in architecture is called 2. ...
  a(n)
    A. cupola   B. finial   C. flying buttress   D. gable
    E. obelisk
3. A gargoyle is   3. ...
    A. a Greek deity, half man and half beast
    B. an ornamentation made by designs sunk below the surface
    C. the decorative top of a Corinthian column
    D. a carved or decorated rainspout
    E. a piece of sculpture placed in the center of a lily pool
4. The triangular part on the front of a building in the classi-4. ...
  cal style is called the
    A. lintel   B. marquee   C. metope   D. pediment   E. pylon
5. In architecture this figure   5. ...
  is known as a
    A. capital
    B. corbel
    C. cusp
    D. fluting
    E. trefoil
6. Sculpture in which the figures stand out slightly from the   6. ...
  background is called
    A. bas relief   B. fresco   C. intaglio   D. medallion
    E. mosaic
7. A dry point is a   7. ...
    A. water color made with a dry brush
    B. kind of etching
    C. rough oil painting
    D. type of fresco
    E. pottery glaze
8. A stencil is a   8. ...
    A. special kind of paintbrush
    B. design stamped from a carved wood or linoleum block
    C. design made by painting through a series of holes cut
       in cardboard or thin metal
    D. spray gun for painting
    E. kind of fabric used for upholstering furniture
9. The skin of a sheep or goat, dressed and prepared for writ- 9. ...
  ing purposes, is called
    A. foolscap   B. holograph   C. papyrus   D. parchment
    E. script

3

10. A series of prints depicting familiar American scenes of   10. ...
    the 19th century was published by
    A. J.J. Audubon   B. Currier and Ives   C. Harper Brothers
    D. Mason and Hamlin   E. McKim, Mead and White

11. This vase is   11. ...
    A. Chinese
    B. Egyptian
    C. Greek
    D. Mexican
    E. Persian

12. Which of these historic decorative designs is Egyptian?   12. ...

    A.   B.   C.   D.   E.

13. According to artistic standards, the BEST space division   13. ...
    is

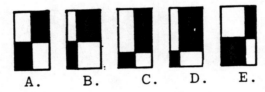

    A.   B.   C.   D.   E.

14. All of the following are principles of art EXCEPT   14. ...
    A. balance B. esthetics C. harmony D. rhythm E. unity

15. All of the following may be used to achieve a center of   15. ...
    interest EXCEPT
    A. balance B. hue C. intensity D. size E. value

16. Which one of the following is NOT a kind of perspective?   16. ...
    A. Angular B. Curvilinear C. Oblique D. Occult
    D. Parallel

17. You are looking at the corner of a house so that you see   17. ...
    the front and the left side at the same time. Your eye le-
    vel is two thirds of the way up the front door. The tops
    of the second-story windows and the upper clapboards on
    the front of the house appear
    A. to slant down to the right
    B. as horizontal, parallel lines
    C. to slant up to the eye level
    D. as slightly curved lines
    E. to slant up to an oblique vanishing point making an
       angle of 15 degrees with the corner of the house

18. When held at a slight distance, alternating blue and yel-   18. ...
    low lines of equal width, drawn close and parallel, will
    appear as
    A. dark yellow B. light blue C. gray D. blue-green
    E. green
19. To subdue a bright color and still-retain its harmony in   19. ...
    a scheme, it is BEST to add a little of
    A. black   B. an adjacent color   C. white
    D. its complement   E. a darker tone of the same color
20. Which of these colors is neutral?   20. ...
    A. Blue   B. Gray   C. Green   D. Red   E. Yellow
21. A stout man will look more slender in a suit   21. ...
    A. with a belt on the coat B. with pronounced stripes
    C. of a solid color   D. with strong checks
    E. with unmatched coat and trousers
22. Which of the following men was a noted craftsman?   22. ...
    A. Thomas Edison   B. Ulysses S. Grant
    C. John Paul Jones   D. Paul Revere
    E. George Washington
23. The former President in whose honor a memorial has been   23. ...
    erected in Washington is
    A. Theodore Roosevelt   B. Abraham Lincoln
    C. Thomas Jefferson   D. James Madison
    E. Woodrow Wilson
24. Which of the following artists is BEST known for his   24. ...
    strong and simple paintings?
    A. George Inness   B. Pablo Picasso
    C. John Singer Sargent   D. Gilbert Stuart
    E. Grant Wood
25. An outstanding illustrator and poster artist who was a   25. ...
    member of the United States Navy in World Wars I and II
    and gave his life for his country in this war about the
    time his last poster was released was
    A. McClelland Barclay   B. Thomas H. Benton
    C. Walt Disney   D. Augustus Saint Gaudens
    E. Ernest Watson

TEST 3

1. One of the FINEST painters of marine pictures is   1. ...
    A. George Bellows   B. John Steuart Curry
    C. El Greco   D. Winslow Homer
    E. James McNeill Whistler
2. A contemporary illustrator whose magazine cover designs   2. ...
    have become known for their interpretation of American
    types and scenes is
    A. Elmore J. Brown   B. Walt Disney
    C. R. John Holmgren   D. Rockwell Kent
    E. Norman Rockwell
3. What American woman painter is known for her use of ex-   3. ...
    quisite colors and abstract representations of flower forms?
    A. Lillian Westcott Hale B. Violet Oakley
    C. Georgia O'Keeffe   D. Marie Danforth Page
    E. Jessie Willcox Smith

4. A painter of decorative, barbaric Tahitian landscapes was   4. ...
   A. Edgar Degas   B. Paul Gauguin
   C. George Inness   D. Pierre Renoir
   E. Vincent Van Gogh
5. In painting or drawing a scene, the MOST important thing to 5. ...
   do is to
   A. represent the scene exactly as it appears to the eye
   B. have all the perspective exact
   C. use a wide variety of colors
   D. plan a good design
   E. lay in the color smoothly
6. Rhythm in a drawing or painting is achieved by   6. ...
   A. repetition of lines
   B. using contrasting colors adjacent to one another
   C. using a variety of straight and curved lines
   D. using the strongest colors for the centers of interest
   E. careful attention to balance
7. Transitional lines are those which   7. ...
   A. are horizontal
   B. tie shapes together to give them unity
   C. are vertical
   D. throw a pattern off balance
   E. repeat a shape
8. Of the six faces of a cube, the GREATEST number that can be 8. ...
   shown in a perspective drawing is
   A. One   B. Two   C. Three   D. Four   E. Five
9. Which of these landscapes shows BEST design?   9. ...

   A.   B.   C.   D.   E.

10. Which candle-and-candlestick combination is MOST artistic? 10. ...

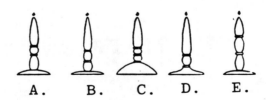

   A.   B.   C.   D.   E.

11. Floor coverings, such as rugs, paint and linoleum, should 11. ...
    be darker in color than the walls because
    A. they are less likely to show soil
    B. they make a better background for furniture
    C. they are warmer
    D. dark dyes do not weaken the fabrics so much as light
       dyes
    E. dark colors are heavy and belong at the bottom

12. The table pictured below is in the style made popular by   12. ...
    A. the Adam brothers
    B. Chippendale
    C. Duncan Phyfe
    D. Paul Revere
    E. Sheraton

13. Painting with the airbrush was perfected by the   13. ...
    A. Dutch School   B. French School   C. Florentine School
    D. English School   E. Commercial art school
14. The VICTORY OF SAMOTHRACE is a famous   14. ...
    A. bas-relief   B. cathedral   C. mural   D. statue
    E. tapestry
15. The raised design on a cameo is an example of   15. ...
    A. bas-relief   B. intaglio   C. modeling   D. sculpture
    E. sgraffito
16. The word *precision* is printed in type known as   16. ...
    A. sans-serif   B. modern   C. roman italic   D. Gothic
    E. old English
17. As a designer of fine type, one of America's foremost con-   17. ...
    tributors to the art of printing has been
    A. Boris Artzybasheff   B. Frederic W. Goudy
    C. Johann Gutenberg   D. Alfred Stieglitz
    E. N.C. Wyeth
18. Which of the following arts BEST expresses the social back-   18. ...
    ground of a period?
    A. Architecture   B. Minor arts   C. Painting   D. Sculpture
    E. Textiles
19. A Florentine sculptor and goldsmith who lived in the 16th   19. ...
    century was
    A. Giovanni Bellini   B. Benvenuto Cellini
    C. Giovanni Cimabue   D. Leonardo DaVinci
    E. Michelangelo
20. In which period of art were stained glass windows intro-   20. ...
    duced for church decoration?
    A. Roman   B. Gothic   C. Renaissance   D. Classical
    E. Futuristic
21. The city of Washington was planned by   21. ...
    A. Ralph Adams Cram   B. Cass Gilbert
    C. Thomas Jefferson   D. Pierre L'Enfant
    E. Frank Lloyd Wright
22. The MOST important American contribution to the develop-   22. ...
    ment of architecture has been
    A. glass brick   B. revolving doors
    C. elevators   D. reinforced concrete
    E. steel-frame construction
23. Which of the following would be designed by an industrial   23. ...
    designer?
    A. A mural   B. A frieze   C. An electric flatiron
    D. A poster   E. The facade of a building

24. Which of the following is a contemporary American indus-   24. ...
    trial designer?
    A. Norman Bel Geddes   B. Thomas Hart Benton
    C. Margaret Bourke-White D. Charles E. Burchfield
    E. Edward Steichen
25. A pioneer in the production of animated cartoons is   25. ...
    A. Malvina Hoffman   B. Diego Rivera
    C. Lee Simonson   D. Paul Terry
    E. Walter Dorwin Teague

TEST 4

1. Which of the following represents 15th century art?   1. ...
   A. The Parthenon   B. The NIGHT WATCH   C. The LAST SUPPER
   D. AMERICAN GOTHIC   E. Portrait of Whistler's Mother
2. MAN WITH THE HOE was painted by   2. ...
   A. Goya   B. Millet   C. Picasso   D. Rembrandt E. Sargent
3. Which of the following is a prominent American sculptor?   3. ...
   A. Dali   B. Lehmbruck   C. Maillol   D. Rodin   E. Zorach
4. The name of a cartoonist who became famous for his draw-   4. ...
   ings of life among the American soldiers during World War II is
   A. Brackman   B. Disney   C. Rockwell   D. Mauldin   E. Young
5. Christopher Wren was a famous   5. ...
   A. architect   B. etcher   C. painter   D. printer E. sculptor
6. Receding parallel lines lying in a horizontal plane   6. ...
   A. seem to diverge   B. meet at a given point
   C. appear to meet at a given point D. become vertical
   E. meet in an oblique plane
7. The FIRST requirement of a good poster is that it   7. ...
   A. inspire action   B. arouse admiration
   C. attract attention   D. create desire
   E. arouse interest in an idea
8. The term *values* as applied to a work of art such as a   8. ...
   painting, illustration or poster refers to
   A. color   B. detail   C. light and dark   D. technique
   E. relationship of line
9. The BEST medium for newspaper reproduction is   9. ...
   A. crayon   B. oils   C. pencil   D. pen and ink
   E. watercolor
10. A foreshortened circle is always either a straight line   10. ...
    or a(n)
    A. ellipse   B. hexagon   C. segment   D. semicircle
    E. tangent
11. Any of the following might be found in "still life" paint-11. ...
    ing EXCEPT a
    A. copper bowl   B. glass bottle   C. pottery elephant
    D. sleeping child E. piece of velvet
12. Which one of the following drawings of a box and dish re- 12. ...
    presents the BEST grouping and CORRECT perspective?

       A.   B.   C.   D.   E.

8

13. Of the following crafts, the OLDEST is   13. ...
     A. furniture B. glass C. metal D. pottery E. weaving
14. All of the following are designers of magazine covers   14. ...
    EXCEPT
     A. Stevan Dohanos   B. John Falter
     C. Quentin Reynolds   D. Norman Rockwell
     E. Meade Schaeffer
15. All of the following are names of type faces EXCEPT   15. ...
     A. Bodoni B. Caslon C. Cheltenham D. Gauguin E. Goudy
16. An artist who painted in the South Sea Islands is   16. ...
     A. Cézanne B. Degas C. Gauguin D. Rousseau
     E. van Gogh
17. The name Norman Bel Geddes is associated with   17. ...
     A. cartooning B. portraiture C. fine lettering
     D. stage design E. flat treatment of landscapes
18. An American sculptor who excels in his interpretation   18. ...
    of the Indian is
     A. George Barnard   B. Gutzon Borglum
     C. Cyrus Edwin Dallin   D. Frederick MacMonnies
     E. Lorado Taft
19. The term *chiton* refers to a gown or tunic once worn by 19. ...
    the people of
     A. Egypt B. England C. France D. Greece E. Turkey
20. The term applied to modern painting that deals with the   20. ...
    product of the subconscious mind is
     A. abstractionism B. cubism C. expressionism
     D. impressionism   E. surrealism
21. The Gothic style of architecture marked the origin of the 21. ...
     A. column   B. dome   C. gargoyle   D. setback
     E. square tower
22. Which of the following sketches shows a gambrel roof?   22. ...

          A.   B.   C.   D.   E.

23. A drawing that makes the receding planes of the object   23. ...
    appear to converge is called a(n)
     A. abstract drawing   B. cabinet drawing
     C. contour drawing   D. isometric drawing
     E. perspective drawing
24. A design fills a space well when it   24. ...
     A. touches the corners
     B. is in the middle of the space
     C. suggests the contour of the space
     D. cuts the space in half
     E. is three-dimensional
25. Objects painted in predominantly warm hues seem to   25. ...
     A. appear distorted   B. come forward
     C. diminish in size   D. flatten out
     E. recede into the picture plane

———

TEST 5

1. The MOST important quality of a good design is   1. ...
   A. color   B. detail   C. size   D. symmetry   E. unity
2. The type of lines by which fantasy can be BEST suggested   2. ...
   is
   A. angular   B. horizontal   C. jagged   D. upward curving
   E. very heavy
3. In order to understand an orthographic projection, it is   3. ...
   necessary to examine
   A. only the side view   B. only the top view
   C. any single view   D. the section view
   E. all views
4. A poster design is MOST effective if it   4. ...
   A. has an analogous color scheme
   B. emphasizes texture
   C. has good dark and light pattern
   D. uses all cool colors
   E. is monochromatic
5. With reference to printing type faces, the term *points* re- 5. ...
   fers to
   A. color   B. serifs   C. shape   D. size   E. style
6. A term applied to pattern in weaving is   6. ...
   A. applique   B. batik   C. Jacquard   D. needlepoint
   E. petit point
7. The modern movement in art started in   7. ...
   A. France   B. Italy   C. Mexico   D. Spain
   E. the United States
8. Fixative is used for   8. ...
   A. blending paints   B. blueprinting
   C. charcoal drawings   D. cleaning paintings
   E. oil painting
9. The French method of painting that uses white pigment   9. ...
   mixed freely with all the colors, giving them an opaque
   quality, is called
   A. Boucher   B. cliché   C. gouache   D. papier-bulle
   E. touché
10. The architectural style that used the pylon extensively   10. ...
    was
    A. Egyptian   B. Gothic   C. Greek   D. Renaissance
    E. Roman
11. In the first centuries of the Christian era, books that   11. ...
    were first put together in pages as we see them today were
    called
    A. booklets   B. codices   C. compositions   D. cuneiforms
    E. pictograms
12. A Dutch painter famous for the dramatic lighting in his   12. ...
    pictures is
    A. Rembrandt   B. Rubens   C. Van Dyck   D. van Gogh
    E. Vermeer
13. An element of design is   13. ...
    A. balance   B. intensity   C. line   D. value   E. variety

14. In which one of the following fields of art expression   14. ...
    has Salvador Dali gained fame as a leader?
    A. Cubism   B. Impressionism   C. Romanticism
    D. Surrealism   E. Symbolism
15. The word that BEST expresses change of shape in a surface   15. ...
    viewed obliquely is
    A. convergence   B. diminution   C. foreshortening
    D. parallelism   E. vanishing
16. A wire or wooden support used in clay modeling is called   16. ...
    a(n)
    A. cone   B. frame   C. template   D. amphora   E. armature
17. Distance as shown by gradations of color is BEST described   17. ...
    as
    A. aerial perspective   B. bird's-eye perspective
    C. linear perspective   D. spherical perspective
    E. worm's-eye perspective
18. The DELPHIC SIBYL was painted to take its place with many   18. ...
    other masterpieces in the
    A. Fountainebleau Palace   B. Louvre Museum
    C. Metropolitan Museum   D. Royal Academy
    E. Sistine Chapel
19. A technique in which no colors are mixed but tones are   19. ...
    built up of a stipple of pure, brilliant color is called
    A. cubistic   B. Gauguinistic   C. neoistic
    D. pointillistic   E. realistic
20. Which one of the following terms refers to writing as a   20. ...
    decorative art?
    A. Calligraphy   B. Cartography   C. Lithography
    D. Serigraphy   E. Typography
21. The part of the modern stage between the curtain and the   21. ...
    orchestra is called the
    A. cyclorama   B. downstage   C. platform   D. proscenium
    E. wing
22. Which one of these painters is known for his soft atmos-   22. ...
    pheric effects, especially in his later paintings?
    A. El Greco   B. George Inness   C. Gilbert Stuart
    D. Michelangelo   E. Titian
23. An equestrian statue is a statue of a   23. ...
    A. charging horse   B. horse and dog
    C. mother and child   D. rider on a horse
    E. soldier with a gun
24. The pen technique that consists of crossing one set of   24. ...
    lines with another is known as
    A. crosshatching   B. mass drawing   C. silhouetting
    D. stippling   E. scratchboard drawing
25. Red and green when combined will produce the SAME color as   25. ...
    A. orange, yellow and violet
    B. red, blue and yellow
    C. red, blue and violet
    D. red and black
    E. yellow and green

―――

KEY (CORRECT ANSWERS)

TEST 1	TEST 2	TEST 3	TEST 4	TEST 5
1. D	1. C	1. D	1. C	1. E
2. C	2. B	2. E	2. B	2. D
3. D	3. D	3. C	3. E	3. E
4. B	4. D	4. B	4. D	4. C
5. A	5. E	5. D	5. A	5. D
6. B	6. A	6. A	6. C	6. C
7. D	7. B	7. B	7. C	7. A
8. D	8. C	8. C	8. C	8. C
9. D	9. D	9. E	9. D	9. C
10. B	10. B	10. D	10. A	10. A
11. C	11. C	11. E	11. D	11. B
12. B	12. A	12. C	12. E	12. A
13. E	13. D	13. E	13. D	13. C
14. B	14. B	14. D	14. C	14. D
15. A	15. A	15. A	15. D	15. C
16. C	16. D	16. C	16. C	16. E
17. D	17. B	17. B	17. D	17. A
18. B	18. E	18. A	18. C	18. E
19. E	19. D	19. B	19. D	19. D
20. A	20. B	20. B	20. E	20. A
21. D	21. C	21. D	21. C	21. D
22. D	22. D	22. E	22. D	22. B
23. E	23. B	23. C	23. E	23. D
24. C	24. E	24. A	24. C	24. A
25. A	25. A	25. D	25. B	25. B

EXAMINATION SECTION

TEST 1

DIRECTIONS: Each question or incomplete statement is followed by several suggested answers or completions. Select the one that BEST answers the question or completes the statement. *PRINT THE LETTER OF THE CORRECT ANSWER IN THE SPACE AT THE RIGHT.*

1. John is $\frac{1}{6}$ of his father's age. In 20 years, he will be $\frac{1}{2}$ of his father's age at that time. How old is the father?   1.___
    A. 24   B. 30   C. 36   D. 42   E. 48

2. $(\frac{.7}{.07})(\frac{49}{100}) = 4 + x \quad x =$ 2.___
    A. 4.9   B. .09   C. .9   D. 3.1   E. 3.95

3. Which is the largest?   3.___
    A. $\frac{23}{25}$ B. $\frac{27}{30}$ C. $\frac{15}{16}$ D. $\frac{14}{15}$ E. $\frac{7}{8}$

4. Clyde received a 10% raise in each of the last two years. His present salary is $21,780. What was his starting salary?   4.___
    A. $18,000   B. $19,000   C. $20,000   D. $21,350   E. $26,354

5. At a convention of dentists, 1,000 dentists are from the east coast. One hundred dentists are women; 60 of the women are not from the east coast. How many male dentists are from the east coast?   5.___
    A. 900   B. 850   C. 800   D. 960   E. 940

6. $\frac{1}{3}$ of $\frac{1}{4}$ is what percent of $\frac{5}{12}$?   6.___
    A. .2   B. 5   C. 12   D. 20   E. 500

7. Which line is parallel to the y axis?   7.___
    A. x = 4y   B. x = $\frac{2}{y}$

    C. x = y + 6   D. xy = 2

    E. xy = 2 + 4y^{-1}

8. The five tires that come with Mary's new car were rotated frequently so that each tire was used for exactly the same amount of time as the others. They were replaced when the odometer read 24,000 miles. How many miles had each been driven?   8.___
    A. 18,000 miles   B. 30,000 miles
    C. 20,000 miles   D. 24,000 miles
    E. 19,200 miles

9. $\dfrac{-\binom{7646}{x}}{4\text{---}}$ What is the smallest number x could be? 9.__

    A. 2647   B. 4000   C. 3000   D. 646   E. 3646

10. A bug sits at the edge of a 12 inch (diameter) phonograph   10.__
record playing at $33\frac{1}{3}$ r.p.m.

Approximately how fast (in feet/minute) is the bug moving?
    A. 3   B. 33   C. 50   D. 100   E. 396

11. An object floats if it weighs less than an equal volume   11.__
of water. One cc of water weighs 1 gram. Each of the
following objects weighs 2 kilograms.
Which ones float? (All dimensions in cm.)

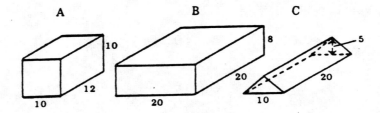

    A. A *only*   B. B *only*   C. C *only*   D. B & C   E. A & B

12. .04 is 25% of   12.__
    A. 0.01   B. 0.16   C. 0.1   D. 1.0   E. 1.6

13. $x^2 + 3x + 2 = 2$, $x < 0$.   13.__
  x =
    A. $\dfrac{3-\sqrt{8}}{2}$ B. -1 C. -2 D. -3 E. -4

14. If $\dfrac{3x}{4y} = \dfrac{1}{8}$, then $\dfrac{4x}{3y} =$ 14.__

    A. $\dfrac{1}{6}$ B. $\dfrac{1}{3}$ C. $\dfrac{2}{3}$ D. 24   E. $\dfrac{2}{9}$

15. .3% of 25% equals   15.__
    A. 7.5   B. .75   C. .075   D. .0075   E. .00075

16. Arrange from least to greatest: 16.__
    I. .07   II. $\sqrt{.49}$ III. .075   IV. $(.835)^2$

The CORRECT answer is:
    A. I, III, IV, II   B. III, I, IV, II
    C. IV, I, II, III   D. I, III, II, IV
    E. IV, II, III, I

17. A television set is priced at $490.00. The installment   17.__
payment contract requires 20% of the price as a down-
payment, plus installments of $47.75 per month over a
period of 10 months to pay for the set, including interest
charges.

What is the total amount of interest charged?
A. $83.00   B. $83.50
C. $85.50   D. $85.75
E. $125.50

18. A florist bought some plants for $150. He sold enough   18.___
at 75 cents to meet the cost and had 100 plants left.
How many were originally purchased by the florist?
A. 150   B. 250   C. 300   D. 350   E. 400

19. If 3x + y = 5 and 5x + y = 6, then y =   19.___
A. $\frac{2}{7}$ B. .5   C. 1   D. 2   E. 3.5

20. A purse contains $3.20 in dimes and quarters. There are   20.___
3 less dimes than quarters. How many dimes are there?
A. 7   B. 10   C. 13   D. 16   E. 20

21. A lawn fertilizer is most effective if 25 pounds is   21.___
spread over 10,000 square feet. A weed killer must be
mixed with the fertilizer but only 3 pounds should be
used on every 15,000 square feet. What should the ratio
be between the fertilizer and the weed killer when mixed?
A. 12.5 to 1   B. 3 to 2
C. 8.33 to 1   D. 5.5 to 1
E. 25 to 3

22. If 1 yard = .9 meters, then 1.5 meters = how many yards?   22.___
A. 1.65   B. 1.80   C. 1.60   D. 1.67   E. 1.35

23. ( ) is to 40 as $\frac{x}{5}$ is to ( ).   23.___

A. 4; $\frac{x}{50}$ B. 10; 40x   C. 8; x   D. 10; 8x   E. 5; $\frac{x}{40}$

24. What is the approximate value of $\sqrt{360}$?   24.___
A. 60   B. 18   C. 6   D. 16   E. 19

25. An auto travels at an average of 45 mi/hr for 1 hour and   25.___
then an average of 60 mi/hr for the next half hour. What
is the average speed for the entire time period in miles/hr.?
A. 47.5   B. 50   C. 52.5   D. 55   E. 62.5

KEY (CORRECT ANSWERS)

1. B	6. D	11. B	16. A	21. A
2. C	7. B	12. B	17. C	22. D
3. C	8. E	13. D	18. C	23. C
4. A	9. A	14. E	19. E	24. E
5. D	10. D	15. E	20. A	25. B

SOLUTIONS TO PROBLEMS

1. Let the father's current age = x and John's current age = $\frac{1}{6}$x.

   In 20 years, their ages will be x + 20 and $\frac{1}{6}$x + 20.

   Then, $\frac{1}{6}$x + 20 = $\frac{1}{2}$(x+20), which becomes $\frac{1}{6}$x + 20 = $\frac{1}{2}$x + 10.

   Solving, x = 30.

2. The left side of this equation becomes (10)(.49) = 4.9
   Now, 4.9 = 4 + x. Solving, x = .9

3. Converting each fraction into a decimal equivalent, we get:
   .92, .9, .9375, .9$\overline{3}$, and .875, respectively. The largest is
   .9375 corresponding to $\frac{15}{16}$.

4. Let x = initial salary. With the first 10% raise, his salary
   is 1.10x. The second 10% raise will bring his salary to
   (1.10x)(1.10) = 1.21x. Now, 1.21x = $21,780. Solving, x = $18,00

5. The number of female dentists from the east coast is
   100 - 60 = 40. Thus, the number of male dentists from the
   east coast must be 1000 - 40 = 960.

6. $\frac{1}{3}$ of $\frac{1}{4}$ means $(\frac{1}{3})(\frac{1}{4})$ = $\frac{1}{12}$. Then, $\frac{1}{12}$ ÷ $\frac{5}{12}$ = $\frac{1}{5}$, and $\frac{1}{5}$ = 20%

7. Any line parallel to the y-axis has no slope, and so must be
   of the form x = c (c is a constant). x = 2/y° can be written
   as x = 2/1 or x = 2.

8. Since only 4 tires are used at the same time, each of the
   5 tires will be used $\frac{4}{5}$ or 80% of the elapsed time before
   replacement. (24,000)(.80) = 19,200.

9. To find the minimum x, we need to find the maximum for the
   answer (since this is a subtraction). The maximum answer
   upon subtracting is 4999. Solving, 7646 - x = 4999, we
   get x = 2647.

10. The circumference = (π)(1 foot) = 3.14 feet (approximately)
    33$\frac{1}{3}$ revolutions = (33$\frac{1}{3}$)(3.14) = 104$\frac{2}{3}$ feet, which is the rate
    per minute.

11. 2 kilograms = 2000 grams. The only object(s) which float must correspond to more than 2000 cc. Object A has a volume of only 1200 cc. Object B has a volume of 3200 cc. Object C has a volume of only $(\frac{1}{2})(10)(5)(20)$ = 500 cc. Object B will float since 3200 cc. of water weighs 3200 grams and 2000 < 3200. Objects A and C will not float.

12. Solve .04 = .25x to get x = .16.

13. Rewrite the equation as x^2 + 3x = 0. Then, x(x+3) = 0. The two answers are x = 0 and x = -3. With the restriction x < 0, we have x = -3.

14. 3x/4y = $\frac{1}{8}$. Dividing both sides by $\frac{3}{4}$, we get $\frac{x}{y}$ = $\frac{1}{6}$.

Now, multiply the entire equation $\frac{x}{y}$ = $\frac{1}{6}$ by $\frac{4}{3}$ to get

4x/3y = $(\frac{1}{6})(\frac{4}{3})$ = $\frac{2}{9}$

15. .3% of 25% becomes (.003)(.25) = .00075

16. The equivalent decimals are .07, .7, .075, and .697225. Arranging from least to greatest: .07, .075, .697225, and .7, which correspond to I, III, IV, and II.

17. The actual payments are (.20)($490) + (10)($47.75) = $575.50 Interest amount = $575.50 - $490 = $85.50

18. The number of plants he sold = $150 ÷ $0.75 = 200. Since he had 100 plants left, he originally purchased 200 + 100 = 300 plants.

19. Subtract the first equation from the second to get 2x = 1. So, x = .5. Substitute this x value in either equation. Choosing the first equation, (3)(.5) + y = 5. Then, y = 3.5

20. Let x = number of dimes, x + 3 = number of quarters. Then, .10x + .25(x+3) = 3.20. Simplifying, .35x + .75 = 3.20. Finally, x = 7

21. For the weed killer, since 3 pounds should be used on 15,000 square feet, this translates into 2 pounds per 10,000 square feet. The ratio on the 10,000 square feet of lawn for fertilizer to weed killer is 25 to 2. This reduces to 12.5 to 1.

22. 1.5 meters = 1.5 ÷ .9 = 1.67 yards

23. Substituting choice C, 8 to 40 = $\frac{1}{5}$ and $\frac{x}{5}$ to x = $\frac{1}{5}$

24. $18^2 = 324$ and $19^2 = 361$. Thus, $\sqrt{360} \approx 19$

25. Total miles = $45 + (\frac{1}{2})(60) = 75$. Total time = $1 + \frac{1}{2} = 1\frac{1}{2}$ hours
    Average speed = $75 \div 1\frac{1}{2} = 50$ mi/hr.

TEST 2

DIRECTIONS: Each question or incomplete statement is followed by several suggested answers or completions. Select the one that BEST answers the question or completes the statement. *PRINT THE LETTER OF THE CORRECT ANSWER IN THE SPACE AT THE RIGHT.*

1. $\frac{1}{3}$ of 15 = 15% of 　　　　1.____

 　　A. $\frac{3}{4}$ 　　　　B. 45 　　　　C. 75 　　　　D. 5 　　　　E. $33\frac{1}{3}$

2. A tree in an apartment building courtyard died, and the cost of cutting down the tree is $350.00. The city will share the cost with the landlord on a 2 to 3 ratio, the landlord paying the larger part. How much will the landlord have to pay?　　　　2.____
 　　A. $233.00 　　　　　　　　B. $175.00
 　　C. $117.00 　　　　　　　　D. $150.00
 　　E. $210.00

3. $\frac{1}{2} + \frac{4}{2x-1} = 6.$　x =　　　　3.____

 　　A. $-\frac{1}{2}$ 　　B. $\frac{13}{22}$ 　　C. $\frac{19}{22}$ 　　D. $-\frac{1}{4}$ 　　E. $-\frac{15}{22}$

4. The capacity of a car's cooling system if 17 quarts. $1\frac{3}{4}$ gallons of antifreeze plus 1 pint of rust inhibitor are required to drop the freezing point to -18°. How much water is required to fill the system to capacity?　　　　4.____
 　　A. 21 pints 　　　　　　　　B. 9 pints
 　　C. 19 pints 　　　　　　　　D. 10 quarts
 　　E. 18 pints

5. If 1 inch = 2.54 cm., $\frac{3}{4}$ cm. = how many inches?　　　　5.____

 　　A. 1.9 　　　　B. 3.39 　　　　C. .75 　　　　D. .19 　　　　E. .3

6. A box has the shape of a rectangular solid, with a base measuring 16 inches by 10 inches and a height of 8 inches. What is the approximate length of the sides of a cubic container having the same volume?　　　　6.____
 　　A. 9.75 inches 　　　　　　　　B. 10.00 inches
 　　C. 10.85 inches 　　　　　　　　D. 12.65 inches
 　　E. 13.15 inches

7. What is a valid formula for the line plotted on the graph?　　　　7.____
 　　A. x = y
 　　B. x = $\frac{10}{y}$

 　　C. x = 10 - y
 　　D. x = $\frac{y}{10}$

 　　E. x = y + 10

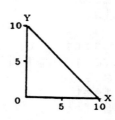

8. In the fraction $\frac{x}{y}$, when 1 is added to the numerator, the
fraction equals $\frac{1}{3}$. When 3 is added to the denominator of
$\frac{x}{y}$, the fraction equals $\frac{1}{6}$. What is $\frac{x}{y}$?

   A. $\frac{2}{6}$ 　　　 B. $\frac{2}{3}$ 　　　 C. $\frac{2}{9}$ 　　　 D. $\frac{6}{17}$ 　　　 E. $\frac{2}{12}$

9. What is the *approximate* value of $\dfrac{(.03)^2(\sqrt{.25} + 3.5)}{.12}$?

   A. .03 　　　 B. .36 　　　 C. .003 　　　 D. 3.0 　　　 E. .0036

10. A woman is now three times as old as her son. In four
years, the son will be one-half as old as the woman is
now. How old is the woman now?
   A. 24 　　　 B. 28 　　　 C. 30 　　　 D. 21 　　　 E. 33

11. $\frac{1}{5}$ of 27 = 25% of

   A. $21\frac{3}{5}$ 　　 B. 5.4 　　 C. 1.35 　　 D. $\frac{105}{5}$ 　　 E. 21.5

12. A rancher had 70 head of cattle. A buyer made four
purchases of cattle from the rancher. The rancher now
has eighteen cattle remaining. On the average, how many
cattle exchanged hands at EACH purchase?
   A. 10.5 　　 B. 13 　　 C. 15 　　 D. 20 　　 E. 52

13. $\sqrt{16 + x} = 4 + 2$ 　　 x =
   A. 36 　　　 B. 4 　　　 C. -10 　　　 D. 20 　　　 E. 2

14. If 10 cc of 20% acid is mixed with 20 cc of 40% acid, the
percentage of acid in the resulting solution is
   A. 50 　　 B. 30 　　 C. $33\frac{1}{3}$ 　　 D. 35 　　 E. 60

15. $\frac{5}{6} + \frac{5}{9} - \frac{2}{3} + x$ = a whole number. Then x = ?

   A. $\frac{5}{18}$ 　　 B. $\frac{13}{16}$ 　　 C. $\frac{17}{18}$ 　　 D. $\frac{18}{13}$ 　　 E. $\frac{2}{9}$

16. A piece of lumber is 63 inches long. It is to be cut
in three pieces. Two pieces are to be of equal length,
while the third piece is to be 9 inches longer than each
of the other two pieces. How long will the longer piece
of lumber be?
   A. 54 inches 　　　　　　 B. 36 inches
   C. 30 inches 　　　　　　 D. 27 inches
   E. 18 inches

17. The sun shining on a tree casts a shadow 45 feet long.
A boy five feet tall standing near the tree has a 2 foot
10 inch shadow. How tall is the tree?
   A. 54 feet 　　　　　　 B. 22.5 feet
   C. 37.5 feet 　　　　　 D. 79.4 feet
   E. 18 feet

18. $\frac{x}{95} = 7.5\%$ $x =$

    A. 12.7   B. 7.1   C. 8.0   D. 1.26   E. 713

    18.___

19. A street light shining on a signpost casts a shadow 6 feet long. A child 5 feet tall standing near the signpost casts a shadow 2 feet 3 inches long. How tall is the signpost?

    A. 13.3 feet   B. 6.6 feet
    C. 12 feet   D. 20 feet
    E. 15.3 feet

    19.___

20. $\frac{(-2)^{15}}{(-2)^{12}} = ?$

    A. −4   B. +4   C. −8   D. +8   E. −16

    20.___

21. Five consecutive whole numbers have a sum of 50. What is the second of the five numbers?

    A. 5   B. 7   C. 9   D. 10   E. 11

    21.___

22. If z = 35% of w, and y = 15% of z, then y = ___% of w.

    A. 2.33   B. 42.9   C. 5.25   D. 2.25   E. 4.3

    22.___

23. If $(y + 2)x = \frac{1}{4}$, $y =$

    A. $\frac{1}{4} - 2x$ B. $\frac{1}{4x} - 2$

    C. $\frac{1}{4x+8}$ D. $\frac{x}{4} - 2$

    E. $\frac{1-8x}{4}$

    23.___

24. A set of drill bits are being sold for $200.00. The bits cost the dealer $160.00, plus a $20.00 shipping fee. What percent of the selling price will be profit for the dealer?

    A. 7%   B. 10%   C. 11%   D. 21%   E. 30%

    24.___

25. Let A be the area of a circle whose diameter is 8. Which of the following numbers is closest to A?

    A. 50   B. 70   C. 100   D. 120   E. 200

    25.___

KEY (CORRECT ANSWERS)

1. E		11. A	
2. E		12. B	
3. C		13. D	
4. C		14. C	
5. E		15. A	
6. C		16. D	
7. C		17. D	
8. C		18. B	
9. A		19. A	
10. A		20. C	

21. C
22. C
23. B
24. B
25. A

SOLUTIONS TO PROBLEMS

1. $\frac{1}{3}$ of 15 = 5.   Then, 5 ÷ .15 = $33\frac{1}{3}$

2. Let 2x = city's cost and 3x = landlord's cost. 2x + 3x = $350
   Solving, x = $70. Then, landlord's cost is (3)($70) = $210

3. Multiplying the equation by (2)(2x-1), we get (1)(2x-1) + (4)(2)
   = (6)(2)(2x-1). Simplifying, 2x - 1 + 8 = 24x - 12.
   This reduces further to 19 = 22x. So, x = $\frac{19}{22}$

4. $1\frac{3}{4}$ gallons = $(1\frac{3}{4})$(4) = 7 quarts = 14 pints of antifreeze.
   The capacity of the cooling system = 17 quarts = 34 pints.
   Since 1 pint of rust inhibitor is needed, the amount of
   water required is 34 - 14 - 1 = 19 pints.

5. $\frac{3}{4}$ cm = $\frac{3}{4}$ ÷ 2.54 = .295 or about .3 inches

6. The volume of the box = (16)(10)(8) = 1280 cubic inches.
   If a cubic container has a volume of 1280 cubic inches,
   each side must be $\sqrt[3]{1280}$ ≈ 10.85 inches.
   (Actually, the answer is slightly closer to 10.86)

7. Since the coordinates of the two given points are (10,0) and
   (0,10), the slope of the line is (10-0) ÷ (0-10) = -1.
   Y = -1x + B, where B is the y-intercept. Now, B = 10 since
   (0,10) lies on this line. Y = -1x + 10 is the equation and
   this can be written as x = 10 - y.

8. From the given information, (x+1)/y = $\frac{1}{3}$ and x/(y+3) = $\frac{1}{6}$
   Rewriting, we have y = 3x + 3 and y = 6x - 3. Adding these
   equations, 2y = 9x. Thus, $\frac{x}{y} = \frac{2}{9}$.

9. $(.03)^2$ = .0009. ($\sqrt{.25}$ + 3.5) = 4.0. The answer becomes
   (.0009)(4)/.12 = .03. (Change the word *approximate* to *exact*.)

10. Let x = woman's age, $\frac{1}{3}$x = son's age. Then, $\frac{1}{3}$x + 4 = ½x.
    This reduces to $\frac{1}{6}$x = 4, so x = 24.

11. $\frac{1}{5}$ of 27 = (.2)(27) = 5.4. Then, 5.4 ÷ .25 = 21.6 = $21\frac{3}{5}$

12. 70 - 18 = 52. Then, 52 ÷ 4 = 13.

13. $\sqrt{16+x}$ = 6. Square both sides to get 16 + x = 36. Then, x = 20

14. The amount of acid in the resulting solution is (.20)(10) + (.40)(20) = 10 cc. The solution is 10 + 20 = 30 cc. Percentage of acid is (10/30)(100) = 33 1/3

15. $\frac{5}{6}$ + $\frac{5}{9}$ - $\frac{2}{3}$ = (15 + 10 - 12)/18 = $\frac{13}{18}$. Since choice A is $\frac{5}{18}$,

    $\frac{13}{18}$ + $\frac{5}{18}$ = $\frac{18}{18}$ = 1, which is a whole number.

16. Let x = length of each shorter piece and x + 9 = length of the longer piece. x + x + x + 9 = 63. Solving, x = 18. So, the longer piece must be 27 inches.

17. The ratio of the boy's height to his shadow is 60 inches to 34 inches = 30 to 17 (reduced). Let x = height of the tree. Then, x/45 = 30/17. Solving, x ≈ 79.4 feet

18. x/95 = .075.   x = (.075)(95) = 7.125 or about 7.1

19. The ratio of the child's height to his shadow is 60 inches to 27 inches = 20 to 9 (reduced). Let x = height of the signpost. Then, x/6 = 20/9. Solving, x - 13.33 or about 13.3 feet.

20. In division, we subtract exponents to get $(-2)^3$ = -8. Of course, the base must remain the same.

21. Let x, x+1, x+2, x+3, x+4 represent the numbers. Then, x + x+1 + x+2 + x+3 + x+4 = 50. Solving, x = 8. The second number must be 9.

22. y = .15z = (.15)(.35)w = .0525w. Thus, y is 5.25% of w.

23. (y+2)(x) = ¼. Dividing both sides by x, we get y + 2 = $\frac{1}{4x}$. Finally, y = $\frac{1}{4x}$ - 2

24. The dealer's total cost is $180 and his profit is $20. The percent profit on the selling price is (20/200)(100) = 10%.

25. A = $(\pi)(4)^2$ = 16π = 50.265 or about 50. Note that the formula is Area = $(\pi)(radius)^2$.

EXAMINATION SECTION

TEST 1

DIRECTIONS: Each question or incomplete statement is followed by several suggested answers or completions. Select the one that BEST answers the question or completes the statement. *PRINT THE LETTER OF THE CORRECT ANSWER IN THE SPACE AT THE RIGHT.*

1. In the number system with base 5, the value of the repeating decimal, .232323...., expressed as a common fraction, is

   A. $\dfrac{44}{344}$ B. $\dfrac{14}{24}$ C. $\dfrac{23}{44}$ D. none of these

   1.___

2. The number 122, base 4, is added to the number 212, base 3. Their sum, when expressed in the base 5, is written

   A. 2,314   B. 334   C. 144   D. 49

   2.___

3. If 13^{52} is multiplied out, the units digit in the final product is

   A. 1   B. 3   C. 7   D. 9

   3.___

4. On a $10,000 order, a merchant has a choice between three successive discounts of 20%, 20%, and 10%, and three successive discounts of 40%, 5%, and 5%.
   By choosing the better offer, he can save

   A. $330   B. $345   C. $360   D. $400

   4.___

5. An article was sold for $21.00 more than it cost.
   If the marked price of this article was 150% of its cost price, and if it was sold at a discount of 30%, then its cost price was

   A. $19.09   B. $70   C. $210   D. $420

   5.___

6. If the statement $202_b = (13_b) \cdot (13_b)$ is true in a number system whose base is b, and b is a natural number, then b is equal to

   A. 5   B. 6   C. 7   D. 8

   6.___

7. A rope 10 yards long is divided into three lengths so that the shortest is equal to the difference in the lengths of the two others.
   Then the LONGEST piece is what part of the whole rope?

   A. 1/4   B. 1/2   C. 2/3   D. 3/4

   7.___

8. Assume that a storekeeper reduces his profit on all merchandise in the store from 40% of the cost to 33 1/3% of the cost.
   If an article originally sold for $14.70, what would its new selling price be?

   A. $9.80   B. $10.78   C. $11.76   D. $14.00

   8.___

9. The numbers 314 and 1011 are written in two different bases. Each number contains the largest digit available on its base.
The sum of these two numbers, if written in base 3, is
   A. 10112   B. 1211002   C. 20220   D. 1011111

10. An automobile covered the first 60 miles of its journey in 1 hour 30 minutes and the next 87 miles in 2 hours. The AVERAGE speed, in miles per hour, for the total trip is
   A. 41 3/4   B. 42   C. 58 4/5   D. 73 1/2

11. If the radius of a circle is increased 50%, the area is INCREASED ____%.
   A. 50   B. 125   C. 200   D. 225

12. Assuming the use of α as a symbol for *ten* and β for *eleven*, the number 283_{ten}, when written in the duodecimal system of numeration, is represented by
   A. $1\beta 7$ B. $1_\alpha 7$ C. 21β D. 21α

13. A owns a house worth $10,000. He sells it to B at a 10% profit. B sells the house back to A at a 10% loss. Then, among the following, which is CORRECT?
   A. A comes out even.   B. A makes $100.
   C. A makes $1,100.   D. B loses $1,000.

14. If the length and width of a rectangle are each doubled, the area is increased by
   A. 100%   B. 200%   C. 300%   D. 400%

15. The list price of an article is $500. On this article, one dealer offers successive discounts of 10% and 20%, while another offers a single discount of 30%.
As a result of these offers, what will the difference be in the selling price of the article be?
   A. No difference   B. $5
   C. $10   D. $15

16. Of a group of pupils, 1/3 walk home, 3/8 of the remaining members go home by bus, and the other 35 use bicycles to go home.
How many pupils are there in the group?
   A. 64   B. 84   C. 120   D. 280

17. A merchant paid $90 for a desk.
At what price should he mark it if he wishes to offer his customers a 10% discount and still make a profit of 20% on the cost?
   A. $108   B. $112   C. $116   D. $120

18. If 16 men require 24 cases of rations for 10 days, then at the same rate of consumption, the number of days that 27 cases of rations will last for 12 men is
   A. 12   B. 15   C. 18   D. 21

19. A man deposits $1,000 in a new account which earns interest at 4% compounded quarterly from the day of deposit.
How much must he deposit in this account three months later in order that the account will contain exactly $2020 six months from the day of the initial deposit?
   A. $940   B. $980   C. $990   D. $1,000

19.___

20. The integer 5x327y, where x and y stand for missing digits, is divisible by 9.
Which of the following could the sum of x and y be?
   A. 5   B. 9   C. 10   D. 11

20.___

——

KEY (CORRECT ANSWERS)

1. B		11. B	
2. C		12. A	
3. D		13. C	
4. B		14. C	
5. D		15. C	
6. C		16. C	
7. B		17. D	
8. D		18. B	
9. A		19. D	
10. B		20. C	

——

SOLUTIONS TO PROBLEMS

1. $.232323\ldots_{\text{base 5}} = (\frac{2}{5} + \frac{3}{25} + \frac{2}{125} + \frac{3}{625} + \frac{2}{3125} + \frac{3}{15625} \ldots)_{\text{base 10}}$
    $.541632$, which approaches $\frac{13}{24}$.   (Ans. B)

2. $122_{\text{base 4}} = 26_{\text{base 10}}$ $\cdot$ $212_{\text{base 3}} = 23_{\text{base 10}}$ $\cdot$ Sum $= 49_{\text{base 10}}$
    which is $144_{\text{base 5}}$.   (Ans. C)

3. $13^1 = 13$, $13^2 = 169$, $13^3 = 2197$, $13^4 = 28561$, $13^5 = 371293$, etc
    The last digit is of a cyclic nature and has the pattern
    3, 9, 7, 1, 3, 9, 7, 1, 3, 9, 7, 1, etc. for consecutive
    powers of 13.
    Now, 13^{62} would end in the same digit as 13^2 which is 9.
    (Ans. D)

4. Under the first option, the merchant would pay
    ($10000)(.8)(.8)(.1) = $5760; but under the second option,
    he would pay ($10000)(.6)(.95)(.95) = $5415. This represents
    a savings of $345.   (Ans. B)

5. Let c = cost. Then, c+21 = selling price and 1.50c = marked
    price. Since the article was sold at a 30% discount (off the
    marked price), c + 21 = .70(1.50c). Solving, c = $420.
    (Ans. D)

6. $202_7 = (2)(7^2) + 2 = 100$ and $13_7 = 10$. Now, $202_7 = (13_7)(13_7)$.

    (Ans. C)

7. Let x = shortest piece, y = second piece. Then, 10 - x - y =
    longest piece. Now, x = (10-x-y) - y. Thus, x + y = 5.
    Then, 10 - x - y must equal 5, and this represents $\frac{1}{2}$ the length
    of the rope.   (Ans. B)

8. Let x = cost. Then, 14.70 = (1.40)(x) and x = 10.50. The new
    selling price is (10.50)(133 1/3%) = $14.00.   (Ans. D)

9. $314_{\text{base 5}} = (3)(25) + (1)(5) + 4 = 84$

    $1011_{\text{base 2}} = (1)(8) + (0)(4) + 1(2) + 1 = 11$

    The sum = 95, which is $10112_{\text{base 3}}$.   (Ans. A)

10. Average speed = total distance/total time = 147/3.5 = 42 mph.
    (Ans. B)

11. If R = original radius, area = πR^2. If new radius = 1.5R, new
    area = $\pi(1.5R)^2 = 2.25\pi R^2$. The area increased $1.25\pi R^2$, which
    represents a 125% increase.   (Ans. B)

12. $\overline{}\,\overline{}\,\overline{}$ The leftmost placeholder represents $12^2 = 144$. Since $283 \div 144 = 1$ with remainder of 139, the first dash = 1. The second dash represents 12, and 139 consists of 11 12's with remainder of 7. Thus, the symbol for 11, β, occupies the second dash. 7 must occupy the rightmost dash. The final answer = 1β7.   (Ans. A)

13.   A sells the house to B for $(\$10,000)(1.10) = \$11,000$. Then, B sells the house to A for $(\$11,000)(.90) = \$9,900$. A nets $1,100.   (Ans. C)

14.   Let L = length, w = width, so that area = Lw. The new length and width are 2L and 2w, and so the new area = 4Lw. The increase in area is 3Lw, which represents 300%.   (Ans. C)

15.   Successive discounts of 10% and 20% would mean that the final price is $(.80)(.90)(\$500) = \$360$. A single discount of 30% would yield a final price of $(.70)(\$500) = \$350$. The difference is $10.   (Ans. C)

16.   Let x = number of students. Then, $x - \frac{1}{3}x - \frac{3}{8}x = 35$. $\frac{7}{24}x = 35$. Solving, x = 120.   (Ans. C)

17.   Let x = marked price. Sale price = .90x, and this price will be 120% of $90. Thus, $.90x = (1.20)(90) = 108$. Solving, x = $120.   (Ans. D)

18.   For 10 days, 12 men would require x rations. $\frac{12}{x} = \frac{16}{24}$.

Then, x = 18. Now, if 18 rations last 10 days, 27 rations

will last y days. $\frac{18}{10} = \frac{27}{y}$. Solving, y = 15.   (Ans. B)

19.   In three months, his account will grow to $\$1000(1.01)^1 = \$1010$. If he deposits x dollars, $(1000+x)(1.01)^1 = 2020$. Solving, x = $1000.   (Ans. D)

20.   Since the sum of all digits = a multiple of 9, 5+x+3+2+7+y = a multiple of 9. Thus, 17 + x + y = a multiple of 9, and so x+y could be 10.   (Ans. C)

———

TEST 2

DIRECTIONS: Each question or incomplete statement is followed by several suggested answers or completions. Select the one that BEST answers the question or completes the statement. *PRINT THE LETTER OF THE CORRECT ANSWER IN THE SPACE AT THE RIGHT.*

1. Which of the following lengths: (A) 2.990 in., (B) 2.998 in., (C) 3.002 in. may be accepted for a part designed to be 3 inches long if a .003 inch tolerance is permitted?
   A. A and B *only*
   B. A and C *only*
   C. B and C *only*
   D. A, B, and C

2. The number 478 (base 10), when changed to base 5 notation, becomes
   A. 3   B. 2390   C. 3403   D. 11102

3. If an article costs $36, the price at which it should be marked to allow a discount of 10% and still make a profit of 20% on the actual selling price is
   A. $40   B. $46   C. $50   D. $54

4. Of the following pairs, the one which is composed of two equivalents is
   A. 1/2 = .5%
   B. 1.01 = 110%
   C. .0001/4 = .0025%
   D. .02/3 = .062/3%

5. A man needs $8000 for the purchase of a business. A loan is available at 6% interest, discounted in advance. The amount he must borrow, to the nearest dollar, to net $8000 repayable at the end of six months is
   A. $8240   B. $8247   C. $8480   D. $8511

6. Of the following, the one which is CLOSEST to the result of the computation of $\dfrac{(.846)^2 \sqrt[3]{18.7}}{3.42}$ is

   A. .5555   B. 5.555   C. 55.55   D. 555.5

7. Which one of the following is NOT a perfect number?
   A. 28
   B. $2^{k-1}(2^k-1)$ (where k is prime)
   C. 15
   D. 6

8. The product of the highest common factor and the lowest common multiple of 18 and 24 is
   A. *equal* to the product of 18 and 24
   B. *equal* to the quotient of 24 and 18
   C. *greater* than the product of 18 and 24
   D. *equal* to half the product of 18 and 24

9. Which one of the following is NOT a characteristic of 9.___
   all *groups*?
      A. Associative law   B. Commutative law
      C. Closure   D. An inverse element

10. Of the following, the set of numbers arranged in 10.___
    ascending order of values is
       A. 114_{five}, 122_{three}, 10110_{two}

       B. 122_{three}, 10110_{two}, 114_{five}

       C. 10110_{two}, 122_{three}, 114_{five}

       D. 10111_{two}, 114_{five}, 122_{three}

11. All of the following numbers are congruent to -14 modulo 11.___
    4, EXCEPT
       A. -8   B. -6   C. 2   D. 6

12. The product of .00000149 and .0000000006 written in 12.___
    scientific notation is
       A. 8.94×10^{-16} B. 8.94×10^{-17}
       C. 8.94×10^{-18} D. 8.94×10^{-19}

13. If an airplane is flying with a ground speed of 200 miles 13.___
    per hour, the number of seconds required for it to travel
    a ground mile is
       A. 1/18   B. 3 1/3   C. 18   D. 60

14. When 148, a numeral to the base 10, is expressed as a 14.___
    numeral to the base 7, it becomes
       A. 103   B. 231   C. 301   D. 321

15. When 231 and 332, numerals expressed to the base 4, are 15.___
    expressed to the base 10, the sum of the two then would be
       A. 107   B. 563
       C. 1225   D. none of these

16. The arithmetic mean of the measures 4.18, 4.23, 4.15, 16.___
    4.17, 4.09 is CLOSEST to which one of the following?
       A. 4.15   B. 4.16   C. 4.17   D. 4.18

17. Of the following pairs, the one containing two equivalent 17.___
    values is
       A. .0375, 3 3/4%   B. 2.75, .02 3/4%
       C. .8 1/3%; 1/12   D. .0125%, .01 1/4

18. Assume that a gasoline tank was half full, and the 18.___
    gasoline was used until the tank is only 1/8 full.
    If the tank is then filled to capacity by putting in
    21 gallons, the capacity of the tank, in gallons, is
       A. 24   B. 42
       C. 56   D. none of these

19. The smallest subdivision on a certain accurately   19.
    calibrated instrument is .01 inch.
    Assuming no human errors in use, the possible error of
    measurement in using the above instrument is
       A. .001"   B. .005"   C. .010"   D. .050"

20. The number 1011 to the base 2, if expressed to the base 10, 20.
    would be
       A. 11   B. 14   C. 22   D. 38

———

KEY (CORRECT ANSWERS)

1. C			11. A	
2. C			12. A	
3. C			13. C	
4. D			14. C	
5. B			15. A	
6. A			16. B	
7. C			17. A	
8. A			18. A	
9. B			19. B	
10. B			20. A	

———

SOLUTIONS TO PROBLEMS

1. $3 \pm .003$ = 2.997 to 3.003. Only choices B and C are acceptable. (Ans. C)

2. In base 5, the name of the columns are units, 5's, 25's, 125's, etc. reading from right to left. Since 478 ÷ 125 gives 3 with remainder 103, the leftmost digit = 3. Then, 103 ÷ 25 gives 4 with remainder 3; so the next digit = 4. Now, 3 ÷ 5 gives 0 with remainder 3; thus the next digit = 0 and the rightmost digit = 3. The number is 3403. (Ans. C)

3. Let x = marked price. With a discount of 10%, the selling price = .90x. To realize a profit of 20% on the selling price, .90x - 36 = .20(.90x). Solving, x = $50. (Ans. C)

4. $\frac{1}{2}$ = 50% ≠ .5%, 1.01 = 101% ≠ 110%, $.000\frac{1}{4}$ = .00025 ≠ .0025%, and $.0\frac{2}{3}$ = $.0\overline{6}$ $\frac{2}{3}$ = $.06\frac{2}{3}$%. (Ans. D)

5. Let x = amount borrowed. Then, .97x = 8000, and x is approximately $8247. (Ans. B)

6. The expression is approximated by $\frac{(.7)(2.6)}{3.4}$, which is about .54. Thus, .5555 is the closest given approximation. (Ans. A)

7. 15 is not a perfect number since the sum of all its factors (except 15) = 1 + 3 + 5 = 9 ≠ 15. (Ans. C)

8. Highest common factor = 6, and the lowest common multiple is 72. Now, (72)(6) = 432, which equals (18)(24). (Ans. A)

9. A group need not be commutative. If it has this property, it is called Abelian. (Ans. B)

10. 122_{three} = 9 + (2)(3) + 2 = 17, 10110_{two} = 16 + 4 + 2 = 22, and 114_{five} = 25 + 5 + 4 = 34. (Ans. B)

11. -8 is NOT congruent to -14 modulo 4 since -8 -(-14) is not a multiple of 4. (Ans. A)

12. $(1.49 \times 10^{-6})(6 \times 10^{-10})$ = 8.94×10^{-16}. (Ans. A)

13. 200 mi/hr = 1 mi/$\frac{1}{200}$ hr. $\frac{1}{200}$ hr. = $(\frac{1}{200})$(3600) = 18 seconds. (Ans. C)

14. $148_{\text{base }10} = 301_{\text{base }7}$, since $301_{\text{base }7} = (3)(49) + 1$.

   (Ans. C)

15. $231_{\text{base }4} = 2(16) + 3(4) + 1 = 45_{\text{base }10}$

   $332_{\text{base }4} = 3(16) + 3(4) + 2 = 62_{\text{base }10}$

   Their sum = 107.   (Ans. A)

16. The arithmetic mean of the 5 numbers $= \dfrac{20.82}{5} = 4.164$, which rounds off to 4.16.   (Ans. B)

17. .0375 is equivalent to 3.75%, which equals 3 3/4%.   (Ans. A)

18. 21 gallons represents $\dfrac{7}{8}$ of the tank's capacity. Thus, the tank's capacity is $(21)(\dfrac{8}{7}) = 24$ gallons.   (Ans. A)

19. The error of measurement $= (\frac{1}{2})(.01) = .005$ inches.   (Ans. B)

20. $1011_{\text{base }2} = 8 + 2 + 1 = 11_{\text{base }10}$.   (Ans. A)

———

TEST 3

DIRECTIONS: Each question or incomplete statement is followed by several suggested answers or completions. Select the one that BEST answers the question or completes the statement. *PRINT THE LETTER OF THE CORRECT ANSWER IN THE SPACE AT THE RIGHT.*

1. If the integers 6 and 3 are interchanged in the number 2635 now expressed to the base seven, the quantity expressed to the base 10 by which the number is reduced is
   A. 21
   B. 30
   C. 147
   D. none of these

   1.___

2. A number of the form $an^4 + bn^2 + cn + d$, where $a = 4$, $b = 2$, $c = 2$, $d = 1$ and $n = 10$, is divisible by
   A. 2
   B. 5
   C. 7
   D. 9

   2.___

3. Of the following, the set in which all are units which may be used for measuring a one-dimensional object is
   A. meter, liter, decimeter, kilometer
   B. meter, kilometer, decimeter, millimeter
   C. liter, decimeter, kilometer, millimeter
   D. meter, liter, millimeter, decimeter

   3.___

4. To arrange the following ruler measurements in order of increasing lengths, the CORRECT arrangement should be

   $A = \frac{27}{32}$ in., $\quad B = \frac{7}{8}$ in., $\quad C = \frac{51}{64}$ in., $\quad D = \frac{13}{16}$ in.

   A. B, D, A, C
   B. D, C, A, B
   C. C, D, A, B
   D. C, A, D, B

   4.___

5. The ratio of 3'6" to 6" is BEST expressed as
   A. 1 to 7
   B. 3.6" to 6"
   C. 6" to 42"
   D. 7 to 1

   5.___

6. A layout of a rectangular foundation for a building is drawn to scale. The 72-foot length of the foundation is represented on the drawing by a line 27 inches long. The length, in inches, of the line needed to represent the 45-foot width of the foundation is

   A. $16 \frac{7}{8}$
   B. $17\frac{1}{4}$
   C. $17 \frac{7}{8}$
   D. $18 \frac{3}{8}$

   6.___

7. A circle graph is to be made to show the parts of the total city budget allocated to each department; the total budget is 2 billion, 100 million dollars.
   If 630 million dollars is allocated for education, the number of degrees on the circle graph which would represent the amount for education is CLOSEST to
   A. 30
   B. 54
   C. 84
   D. 108

   7.___

8. The screw which advances the thimble of a micrometer has 8.
   40 threads to the inch.
   If the thimble is turned exactly 3 threads, the micrometer
   will be opened by ____ inches.
   A. 0.025   B. 0.075   C. 0.340   D. 0.750

9. A voltmeter scale is divided into ten major divisions, 9.
   each of which is divided into five minor divisions. Full-
   scale deflection occurs when 30 volts are across the meter.
   The number of volts indicated when the needle is on the
   second minor division beyond the sixth major division is
   A. 6.4   B. 16.4   C. 18.6   D. 19.2

10. The number of rectangular cards 11 inches long and 8 10.
    inches wide that can be cut from a sheet 33 inches long
    and 27 inches wide with a minimum of waste is
    A. 6   B. 9   C. 10   D. 12

11. Of the following four fractions, the one that is CLOSEST 11.
    in value to $\sqrt{5}$ is

    A. $2\frac{1}{10}$ B. $2\frac{1}{5}$ C. $2\frac{1}{8}$ D. $2\frac{1}{2}$

12. During a transfer of oil from one tank to another, 12.
    $1\frac{1}{2}$ gallons were lost through leaks in the hose. This
    represented 0.3 percent of the capacity of the first tank.
    The capacity of this tank, in gallons, is
    A. 50   B. 200   C. 450   D. 500

13. Using six number punches with digits 1, 2, 3, 4, 5, and 13.
    6, the number of differently numbered tags that can be
    made with three-digit numbers on each tag is
    A. 120   B. 216   C. 278   D. 556

14. A junior high school class studying the metric system 14.
    came to the following conclusions. Of these, it is
    INCORRECT to conclude that a(n)
    A. basketball player can be 2 meters tall
    B. football player can weigh 100 kilograms
    C. track star can run 2 kilometers in 1 minute
    D. automobile gasoline tank can hold 80 liters of gasoline

15. The product of 32,000,000 and .000028 is 15.
    A. 8.96×10^{-2} B. 896×10^{-2}
    C. 8.96×10^{2} D. 896×10^{2}

16. Which of the following is its own multiplicative inverse? 16.
    I. -1   II. 0   III. +.1   IV. +1

    A. I, IV   B. II, IV   C. III, IV   D. IV *only*

17. If 1 inch ≈ 2.5 centimeters, then the number of yards in   17.___
    a kilometer can be found by computing the fraction

    A. $\dfrac{36 \times 100,000}{2.5}$ B. $\dfrac{1000}{2.5 \times 36}$

    C. $\dfrac{100,000}{2.5 \times 36}$ D. $\dfrac{2.5 \times 36 \times 100}{1000}$

18. A man invested $120,000 in a new business enterprise.   18.___
    The first year, he lost 37½% of the original investment.
    The next year, he made a profit of 40% of his net worth at the
    beginning of that year.
    His net worth at the end of the second year was what
    percent of his original investment?
    A. 62½   B. 75   C. 87½   D. 97½

19. The arithmetic mean (average) of a set of 50 numbers is   19.___
    38.
    If two numbers 45 and 55 are discarded, the mean of the
    remaining set of numbers is
    A. 36.5   B. 37.0   C. 37.24   D. 37.5

20. Which of the following numbers is 26^9?   20.___
    A. 5,011,849,549,824   B. 5,429,503,678,976
    C. 5,847,157,808,128   D. 5,638,330,743,552

KEY (CORRECT ANSWERS)

1. D		11. B	
2. D		12. D	
3. B		13. B	
4. C		14. C	
5. D		15. C	
6. A		16. A	
7. D		17. C	
8. B		18. C	
9. D		19. D	
10. B		20. B	

SOLUTIONS TO PROBLEMS

1. $2635_{\text{base } 7} = (2)(343) + (6)(49) + (3)(7) + 5 = 1006_{\text{base } 10}$ and

   $2365_{\text{base } 7} = (2)(343) + (3)(49) + (6)(7) + 5 = 880_{\text{base } 10}$.

   The amount reduction is 126.　(Ans. D)

2. The number's value is $4 \times 10^4 + 2 \times 10^2 + 2 \times 10 + 1 = $
   40,221.　Since the sum of the digits of this number is
   divisible by 9, then so must the number be divisible by 9.
   (Ans. D)

3. All four of the units meter, kilometer, decimeter, and
   millimeter are linear measurements.　Thus, they can be used
   to measure one-dimensional objects.　(Ans. B)

4. Convert all fractions to like demonimators:　$A = \dfrac{54}{64}$ in.,

   $B = \dfrac{56}{64}$ in., $C = \dfrac{51}{64}$ in., $D = \dfrac{52}{64}$ in.　Thus, in increasing

   length, the arrangement is C, D, A, B.　(Ans. C)

5. Change 3'6" to 42".　Then, 42" to 6" = 7 to 1.　(Ans. D)

6. Let x = required line.　Then $\dfrac{27}{x} = \dfrac{72}{45}$, and $x = 16\dfrac{7}{8}$ in.
   (Ans. A)

7. The ratio of 630 million to 2 billion, 100 million is

   630 to 2100 = $\dfrac{3}{10}$.　$(\dfrac{3}{10})(360°) = 108°$.　(Ans. D)

8. $3 \div 40 = .075$ inches.　NOTE correction of problem.　(Ans. B)

9. Each major division is $\dfrac{30}{10} = 3$ volts.　Each minor division is $\dfrac{3}{5}$

   .6 volts.　6 major + 2 minor divisions = $(6)(3) + (2)(.6) = $
   19.2 volts.　(Ans. D)

10. $33 \div 11 = 3$ columns by $27 \div 8$ rounded down to 3 rows.
    $(3)(3) = 9$.　(Ans. B)

11. $\sqrt{5} = 2.236$ approx.　Finding the absolute value of the difference
    between 2.236 and each of 2.1, 2.2, 2.125, and 2.5 yields .136,
    .036, .111, and .264, respectively.　Thus, 2.2 (or $2\dfrac{1}{5}$) is
    closest to $\sqrt{5}$.　(Ans. B)

12. Use a proportion: $\dfrac{1\frac{1}{2}}{x} = \dfrac{.3\%}{100\%} = \dfrac{.003}{1}$, where x = capacity of the tank. Solving, x = 500. (Ans. D)

13. Total number of permutations = (6)(6)(6) = 216. (Ans. B)

14. 2 kilometers = 1.24 miles, which would require a MINIMUM of over $4\frac{1}{2}$ minutes for a superior athlete. (Ans. C)

15. 32,000,000 = 3.2×10^7 and .000028 = 2.8×10^{-5}. Then, $(3.7 \times 10^7)(2.8 \times 10^{-5}) = 8.96 \times 10^2$. (Ans. C)

16. +1 and -1 are their own multiplicative inverses. The multiplicative inverse of 0 doesn't exist. The multiplicative inverse of +.1 is +10. (Ans. A)

17. There are 100,000 centimeters in a kilometer. Since 1 inch ≈ 2.5 centimeters, 1 yard ≈ (36)(2.5) = 90 centimeters. Thus, the number of yards in 100,000 centimeters = 100,000/90 = (100,000)/[(36)(2.5)]. (Ans. C)

18. His net worth after 1 year = ($120,000)(.625) = $75,000. His net worth after 2 years = (75,000)(1.40) = $105,000. Thus, $105,000/$120,000 = .875 = $87\frac{1}{2}\%$. (Ans. C)

19. The sum of all fifty numbers = (50)(38) = 1900. By discarding the numbers 45 and 55, the new sum is 1800 for 48 numbers. The mean is then 1800/48 = 37.5. (Ans. D)

20. Any number ending in a 6 which is raised to a positive integral value will still have 6 as its last digit. Only choice B ends in a 6. (Ans. B)

———

TEST 4

DIRECTIONS: Each question or incomplete statement is followed by several suggested answers or completions. Select the one that BEST answers the question or completes the statement. *PRINT THE LETTER OF THE CORRECT ANSWER IN THE SPACE AT THE RIGHT.*

1. A dealer sold two calculators for $15 each, one at a profit of 25% of its cost, the second at a loss of 25% of its cost.
   The COMBINED effect of the two transactions is
   A. no gain or loss   B. a gain of $2
   C. a gain of $3   D. a loss of $2

2. One hundred dollars is invested at a rate of interest of 8% per annum compounded semi-annually.
   The TOTAL value of the investment, in dollars, at the end of one year will be
   A. 116.64   B. 108.16   C. 108.08   D. 108.00

3. If the distance from the earth to the moon is approximately 380,000 kilometers, then this distance, in meters, is
   A. 3.8×10^8 B. 3.8×10^7 C. 3.8×10^5 D. 3.8×10^2

4. If 14_{five} is subtracted from 123_{four}, the result, in base ten, is
   A. 18   B. 63   C. 109   D. 1299

5. Two junior high school classes took the same test. The first class of 20 students attained an average grade of 80%. The second class of 30 students attained an average grade of 70%.
   The AVERAGE grade for all students in both classes is
   A. 75%   B. 74%   C. 73%   D. 72%

6. In a class studying the relationship between the metric system and the English system, the following statements were made by students: a
   I. meter is a little more than a yard
   II. liter is a little more than a quart
   III. kilometer is more than a mile
   IV. kilogram is more than a pound

   Which of these statements if FALSE?
   A. I   B. II   C. III   D. IV

7. A pupil adds his test scores and divides the sum by the number of scores.
   The result of this procedure would be the
   A. arithmetic mean   B. median
   C. mode   D. standard deviation

8. If the product of two positive integers is divisible by 6, which of the following must be TRUE?   8.___
   A. One integer must be divisible by 2, and the other integer must be divisible by 3.
   B. At least one of the integers must be divisible by 6.
   C. At least one of the integers must be an even number.
   D. Neither of the integers can be a prime number.

9. A gas tank with a capacity of 15 gallons is $\frac{5}{16}$ full.   9.___

How many gallons of fuel must be added to the tank for it to be $\frac{5}{8}$ full?

   A. $4\frac{11}{16}$ B. $5\frac{5}{8}$ C. $9\frac{3}{8}$ D. $10\frac{5}{16}$

10. Mr. Jones bought a house for $50,000. He sold the house at a profit of 20% of his original cost. The house was resold by the new purchaser at a profit of 20% of his cost.   10.___
What percent of Mr. Jones' original purchase price is the final selling price of the house?
   A. 44%   B. 122%   C. 140%   D. 144%

11. A man invested $1000 at 12% per year, compounded quarterly, for a period of 5 years.   11.___
Which of the following represents the total of his investment at the end of that time?
   A. $1000 (1.03)^{20}$ B. $1000 (1.05)^{12}$
   C. $1000 (1.12)^{5}$ D. $1000 (1.12)^{20}$

12. The number designated by 2021_{three} can be denoted in the binary system by   12.___
   A. 111101_{two} B. 101011_{two}
   C. 110111_{two} D. 101111_{two}

13. A representation for the number .00792 in scientific notation is   13.___
   A. 7.92×10^{-3} B. 7.92×10^{-4}
   C. 7.92×10^{2} D. 7.92×10^{3}

14. An eleventh year mathematics class studying positive and negative exponents examined a number of relationships in the metric system.   14.___
Which of the following is NOT a correct relationship?
   A. $1 \text{ mm} = 10^{-2} \text{ cm}$ B. $1 \text{ cm}^3 = 10^{-3}L$
   C. $1 \text{ kg} = 10^{6} \text{ mg}$ D. $1 \text{ cm} = 10^{-5}\text{km}$

15. The last digit of 7^{253} is   15.___
   A. 1   B. 5   C. 7   D. 9

16. Of the following, the property that the set {-1,0,1} does
    NOT possess is
    A. closure under addition
    B. closure under multiplication
    C. an identity element for multiplication
    D. inverse elements for addition

17. A pupil is informed that his percentile rank on a test
    given to a certain group is 70.
    This means that
    A. his score is in the upper 30% of the test scores of
       the group
    B. his score is in the lower 30% of the test scores of
       the group
    C. he answered 70 of the items correctly
    D. he answered 70% of the items correctly

18. A number written in base 7 is 1231_{seven}.

    This number written in base 5 is
    A. 3323_{five} B. 3233_{five} C. 1321_{five} D. 463_{five}

19. A television console is listed in a catalog for $1000.
    If the set is sold with successive discounts of 20% and
    10%, the ACTUAL selling price will be
    A. $700   B. $720   C. $780   D. $850

20. At a certain college, 1/3 of all applications sent to
    prospective students were never returned. Of those re-
    turned, 2/5 were rejected and 1/6 of those accepted decided
    not to attend.
    How many applications were sent out if 1,000 freshmen were
    admitted?
    A. 6000   B. 2000   C. 3000   D. 4500

KEY (CORRECT ANSWERS)

1. D		11. A	
2. B		12. A	
3. A		13. A	
4. A		14. A	
5. B		15. C	
6. C		16. A	
7. A		17. A	
8. C		18. A	
9. A		19. B	
10. D		20. C	

SOLUTIONS TO PROBLEMS

1. The first calculator's cost to the dealer = $15 ÷ 1.25 = $12.
    The second calculator's cost to the dealer = $15 ÷ .75 = $20.
    The combined effect for the dealer was ($15+$15) − ($12+$20) =
    −$2; thus a loss of $2.   (Ans. D)

2. Total value at the end of one year = $100(1.04)^2 = $108.16.
    (Ans. B)

3. Since 1 kilometer = 1000 meters, 380,000 km = (380,000)(1000) =
    380,000,000 or 3.8×10^8 m.   (Ans. A)

4. 14_{five} = (1)(5) + 4 = 9_{ten}. 123_{four} = (1)(16) + (2)(4) + 3 =

    27_{ten}.   The difference is 18, base 10.   (Ans. A)

5. Average = $\dfrac{(20)(.80) + (30)(.70)}{50}$ = .74 or 74%.   (Ans. B)

6. A kilometer is about $\dfrac{5}{8}$ of a mile.   (Ans. C)

7. The arithmetic mean = sum of numbers divided by the number
    of numbers.   (Ans. A)

8. If (A)(B)/6 is a whole number, we can conclude that either A
    or B or both A,B is(are) even. Furthermore, at least one of
    A,B must be divisible by 3.   (Ans. C)

9. The required amount of fuel = $15(\dfrac{5}{8} - \dfrac{5}{16})$ = $4\dfrac{11}{16}$.   (Ans. A)

10. Mr. Jones sold his house for ($50,000)(1.20) = $60,000.
    The new buyer sold the house for ($60,000)(1.20) = $72,000.
    Now, $72,000 is (72,000/50,000) × 100 = 144% of $50,000.
    (Ans. D)

11. $T = P(1 + \dfrac{R}{n})^{nt}$, where T = total, P = principal (investment),

    R = annual compounded rate, n = number of times per year being
    compounded, t = number of years.
    Thus, $T = 1000(1.03)^{20}$.   (Ans. A)

12. 2021_{three} = 2(27) + 0(9) + 2(3) + 1 = 61 in base 10. This is

    equivalent to 111101_{two}.   (Ans. A)

13. .00792 = 7.92 × .001 = 7.92×10^{-3}.   (Ans. A)

14. The CORRECT statement for A is 1 mm = 10^{-1} cm. (Ans. A)

15. 7^1 ends in 7, 7^2 ends in 9, 7^3 ends in 3, 7^4 ends in 1. This cycle is repeated, so that in order to find the last digit of 7^{253}, divide 253 by 4. The remainder of this division is 1, and thus corresponds to 7^1 which ends in 7. (Note that if there were no remainder, this would have been equivalent to a remainder of 4, corresponding to 7^4 which ends in 1.) (Ans. C)

16. Use the example 1 + 1 = 2, and 2 is not an element of {-1,0,1}. (Ans. A)

17. A percentile rank indicates the *relative* position of a score when the scores are arranged from LOWEST to HIGHEST. 70, as a percentile, means that *approximately* 70% of all the scores are LOWER and 30% of all the scores are HIGHER. (Ans. A)

18. 1231_{seven} = (1)(343) + (2)(49) + (3)(7) + 1 = 463.

    With base 5, the rightmost column is ones, next column is fives, next column is twenty-fives, fourth column is 125's. Now, 463 = (3)(125) + (3)(25) + (2)(5) + 3(1), so the answer is 3323_{five}. (Ans. A)

19. Discount of 20% = ($1000)(.80) + $800, followed by a Discount of 10%= ($800)(.90) = $720 = answer. (Ans. B)

20. Let x = number of applications sent out. Then, 2/3x = number of applications returned; (3/5)(2/3x) = 2/5x = number of applicants accepted; (5/6)(3/5x) = 1/3x decided to attend. Thus, 1/3x = 1000 and so x = 3000. (Ans. C)

———

TEST 5

DIRECTIONS: Each question or incomplete statement is followed by several suggested answers or completions. Select the one that BEST answers the question or completes the statement. *PRINT THE LETTER OF THE CORRECT ANSWER IN THE SPACE AT THE RIGHT.*

1. In a three digit number, the units digit is two more than the tens digit. The sum of the digits is 12. The number with the digits reversed is 198 less than the original number.
   The original number must be between
   A. 100 and 200   B. 200 and 300
   C. 400 and 500   D. 600 and 700

   1.___

2. If the tenth term of an arithmetic sequence is 15 and the twentieth term is 35, then the thirtieth term is
   A. 525   B. 50   C. 55   D. 61

   2.___

3. The expressions a+bc and (a+b)(a+c) are
   A. *never* equal   B. equal when a+b+c = 1
   C. *always* equal   D. equal when a+b+c = 0

   3.___

4. Four pupils answered a question. Pupil A's answer was 37.5×10^{-6}, Pupil B's answer was $\frac{3}{8} \times 10^{-6}$, Pupil C's answer was $\frac{15}{4} \times 10^{-5}$, and Pupil D's answer was $.000037\frac{1}{2}$.

   The answer that was NOT equivalent to the others was that of Pupil
   A. A   B. B   C. C   D. D

   4.___

5. If the original selling price of a certain article, including a profit of 40% of the cost, were $18.20, and if the profit were to be reduced to 30% of the cost, the selling price would become
   A. $13.39   B. $13.65   C. $16.38   D. $16.90

   5.___

6. If a 4% stock whose par value is $60.00 is purchased at a price that will make the investment yield a return of 5%, the purchase price is
   A. $30   B. $48   C. $75   D. $82

   6.___

7. If a piece of property was sold for $5,780 at a loss of 15% of the cost, the cost of the property was
   A. $4,913   B. $6,647   C. $6,800   D. $7,200

   7.___

8. If the single discount equivalent to three successive discounts is 38.8% and the first two discounts are 20% and 10%, then the third discount, in percent, is
   A. 8.8   B. 15   C. 17   D. 30

   8.___

9. The SMALLEST integral value of k (k≠0) that will make   9.
   8820k the cube of a positive integer is
      A. 100   B. 150   C. 1000   D. 1050

10. A wholesaler sells a certain article to the retailer at   10.
    a profit of 60% of the cost. The retailer then sells this
    article to the consumer at a profit of 25% of his cost.
    The consumer pays $14.40.
    The cost to the wholesaler was
       A. $7.20   B. $7.78   C. $10.80   D. $12.24

11. Two bicycles start traveling from the same point at the   11.
    same time. One heads due west at 8 mph and the other
    heads due south at 15 mph.
    They will be 51 miles apart in _____ hours.
       A. 2   B. approximately $2\frac{1}{4}$
       C. 3   D. 9

12. At the end of the first two years of school, a pupil   12.
    attains an average of 83% in eight majors.
    The average required in five majors in the third year
    at school in order to achieve an overall average of 85%
    is
       A. 86.5%   B. 87%   C. 88.2%   D. 89%

13. To win an election, a candidate needs 3/4 of the votes   13.
    cast.
    If after 2/3 of the votes have been counted, a candidate
    has 5/6 of what he needs, what part of the remaining votes
    does he still need?
       A. 1/8   B. 1/4   C. 3/8   D. 1/2

14. A sells an article for D dollars, less 20% and 10%. B   14.
    sells the same article for D dollars less 25%.
    What additional discount should B allow in order to match
    A's selling price?
       A. 1.8%   B. 2%   C. 4%   D. 5%

15. A radioactive isotope loses 1/3 of its strength during   15.
    the first minute of its existence, 1/3 of its remaining
    strength during the second minute, 1/3 of its remaining
    strength during the third minute, etc.
    How long, to the nearest minute, will it be before the
    isotope will have lost 87% of its original activity?
    _____ minutes.
       A. 2   B. 3   C. 4   D. 5

16. A refrigerator was originally marked to sell at a profit   16.
    of 66 2/3% of the cost. It was finally sold at a profit
    of 33 1/3% of the cost.
    What percent discount did the purchaser receive on the
    marked price?
       A. 15   B. 20   C. 25   D. 33 1/3

17. A store offers a discount of 30%. An additional discount, in percent, to make the combined discount equivalent to a single discount of 37% would be
    A. 7 B. 10 C. 23 D. 67

17. ___

18. A sample of brass contained $1\frac{3}{4}$ pounds of copper, $1\frac{1}{4}$ pounds of zinc, and 2 ounces of impurities.
    The number of pounds of copper in one ton of this type of brass is
    A. 560 B. 800 C. 1080 D. 1120

18. ___

19. When the temperature drops from 37°F to -8°F, the number of degrees the temperature on the Centigrade scale will fall during the same period is

    A. $7\frac{2}{9}$ B. 25 C. 49 D. 57

19. ___

20. As part of its aircraft officer training program, the Navy sends sailors to radio school. Of those who are sent to radio school, 1/3 drop out during the course. Of those who graduate, 4/5 are assigned to aircraft carriers.
    If 3/4 of these become officers, how many sailors should the Navy send to radio school if it needs 60 aircraft officers?
    A. 120 B. 150 C. 180 D. 300

20. ___

KEY (CORRECT ANSWERS)

1. D		11. C	
2. C		12. C	
3. C		13. C	
4. B		14. C	
5. D		15. D	
6. B		16. B	
7. C		17. B	
8. B		18. D	
9. D		19. B	
10. A		20. B	

SOLUTIONS TO PROBLEMS

1. Any three digit number can be represented as 100h + 10t + u.
    From the conditions of the problem, we get three equations:
    1) u - t = 2
    2) u + t + h = 12
    3) 100h + 10t + u = 100 u + 10t + h + 198 which reduces
       to -u + h = 2
    Solving, u = 4, t = 2, h = 6; so the answer is 624.
    (Ans. D)

2. The nth term of an arithmetic progression with first term x
    and difference d is x + (n-1)d. Thus, x + 9d = 15 and
    x + 19d = 35. Solving, x = -3 and d = 2. The thirtieth
    term is -3 + (29)(2) = 55. (Ans. C)

3. $(a+b)(a+c) = a^2 + ab + ac + bc$. In order for this expression
    to equal a+bc, we need $a^2 + ab + ac = a$, which implies
    a(a+b+c-1) = 0. Now, either a = 0 or a+b+c-1 = 0; i.e.,
    a+b+c = 1. Note that choice C does NOT give the FULL answer
    but is the BEST choice. (Ans. C)

4. Pupils A, C, and D have answers equivalent to .0000375,
    whereas Pupil B's answer is .000000375. (Ans. B)

5. Let C = cost. $18.20 = (1.40)(C), so C = $13.00.
    Now, the new profit = (13)(1.30) = $16.90. (Ans. D)

6. Let x = purchase price. Then, (60)(.04) = (x)(.05).
    Solving, x = $48. (Ans. B)

7. Let x = cost. 5780 = .85x. Thus, x = $6800. (Ans. C)

8. Let the original price = 1 (for simplicity). A single discount
    of 38.8% means the final sale price = .612. Two successive
    discounts of 20% and 10% would amount to a price of
    (.8)(.9) = .72. Letting x be the third discount, the final
    price = $.72(1 - \frac{x}{100})$. Thus, $.612 = .72(1 - \frac{x}{100})$.
    Solving, x = 15. (Ans. B)

9. $8820 = 2^2 \cdot 3^2 \cdot 5 \cdot 7^2$. In order to multiply this product by
    some factor so that the new number will be a perfect cube
    (and smallest non-zero perfect cube), the factor would be
    $2 \cdot 3 \cdot 5^2 \cdot 7 = 1050$. Note that (8820)(1050) = 9,261,000, which
    is $(210)^3$. (Ans. D)

10. Let c = wholesaler cost. The cost to the retailer = 1.6c and
    so the cost to the consumer becomes (1.6c)(1.25) = 2c.
    If 2c = $14.40, c = 7.20. (Ans. A)

11. Let h = number of hours. Then, $(8h)^2 + (15h)^2 = 51^2$, since
    the Pythagorean Theorem can be used. Solving, h = 3. (Ans. C)

12. An average of 83% for eight subjects means a total of 664 percentage points. Let x = average for the next five subjects, so that 5x = the total percentage points for these 5 subjects. To average 85% for all 13 subjects, 85% = (664+5x)/13. Solving, x = 88.2%. (Ans. C)

13. Let V = number of votes to be cast. After $\frac{2}{3}$V have been tallied, the candidate has $\frac{5}{6}$ of the $\frac{3}{4}$V he needs to win. $(\frac{5}{6})(\frac{3}{4}V) = \frac{5}{8}V$. From the remaining $\frac{1}{3}V$ votes he needs to be nominated, $\frac{3}{4}V - \frac{5}{8}V = \frac{1}{8}V$ times. Finally, $\frac{1}{8}V / \frac{1}{3}V = \frac{3}{8}$. (Ans. C)

14. Two consecutive discounts of 20% and 10% on D dollars means .90(.80D)= .72D is the selling price. If the first discount is 25%, the selling price is then .75D (B's first discount). In order to match .72D as the final selling price, a second discount of x% means (100-x)(.75D) = .72D. Then, x = 4%. (Ans. C)

15. Let x = number of minutes required. After x minutes, the isotope will retain $(\frac{2}{3})^x \cdot S$ of its strength, where S = original strength. We seek x such that the retention will be $\frac{13}{100} \cdot S$. Solving, $(\frac{2}{3})^x = \frac{13}{100}$ by Logs yields x = 5.03 or about 5 minutes. (Ans. D)

16. Let C = cost. Then, $1\frac{2}{3}C$ = original marked price. The item was finally sold at $1\frac{1}{3}C$. The percent discount on the marked price is $[(1\frac{2}{3} - 1\frac{1}{3})/1\frac{2}{3}][100]$ = 20%. (Ans. B)

17. Let P = original price. After one discount of 30%, the price is .708. If the second discount is x%, then the new price is $(\frac{100-x}{100})(.70P)$. Since the combined discount is equivalent to one 37% discount, $(\frac{100-x}{100})(.70P) = .63P$. Solving, x = 10. (Ans. B)

18. This sample contains $1\frac{3}{4} + 1\frac{1}{4} + \frac{1}{8} = 3\frac{1}{8}$ lbs. Let x = number of pounds of copper in 1 ton of this brass sample. $\frac{x}{2000} = \frac{1.75}{3.125}$. Solving by cross-multiplication, x = 1120. (Ans. D)

19. Use $C = \frac{5}{9}(F-32)$. 37°F converts to $2\frac{7}{9}$°C and -8°F converts to $-22\frac{1}{9}$°C. The drop is $24\frac{8}{9}$° or approx. 25°. (Ans. B)

20. Let x = number of sailors sent to school. Then, $\frac{2}{3}$x graduate. Subsequently, $(\frac{4}{5})(\frac{2}{3}x) = \frac{8}{15}x$ are assigned to aircraft carriers. Finally, $(\frac{3}{4})(\frac{8}{15}x) = \frac{2}{5}x$ = number of officers = 60. Thus, x = 150. (Ans. B)

READING COMPREHENSION
UNDERSTANDING WRITTEN MATERIAL

COMMENTARY

Questions on reading comprehension -- the ability to understand and interpret written materials -- are now universal, staple parts of almost all aptitude and achievement tests, as well as tests of general and mental ability.

By its very nature, the reading comprehension question is the most difficult of the question-types to cope with successfully, and, accordingly, it is usually weighted more heavily (assigned more credits) than other questions.

Generally, tests of aptitude and/or achievement derive their reading selections ("passages")from the several disciplines -- art, biology, chemistry, economics, education, engineering, history, literature, mathematics, music, philosophy, physics, political science, psychology, and sociology. Thus, the student or applicant is *not* being tested for specific knowledge of, or proficiency in, these areas. Rather, he is being tested on his understanding and comprehension of the meaning of the materials contained in the specific passages presented, the theory being that his mental ability will be *best* tested by his reading power, not by his training or acquired knowledge in the different fields,since it may be reasonably expected that such training and/or knowledge will differ among the candidates for a variety of reasons. The great equalizing element is the reading comprehension test. Therefore, all the information and material needed for answering the questions are imbedded in the passages themselves. *The power or skill or ability of the testee, then, is to be shown in the extent and degree to which he succeeds in making the correct answers to the questions in the reading passages.*

Historically, many colleges and universities, leaning on the theory of transfer of training, regard the reading comprehension factor as, perhaps the most important of all criteria in measuring scholastic aptitude since, according to this view, the ability to read with understanding and to go on from this point, is basic to all academic professional, graduate, and research work.

Let us examine just what reading comprehension means in the context described above and analyze its basic components.

The factor of reading ability is a complex one which may be tested and measured at several discrete levels of ability.

Comparatively, the easiest type of reading question is that which tests understanding of the material to be read -- to list facts or details as described in the passage, to explain the meanings of words or phrases used, to clarify references, etc.

The next level of difficulty is reached when the student is confronted with questions designed to show his ability to interpret and to analyze the material to be read, e.g., to discover the central thought of the passage, to ascertain the mood or point of view of the author, to note contradictions, etc.

The third stage consists of the ability to apply the principles and/or opinions expressed in the article, e.g., to surmise the recommendations that the writer may be expected to make later on or to formulate his stand on related issues.

The final and highest point is attained when the student is called upon to evaluate what he has read -- to agree with or to differ with the point of view of the writer, to accept or to refute the evidences or methods employed, to judge the efficacy or the inappropriateness of different proposals, etc.

All these levels will be broached and tested in this reading section.

SAMPLE PASSAGES - QUESTIONS AND ANSWERS

PASSAGE 1

(1) Our ignorance of the complex subject of social insurance was and remains colossal. (2) For years American business leaders delighted in maligning the British social insurance schemes. (3) Our industrialists condemned them without ever finding out what they were about. (4) Even our universities displayed no interest. (5) Contrary to the interest in this subject taken by organized labor abroad, our own labor movement bitterly opposed the entire program of social insurance up to a few years ago. (6) Since the success of any reform depends largely upon a correct public understanding of the principles involved, the adoption of social insurance measures presented peculiar difficulties for the United States under our Federal type of government of limited powers, our constitutional and judicial handicaps, our long conditioning to individualism, the traditional hostility to social reform by both capital and labor, the general inertia, and our complete lack of trained administrative personnel without which even the best law can be ineffective. (7) Has not bitter experience taught us that far more important than the passage of a law, which is at best only a declaration of intention, is a ready public opinion prepared to enforce it?

1. According to this writer, what attitude have we shown in this country toward social insurance?
   A. We have been extremely doubtful that it will work, but have been willing to give it a chance
   B. We have opposed it on the ground of a careful study of its defects
   C. We have shown an unintelligent and rather blind antagonism toward it
   D. We have been afraid that it would not work under our type of government
   E. We have resented it because of the extensive propaganda in favor of it

2. To what does the phrase, "our long conditioning to individualism," refer?
    A. Our habit of depending upon ourselves
    B. Our increasing dependence on the Federal Government
    C. Our long established distrust of "big business"
    D. Our policies of high protective tariff
    E. Our unwillingness to accept reforms

3. Which of these ideas is expressed in this passage?
    A. The surest way to cure a social evil is to get people to pass a law against it
    B. Legislation alone cannot effect social reforms
    C. The American people are seriously uninformed about all social problems
    D. Our type of government makes social reform practically impossible
    E. Capital and labor retard social progress

ANALYSIS

These are the steps you must take to answer the questions:
First, scan the passage quickly, trying to gather at a glance the general import.
Then, read the passage carefully and critically, underlining with a pencil, what are apparently leading phrases and concepts.
Next, read each question carefully, and seek the answer in definite parts -- sentences, clauses, phrases, figures of speech, adverbs, adjectives, etc. -- in the text of the passage.
Finally, select the one answer which *best* answers the question, that is, it *best* matches what the paragraph says or is *best* supported by something in the passage.

The passage is concerned with the advent of social insurance to the United States. The author makes several points in this connection:
    1. Our gross ignorance of, and lack of interest in, the subject.
    2. The bitter opposition to social insurance in this country, particularly, of organized labor.
    3. Special and augmented difficulties in the United States in respect to this area; enumeration of these factors.
    4. The ultimate, certain method of achieving reform.

Having firmly encompassed the central meaning and basic contents of the passage, let us now proceed to examine each of the stated questions and proposed answers.

Question 1. According to this writer, what attitude have we shown in this country toward social insurance?
    A. We have been extremely doubtful that it will work, but have been willing to give it a chance
        Sentences 1,2,3,4,5 drastically negate the second clause of this statement ("but we have been willing to give it a chance").

3

B. We have opposed it on the ground of a careful study of its defects
   This statement is completely refuted by sentences 2 and 3.

C. We have shown an unintelligent and rather blind antagonism toward it
   Just as A is fully denied by sentences 1-5, so these sentences fully affirm the validity of this statement.

D. We have been afraid that it would not work under our type of government
   This is one -- and only one -- of the several difficulties facing the success of social insurance. Thus, this answer is only *partially* true

E. We have resented it because of the extensive propaganda in favor of it
   Quite the contrary. Again, see sentences 1-5.

————

Looking back, you now see that the one suggested answer of the five (5) offered that *BEST* answers the question is item C., We have shown an unintelligent and rather blind antagonism toward it. The CORRECT answer, then, is C.

Question 2. To what does the phrase, "our long conditioning to individualism," refer?
   A. Our habit of depending upon ourselves
      When a phrase is quoted from the text, as in this question, we should immediately locate it, review the context, and then consider it *in the light of the meaning of the passage as a whole.*
      We find the quoted phrase in long sentence 6, beginning "Since the success ..."
      A is clearly the answer to question 2.
   Items B, C, D, E have little or no merit with reference to the meaning of the quoted phrase within the passage, and are, therefore, to be discarded as possible answers.

Question 3. Which of these ideas is expressed in this passage?
   A. The surest way to cure a social evil is to get people to pass a law against it
      This is clearly refuted by the last sentence, "Has not bitter experience ...... it?"
   B. Legislation alone cannot effect social reforms
      This is just as clearly supported by this same last sentence.
   C. The American people are seriously uninformed about all social problems
      There is no evidence in the passage to support this statement.
   D. Our type of government makes social reform practically impossibl
      Our democratic form of government does present serious handi-

4

caps to social reform, as stated in the next-to-last sentence, but does *not* make social reform "practically impossible."
E. Capital and labor retard social progress

    American business leaders and the labor movement both opposed social *insurance*. They did not, however, retard social *progress*.

PASSAGE 2

    Questions testing your ability to understand what you have read are included in most tests because this ability is essential in carrying out the duties of administrative, professional, and technical jobs. To do such jobs, employees must be able to read and interpret manuals and carry out various assignments in accordance with them.

    Here is a reading comprehension question. This sample is fairly difficult; it was answered correctly by less than half of a college sample. To answer this question, read the following paragraph and find the choice that is best supported by the paragraph.

    Most tropical forests are composed of a wide variety of species of trees, intermingled in great confusion. They can be exploited economically only if practically all the important species can be utilized. Only a few of them are now known on the world's markets, and those are chiefly cabinet woods, of which the supply and the possibilities for utilization are more or less limited. To market large quantities of the less-known timbers, particularly those which are more suited for common lumber and construction, a long process of education and economic pressure will be necessary to overcome the established habits and idiosyncrasies of the consuming nations.

1. *Select the alternative that is best supported by the passage.*
The trees that grow in tropical forests
    A. furnish many rare woods that are in great demand on world markets
    B. are in great part unsuited to general construction uses
    C. defy profitable economic marketing because of the profusion and confusion of their growth
    D. are susceptible of considerably wider use on world markets
    E. furnish the major part of the total amount of cabinet woods consumed in industry
                              ANALYSIS
    The first part of the sentence, "The trees that grow in tropical forests," precedes every one of the five choices, and you must decide which of the choices lettered A,B,C,D, or E to use in completing the sentence.
    D. "... are susceptible of considerably wider use on world markets" is the best choice. This sentence seems to mean that more tropical trees could be used in other countries. The last sentence in the paragraph says that under certain conditions there would be a market for large quantities of lesser known timbers. D is the answer.

5

A. "... furnish many rare woods that are in great demand on world markets" is wrong. The paragraph says, "Only a few of them are now known on the world's markets."

B. "... are in great part unsuited to general construction uses" is wrong. The paragraph states that more education and economic pressure are needed before wood from tropical trees can be marketed for general construction use, but it does not say that the trees are unsuitable for such use.

C. "... defy profitable economic marketing because of the profusion and confusion of their growth" is wrong. Although the paragraph does state some of the difficulties of profitably marketing wood from tropical forests, it does not say that the problem defies solution because of the profusion and intermingling of many species of trees.

E. "... furnish the major part of the total amount of cabinet woods consumed in industry" is wrong. E is not supported by the paragraph; it is a misinterpretation of a statement in the paragraph. The paragraph states that the tropical wood now known and used are chiefly cabinet woods (of which fine furniture is made); it does not say or imply that the greatest proportion of the wood used in cabinetmaking is tropical wood.

SUGGESTIONS FOR ANSWERING THE READING COMPREHENSION QUESTION

1. Be sure to answer the questions *only* on the basis of the passage, and not from any other source, unless specifically directed to do otherwise.
2. Note that the answers may not be found directly in the text. For the more difficult reading questions, answers are generally to be *inferred* or *derived* from the sense of one or more sentences, clauses, and even paragraphs.
3. Do not expect to find the bases for the answers in sequential parts of the textual material. The difficulty of questions is increased when the candidate is required to skip from one part of the passage to another without any order, i.e., Question 1 may have its root in the last sentence of the paragraph, let us say, and Question 5 may be based upon the second sentence, for example. This is a method of increasing the difficulty of the research and investigation required of the candidate.
4. When the question refers to a specific line, sentence, paragraph, or quotation, be sure to find this reference and to re-read it thoroughly. The answer to such a question is almost certain to be found in or near this reference in the passage.
5. Time for the reading question is limited, as it is for the examination as a whole. In other words, one must work speedily as well as effectively. The candidate, in seeking the answers to the reading questions, is not expected to go through all of the items in the thorough way presented in the sample questions above. That is, he has only to suit himself. It suffices, in order to attain to the right answer, to note mentally the basis for the answer in the text. There is no need to annotate your answer or to write out reasons for your answer. What we have attempted to do in the samples is to show that there is a definite and logical attack on this type of question, which, principally, consists of careful, critical

reading, research and investigation, and evaluation of the material. One must learn to arrive at the correct answer through this process rather than through hit-or-miss tactics or guessing. There is no reading comprehension question, logically or fairly devised, which cannot be answered by the candidate provided he goes about this task in a systematic, sustained manner.

6. The candidate may be assisted by this advanced technique. Often, the general sense of the passage when fully captured, rather than specific parts in the passage, will lead to the correct answer. Therefore, it is most important that the candidate read the passage for total meaning first. This type of general understanding will be most helpful in answering those questions which have no specific background in the text but, rather, must be inferred from what has been read.

7. Beware of the following pitfalls:

A. The categorical statement. -- You can almost be sure that any answer which uses the words solely, wholly, always, never, at all times, forever, etc., is wrong.

B. The too-easy answer. -- When the question appears to be so simple that it can be answered almost word for word by reference to the text, be particularly on your guard. You will, probably, find that the language of the question may have been inverted or changed or that some important word has been added or omitted, so that you are being tested for alertness and attention to details. For example, if, in a passage, a comparison is made between Country A and Country B, and you are told that Country A has twice the area of Country B, and the question contains an item which states that "it is clear that the area of Country B is greater than Country A," note how easily you can be beguiled into accepting this statement as true.

C. Questions requiring that the candidate show his understanding of the main point of a passage, e.g., to state the central theme, or to suggest a worthy title, must be answered on that basis alone. You may be sure that other worthy possibilities are available, but you should examine your choice from the points of view of both appropriateness and breadth. For the most part, answers that are ruled out will contain one, but not both of these characteristics.

D. Make up your mind now that some, but not all, of the material in the various passages in the reading comprehension questions will be useful for finding the answer. Sometimes, passages are made purposely long to increase the difficulty and to further confuse the harried candidates. However, do not disregard any of the textual material without first having given it a thorough reading.

E. If the question requires that you give the writer's opinion or feelings on possible future action, do just that, and do not substitute your own predilections or antidotes. Similarly, do not make inferences if there exists in the text a clear-cut statement of facts. Base your answer, preferably, on the facts; make inferences or assumptions when they are called for, or as necessary.

F. Do not expect the passages to deal with your subject field(s) alone. The passages offered will illustrate all the academic areas. While interest is a major factor in attaining to success, resolve now that you are going to wade through all the passages, in a thorough way, be they science or mathematics or economics or art. Unfamiliarity with a subject is no excuse on this type of test since the answers are to be based upon the reading passage alone.

In corollary fashion, should you encounter a passage dealing with a field with which you are familiar, do not permit your special knowledge to play a part in your answer. Answer only on the basis of the passage, as directed.

G. The hardest type of reading question is the one in which the fifth choice presented is "none of these." Should this phrase prove to be the correct answer, it would require a thorough, albeit rapid, examination of ALL the possibilities. This, of course, is time consuming and often frustrating.

H. A final word of advice at this point. On the Examination, leave the more difficult reading questions for the end. Try to answer those of lesser difficulty first. In this way, you will leave yourself maximum time for the really difficult part of the Examination

—

In accordance with the special challenge of the reading comprehension question, several selected passages, varying in subject matter style, length, and form, are presented for solution by the candidate However, the passages are all alike in one respect: they extend to the highest ranges of difficulty.

—

READING COMPREHENSION
EXAMINATION SECTION

DIRECTIONS FOR THIS SECTION:
  Each question or incomplete statement is followed by several suggested answers or completions. Select the one that *BEST* answers the question or completes the statement. *PRINT THE LETTER OF THE CORRECT ANSWER IN THE SPACE AT THE RIGHT.*

TEST 1

  In its current application to art, the term "primitive" is as vague and unspecific as the term "heathen" is in its application to religion. A heathen sect is simply one which is not affiliated with one or another of three or four organized systems of theology. Similarly, a primitive art is one which flourishes outside the small number of cultures which we have chosen to designate as civilizations. Such arts differ vastly and it is correspondingly difficult to generalize about them. Any statements which will hold true for such diverse aesthetic experiences as the pictographs of the Australians, the woven designs of the Peruvians, and the abstract sculptures of the African Negroes must be of the broadest and simplest sort. Moveover, the problem is complicated by the meaning attached to the term "primitive" in its other uses. It stands for something simple, undeveloped, and, by implication, ancestral to more evolved forms. Its application to arts and cultures other than our own is an unfortunate heritage from the nineteenth-century scientists who laid the foundations of anthropology. Elated by the newly enunciated doctrines of evolution, these students saw all cultures as stages in a single line of development and assigned them to places in this series on the simple basis of the degree to which they differed from European culture, which was blandly assumed to be the final and perfect flower of the evolutionary process. This idea has long since been abandoned by anthropologists, but before its demise it diffused to other social sciences and became a part of the general body of popular misinformation. It still tinges a great deal of the thought and writing about the arts of non-European peoples and has been responsible for many misunderstandings.

1. The *MAIN* purpose of the passage is to   1. ...
   A. explain the various definitions of the term "primitive"
   B. show that the term "primitive" can be applied validly
      to art
   C. compare the use of the term "primitive" to the use of
      the term "heathen"
   D. deprecate the use of the term "primitive" as applied
      to art
   E. show that "primitive" arts vary greatly among themselves
2. The nineteenth-century scientists believed that the theory 2. ...
   of evolution
   A. could be applied to the development of culture
   B. was demonstrated in all social sciences
   C. was substantiated by the diversity of "primitive" art
   D. could be applied only to European culture
   E. disproved the idea that some arts are more "primitive"
      than others
3. With which of the following would the author agree?   3. ...
   A. The term "primitive" is used only by the misinformed.

1

    B. "Primitive" arts may be as highly developed as "civilized" arts.

    C. The arts of a culture often indicated how advanced that culture was.

    D. Australian, Peruvian, and African Negro arts are much like the ancestral forms from which European art evolved.

    E. A simple culture is likely to have a simple art.

4. According to the author, many misunderstandings have been   4. ...
caused by the belief that

    A. most cultures are fundamentally different

    B. inferior works of art in any culture are "primitive" art

    C. "primitive" arts are diverse

    D. non-European arts are diverse

    E. European civilization is the final product of the evolutionary process

---

TEST 2

One of the ways the intellectual *avant-garde* affects the technical intelligentsia is through the medium of art, and art is, if only implicitly, a critique of experience. The turning upon itself of modern culture in the forms of the new visual art, the utilization of the detritus of daily experience to mock that experience, constitutes a mode of social criticism. Pop art, it is true, does not go beyond the surface of the visual and tactile experience of an industrial (and a commercialized) culture. Dwelling on the surface, it allows its consumers to mock the elements of their daily life, without abandoning it. Indeed, the consumption of art in the organized market for leisure serves at times to encapsulate the social criticism of the *avant-garde*. However, the recent engagement of writers, artists and theater people in contemporary issues suggests that this sort of containment may have begun to reach its limits.

In an atmosphere in which the intellectually dominant group insists on the contradictions inherent in daily experience, the technical intelligentsia will find it difficult to remain unconscious of those contradictions. The technical intelligentsia have until now avoided contradictions by accepting large rewards for their expertise. As expertise becomes increasingly difficult to distinguish from ordinary service on the one hand, and merges on the other with the change of the social environment, the technical intelligentsia's psychic security may be jeopardized. Rendering of labor services casts it back into spiritual proletarianization; a challenge to the social control exercised by elites, who use the technical intelligentsia's labor power, pushes it forward to social criticism and revolutionary politics. That these are matters, for the moment, of primarily spiritual import does not diminish their ultimate political significance. A psychological precondition for radical action is usually far more important than an "objectively" revolutionary situation -- whatever that may be.

The chances for a radicalization of the technical intelligentsia, thus extending the student revolt, cannot be even approximated. I believe I have shown there is a chance.

1. It may be *inferred* that the technical intelligentsia are: 1. ...
    I. The executives and employers in society
   II. Critics of *avant-garde* art
  III. Highly skilled technical workers
  The *CORRECT* answer is:
   A. I *only*   B. I and III C. I, II, and III
   D. III *only*   E. I and II
2. The engagement of the intellectual *avant-garde* in con-   2. ...
   temporary issues
    A. indicates that people tire of questioning the contra-
       dictions inherent in day-to-day living
    B. indicates that the technical intelligentsia are close
       to the point where they will rebel against the *avant-garde*
    C. could cause a challenge to the social control of the
       elites
    D. could cause the public to become more leisure-oriented
    E. could cause an increase in the consumption of art in
       the organized market for leisure services
3. The *possible* effect of the intellectual *avant-garde* on   3. ...
   the technical intelligentsia is that
    A. the intellectual *avant-garde* makes the technical
       intelligentsia conscious of society's contradictions
    B. rapid curtailment of large rewards for expertise will
       result
    C. it may cause a strong likelihood of a radicalization
       of the technical intelligentsia
    D. the *avant-garde* will replace the employment of the
       technical intelligentsia in contemporary issues
    E. the rendering of labor services will be eliminated
4. If it is assumed that the technical intelligentsia become   4. ...
   fully aware of the contradictions of modern life, it is
   the author's position that
    A. revolution will result
    B. the technical intelligentsia may refuse to perform
       manual labor
    C. the technical intelligentsia will be pushed forward
       to social criticism and revolutionary politics
    D. the technical intelligentsia will experience some
       psychic dislocation
    E. ordinary service will replace technical expertise
5. According to the author,   5. ...
    A. the state of mind of a particular group may have more
       influence on its action than the effect of environmental
       factors
    B. the influence of art will often cause social upheaval
    C. matters of primarily spiritual import necessarily lack
       political significance
    D. the detritus of day-to-day living should be mocked by
       the intellectual *avant-garde*
    E. the technical intelligentsia can only protect their
       psychic security by self-expression through art

6. *With which* of the following would the author *agree*?   6. ...
   I. As contradictions are less contained, the psychic
     security of all members of the working class would
     be jeopardized.
  II. The expertise of the technical intelligentsia evolved
     from the ownership and management of property.
 III. The technical intelligentsia are not accustomed to
     rendering labor services.
The *CORRECT* answer is:
  A. I only   B. III only   C. I and III
  D. II only   E. None of the above

7. The *MAIN* purpose of the passage is to   7. ...
  A. discuss the influence of the *avant-garde* art form on
    the expertise of the technical intelligentsia
  B. discuss the effect of the intellectual *avant-garde* on
    the working classes
  C. discuss the social significance of the technical
    intelligentsia
  D. discuss the possible effects of the deencapsulation
    of *avant-garde* social criticism
  E. point out that before a change psychological precon-
    ditions are first established

TEST 3

Turbulent flow over a boundary is a complex phenomenon for which
there is no really complete theory even in simple laboratory cases.
Nevertheless, a great deal of experimental data has been collected
on flows over solid surfaces, both in the laboratory and in nature,
so that, from an engineering point of view at least, the situation
is fairly well understood. The force exerted on a surface varies
with the roughness of that surface and approximately with the square
of the wind speed at some fixed height above it. A wind of 10 meters
per second (about 20 knots, or 22 miles per hour) measured at a heigh
of 10 meters will produce a force of some 30 tons per square kilomete
on a field of mown grass or of about 70 tons per square kilometer on
ripe wheat field. On a really smooth surface, such as glass, the for
is only about 10 tons per square kilometer.

When the wind blows over water, the whole thing is much more complicated. The roughness of the water is not a given characteristic
of the surface but depends on the wind itself. Not only that, the
elements that constitute the roughness - the waves - themselves move
more or less in the direction of the wind. Recent evidence indicates
that a large portion of the momentum transferred from the air into
the water goes into waves rather than directly into making currents
in the water; only as the waves break, or otherwise lose energy, does
their momentum become available to generate currents, or produce
Ekman layers. Waves carry a substantial amount of both energy and
momentum (typically about as much as is carried by the wind in a laye
about one wavelength thick), and so the wave-generation process is fa
from negligible.

A violently wavy surface belies its appearance by acting, as far
as the wind is concerned, as though it were very smooth. At 10 meter

per second, recent measurements seem to agree, the force on the surface is quite a lot less than the force over mown grass and scarcely more than it is over glass; some observations in light winds of two or three meters per second indicate that the force on the wavy surface is less than it is on a surface as smooth as glass.   In some way the motion of the waves seems to modify the airflow so that air slips over the surface even more freely than it would without the waves. This seems not to be the case at higher wind speeds, above about five meters per second, but the force remains strikingly low compared with that over other natural surfaces.

One serious deficiency is the fact that there are no direct ob-servations at all in those important cases in which the wind speed is greater than about 12 meters per second and has had time and fetch (the distance over water) enough to raise suhstantial waves. The few indirect studies indicate that the apparent roughness of the surface increases somewhat under high-wind conditions, so that the force on the surface increases rather more rapidly than as the square of the wind speed.

Assuming that the force increases at least as the square of the wind speed, it is evident that high-wind conditions produce effects far more important than their frequency of occurrence would suggest. Five hours of 60-knot storm winds will put more momentum into the water than a week of 10-knot breezes. If it should be shown that, for high winds, the force on the surface increases appreciably more rapidly than as the square of the wind speed, then the transfer of momentum to the ocean will turn out to be dominated by what happens during the occasional storm rather than by the long-term average winds.

1. According to the passage, several hours of storm winds   1. ...
   (60 miles per hour) over the ocean would
     A. be similar to the force exerted by light winds for
        several hours over glass
     B. create an ocean roughness which reduces the force
        exerted by the high winds
     C. have proved to be more significant in creating ocean
        momentum than light winds
     D. create a force not greater than 6 times the force of
        a 10-mile-per-hour wind
     E. eventually affect ocean current
2. According to the passage, a rough-like ocean surface   2. ...
     A. is independent of the force of the wind
     B. has the same force exerted against it by high and
        light winds
     C. is more likely to have been caused by a storm than
        by continuous light winds
     D. nearly always allows airflow to be modified so as to
        cause the force of the wind to be less than on glass
     E. is a condition under which the approximate square of
        wind speed can never be an accurate figure in measur-
        ing the wind force

3. The author indicates that, where a hurricane is followed   3. ...
by light winds of 10 meters per second or less,
  I. ocean current will be unaffected by the light winds
 II. ocean current will be more affected by the hurricane
    winds than the following light winds
III. the force of the light winds on the ocean would be
    less than that exerted on a wheat field
The *CORRECT* combination is:
  A. I only   B. III only   C. II and III
  D. I and III   E. II only
4. The *MAIN* purpose of the passage is to discuss   4. ...
  A. oceanic momentum and current
  B. turbulent flow of wind over water
  C. wind blowing over water as related to causing tidal
    flow
  D. the significance of high wind conditions on ocean
    momentum
  E. experiments in wind force
5. The author would be *incorrect* in concluding that the   5. ...
transfer of momentum to the ocean is dominated by the
occasional storm if
  A. air momentum went directly into making ocean current
  B. high speed winds slipped over waves as easily as low
    speed winds
  C. waves did not move in the direction of wind
  D. the force exerted on a wheat field was the same as
    on mown grass
  E. the force of wind under normal conditions increased
    as the square of wind speed
6. A wind of 10 meters per second measured at a height of   6. ...
10 meters will produce a force close to 30 tons per square
mile on *which* of the following?
  A. Unmown grass   B. Mown grass   C. Glass
  D. Water   E. A football field

TEST 4

Political scientists, as practitioners of a negligibley formalize
discipline, tend to be accommodating to formulations and suggested
techniques developed in related behavioral sciences. They even tend
on occasion, to speak of psychology, sociology and anthropology as
"hard core sciences." Such a characterization seems hardly justifie
The disposition to uncritically adopt into political science non-
indigenous sociological and general systems concepts tends, at times,
to involve little more than the adoption of a specific, and sometime
barbarous, academic vocabulary which is used to redescribe reasonabl
well-confirmed or intuitively-grasped low-order empirical generaliza
tions.

At its worst, what results in such instances is a runic explanation, a redescription in a singular language style, i.e., no explanation at all. At their best, functional accounts as they are
found in the contemporary literature provide explanation sketches,
the type of elliptical explanation characteristic of historical and

psychoanalytic accounts. For each such account there is an in-determinate number of equally plausible ones, the consequence of either the complexity of the subject matter, differing perspectives, conceptual vagueness, the variety of sometimes mutually exclusive empirical or quasi-empirical generalizations employed,or syntactical obscurity, or all of them together.

Functional explanations have been most reliable in biology and physiology (where they originated) and in the analysis of servo-mechanical and cybernetic systems (to which they have been effec-tively extended). In these areas we possess a well-standardized body of lawlike generalizations. Neither sociology nor political science has as yet the same resource of well-confirmed lawlike statements. Certainly sociology has few more than political science. What passes for functional explanation in sociology is all too frequently para-sitic upon suggestive analogy and metaphor, trafficking on our familiarity with goal directed systems.

What is advanced as "theory" in sociology is frequently a non-theoretic effort at classification or "codification," the search for an analytic conceptual schema which provides a typology or a classificatory system serviceable for convenient storage and ready retrieval of independently established empirical regularities. That such a schema takes on a hierarchic and deductive character, impart-ing to the collection of propositions a *prima facie* theoretical appearance, may mean no more than that the terms employed in the high-order propositions are so vague that they can accommodate al-most any inference and consequently can be made to any conceivable state of affairs.

1. The author *implies* that, when the political scientist is   1. ...
   at his best, his explanations
   A. are essentially a retelling of events
   B. only then form the basis of an organized discipline
   C. plausibly account for past occurrences
   D. are prophetic of future events
   E. are confirmed principles forming part of the
      political scientist's theory
2. With *which* of the following would the author probably   2. ...
   agree?
   I. Because of an abundance of reasonable explanations
      for past conduct, there is the possibility of contend-
      ing schools within the field of political science
      developing.
   II. Political science is largely devoid of predictive power.
   III. Political science has very few verified axioms.
   The *CORRECT* answer is:
   A. III only   B. I and III   C. I and II
   D. I, II, and III E. I only
3. The passage *implies* that many sociological theories   3. ...
   A. are capable of being widely applied to various situations
   B. do not even appear to be superficially theoretical in
      appearance
   C. contrast with those of political science in that there
      are many more confirmed lawlike statements
   D. are derived from deep analysis and exhaustive research
   E. appear theoretical but are really very well proved

4. The author's thesis would be *UNSUPPORTABLE if*   4. ...
    A. the theories of the political scientist possessed
       predictive power
    B. political science did not consist of redescription
    C. political scientists were not restricted to "hard
       core sciences"
    D. political science consisted of a body of theories
       capable of application to any situation
    E. None of the above
5. The author believes that sociology   5. ...
    A. as a "hard core science,"contains reliable and func-
       tional explanations
    B. is never more than a compilation of conceptual schema
    C. is in nearly every respect unlike political science
    D. is a discipline which allows for varied inferences to be
       drawn from its general propositions
    E. is a science indigenous to *prima facie* theoretical ap-
       pearance, containing very little codification posing
       as theory

TEST 5

James's own prefaces to his works were devoted to structural composition and analytics and his approach in those prefaces has only
recently begun to be understood. One of his contemporary critics,
with the purest intention to blame, wrote what might be recognized
today as sophisticated praise when he spoke of the later James as
"an impassioned geometer" and remarked that "what interested him was
not the figures but their relations, the relations which alone make
pawns significant." James's explanations of his works often are so
bereft of interpretation as to make some of our own austere defenses
against interpretation seem almost embarrassingly rich with psycholog
cal meanings. They offer, with a kind of brazen unselfconsciousness,
an astonishingly artificial, even mechanical view of novelistic in-
vention. It's not merely that James asserts the importance of technique; more radically, he tends to discuss character and situation
almost entirely as functions of technical ingenuities. The very
elements in a Jamesian story which may strike us as requiring the
most explanation are presented by James either as a *solution* to a
problem of compositional harmony or else as the *donnee* about which
it would be irrelevant to ask any questions at all.

James should constantly be referred to as a model of structuralist
criticism. He consistently redirects our attention from the referential aspect of a work of art (its extensions into "reality") to its
own structural coherence as the principal source of inspiration.

What is most interesting about James's structurally functional
view of character is that a certain devaluation of what we ordinarily
think of as psychological interest is perfectly consistent with an
attempt to portray reality. It's as if he came to feel that a kind
of autonomous geometric pattern, in which the parts appeal for their
value to nothing but their contributive place in the essentially abstract pattern, is the artist's most successful representation of
life. Thus he could perhaps even think that verisimilitude - a word
he liked - has less to do with the probability of the events the

novelist describes than with those processes, deeply characteristic of life, by which he creates sense and coherence from *any* event. The only faithful picture of life in art is not in the choice of a significant subject (James always argues against the pseudorealistic prejudice), but rather in the illustration of sense-, of design-making processes. James proves the novel's connection with life by deprecating its derivation from life; and it's when he is most abstractly articulating the growth of a structure that James is almost most successfully defending the mimetic function of art (and of criticism). His deceptively banal position that only execution matters means most profoundly that verisimilitude, properly considered, is the grace and the truth of a formal unity.

1. The author suggests that James, in explanations of his own art,
   A. was not bound by formalistic strictures but concentrated on verisimilitude
   B. was deeply psychological and concentrated on personal insight
   C. felt that his art had a one-to-one connection with reality
   D. was basically mechanical and concentrated on geometrical form
   E. was event-and-character-oriented rather than technique-oriented

   1. ...

2. The passage indicates that James's method of approaching reality was
   A. that objective reality did not exist and was patterned only by the mind
   B. that formalism and pattern were excellent means of approaching reality
   C. not to concentrate on specific events but rather on character development
   D. that the only objective reality is the psychological processes of the mind
   E. that in reality events occur which are not structured but rather as random occurrences

   2. ...

3. The *MAIN* purpose of the paragraph is to
   A. indicate that James's own approach to his work is only now beginning to be understood
   B. deprecate the geometrical approach towards the novel
   C. question whether James's novels were related to reality
   D. indicate that James felt that society itself could be seen as a geometric structure
   E. discuss James's explanation of his works

   3. ...

4. In discussing his own works, James
   I. talks of people and events as a function of technique to the exclusion of all else
   II. is quick to emphasize the referential aspect of the work
   III. felt that verisimilitude could be derived not from character but rather from the ordering of events
   The *CORRECT* answer is:
   A. I *only*   B. II *only*   C. III *only*
   D. I and III   E. I and II

   4. ...

5. The author   5. ...
   A. *approves* of James's explanations of his own work but
      disapproves his lack of discussion into the psycho-
      logical makings of his characters
   B. *disapproves* of James's explanation of his own work
      and his lack of discussion into the psychological
      makings of his characters
   C. *approves* of James's explanations of his works in
      terms of structure as being well related to life
   D. *disapproves* of James's explanation of his works in
      terms of structure as lacking verisimilitude
   E. *approves* of James's explanation of his works because
      of the significance of the subjects chosen
6. The *following* is *NOT* true of James's explanation of his   6. ...
   own works: He
   A. did not explain intriguing elements of a story except
      as part of a geometric whole
   B. felt the artist could represent life by its patterns
      rather than its events
   C. defended the imitative function of art by detailing
      the growth of a structure
   D. attempted to give the reader insight into the psychology
      of his characters by insuring that his explanation fol-
      lowed a strict geometrical pattern
   E. was able to devalue psychological interest and yet be
      consistent with an attempt to truly represent life
7. James believed it to be *essential* to   7. ...
   A. carefully choose a subject which would lend itself
      to processes by which sense and cohesion is achieved
   B. defend the mimetic function of art by emphasizing
      verisimilitude
   C. emphasize the manner in which different facets of a
      story   could fit together
   D. explain character in order to achieve literary harmony
   E. be artificial and unconcerned with representing life

TEST 6

The popular image of the city as it is now is a place of decay,
crime, of fouled streets, and of people who are poor or foreign or
odd. But what is the image of the city of the future? In the plans
for the huge redevelopment projects to come, we are being shown a
new image of the city. Gone are the dirt and the noise - and the
variety and the excitement and the spirit. That it is an ideal
makes it all the worse; these bleak new utopias are not bleak because they have to be; they are the concrete manifestation - and
how literally - of a deep, and at times arrogant, misunderstanding
of the function of the city.

Being made up of human beings, the city is, of course, a wonder-
fully resilient institution. Already it has reasserted itself as
an industrial and business center. Not so many years ago, there
was much talk of decentralizing to campus-like offices, and a wholesale exodus of business to the countryside seemed imminent. But a
business pastoral is something of a contradiction in terms, and for

the simple reason that the city is the center of things because it is a center, the suburban heresy never came off. Many industrial campuses have been built, but the overwhelming proportion of new office building has been taking place in the big cities.

But the rebuilding of downtown is not enough; a city deserted at night by its leading citizens is only half a city. If it is to continue as the dominant cultural force in American life, the city must have a core of people to support its theatres and museums, its shops and its restaurants - even a Bohemia of sorts can be of help. For it is the people who like living in the city who make it an attraction to the visitors who don't. It is the city dwellers who support its style; without them there is nothing to come downtown to.

The cities have a magnificant opportunity. There are definite signs of a small but significant move back from suburbia. There is also evidence that many people who will be moving to suburbia would prefer to stay in the city - and it would not take too much more in amenities to make them stay.

But the cities seem on the verge of muffing their opportunity - and muffing it for generations to come. In a striking failure to apply marketing principles and an even more striking failure of aesthetics, the cities are freezing on a design for living ideally calculated to keep everybody in suburbia. These vast, barracks-like superblocks are not designed for people who *like* cities, but for people who have no other choice. A few imaginative architects and planners have shown that redeveloped blocks don't have to be repellent to make money, but so far their ideas have had little effect. The institutional approach is dominant, and unless the assumptions embalmed in it are re-examined, the city is going to be turned into a gigantic bore.

1. The author would *NOT* be pleased with   1. ...
   A. a crowded, varied, stimulating city
   B. the dedication of new funds to the reconstruction of
      the cities
   C. a more detailed understanding of the poor
   D. the elimination of assumptions which do not reflect
      the function of the city
   E. the adoption of a laissez faire attitude by those in
      charge of redevelopment.
2. "The rebuilding of downtown" (1st sentence, 3d paragraph)   2. ...
   refers to
   A. huge redevelopment projects to come
   B. the application of marketing and aesthetic principles
      to rejuvenating the city
   C. keeping the city as the center of business
   D. attracting a core of people to support the city's
      functions
   E. the doing away with barracks-like structures
3. According to the author, the city, in order to better it-   3. ...
   self, *must*
   A. increase its downtown population
   B. attract an interested core of people to support its
      cultural institutions

C. adhere to an institutional approach rather than be
   satisfied with the status quo
D. erect campus-like business complexes
E. establish an ideal for orderly future growth

4. The *MAIN* purpose of the passage is to   4. ...
    A. show that the present people inhabiting the city do
       not make the city viable
    B. discuss the types of construction which should and
       should not take place in the city's future
    C. indicate that imaginative architects and planners have
       shown that redeveloped areas don't have to be ugly to
       make money
    D. discuss the human element in the city
    E. point out the lack of understanding by many city plan-
       ners of the city's functions

5. The author's thesis would be *LESS* supportable *if*   5. ...
     I. city planners presently understood that stereotyped
        reconstruction is doomed to ultimate failure
    II. the institutional approach referred to in the passage
        was based upon assumptions which took into account
        the function of the city
   III. there were signs that a shift back to the city from
        suburbia were occurring
   The *CORRECT* answer is:
       A. II *only*   B. II and III   C. I and II
       D. I *only*   E. III *only*

TEST 7

In estimating the child's conceptions of the world, the first
question is to decide whether external reality is as external and
objective for the child as it is for adults. In other words, can
the child distinguish the self from the external world? So long as
the child supposes that everyone necessarily thinks like himself,
he will not spontaneously seek to convince others, nor to accept
common truths, nor, above all, to prove or test his opinions. If
his logic lacks exactitude and objectivity it is because the social
impulses of maturer years are counteracted by an innate egocentricity
In studying the child's thought, not in this case in relation to
others but to things, one is faced at the outset with the analogous
problem of the child's capacity to dissociate thought from self in
order to form an objective conception of reality.

The child, like the uncultured adult, appears exclusively concerned with things. He is indifferent to the life of thought and
the originality of individual points of view escapes him. His
earliest interests, his first games, his drawings are all concerned
solely with the imitation of what is. In short, the child's thought
has every appearance of being exclusively realistic.

But realism is of two types, or, rather, objectivity must be distinguished from realism. Objectivity consists in so fully realizing
the countless intrusions of the self in everyday thought and the
countless illusions which result - illusions of sense, language,
point of view, value, etc. - that the preliminary step to every
judgment is the effort to exclude the intrusive self. Realism, on

the contrary, consists in ignoring the existence of self and thence regarding one's own perspective as immediately objective and absolute. Realism is thus anthropocentric illusion, finality - in short, all those illusions which teem in the history of science. So long as thought has not become conscious of self, it is a prey to perpetual confusions between objective and subjective, between the real and the ostensible; it values the entire content of consciousness on a single plane in which ostensible realities and the unconscious interventions of the self are inextricably mixed. It is thus not futile, but, on the contrary, indispensable to establish clearly and before all else the boundary the child draws between the self and the external world.

1. The result of a child's not learning that others think   1. ...
   differently than he does is that
      A. the child will not be able to function as an adult
      B. when the child has matured, he will be innately
         egocentric
      C. when the child has matured, his reasoning will be poor
      D. upon maturity, the child will not be able to distinguish
         thought from objects
      E. upon maturity, the child will not be able to make non-
         ego-influenced value judgments
2. Objectivity is the ability to   2. ...
      A. distinguish ego from the external world
      B. dissociate oneself from others
      C. realize that others have a different point of view
      D. distinguish illusion from realism
      E. dissociate ego from thought
3. When thought is *not* conscious of self,   3. ...
      A. one is able to draw the correct conclusions from his
         perceptions
      B. the apparent may not be distinguishable from the actual
      C. conscious thought may not be distinguishable from the
         unconscious
      D. the ego may influence the actual
      E. ontogony recapitulates phylogony
4. The *MAIN* purpose of the passage is to   4. ...
      A. argue that the child should be made to realize that
         others may not think like he does
      B. estimate the child's conception of the world
      C. explain the importance of distinguishing the mind
         from external objects
      D. emphasize the importance of non-ego-influenced per-
         spective
      E. show how the child establishes the boundary between
         himself and the external world
5. The author *implies* that, if an adult is to think logically, 5. ...
      A. his reasoning, as he matures, must be tempered by
         other viewpoints
      B. he must be able to distinguish one physical object
         from another
      C. he must be exclusively concerned with thought in-
         stead of things

D. he must be able to perceive reality without the intrusions of the self

E. he must not value the content of consciousness on a single plain

6. Realism, according to the passage, is   6. ...
   A. the realization of the countless intrusions of the self
   B. final and complete objectivity
   C. a desire to be truly objective and absolute
   D. the ability to be perceptive and discerning
   E. none of the above

7. The child who is exclusively concerned with things   7. ...
   A. thinks only objectively
   B. is concerned with imitating the things he sees
   C. must learn to distinguish between realism and anthropomorphism
   D. has no innate ability
   E. will, through interaction with others, often prove his opinions

TEST 8

Democracy is not logically antipathetic to most doctrines of natural rights, fundamental or higher law, individual rights, or any similar ideals - but merely asks citizens to take note of the fact that the preservation of these rights rests with the majority, in political processes, and does not depend upon a legal or constitutional Maginot line. Democracy may, then, be supported by believers in individual rights providing they believe that rights - or any transcendental ends - are likely to be better safeguarded under such a system. Support for democracy on such instrumental grounds may, of course, lead to the dilemma of loyalty to the system vs. loyality to a natural right - but the same kind of dilemma may arise for anyone, over any prized value, and in any political system, and is insoluble in advance.

There is unanimous agreement that - as a matter of fact and law, not of conjecture - no single right can be realized, except at the expense of other rights and claims. For that reason their absolute status, in some philosophic sense, is of little political relevance. Political policies involve much more than very general principles or rights. The main error of the older natural rights school was not that it had an absolute right, but that it had too many absolute rights. There must be compromise, and, as any compromise destroys the claim to absoluteness, the natural outcome of experience was the repudiation of all of them. And now the name of "natural right" can only creep into sight with the reassuring placard, "changing content gurranteed." Nor is it at all easy to see how any doctrine of inalienable, natural, individual rights can be reconciled with a political doctrine of common consent - except in an anarchist societ or one of saints. Every natural right ever put forward, and the lis are elusive and capricious, is every day invaded by governments, in the public interest and with widespread public approval.

To talk of relatively attainable justice or rights in politics is not to plump for a moral relativism - in the sense that all values are equally good. But while values may be objective, the specific value judgments and policies are inevitably relative to a context, and it is only when a judgment divorces context from general principle that it looks like moral relativism. Neither, of course, does the fact of moral diversity invalidate all moral rules.

Any political system, then, deals only with relatively attainable rights, as with relative justice and freedoms. Hence we may differ in given instances on specific policies, despite agreement on broad basic principles such as a right or a moral "ought"; and, per contra, we may agree on specific policies while differing on fundamental principles or long-range objectives or natural rights. Politics and through politics, law and policies, give these rights - and moral principles - their substance and limits. There is no getting away from the political nature of this or any other prescriptive ideal in a free society.

1. With *which* of the following would the author *agree?*   1. ...
    A. Natural and individual rights can exist at all only
       under a democracy.
    B. While natural rights may exist, they are only relative-
       ly attainable.
    C. Civil disobedience has no place in a democracy where
       natural rights have no philosophic relevance.
    D. Utilitarianism, which draws its criteria from the hap-
       piness and welfare of individuals, cannot logically be
       a goal of a democratic state.
    E. Some natural rights should never be compromised for
       the sake of political policy.
2. It can be *inferred* that a democratic form of government   2. ...
    A. can be supported by natural rightists as the best
       pragmatic method of achieving their aims
    B. is a form of government wherein fundamental or higher
       law is irrelevant
    C. will in time repudiate all inalienable rights
    D. forces a rejection of moral absolutism
    E. will soon exist in undeveloped areas of the world
3. The *MAIN* purpose of the passage is to   3. ...
    A. discuss natural rights doctrine
    B. compare and contrast democracy to individual rights
    C. discuss the reconciliation of a doctrine of inalien-
       able natural rights with a political system
    D. discuss the safegurrding of natural rights in a
       democratic society
    E. indicate that moral relativism is antipathetic to
       democracy
4. The author indicates that natural rights   4. ...
      I. are sometimes difficult to define
     II. are easily definable but at times unreconcilable with
         a system of government predicated upon majority rule
    III. form a basis for moral relativism
    The *CORRECT* answer is:
      A. I *only*   B. I *only*   C. I and II
      D. III *only*   E. II and III

5. The fact that any political system deals with relatively   5. ...
   attainable rights
   A. shows that all values are equally good or bad
   B. is cause for divorcing political reality from moral
      rules
   C. shows·that the list of natural rights is elusive and
      capricious
   D. is inconsistent with the author's thesis
   E. does not necessarily mean that natural rights do not
      exist
6. The passage indicates that an important conflict which   6. ...
   can exist in a democracy is the
   A. rights of competing groups, i.e., labor versus manage-
      ment
   B. adherence to the democratic process versus non-democratic
      actions by government
   C. difficulty in choosing between two effective compromises
   D. adherence to the democratic process versus the desire
      to support a specific right
   E. difficulty in reconciling conflict by natural rights

KEYS (CORRECT ANSWERS)

TEST 1	TEST 2	TEST 3	TEST 4
1. D	1. D	1. E	1. C
2. A	2. C	2. C	2. D
3. B	3. A	3. C	3. A
4. E	4. D	4. B	4. A
	5. A	5. B	5. D
	6. B	6. A	
	7. D		

TEST 5	TEST 6	TEST 7	TEST 8
1. D	1. D	1. C	1. B
2. B	2. C	2. E	2. A
3. E	3. B	3. B	3. C
4. C	4. E	4. D	4. A
5. C	5. C	5. A	5. E
6. D		6. E	6. D
7. C		7. B	

LISTENING COMPREHENSION

EXAMINATION SECTION

TEST 1

DIRECTIONS: In this part a passage will be read orally to you.
It is NOT written out in the test booklet so you
will have to listen carefully. After the reading of the
passage, you will answer the questions that follow.
Each question or incomplete statement is followed by
several suggested answers or completions. Select the
one that BEST answers the question or completes the
statement. *PRINT THE LETTER OF THE CORRECT ANSWER IN
THE SPACE AT THE RIGHT.*

Listening Passage

(The following passage is adopted from Paddy Chayefsky's television play *Printer's Measure*. Prior to this scene the father
has died, and now the mother is talking to her seventeen-year-
old son.)

I know you feel bitter against your sister, Tom. I know
you do. I can see every thought in your mind. You're going to
have to scrape and scrimp to put a sister through college. And
you're only seventeen years old. You'd like to be out kissing
girls instead of worrying under the burden of a grown man. Well,
it'll only be two years. She'll crowd in as much as humanly
possible and finish it off quick. She's very good at this physics,
and someday she may poke out some radium like Madame Curie, and
they'll make a moving picture out of her. You're as old-fashioned
as your father, and all that you see in women is a drudge to cook
your stew. Well, times have changed, and it's something marvel-
ous that a sister of yours has a turn of mind to explore atoms. I
can't tell you the pleasure it gives me to see her bent over her
books, and when she's not home, sometimes I open up her notes and
see these fantastic diagrams and pictures, and I never get over
the shock of it. If she was just an average student, I'd have
said to her long since, you've got to go to work. But she's
strong at this physics, Tom. She'll make something out of it.
They may not do a movie about her, but somewhere in some fine
thing for mankind, she'll have a finger. I'm not going to argue
from day to night about this with you, Tom, as I did with your
father. It's got to be clear between us.
When I was a girl, your father came to my father's house and
knocked at the door, and announced: "I'm after a bride." And he
and my father went into the other room and talked it out, and I
sat in the kitchen with my hands in my lap and waited to hear.
I thought nothing of it, because it was done that way when I was
a girl. But the world is changing, and if a woman's got a spark,
it's her right and privilege to make a thing of herself. It's
like this old friend of yours in the shop. The machine is there,
but he won't accept it. I'm not saying that it's good or bad that
a machine does a man out of his work, but the machine is here.

It's part of our world, and the thing to do is to make our lives better with the machine, not worse. If we cannot hold on to old things, we must make peace with the new. Your sister has a talent. You had best make peace with that, Tom.

1. The mother clearly realizes that her son   1.____
   A. wants a lot of money for himself
   B. is too young to understand the situation
   C. is jealous of his sister
   D. would rather have fun than have responsibility

2. The mother most likely holds this conversation with her   2.____
   son because she
   A. wants no more arguments
   B. is unsure of his response
   C. was asked to by the father
   D. needs to feel better about herself

3. The father's attitude toward his daughter's education   3.____
   could best be described as
   A. uninformed   B. questioning
   C. negative   D. indifferent

4. The mother supports her idea that times are changing by   4.____
   referring to
   A. Madame Curie   B. her own marriage
   C. motion pictures   D. science

5. Which words best describes how the mother felt about her   5.____
   own marriage?
   A. Disappointed   B. Resentful
   C. Satisfied   D. Accepting

6. The example of the son's friend in the machine shop sup-   6.____
   ports the idea that machines
   A. will not last very long
   B. must be used for peaceful purposes
   C. must be integrated into our world
   D. are not being accepted

7. The mother firmly believes that in the future her daughter 7.____
   will
   A. make a contribution to humanity
   B. be like Madame Curie
   C. be the subject of a movie
   D. marry a scientist

8. Which word best describes the mother's attitude toward   8.____
   her son?
   A. Protective   B. Approving
   C. Sympathetic   D. Apathetic

9. Compared with the father's thinking, the mother's thinking 9.____
   in this scene from the play could best be described as
   A. judgmental   B. progressive
   C. biased   D. faulty

10. Which statement best describes the mother's approach to 10.____
    life?
    A. Plan for the future.
    B. Remember the past.
    C. Take life one day at a time.
    D. Question your own decisions.

———

KEY (CORRECT ANSWERS)

1.	D	6.	C
2.	A	7.	A
3.	C	8.	C
4.	B	9.	B
5.	D	10.	A

———

TEST 2

DIRECTIONS: In this part a passage will be read orally to you.
It is NOT written out in the test booklet so you
will have to listen carefully. After the reading of the
passage, you will answer the questions that follow.
Each question or incomplete statement is followed by
several suggested answers or completions. Select the
one that BEST answers the question or completes the
statement. *PRINT THE LETTER OF THE CORRECT ANSWER IN
THE SPACE AT THE RIGHT.*

Listening Passage

(The following speech has been adapted from *A Citizen Is Entitled
to Vote* by Susan B. Anthony. At the time of the speech, women
were not guaranteed the right to vote.)

Friends and fellow citizens: — I stand before you tonight
under indictment for the alleged crime of having voted at the
last presidential election, without having a lawful right to vote.
It shall be my work this evening to prove to you that in thus
voting, I not only committed no crime, but, instead, simply exercised my *citizen's rights,* guaranteed to me and all United States
citizens by the National Constitution, beyond the power of any
State to deny.
The preamble of the Federal Constitution says:
"We, the people of the United States, in order to form a
more perfect union, establish justice, insure *domestic* tranquility,
provide for the common defense, promote the general welfare, and
secure the blessing of liberty to ourselves and our posterity, do
ordain and establish this Constitution for the United States of
America."
It was we, the people; not we, the white male citizens; but
we, the whole people, who formed the Union. And we formed it, not
to give the blessings of liberty, but to secure them; not to the
half of ourselves and the half of our posterity but to the whole
people — women as well as men. And it is a downright mockery to
talk to women of their enjoyment of the blessings of liberty while
they are denied the use of the only means of securing them provided by this democratic-republican government — the ballot.
For any State to make sex a qualification that must ever
result in the disfranchisement of one entire half of the people
is a violation of the supreme law of the land. By it the blessings
of liberty are forever withheld from women and their female posterity. To them this government has no just powers derived from
the consent of the governed. To them this government is not a
democracy. It is not a republic. It is a hateful oligarchy of
sex. An oligarchy of learning, where the educated govern the
ignorant, might be endured; but this oligarchy of sex, which makes
father, brothers, husband, sons, the oligarchs or rulers over the

mother and sisters, the wife and daughters of every household —
which ordains all men sovereigns, all women subjects, carries
dissension, discord and rebellion into every home of the nation.

Webster's Dictionary defines a citizen as a person in the
United States, entitled to vote and hold office.

The only question left to be settled now is: Are women
persons? And I hardly believe any of our opponents will have
the hardihood to say they are not. Being persons, then, women
are citizens; and no State has a right to make any law, or to
enforce any old law, that shall abridge their privileges or
immunities. Hence, every discrimination against women in the
constitutions and laws of the several States is today null and
void.

1. The speaker talks as if she were a   1._____
   A. defendant on trial
   B. chairperson of a committee
   C. legislator arguing for a new law
   D. judge ruling at a trial

2. The speaker broadens her appeal to her audience by   2._____
   showing how her case could affect all
   A. existing laws
   B. United States citizens
   C. women
   D. uneducated persons

3. The speaker quotes the preamble to the Constitution in   3._____
   order to
   A. impress the audience with her intelligence
   B. share common knowledge with her audience
   C. point out which part of the preamble needs to be
      changed
   D. add force to her argument

4. According to this speech, one reason for forming the   4._____
   Union was to
   A. establish aristocracy
   B. limit the powers of the states
   C. insure domestic harmony
   D. draw up a Constitution

5. According to the speaker, who formed the Union?   5._____
   A. Only one-half of the people.
   B. The whole people.
   C. White male citizens, *only*.
   D. Only the male citizens of all races.

6. When the speaker says that the blessings of liberty are   6._____
   forever withheld from women and their female posterity,
   she means that
   A. women of the present and the future will suffer
   B. all classes of women are discriminated against
   C. women of the past have been victimized
   D. female children of the poor will be the only ones
      affected

7. The speaker argues that government which denies women   7._____
the right to vote is not a democracy because its powers
do not come from the
    A. Constitution of the United States
    B. rights of the states
    C. consent of the governed
    D. vote of the majority

8. According to this speech, an oligarchy of sex would cause 8._____
    A. women to rebel against the government
    B. men to desert their families
    C. poor women to lose hope
    D. problems to develop in every home

9. In this speech, a citizen is defined as a person who has   9._____
the right to vote and also the right to
    A. change laws   B. acquire wealth
    C. speak publicly   D. hold office

10. The speaker argues that state laws which discriminate   10._____
against women are
    A. being changed   B. null and void
    C. helpful to the rich   D. supported only by men

KEY (CORRECT ANSWERS)

1.	A	6.	A
2.	B	7.	C
3.	D	8.	D
4.	C	9.	D
5.	B	10.	B

TEST 3

DIRECTIONS: In this part a passage will be read orally to you.
It is NOT written out in the test booklet so you
will have to listen carefully. After the reading of the
passage, you will answer the questions that follow.
Each question or incomplete statement is followed by
several suggested answers or completions. Select the
one that BEST answers the question or completes the
statement. *PRINT THE LETTER OF THE CORRECT ANSWER IN
THE SPACE AT THE RIGHT.*

Listening Passage

(The following passage is adapted from a speech entitled "Government Services — A Dangerous Addiction" delivered by Gerald J.
Thompson, secretary of the State of Washington Department of Social
and Health Services.)

We have a habit in this state — in the whole nation, for
that matter — a habit of turning our problems over to the government. As the head of a government agency which is expected
to deal with some of the worst of those problems, I've come to
see this as a dangerous habit — an addiction to government services which has all the characteristics normally associated with
serious drug addiction — the high cost and the prospect for a
painful withdrawal if and when we ever get around to kicking the
habit.
    We're hooked. We're a society of government-service junkies.
And I use the pronoun "we" deliberately. It's not the recipients
of services who are the real users. It's not the deaf, the blind,
the mentally retarded or the physically handicapped. It's not
the emotionally disturbed father or the deserted mother or the
confused and angry adolescent. It's not the abused child or the
neglected grandparent. They're the recipients, not the real users.
The real users are the rest of us, who use government services as
a substitute for individual and collective action on a direct and
personal scale. We allow problems to develop in our families, our
friends, our neighborhoods, our businesses and our communities —
and then when those problems reach crisis proportions, when they're
so obvious they can no longer be ignored, we hand them over to the
State or the Federal Government and say, "Here, you deal with this.
It's too much for us."...
    We've all heard of doctors who get a reputation as a "soft
touch" for prescriptions. You just go to one of them and complain
enough about almost anything, and he'll write out a prescription
for you. Sometimes I feel like one of those doctors; I feel that
the Department of Social and Health Services has a reputation as
a soft touch, only we deal in programs rather than pills.
    As far as I'm concerned, those days are over. We're con-
cerned about the problems and about our clients, but we're not
going to cave in every time somebody comes to us with a request —
or a demand — for new programs to deal with some crisis that
should have been addressed by the community.

We're pouring a billion dollars a year into management of crises, and we could probably double that and still not get a handle on the problems. If somebody in our society — not the government — began putting that sort of effort into attacking the root cause of these problems, then we'd begin to see some real improvements — a reduction in the incidence of alcoholism, fewer abused children, less crime, less family strife, a better life for the elderly. But I'm convinced we'll never see that sort of effort as long as we continue to provide marginally effective, crisis-oriented services which erode personal responsibilities and foster dependency.

What I'm proposing is not a miracle cure. I'm proposing that we all make some tough decisions about who's responsible for what, and then begin placing that responsibility where it belongs.

1. The speaker gains the attention of the audience at the   1.____
   beginning of the speech through the use of a
      A. rhetorical question   B. comparison
      C. patriotic appeal   D. personal example

2. The speaker believes that those who are truly responsible 2.____
   for the growth of social service programs are the
      A. worthy recipients who receive help
      B. powerful lobby groups who demand action
      C. government bureaucrats who are protecting their jobs
      D. individuals who refuse to accept social responsibility

3. According to the speaker, government has been a "soft   3.____
   touch" because it has
      A. developed too many programs for too many problems
      B. been too lenient in developing program guidelines
      C. shown more concern for the needs of recipients than
         the needs of taxpayers
      D. been spoiled by the willingness of the public to fund
         worthwhile programs

4. According to the speaker, fewer State and Federal pro-   4.____
   grams should be developed in the future because
      A. less money might be available for the programs
      B. the number of needy people is decreasing
      C. existing programs are becoming more effective
      D. problem solving should become a community responsibility

5. The speaker believes that doubling the amount of money   5.____
   spent on crisis management would be
      A. justifiable   B. unappreciated
      C. ineffective   D. wise

6. According to this speech, fewer government services would 6.____
   be necessary if
      A. problems were handled more efficiently in their
         early stages
      B. public officials were held more accountable for the
         programs

C. stricter eligibility requirements were used to define needs

D. costly duplication of services was eliminated

7. Marginally effective programs are those programs which the speaker feels   7.____
    A. treat only the visible signs of a crisis
    B. show the greatest cost savings
    C. work to reduce the number of people serviced by the program
    D. provide a minimum of services to a maximum of people

8. According to the speaker, present government programs tend to encourage the public's   8.____
    A. responsibility   B. anger
    C. dependency   D. despair

9. According to the speaker, the reduction of government services is   9.____
    A. a dream that will never be achieved
    B. a painful necessity that must be attempted
    C. a cruel approach to dealing with a problem
    D. an impossible task for a responsive government

10. The speaker's attitude might be considered somewhat surprising since his position is that of a   10.____
    A. political reporter
    B. candidate for office
    C. head of a government agency
    D. leader of a lobbying organization

KEY (CORRECT ANSWERS)

1.	B	6.	A
2.	D	7.	A
3.	A	8.	C
4.	D	9.	B
5.	C	10.	C

TEST 4

DIRECTIONS: In this part a passage will be read orally to you.
It is NOT written out in the test booklet so you
will have to listen carefully. After the reading of the
passage, you will answer the questions that follow.
Each question or incomplete statement is followed by
several suggested answers or completions. Select the
one that BEST answers the question or completes the
statement. *PRINT THE LETTER OF THE CORRECT ANSWER IN
THE SPACE AT THE RIGHT.*

Listening Passage

(The following passage has been adapted from "The Figgerin' of
Aunt Wilma" by James Thurber.)

When I was quite young, John Hance's grocery stood on the
south side of Town Street, just east of Fourth, in the Central
Market region of Columbus, Ohio. It was an old store even then,
forty-five years ago, and its wide oak floorboards had been worn
pleasantly smooth by the shoe soles of three generations of
customers. The place smelled of coffee, peppermint, vinegar, and
spices. Just inside the door on the left, a counter with a rounded
glass front held all the old-fashioned penny candies — gumdrops,
licorice whips, horehound, and the rest — some of them a little
pale with age.
Once, Mr. Hance gave me a stick of Yucatan gum, an astonishing
act of generosity since he had a sharp sense of the value of a
penny. Thrift was John Hance's religion. His store was run on
a strictly cash basis.
Mr. Hance was nearly seventy, a short man with white hair and
a white mustache and the most alert eyes that I can remember,
except perhaps Aunt Wilma Hudson's. Aunt Wilma lived on South
Sixth Street and always shopped at Mr. Hance's store. Mr. Hance's
eyes were blue and capable of a keen concentration that could
make you squirm. Aunt Wilma had black agate eyes that moved
restlessly and scrutinized everybody with bright suspicion. In
church, her glance would dart around the congregation seeking out
irreverent men and women whose expressions showed that they were
occupied with worldly concerns, or even carnal thoughts, in the
holy place. If she lighted on a culprit, her heavy, dark brows
would lower, and her mouth would tighten in righteous disapproval.
Aunt Wilma was as honest as the day is long, and as easily confused, when it came to what she called figgerin', as the night is
dark. Her clashes with Mr. Hance had become a family legend. He
was a swift and competent calculator, and nearly fifty years of
constant practice had enabled him to add up a column of figures
almost at a glance. He set down his columns swiftly on an empty
paper sack with a stubby black pencil. Aunt Wilma, on the other
hand, was slow and painstaking when it came to figgerin'. She
would go over and over a column of numbers, her glasses far down
on her nose, her lips moving soundlessly. To her, rapid calcula-
tion, like all the other reckless and impulsive habits of men,

was tainted with a kind of godlessness. Mr. Hance always sighed
when he looked up and saw her coming into his store. He knew that
she could lift a simple dollar transaction into a dim and mystic
realm of confusion all her own.

1. The speaker emphasizes the age of the store by remarking   1.____
   on the
       A. smells of the spices
       B. smoothness of the floorboards
       C. availability of penny candy
       D. presence of a coffeegrinder

2. What was the speaker's first reaction when Mr. Hance   2.____
   gave him a stick of Yucatan gum?
       A. Suspicion   B. Pride
       C. Delight   D. Amazement

3. One characteristic which Mr. Hance and Aunt Wilma shared   3.____
   was
       A. an enthusiasm for religion
       B. an ability to calculate swiftly
       C. the alertness of their eyes
       D. a sense of humor

4. Aunt Wilma thought that many people in church were   4.____
       A. praying to become better persons
       B. thinking unworthy thoughts
       C. sleeping during the sermon
       D. looking to her as a model

5. From this passage, the listener can most safely assume   5.____
   that when the speaker was in church he often
       A. looked at the other worshipers
       B. disagreed with the sermon
       C. whispered to others
       D. fell asleep

6. The speaker's amusement at the clashes between Mr. Hance   6.____
   and Aunt Wilma was shared by
       A. his neighbors   B. fellow church members
       C. his family   D. other customers

7. The relationship between Aunt Wilma and Mr. Hance was   7.____
   characterized by their
       A. suspicion of each other's honesty
       B. respect for each other's intelligence
       C. dislike of each other's personality
       D. distrust over each other's arithmetic

8. Aunt Wilma thought the ability to do arithmetical calcu-   8.____
   lations quickly was
       A. dishonest   B. magic
       C. unholy   D. lucky

9. What was the speaker's attitude toward Aunt Wilma?   9.____
   A. Affectionate   B. Disapproving
   C. Confused   D. Proud

10. In this passage, the speaker demonstrates his ability to 10.____
    A. create suspense   B. recall people
    C. communicate opinions   D. describe action

KEY (CORRECT ANSWERS)

1.	B	6.	C
2.	D	7.	D
3.	C	8.	C
4.	B	9.	A
5.	A	10.	B

English Expression
CHOICE OF EXPRESSION
COMMENTARY

One special form of the English Expression multiple-choice question in current use requires the candidate to select from among five (5) versions of a particular part of a sentence (or of an entire sentence), the one version that expresses the idea of the sentence most clearly, effectively, and accurately. Thus, the candidate is required not only to recognize errors, but also to choose the best way of phrasing a particular part of the sentence.

This is a test of choice of expression, which assays the candidate's ability to express himself correctly and effectively, including his sensitivity to the subleties and nuances of the language.

SAMPLE QUESTIONS

DIRECTIONS: In each of the following sentences some part of the sentence or the entire sentence is underlined. The underlined part presents a problem in the appropriate use of language. Beneath each sentence you will find five ways of writing the underlined part. The first of these indicates no change (that is, it repeats the original), but the other four are all different. If you think the original sentence is better than any of the suggested changes, you should choose answer A; otherwise you should mark one of the other choices. Select the best answer and blacken the corresponding space on the answer sheet.

This is a test of correctness and effectiveness of expression. In choosing answers, follow the requirements of standard written English; that is, pay attention to acceptable usage in grammar, diction (choice of words), sentence construction, and punctuation. Choose the answer that produces the most effective sentence -- clear and exact, without awkwardness or ambiguity. Do not make a choice that changes the meaning of the original sentence.

SAMPLE QUESTION 1

Although these states now trade actively with the West, and although they are willing to exchange technological information, their arts and thought, and social structure remains substantially similar to what it has always been.
A. remains substantially similar to what it has always been
B. remain substantially unchanged
C. remains substantially unchanged
D. remain substantially similar to what they have always been
E. remain substantially without being changed

The purpose of questions of this type is to determine the candidate's ability to select the clearest and most effective means of expressing what the statement attempts to say. In this example, the phrasing in the statement, which is repeated in **A**, presents a problem of agreement between a subject and its verb (their arts and thought and social structure and remains), a problem of agreement between a pronoun and its antecedent (their arts and thought and social structure and it), and a problem of precise and concise phrasing (remains substantially similar to what it has always been for remains substantially unchanged). Each of the four remaining choices in some way corrects one or more of the faults in the sentence, but only one deals with all three prob-

1

lems satisfactorily. Although C presents a more careful and concise wording of the phrasing of the statement and, in the process, eliminates the problem of agreement between pronoun and antecedent, it fails to correct the problem of agreement between the subject and its verb. In D, the subject agrees with its verb and the pronoun agrees with its antecedent, but the phrasing is not so accurate as it should be. The same difficulty persists in E. Only in B are all the problems presented corrected satisfactorily.

The question is not difficult.

SAMPLE QUESTION 2

Her latest novel is the largest in scope, the most accomplished in technique, and <u>it is more significant in theme than anything</u> she has written.

    A. it is more significant in theme than anything
    B. it is most significant in theme of anything
    C. more significant in theme than anything
    D. the most significant in theme than anything
    E. the most significant in theme of anything

This question is of greater difficulty than the preceding one.

The problem posed in the sentence and repeated in A, is essentially one of parallelism: Does the underlined portion of the sentence follow the pattern established by the first two elements of the series (<u>the largest</u> ... <u>the most accomplished</u>)? It does not, for it introduces a pronoun and verb (<u>it is</u>) that the second term of the series indicates should be omitted and a degree of comparison (<u>more significant</u>) that is not in keeping with the superlatives used earlier in the sentence. B uses the superlative degree of <u>significant</u> but retains the unnecessary <u>it is</u>; C removes the <u>it is</u>, but retains the faulty comparative form of the adjective. D corrects both errors in parallelism, but introduces an error in idiom (<u>the most</u> ...<u>than</u>). Only E corrects all the problems without introducing another fault.

SAMPLE QUESTION 3

Desiring to insure the continuity of their knowledge, <u>magical lore is transmitted by the chiefs</u> to their descendants.

    A. magical lore is transmitted by the chiefs
    B. transmission of magical lore is made by the chiefs
    C. the chiefs' magical lore is transmitted
    D. the chiefs transmit magical lore
    E. the chiefs make transmission of magical lore

The CORRECT answer is D.

SAMPLE QUESTION 4

<u>As Malcolm walks quickly and confident</u> into the purser's office, the rest of the crew wondered whether he would be charged with the theft.

    A. As Malcolm walks quickly and confident
    B. As Malcolm was walking quick and confident
    C. As Malcolm walked quickly and confident
    D. As Malcolm walked quickly and confidently
    E. As Malcolm walks quickly and confidently

The CORRECT answer is D.

The chairman, <u>granted the power to assign any duties to whoever he</u> <u>wished</u>,was still unable to prevent bickering.
  A. granted the power to assign any duties to whoever he wished
  B. granting the power to assign any duties to whoever he wished
  C. being granted the power to assign any duties to whoever he wished
  D. having been granted the power to assign any duties to whosoever he wished
  E. granted the power to assign any duties to whomever he wished

The CORRECT answer is E.

SAMPLE QUESTION 6
Certainly, well-seasoned products are more expensive, <u>but those</u> <u>kinds prove cheaper</u> in the end.
  A. but those kinds prove cheaper
  B. but these kinds prove cheaper
  C. but that kind proves cheaper
  D. but those kind prove cheaper
  E. but this kind proves cheaper

The CORRECT answer is A.

SAMPLE QUESTION 7
"We shall not," he shouted, "whatever the <u>difficulties," "lose</u> <u>faith in the success of our plan</u>!"
  A. difficulties," "lose faith in the success of our plan!"
  B. difficulties, "lose faith in the success of our plan"!
  C. "difficulties, lose faith in the success of our plan!"
  D. difficulties, lose faith in the success of our plan"!
  E. difficulties, lose faith in the success of our plan!"

The CORRECT answer is E.

SAMPLE QUESTION 8
<u>Climbing up the tree</u>, the lush foliage obscured the chattering monkeys.
  A. Climbing up the tree
  B. Having climbed up the tree
  C. Clambering up the tree
  D. After we had climbed up the tree
  E. As we climbed up the tree

The CORRECT answer is E.

EXAMINATION SECTION

DIRECTIONS FOR THIS SECTION:
  See DIRECTIONS for Sample Questions on page 1. *PRINT THE LETTER OF THE CORRECT ANSWER IN THE SPACE AT THE RIGHT.*

TEST 1

1. At the opening of the story, Charles Gilbert <u>has just come</u>   1. ...
   to make his home with his two unmarried aunts.
   - A. No change   B. hadn't hardly come   C. has just came
   - D. had just come   E. has hardly came
2. The sisters, who are no longer young, <u>are use to living</u> quiet 2. ...
   lives.
   - A. No change   B. are used to live
   - C. are use'd to living   D. are used to living
   - E. are use to live
3. They <u>willingly except</u> the child.   3. ...
   - A. No change   B. willingly eccepted
   - C. willingly accepted   D. willingly acepted
   - E. willingly accept
4. As the months pass, Charles' presence <u>affects many changes</u>   4. ...
   in their household.
   - A. No change   B. affect many changes
   - C. effects many changes   D. effect many changes
   - E. affected many changes
5. These changes <u>is not all together</u> to their liking.   5. ...
   - A. No change   B. is not altogether
   - C. are not all together   D. are not altogether
   - E. is not alltogether
6. In fact, they have some difficulty in adapting <u>theirselves</u>   6. ...
   to these changes.
   - A. No change   B. in adopting theirselves
   - C. in adopting themselves   D. in adapting theirselves
   - E. in adapting themselves
7. That is the man <u>whom I believe</u> was the driver of the car.   7. ...
   - A. No change   B. who I believed   C. whom I believed
   - D. who to believe E. who I believe
8. John's climb to fame was more rapid <u>than his brother's.</u>   8. ...
   - A. No change   B. than his brother
   - C. than that of his brother's D. than for his brother
   - E. than the brother
9. We knew that he <u>had formerly swam</u> on an Olympic team.   9. ...
   - A. No change   B. has formerly swum
   - C. did formerly swum   D. had formerly swum
   - E. has formerly swam
10. Not one of us loyal supporters <u>ever get a pass</u> to a game   10. ...
    - A. No change   B. ever did got a pass
    - C. ever has get a pass   D. ever had get a pass
    - E. ever gets a pass
11. He <u>was complemented</u> on having done a fine job.   11. ...
    - A. No change   B. was compliminted
    - C. was compleminted   D. was complimented
    - E. did get complimented

4

12. This play is different from the one we <u>had seen</u> last night.   12. ...
    A. No change   B. have seen   C. had saw
    D. have saw   E. saw

13. A row of trees <u>was planted</u> in front of the house.   13. ...
    A. No change   B. was to be planted C. were planted
    D. were to be planted E. are planted

14. The house <u>looked its age</u> in spite of our attempts to beauti-   14. ...
    fy it.
    A. No change   B. looks its age C. looked its' age
    D. looked it's age   E. looked it age

15. I do not know <u>what to council</u> in this case.   15. ...
    A. No change   B. where to council
    C. when to councel   D. what to counsel
    E. what to counsil

16. She is more capable <u>than any other girl</u> in the office.   16. ...
    A. No change   B. than any girl
    C. than any other girls   D. than other girl
    E. than other girls

17. At the picnic the young children <u>behaved very good</u>.   17. ...
    A. No change   B. behave very good
    C. behaved better   D. behave very well
    E. behaved very well

18. I resolved <u>to go irregardless of</u> the consequences.   18. ...
    A. No change   B. to depart irregardless of
    C. to go regarding of   D. to go regardingly of
    E. to go regardless of

19. The new movie has a number of actors <u>which have been famous</u>   19. ...
    on Broadway.
    A. No change   B. which had been famous
    C. who had been famous   D. that are famous
    E. who have been famous

20. I am certain that these books <u>are not our's</u>.   20. ...
    A. No change   B. have not been ours'
    C. have not been our's   D. are not ours
    E. are not ours'

21. <u>Each of your papers is filed</u> for future reference.   21. ...
    A. No change
    B. Each of your papers are filed
    C. Each of your papers have been filed
    D. Each of your papers are to be filed
    E. Each of your paper is filed

22. I wish that <u>he would take his work more serious</u>.   22. ...
    A. No change
    B. he took his work more serious
    C. he will take his work more serious
    D. he shall take his work more seriously
    E. he would take his work more seriously

23. <u>After the treasurer report had been read</u>, the chairman   23. ...
    called for the reports of the committees.
    A. No change
    B. After the treasure's report had been read
    C. After the treasurers' report had been read
    D. After the treasurerer's report had been read
    E. After the treasurer's report had been read

24. Last night the stranger <u>lead us down the mountain</u>.   24. ...
    A. No change
    B. leaded us down the mountain
    C. let us down the mountain
    D. led us down the mountain
    E. had led us down the mountain
25. It would not be safe <u>for either you or I</u> to travel in Viet   25. ...
Nam.
    A. No change   B. for either you or me
    C. for either I or you   D. for either of you or I
    E. for either of I or you

TEST 2

1. Both the body and the mind <u>needs exercise</u>.   1. ...
    A. No change   B. have needs of exercise
    C. is needful of exercise   D. needed exercise
    E. need exercise
2. <u>It's paw injured</u>, the animal limped down the road.   2. ...
    A. No change   B. It's paw injured
    C. Its paw injured   D. Its' paw injured
    E. Its paw injure
3. The butter <u>tastes rancidly</u>.   3. ...
    A. No change   B. tastes rancid
    C. tasted rancidly   D. taste rancidly
    E. taste rancid
4. <u>Who do you think</u> has sent me a letter?   4. ...
    A. No change   B. Whom do you think
    C. Whome do you think   D. Who did you think
    E. Whom can you think
5. If more nations <u>would have fought</u> against tyranny, the   5. ...
course of history would have been different.
    A. No change   B. would fight
    C. could have fought   D. fought
    E. had fought
6. Radio and television programs, along with other media of   6. ...
communication, <u>helps us to appreciate the arts and to keep
informed</u>.
    A. No change
    B. helps us to appreciate the arts and to be informed
    C. helps us to be appreciative of the arts and to keep
       informed
    D. helps us to be appreciative of the arts and to be
       informed
    E. help us to appreciate the arts and to keep informed
7. Music, <u>for example most always</u> has listening and viewing   7. ...
audiences numbering in the hundreds of thousands.
    A. No change   B. for example, most always
    C. for example, almost always D. for example nearly always
    E. for example, near always
8. When operas are performed on radio or television, <u>they</u>   8. ...
<u>effect the listener</u>.
    A. No change   B. they inflict the listener
    C. these effect the listeners D. they affects the listeners
    E. they affect the listener

9. <u>After hearing them the listener wants</u> to buy recordings   9. ...
of the music.
    A. No change
    B. After hearing them, the listener wants
    C. After hearing them, the listener want
    D. By hearing them the listener wants
    E. By hearing them, the listener wants

10. <u>To we Americans</u> the daily news program has become important. 10. ...
    A. No change   B. To we the Americans
    C. To us Americans   D. To us the Americans
    E. To we and us Americans

11. This has resulted from <u>it's coverage of a days' events</u>.   11. ...
    A. No change
    B. from its coverage of a days' events
    C. from it's coverage of a day's events
    D. from its' coverage of a day's events
    E. from its coverage of a day's events

12. In schools, <u>teachers advice their students</u> to listen to or   12. ...
to view certain programs.
    A. No change
    B. teachers advise there students
    C. teachers advise their students
    D. the teacher advises their students
    E. teachers advise his students

13. In these ways <u>we are preceding toward the goal</u> of an edu-   13. ...
cated and an informed public.
    A. No change
    B. we are preeceding toward the goal
    C. we are preceeding toward the goal
    D. we are proceding toward the goal
    E. we are proceeding toward the goal

14. The cost of living <u>is raising again</u>.   14. ...
    A. No change   B. are raising again
    C. is rising again   D. are rising again
    E. is risen again

15. We did not realize that the boys' father <u>had forbidden</u>   15. ...
<u>them to keep there puppy</u>.
    A. No change
    B. had forbade them to keep there puppy
    C. had forbade them to keep their puppy
    D. has forbidden them to keep their puppy
    E. had forbidden them to keep their puppy

16. <u>Her willingness to help others'</u> was her outstanding char-   16. ...
acteristic.
    A. No change
    B. Her willingness to help other's,
    C. Her willingness to help others's
    D. Her willingness to help others
    E. Her willingness to help each other

17. Because he did not have an invitation, <u>the girls objected</u>   17. ...
to him going,
    A. No change
    B. the girls object to him going
    C. the girls objected to him's going
    D. the girls objected to his going
    E. the girls object to his going

18. Weekly dances <u>have become a popular accepted feature</u> of   18. ...
    the summer schedule.
    A. No change
    B. have become a popular accepted feature
    C. have become a popular excepted feature
    D. have become a popularly excepted feature
    E. have become a popularly accepted feature

19. I <u>couldn't hardly believe</u> that he would desert our party.   19. ...
    A. No change   B. would hardly believe
    C. didn't hardly believe D. should hardly believe
    E. could hardly believe

20. I found the place in the book <u>more readily than she.</u>   20. ...
    A. No change   B. more readily than her
    C. more ready than she   D. more quickly than her
    E. more ready than her

21. A good example of American outdoor activities <u>are sports.</u>   21. ...
    A. No change   B. is sports   C. are sport
    D. are sports events   E. are to be found in sports

22. My point of view is <u>much different from your's.</u>   22. ...
    A. No change
    B. much different than your's
    C. much different than yours
    D. much different from yours
    E. much different than yours'

23. The cook <u>was suppose to use two spoonfuls</u> of dressing for   23. ...
    each serving.
    A. No change
    B. was supposed to use two spoonsful
    C. was suppose to use two spoonsful
    D. was supposed to use two spoonsfuls
    E. was supposed to use two spoonfuls

24. If anyone has any doubt about the values of the tour,<u>refer</u>   24. ...
    <u>him to me.</u>
    A. No change   B. refer him to I   C. refer me to he
    D. refer them to me   E. refer he to I

25. We expect that the affects of <u>the trip will be beneficial.</u>   25. ...
    A. No change
    B. the effects of the trip will be beneficial
    C. the effects of the trip should be beneficial
    D. the affects of the trip would be beneficial
    E. the effects of the trip will be benificial

TEST 3

1. <u>That, my friend</u> is not the proper attitude.   1. ...
    A. No change   B. That my friend
    C. That my friend,   D. That -- my friend
    E. That, my friend,

2. The girl refused <u>to admit that the not was her's.</u>   2. ...
    A. No change   B. that the note were her's
    C. that the note was hers'   D. that the note was hers
    E. that the note might be hers

8

3. There <u>were fewer candidates that we had been lead</u> to expect.   3. ...
   A. No change
   B. was fewer candidates than we had been lead
   C. were fewer candidates than we had been lead
   D. was fewer candidates than we had been led
   E. were fewer candidates than we had been led

4. When I first saw the car, <u>its steering wheel was broke</u>.   4. ...
   A. No change
   B. its' steering wheel was broken
   C. it's steering wheel had been broken
   D. its steering wheel were broken
   E. its steering wheel was broken

5. I find that the essential spirit for <u>we beginners is missing</u>.   5. ...
   A. No change
   B. we who begin are missing
   C. us beginners are missing
   D. us beginners is missing
   E. we beginners are missing

6. I believe that <u>you had ought</u> to study harder.   6. ...
   A. No change   B. you should have ought
   C. you had better   D. you ought to have
   E. you ought

7. This is <u>Tom, whom I am sure</u>, will be glad to help you.   7. ...
   A. No change   B. Tom whom, I am sure,
   C. Tom, whom I am sure, D. Tom who I am sure,
   E. Tom, who, I am sure,

8. His father or his mother <u>has read to him</u> every night since   8. ...
   he was very small.
   A. No change   B. did read to him
   C. have been reading to him D. had read to him
   E. have read to him

9. He <u>become</u> an authority on the theater and its great person-   9. ...
   alities.
   A. No change   B. becomed an authority
   C. become the authority D. became an authority
   E. becamed an authority

10. I know of no other person in the club <u>who is more kind-</u>   10. ...
    <u>hearted than her</u>.
    A. No change
    B. who are more kind-hearted than they
    C. who are more kind-hearted than them
    D. whom are more kind-hearted than she
    E. who is more kind-hearted than she

11. After Bill <u>had ran the mile</u>, he was breathless.   11. ...
    A. No change   B. had runned the mile
    C. has ran the mile   D. had ranned the mile
    E. had run the mile

12. Wilson <u>has scarcely no equal</u> as a pitcher.   12. ...
    A. No change   B. has scarcely an equal
    C. has hardly no equal D. had scarcely no equal
    E. has scarcely any equals

13. It <u>was the worse storm</u> that the inhabitants of the island   13. ...
    could remember.
    A. No change   B. were the worse storm
    C. was the worst storm D. was the worsest storm
    E. was the most worse storm

9

14. If only <u>we had began</u> before it was too late!   14. ...
    A. No change   B. we had began
    C. we would have begun   D. we had begun
    E. we had beginned
15. <u>Lets evaluate</u> our year's work.   15. ...
    A. No change   B. Let us' evaluate
    C. Lets' evaluate   D. Lets' us evaluate
    E. Let's evaluate
16. This is an organization <u>with which I wouldn't want to be</u>   16. ...
    <u>associated with</u>.
    A. No change
    B. with whom I wouldn't want to be associated with
    C. that I wouldn't want to be associated
    D. with which I would want not to be associated with
    E. with which I wouldn't want to be associated
17. The enemy fled in many directions, <u>leaving there weapons</u>   17. ...
    on the field.
    A. No change   B. leaving its weapons
    C. letting their weapons   D. leaving alone there weapons
    E. leaving their weapons
18. I hoped that John <u>could effect a compromise between</u> the   18. ...
    approved forces.
    A. No change
    B. could accept a compromise between
    C. could except a compromise between
    D. would have effected a compromise among
    E. could effect a compromise among
19. I was surprised to learn <u>that he has not always spoke Eng-</u>   19. ...
    <u>lish</u> fluently.
    A. No change
    B. that he had not always spoke English
    C. that he did not always speak English
    D. that he has not always spoken English
    E. that he could not always speak English
20. The lawyer promised <u>to notify my father and I</u> of his plans   20. ...
    for a new trial.
    A. No change
    B. to notify I and my father
    C. to notify me and our father
    D. to notify my father and me
    E. to notify mine father and me
21. The most important feature of the series of tennis lessons   21. ...
    <u>were the large amount</u> of strokes taught.
    A. No change
    B. were the large number
    C. was the large amount
    D. was the largeness of the amount
    E. was the large number
22. That the prize proved to be beyond her reach <u>did not sur-</u>   22. ...
    <u>prise him</u>.
    A. No change
    B. has not surprised him
    C. had not ought to have surprised him
    D. should not surprise him
    E. would not have surprised him

23. I am not <u>all together in agreement</u> with the author's point   23. ...
    of view.
      A. No change   B. all together of agreement
      C. all together for agreement D. altogether with agreement
      E. altogether in agreement
24. Windstorms have recently established a record which meteor- 24. ...
    ologists hope <u>will not be equal</u> for many years to come.
      A. No change   B. will be equal
      C. will not be equalized D. will be equaled
      E. will not be equaled
25. A large number of Shakespeare's soliloquies must be consi- 25. ...
    dered <u>as representing thought</u>, not speech.
      A. No change
      B. as representative of speech, not thought
      C. as represented by thought, not speech
      D. as indicating thought, not speech
      E. as representative of thought, more than speech

TEST 4

1. A sight to inspire fear <u>are wild animals on the lose</u>.   1. ...
     A. No change
     B. are wild animals on the loose
     C. is wild animals on the loose
     D. is wild animals on the lose
     E. are wild animals loose
2. For many years, the settlers <u>had been seeking to workship as</u> 2. ...
   <u>they please</u>.
     A. No change
     B. had seeked to workship as they pleased
     C. sought to workship as they please
     D. sought to have worshiped as they pleased
     E. had been seeking to worship as they pleased
3. The girls stated that the dresses were <u>their's</u>.   3. ...
     A. No change B. there's C. theirs   D. theirs'
     E. there own
4. <u>Please fellows</u> don't drop the ball.   4. ...
     A. No change B. Please, fellows C. Please fellows;
     D. Please, fellows,   E. Please! fellows
5. Your sweater <u>has laid</u> on the floor for a week.   5. ...
     A. No change   B. has been laying
     C. has been lying   D. laid
     E. has been lain
6. I wonder whether <u>you're sure that scheme of yours'</u> will work. 6. ...
     A. No change
     B. your sure that scheme of your's
     C. you're sure that scheme of yours
     D. your sure that scheme of yours
     E. you're sure that your scheme's
7. Please let <u>her and me</u> do it.   7. ...
     A. No change   B. she and I   C. she and me
     D. her and I   E. her and him

8. I expected him to be angry <u>and to scold</u> her.   8. ...
   A. No change   B. and that he would scold
   C. and that he might scold D. and that he should scold
   E. , scolding

9. Knowing little about algebra, <u>it was difficult to solve the</u>   9. ...
<u>equation</u>.
   A. No change
   B. the equation was difficult to solve
   C. the solution to the equation was difficult to find
   D. I found it difficult to solve the equation
   E. it being difficult to solve the equation

10. He <u>worked more diligent</u> now that he had become vice presi-   10. ...
dent of the company.
   A. No change   B. works more diligent
   C. works more diligently   D. began to work more diligent
   E. worked more diligently

11. <u>Flinging himself at the barricade</u> he pounded on it furious-   11. ...
ly.
   A. No change
   B. Flinging himself at the barricade: he
   C. Flinging himself at the barricade - he
   D. Flinging himself at the barricade; he
   E. Flinging himself at the barricade, he

12. When he <u>begun to give us advise,</u> we stopped listening.   12. ...
   A. No change   B. began to give us advise
   C. begun to give us advice   D. began to give us advice
   E. begin to give us advice

13. John was only one of the boys <u>whom as you know was</u> not   13. ...
eligible.
   A. No change   B. who as you know were
   C. whom as you know were   D. who as you know was
   E. who as you know is

14. Why <u>was Jane and he</u> permitted to go?   14. ...
   A. No change   B. was Jane and him
   C. were Jane and he   D. were Jane and him
   E. weren't Jane and he

15. <u>Take courage Tom: we</u> all make mistakes.   15. ...
   A. No change   B. Take courage Tom - we
   C. Take courage, Tom; we   D. Take courage, Tom we
   E. Take courage! Tom: we

16. Henderson, the president of the class and <u>who is also cap-</u>   16. ...
<u>tain of the team</u>, will lead the rally.
   A. No change
   B. since he is captain of the team
   C. captain of the team
   D. also being captain of the team
   E. who be also captain of the team

17. Our car has always <u>run good</u> on that kind of gasoline.   17. ...
   A. No change   B. run well   C. ran good
   D. ran well   E. done good

18. There was a serious difference of opinion <u>among her and I</u>.   18. ...
   A. No change   B. among she and I
   C. between her and I   D. between her and me
   E. among her and me

19. "This is most unusual," said <u>Helen, "the</u> mailman has never   19. ...
    been this late before."
    A. No change   B. Helen, "The   C. Helen - "The
    D. Helen; "The   E. Helen." The
20. The three main characters in the story are Johnny Hobart a   20. ...
    <u>teenager, his mother a widow, and</u> the local druggist.
    A. No change
    B. teenager; his mother, a widow; and
    C. teenager; his mother a widow; and
    D. teenager, his mother, a widow and
    E. teenager, his mother, a widow; and
21. How much <u>has food costs raised</u> during the past year?   21. ...
    A. No change
    B. have food costs rose
    C. have food costs risen
    D. has food costs risen
    E. have food costs been raised
22. "Will you come <u>too" she pleaded</u>?   22. ...
    A. No change   B. too,?"she pleaded.
    C. too?" she pleaded.   D. too," she pleaded?
    E. too, she pleaded?"
23. If he <u>would have drank</u> more milk, his health would have been   23. ...
    better.
    A. No change   B. would drink   C. had drank
    D. had he drunk E. had drunk
24. Jack had <u>no sooner laid down and fallen asleep when</u> the   24. ...
    alarm sounded.
    A. No change
    B. no sooner lain down and fallen asleep than
    C. no sooner lay down and fell asleep when
    D. no sooner laid down and fell asleep than
    E. no sooner lain down than he fell asleep when
25. Jackson is <u>one of the few Sophomores, who has</u> ever made the   25. ...
    varsity team.
    A. No change
    B. one of the few Sophomores, who have
    C. one of the few sophomores, who has
    D. one of the few sophomores who have
    E. one of the few sophomores who has

—

TEST 5

1. The lieutenant had ridden almost a kilometer when the scat-   1. ...
   tering shells <u>begin landing</u> uncomfortably close.
   A. No change   B. beginning to land C. began to land
   D. having begun to land   E. begin to land
2. <u>Having studied eight weeks</u>, he now feels sufficiently pre-   2. ...
   pared for the examination.
   A. No change
   B. For eight weeks he studies so
   C. Due to eight weeks of study
   D. After eight weeks of studying
   E. Since he's been spending the last eight weeks in study

13

3. <u>Coming from the Greek, and the word "democracy" means govern-</u>   3. ...
   <u>ment by the people.</u>
      A. No change
      B. "Democracy," the word which comes from the Greek, means
         government by the people.
      C. Meaning government by the people, the word "democracy"
         comes from the Greek.
      D. Its meaning being government by the people in Greek, the
         word is "democracy."
      E. The word "democracy" comes from the Greek and means go-
         vernment by the people.

4. Moslem universities were one of the chief agencies <u>in the de-</u>   4. ...
   <u>velopment</u> and spreading Arabic civilization.
      A. No change   B. in the development of
      C. to develop   D. in developing
      E. for the developing of

5. The water of Bering Strait <u>were closing</u> to navigation by ice   5. ...
   early in the fall.
      A. No change   B. has closed   C. have closed
      D. had been closed   E. closed

6. The man, <u>since he grew up</u> on the block, felt sentimental when   6. ...
   returning to it.
      A. No change   B. having grown up
      C. growing up   D. since he had grown up
      E. whose growth had been

7. <u>Jack and Jill watched the canoe to take their parents out of</u>   7. ...
   <u>sight round the bend of the creek.</u>
      A. No change
      B. The canoe, taking their parents out of sight, rounds the
         bend as Jack and Jill watch.
      C. Jack and Jill watched the canoe round the bend of the
         creek, taking their parents out of sight.
      D. The canoe rounded the bend of the creek as it took their
         parents out of sight, Jack and Jill watching.
      E. Jack and Jill watching, the canoe is rounding the bend of
         the creek to take their parents out of sight.

8. Chaucer's best-known work is THE CANTERBURY TALES, a collec-   8. ...
   tion of stories <u>which he tells</u> with a group of pilgrims as
   they travel to the town of Canterbury.
      A. No change   B. which he tells through   C. who tell
      D. told by   E. told through

9. The Estates-General, the old feudal assembly of France, <u>had</u>   9. ...
   <u>not met</u> for one hundred and sevety-five years when it con-
   vened in 1789.
      A. No change   B. has not met   C. has not been meeting
      D. had no meeting   E. has no meeting

10. Just forty years ago, <u>there had been</u> fewer than one hundred   10. ...
    symphony orchestras in the United States.
       A. No change   B. there had   C. there were
       D. there was   E. there existed

11. Mrs. Smith complained that her son's temper tantrums <u>aggra-</u>   11. ...
    <u>gravated her</u> and caused her to have a headache.
       A. No change   B. gave her aggravation
       C. were aggravating to her   D. aggravated her condition
       E. instigated

12. A girl <u>like I</u> would never be seen in a place like that.   12. ...
    A. No change   B. as I   C. as me   D. like I am   E. like me
13. <u>Between you and me</u>, my opinion is that this room is certain- 13. ...
    ly nicer than the first one we saw.
        A. No change   B. between you and I   C. among you and me
        D. betwixt you and I   E. between we
14. It is important to know for <u>what kind of a person you are</u>   14. ...
    <u>working.</u>
        A. No change
        B. what kind of a person for whom you are working
        C. what kind of person you are working
        D. what kind of person you are working for
        E. what kind of a person you are working for
15. I had <u>all ready</u> finished the book before you came in.   15. ...
    A. No change   B. already   C. previously   D. allready   E. all
16. <u>Ask not for who the bell tolls, it tolls for thee.</u>   16. ...
        A. No change
        B. Ask not for whom the bell tolls, it tolls for thee.
        C. Ask not whom the bell tolls for; it tolls for thee.
        D. Ask not for whom the bell tolls; it tolls for thee.
        E. Ask not who the bell tolls for: It tolls for thee.
17. It is a far better thing I do, than <u>ever I did</u> before.   17. ...
        A. No change   B. never I did   C. I have ever did
        D. I have ever been done   E. ever have I done
18. <u>Ending a sentence with a preposition is something up with</u>   18. ...
    <u>which I will not put.</u>
        A. No change
        B. Ending a sentence with a preposition is something with
           which I will not put up.
        C. To end a sentence with a preposition is that which I
           will not put up with.
        D. Ending a sentence with a preposition is something of
           which I will not put up.
        E. Something I will not put up with is ending a sentence
           with a preposition.
19. Everyone <u>took off their hats and stand up</u> to sing the nation-19. ...
    al anthem.
        A. No change
        B. took off their hats and stood up
        C. take off their hats and stand up
        D. took off his hat and stood up
        E. have taken off their hats and standing up
20. <u>She promised me that if she had the opportunity she would</u>   20. ...
    <u>have came irregardless of the weather.</u>
        A. No change
        B. She promised me that if she had the opportunity she
           would have come regardless of the weather.
        C. She assured me that had she had the opportunity she
           would have come regardless of the weather.
        D. She assured me that if she would have had the opportu-
           nity she would have come regardless of the weather.
        E. She promised me that if she had had the opportunity she
           would have came irregardless of the weather.

21. The man decided it would be advisable to marry a girl some-   21. ...
    what younger than him.
        A. No change   B. somehow younger than him
        C. some younger than him   D. somewhat younger from him
        E. somewhat younger than he

22. Sitting near the campfire, the old man told John and I about 22. ...
    many exciting adventures he had had.
        A. No change
        B. John and me about many exciting adventures he had.
        C. John and I about much exciting adventure which he'd had.
        D. John and me about many exciting adventures he had had.
        E. John and me about many exciting adventures he has had.

23. If you had stood at home and done your homework, you would   23. ...
    not have failed the course.
        A. No change
        B. If you had stood at home and done you're homework,
        C. If you had staid at home and done your homework,
        D. Had you stayed at home and done your homework,
        E. Had you stood at home and done your homework,

24. The children didn't, as a rule, do anything beyond what   24. ...
    they were told to do.
        A. No change   B. do hardly anything beyond
        C. do anything except   D. do hardly anything except for
        E. do nothing beyond

25. Either the girls or him is right.   25. ...
        A. No change
        B. Either the girls or he is
        C. Either the girls or him are
        D. Either the girls or he are
        E. Either the girls nor he is

KEYS (CORRECT ANSWERS)

TEST 1		TEST 2		TEST 3		TEST 4		TEST 5	
1. A	11. D	1. E	11. E	1. E	11. E	1. C	11. E	1. C	11.
2. D	12. E	2. C	12. C	2. D	12. B	2. E	12. D	2. A	12.
3. E	13. A	3. B	13. E	3. E	13. C	3. C	13. B	3. E	13.
4. C	14. A	4. A	14. C	4. E	14. D	4. D	14. C	4. D	14.
5. D	15. D	5. E	15. E	5. D	15. E	5. C	15. C	5. D	15.
6. E	16. A	6. E	16. D	6. E	16. E	6. C	16. C	6. B	16.
7. E	17. E	7. C	17. D	7. E	17. E	7. A	17. B	7. C	17.
8. A	18. E	8. E	18. E	8. A	18. A	8. A	18. D	8. D	18.
9. D	19. E	9. B	19. E	9. D	19. D	9. D	19. E	9. A	19.
10. E	20. D	10. C	20. A	10. E	20. D	10. E	20. B	10. C	20.
	21. A		21. B		21. E		21. C		21. E
	22. E		22. D		22. A		22. C		22. D
	23. E		23. E		23. E		23. E		23. D
	24. D		24. A		24. E		24. B		24. A
	25. B		25. B		25. A		25. D		25. B

WRITTEN ENGLISH EXPRESSION
EXAMINATION SECTION

TEST 1

1. The revised procedure was quite different than the one   1.___
                   A   B   C
    which was employed up to that time.   No error
          D   E

2. Blinded by the storm that surrounded him, his plane   2.___
       A   B
    kept going in circles.   No error
         C   D   E

3. They should give the book to whoever they think deserves   3.___
            A   B   C
    it.   No error
    D   E

4. The government will not consent to your firm sending that   4.___
         A   B   C
    package as second class matter.   No error
                D   E

5. She would have avoided all the trouble that followed if   5.___
        A   B
    she would have waited ten minutes longer.   No error
        C   D   E

6. His poetry, when it was carefully examined, showed   6.___
    A   B
    characteristics not unlike Wordsworth.   No error
        C   D   E

7. <u>In my opinion</u>, based upon long years of research, <u>I think</u>
     A   B
   the plan offered by my opponent is <u>unsound</u>, because it is
                                       C
   not <u>founded</u> on true facts.   <u>No error</u>
         D   E

8. The soldiers of <u>Washington's</u> army at Valley Forge <u>were</u> men
                A   B
   ragged in <u>appearance</u> but <u>who were</u> noble in character.
               C   D
   <u>No error</u>
     E

9. Rabbits <u>have a distrust</u> of man <u>due to</u> the fact <u>that</u> they
              A   B   C
   are <u>so often</u> shot.   <u>No error</u>
        D   E

10. <u>This</u> is the man <u>who</u> I believe <u>is</u> best <u>qualified</u> for the
    A   B   C   D
   position.   <u>No error</u>
              E

11. Her voice was <u>not only</u> <u>good</u>, but <u>she</u> also very clearly
               A   B   C
   <u>enunciated</u>.   <u>No error</u>
     D   E

12. <u>Today he</u> is wearing a <u>different</u> suit <u>than</u> the <u>one</u> he wore
    A   B   C   D
   yesterday.   <u>No error</u>
              E

13. Our work <u>is</u> to improve the club; if anybody <u>must</u> resign,
           A   B
   let it <u>not</u> be you or <u>I</u>.   <u>No error</u>
         C   D   E

14. There was so much talking <u>in back of</u> me <u>as</u> I <u>could</u> not
                            A   B   C
   <u>enjoy</u> the music.   <u>No error</u>
     D   E

15. <u>Being that</u> he is that <u>kind of boy</u>, he cannot be blamed
      A   B   C
   <u>for</u> the mistake.   <u>No error</u>
    D   E

16. The king, having read the speech, he and the queen   16.___
              A   B   C
    departed.   No error
       D   E

17. I am so tired I can't scarcely stand.   No error   17.___
    A   B   C   D   E

18. We are mailing bills to our customers in Canada, and,   18.___
             A   B
    being eager to clear our books before the new season opens,
    C
    it is to be hoped they will send their remittances promptly.
          D
    No error
      E

19. I reluctantly acquiesced to the proposal. No error   19.___
    A   B   C   D   E

20. It had lain out in the rain all night. No error   20.___
    A   B   C   D   E

21. If he would have gone there, he would have seen a   21.___
           A   B   C
    marvelous sight. No error
       D   E

22. The climate of Asia Minor is somewhat like Utah. No error   22.___
            A   B   C   D   E

23. If everybody did unto others as they would wish others to   23.___
      A   B   C   D
    do unto them, this world would be a paradise. No error
                                     E

24. This was the jockey whom I saw was most likely to win the   24.___
    A   B   C   D
    race. No error
         E

25. The only food the general demanded was potatoes. No error   25.___
      A   B   C   D   E

KEY (CORRECT ANSWERS)

1. C		11. C	
2. A		12. C	
3. E		13. D	
4. B		14. B	
5. C		15. A	
6. D		16. A	
7. B		17. C	
8. D		18. C	
9. B		19. E	
10. E		20. E	

21. A
22. D
23. D
24. B
25. E

TEST 2

DIRECTIONS: In each of the sentences below, four portions are underlined and lettered. Read each sentence and decide whether any of the UNDERLINED parts contains an error in spelling, punctuation, or capitalization, or employs grammatical usage which would be inappropriate for carefully written English. If so, note the letter printed under the unacceptable form and indicate this choice in the space at the right. If all four of the underlined portions are acceptable as they stand, select the answer E.
(No sentence contains more than ONE unacceptable form.)

1. A party like that only comes once a year. No error
          A   B   C   D   E
                                                      1.___

2. Our's is a swift moving age. No error
    A   B C   D   E
                                                    2.___

3. The healthy climate soon restored him to his accustomed
        A   B   C   D
   vigor. No error
         E
                                                    3.___

4. They needed six typists and hoped that only that many
    A   B   C
   would apply for the position. No error
    D   E
                                                    4.___

5. He interviewed people whom he thought had something
      A   B   C
   to impart. No error
    D   E
                                                  5.___

6. Neither of his three sisters is older than he. No error
    A   B   C D   E
                                                  6.___

7. Since he is that kind of a boy, he cannot be expected to
    A   B   C   D
   cooperate with us. No error
                  E
                                                7.___

8. When passing through the tunnel, the air pressure affected
    A   B   C
   our ears. No error
    D   E
                                                8.___

9. The story having a sad ending, it never achieved popularity   9.
   A   B   C
   among the students.   No error
   D   E

10. Since we are both hungry, shall we go somewhere for lunch?   10.
    A   B   C   D
    No error
    E

11. Will you please bring this book down to the library and   11.
    A   B   C
    give it to my friend, who is waiting for it?   No error
                   D   E

12. You may have the book; I am finished with it.   No error   12.
        A   B   C   D   E

13. I don't know if I should mention it to her or not.   13.
      A   B   C   D
    No error
    E

14. Philosophy is not a subject which has to do with philo-   14.
                        A   B   C
    sophers and mathematics only.   No error
                            D   E

15. The thoughts of the scholar in his library are little   15.
                                A
    different than the old woman who first said, "It's no use
              B   C
    crying over spilt milk."   No error
                        D   E

16. A complete system of philosophical ideas are implied in   16.
               A   B   C
    many simple utterances.   No error
                D   E

17. Even if one has never put them into words, his ideas   17.
         A   B   C
    compose a kind of a philosophy.   No error
    D   E

18. Perhaps it is well enough that most people do not attempt   18.
             A   B   C
    this formulation.   No error
         D   E

19. <u>Leading their</u> ordered lives, this <u>confused</u> <u>body</u> of ideas
       A   B   C
    and feelings <u>is</u> sufficient.   <u>No error</u>   19.___
                 D   E

20. Why <u>should</u> we <u>insist upon</u> <u>them</u> <u>formulating</u> it? <u>No error</u> 20.___
         A   B   C   D   E

21. <u>Since</u> it includes <u>something</u> of the wisdom of the ages, it 21.___
     A   B
    is <u>adequate</u> for the <u>purposes</u> of ordinary life. <u>No error</u>
        C   D   E

22. Therefore, I <u>have sought</u> to make a pattern <u>of mine,</u> <u>and so</u> 22.___
                  A   B   C
    there were early moments of <u>my trying</u> to find out what were
                                 D
    the elements with which I had to deal. <u>No error</u>
                                              E

23. I <u>wanted</u> <u>to get</u> <u>what</u> knowledge I <u>could</u> about the general 23.___
       A   B   C   D
    structure of the universe. <u>No error</u>
                                  E

24. I wanted to <u>know</u> <u>if</u> life <u>per se</u> had any meaning or 24.___
                 A   B   C
    <u>whether</u> I must strive to give it one. <u>No error</u>
     D   E

25. <u>So,</u> in a <u>desultory</u> way, I <u>began</u> <u>to read.</u> <u>No error</u> 25.___
     A   B   C   D   E

KEY (CORRECT ANSWERS)

1. C		11. B	
2. A		12. C	
3. A		13. B	
4. C		14. D	
5. B		15. B	
6. A		16. B	
7. D		17. A	
8. A		18. C	
9. A		19. A	
10. E		20. C	

21. E
22. C
23. C
24. B
25. E

TEST OF STANDARD WRITTEN ENGLISH *(ESSAY)*

QUESTIONS AND MODEL ANSWERS

CONTENTS

QUESTIONS AND MODEL ANSWERS

QUESTION I – EXCELLENCE IN EDUCATION

The modern school is a cooperative venture in education, involving the child, the parent, the school administration, and the community.

In a well-organized essay of *at least 450 words*, discuss the ways in which each of the four mentioned above may contribute to the objective of excellence in education.

ANALYSIS OF THE QUESTION

1. Your composition is to be a *well-organized essay*. Since the question itself gives you the four major areas to be discussed, a good arrangement is to have an introductory paragraph, four middle paragraphs devoted to the topics stated, and a paragraph of conclusion.
2. The beginning paragraph should restate and comment on the *objective of excellence in education* and indicate that each of the areas will be analyzed and developed.
3. In developing the four middle paragraphs, be sure to include logically reasoned concepts and to link them all together with skillful transitions. You are asked to see each area in itself and in its relationship to the others in a *cooperative venture*.
4. The concluding paragraph should reaffirm the central idea of *cooperation* and indicate its importance.
5. Although it is stated that the paper will be rated ONLY for written English, be sure to deal with the matter of the question DIRECTLY AND SPECIFICALLY. You may lose much credit by wandering from the point, because you would then not really be answering the question.
6. Arouse and maintain interest in each of your central paragraphs by using topic sentences and clincher sentences which vitalize the concept.
7. Do not talk vaguely of the child, the parent, and such. The question asks for *ways in which they contribute to excellence in education*.
8. In meeting the requirement of length, plan carefully to include all designated areas.

PLAN OF THE ESSAY

The overall plan of the model below consists of:

1. An opening paragraph which goes directly to the topic, the components of excellence in education.

2. A body which devotes separate paragraphs to the:
    a. child, his interests and aptitudes;
    b. parent, his role in school matters;
    c. school administration, its plans and programs;
    d. community, adjunct to the school and cultural resource.

3. A brief statement of conclusion which stresses the idea of balance among all cooperating forces.

———

MODEL ANSWER

POINT-SCORING ELEMENTS   PARAGRAPH NUMBER

Statement of theme suggested in question

(1) The goal of excellence in education is an objective that calls for united effort. The important ingredients in this endeavor are four vital forces, each of which must make its contribution -- the child, the parent, the school administration, and the community. Each has its own <u>role</u> to play, and all must work together cohesively in the <u>drama</u> of the educational process.

Interesting diction: use of metaphor

Note varied types of subordinate clauses

(2) The child occupies the <u>center of the stage.</u> It is the child whose trials and successes indicate the value of our schools. When the child responds to the lure of learning, he is well on his way to the development of his potential. It is most important, therefore, that the child do all he can to learn essential skills, increase his store of learning, and strengthen attitudes and traits of character. If, for some reason, the child is out of tune with the purposes of education or reluctant to apply himself to the tasks placed before him, there is a serious obstacle to be overcome. One might say that in a very real sense all education is self-education. The willing participation of the child is basic.

Parallel structure

Pointed summary sentence

Transition

Introductory modifer

(3) Behind the child is the parent. In the modern world, the parent's function is clear. Aware that the primary concern during the childhood years is success in school, the parent undertakes to prepare his offspring for the daily tasks. He develops tactfully in the youngster the habits of punctuality and readiness which are the foundation of good performance. He helps him to obtain and care for his materials of learning. He inquires about his progress in school. He supports him in difficulty. He meets with the teacher in order to share information which will be helpful in motivation and correction. Without an active parent on the scene, a strong strand of guidance is missing. The parent's cooperation is vital.

Effectivenesss through repetition of "He...."

Summary

3

POINT-SCORING ELEMENTS PARAGRAPH NUMBER

Simple sentence

Compound sentence

*Mature diction:
"function," "interpersonal patterns," "gauge," "environment"*

Summary

Examples

Imaginative diction

(4) Within the school building, the contact between pupil and teacher is at the core of learning. The teachers are devoted to the task in their personal ways, but it is the school administration which performs a special <u>function</u>. The school leader ship provides direction in laying ou the whole scheme of activities in th various subject areas. It groups students in <u>interpersonal patterns</u> calculated to stimulate effort. It uses testing procedures to diagnose aptitudes and to <u>gauge</u> achievement. It arranges guidance services for those who need special help. A well run school is, <u>in a word</u>, the perfec <u>environment</u> for education.

(5) More and more, in our time, the community is a powerful factor in the educational setting. The resources of the community -- its library, its museums, its public services, and it citizens -- are <u>avenues of instructi</u> which the school wisely utilizes. T community represents the <u>segment of world</u> which gives breadth and realit to the ideas found in books. It is the <u>classroom outside the school</u>, to which students go for motivation and application of skills and knowledges learned.

(6) The balance established among these four essential factors is evidenced by the cooperation shown by each element. All must work together in cooperative venture to make and to stabilize the school as an effective social institution basic to democrac

QUESTION 2 - MEETING THE NEEDS OF ALL THE CHILDREN

Great emphasis in recent years has been placed on the training of teachers for a role particularly attuned to the needs of children in large-city schools.

In a well-organized essay of *at least 450 words*, discuss the specific needs of children in an urban environment and the various approaches the classroom teacher might use in meeting the needs of all the children.

ANALYSIS OF THE QUESTION

1. You are asked to write an *essay*. Be sure then that you observe the requirement that your composition have a beginning, a middle, and an end.
2. The beginning should address itself directly to the question, considering it broadly, reflecting on its importance, and leading to various aspects to be developed in the middle or body. What is called for here is a picture of urban education in our times and its relation to contemporary life.
3. The middle of the essay should rightly be concerned with a detailed analysis of pupil needs, teacher skills and attitudes, and teacher training objectives.
4. The conclusion should leave the reader with a reinforced emphasis on the heart of the matter, namely, the role of the teacher in the advancement of our society.
5. Although it is indicated that the paper will be rated ONLY for written English, be sure to deal with the matter of the question DIRECTLY AND SPECIFICALLY. You may lose much credit by wandering from the point, because you would then not really be answering the question.
6. Note that *specific needs of children in an urban environment* and *various approaches the classroom teacher may use* are called for. Arouse and maintain interest in each of your examples through the introduction of varied concepts and through skillful transitions.
7. In meeting the requirement of length, plan carefully to include all important aspects of the question.

PLAN OF THE ESSAY

The overall plan of the model below consists of:

1. An introduction which goes directly to the topic, the problem of education in today's cities.

2. A body which devotes separate paragraphs to the:
    a. needs of children, as shown in their family heritage, language background, class attitudes, and way of life.
    b. skills teachers should have in teaching basic subjects in remediation techniques, and in guidance orientation

3. A conclusion which summarizes the essentials of the problem and reaffirms the concept of teacher training as a prime requisite.

MODEL ANSWER

POINT-SCORING ELEMENTS   PARAGRAPH NUMBER

Direct attack on the nub of the question

Cohesiveness with previous sentence

Parallel structure

(1) In recent years, the problem of educating children in large-city schools has been the object of much inquiry. These schools reflect in a marked degree the major social developments of the post-war world, such as the influx of migrants from Puerto Rico and other areas of the world, the move toward an integrated society, and the phenomenon of poverty amid prosperity. As legislators attempt to come to grips with the implementation of civil rights, with traditional practices in housing and employment, and with the improvement of health and welfare standards, educators must deal with the children of families whose lot in life cries out for betterment.

Question for interest
Key sentence directing division within paragraph

Short sentence for effect
Connectors then, too; lastly

Semicolon between coordinate clauses

(2) What are the needs of these children? Specifically, there is great need for such important learning factors as remedial instruction, broadening of horizons, and guidance-oriented teaching. Remedial instruction in the basic subjects of reading and arithmetic should be used to raise achievement levels up to grade. These skills may have suffered as a result of a language barrier, such as the use of Spanish at home, or because of an impoverished background. They must be improved. Then, too, horizons should be broadened. It is a known fact that big-city children are largely provincial in experience and outlook. Their world is bounded by their own neighborhood; they have not had contact with the cultural resources of the city. Lastly, the teacher finds that many of these children are not responsive to the ordinary classroom situation. They need the understanding treatment which could come only from teachers who recognize the impairments resulting from environment and can and want to deal with them.

Topic sentence, connecting with previous paragraph and leading to new aspect

(3) It is indeed the teacher who is vital here. The teacher of big-city children must be skilled in teaching reading and number skills; he must be able to diagnose each child's problems in these areas of study and select tools and

POINT-SCORING ELEMENTS   PARAGRAPH NUMBER

Use of examples introduced by for example, such as, for instance, finally

Mature diction, elicit, rapport, value level, focal point

Interesting conclusion: summary and application

methods to move the child on to re-
mediation and further development.
He must be able to interest the chil
in making progress in book subjects.
He might do this, for example, by
taking his class on trips to communi
facilities, such as the firehouse, t
post office, and the museum. These
excursions from the school proper
should be conducted in such a way as
to provide not mere entertainment bu
real learning experiences, for insta
the construction of an experience ch
Finally, the teacher should be able
approach each child knowing enough o
the family background to elicit from
the child his very best effort towar
learning. This can mean a knowledge
of home conditions, the degree of
rapport within the family, the value
level on which the child operates,
and the personal, social, and econom
factors which influence his life. I
this way, the teacher uses the best
guidance techniques to stimulate and
encourage learning.

(4) The training of teachers for this
challenging task has become a focal
point of teacher education, a fact
which the colleges clearly recognize
Because of his disadvantaged background in basic skills, in community
contact, and in personal orientation
the big-city child poses a problem
of serious dimensions. The teacher
who holds the key to this problem
must have the special aptitudes that
can bring about quality education in
every potential member of our democratic society.

QUESTION 3 - MOTIVATING LEARNING

Advertising firms have been interested in motivational research. Teachers, too, are interested in what will make learning attractive to children.

In a well-organized essay of *at least 450 words*, discuss interests of children that may be utilized by a teacher in the approach to learning, giving specific illustrations in any or all subject areas.

ANALYSIS OF THE QUESTION

1. Note that the piece of writing called for is an *essay*. Be sure that your composition is an orderly succession of paragraphs with a beginning, middle, and end.
2. Although it is indicated that the paper will be rated ONLY for written English, be sure to deal with the matter of the question DIRECTLY AND SPECIFICALLY. You may lose much credit by wandering from the point, because you would then not really be answering the question.
3. Strive for correctness in all details as indicated, namely, sentence structure, grammar, spelling, idiomatic usage, etc. With respect to sentence structure, be sure every sentence is a complete one and meets the requirements of formal style. Do not use the run-on sentence or the fragment permitted in informal style and fiction.
4. Give some maturity to your style by using varied sentence patterns, both simple and complex.
5. Note that specific illustrations in subject areas are called for. Do not make this a mere factual listing in your essay. Arouse and maintain interest in each of your examples through the introduction of varied concepts and through skillful transitions. In this connection, too, the most important factor is the clear reference to a pupil interest which leads to, or may be involved in, a subject field.
6. Be sure to conform to the requirement of length. Do not be careless about this.

PLAN OF THE ESSAY

The overall plan of the model below consists of:

1. An introduction which goes directly to the topic, that of motivation in learning.

2. **A** transitional paragraph which opens up the idea of *pupil interests*.

3. An enumeration of recommended devices, each paragraph dealing with one device, and showing its usefulness in a particular subject area, viz.:
   a. story-telling - reading and language arts
   b. pupil experiences - arithmetic
   c. projects and constructions - social studies
   d. trips - science, music, art
   e. holidays - general achievement

4. A brief statement of conclusion with a short reference to the advertising practices mentioned in the question.

MODEL ANSWER

POINT-SCORING ELEMENTS	PARAGRAPH NUMBER

Sentence pattern: complex, simple, compound-complex

(1) Teachers know that their task is to effect a pleasant and profitable meeting between the child and learning. This is the daily challenge. To meet it, they think in terms of *motivating* the pupils, and they are agreed that the best stimulation is an attractive learning experience.

Use of question
Transitional sentence

(2) How can the educative act be made appealing? There are a number of pupil interests which may be utilized to bring about this result.

Mature and precise diction: device, imaginative, venture, sure-fire, compensations

(3) Children like well-told stories. Oral story-telling is, therefore, an effective device in the teaching of reading and the language arts. The experienced and imaginative teacher stores up accounts of personal experiences and uses these at the appropriate time, usually at the beginning of a new reading venture. In addition, she has a fund of sure-fire tales to read to the class. Her enthusiasm for reading leads the pupils to explore library resources and to find similar compensations.

Parallel structure in phrases of a simple sentence

(4) In any field, the best approach is usually made through the use of pupil knowledge and experience. In arithmetic, number concepts and computing operations are concretized in terms of what pupils know from daily living. Problems deal with money, with store purchases, with game materials, with houses and home living, with the division of pies and cakes into fractional parts, and the like. The funda-

Note semi-colon

mental principle here is the use of an apperceptive basis for learning; in other words, that which is to be learned must be related to that which is already known.

Transitional word, another

(5) Another writing path to new knowledge is provided by means of projects which call for construction, for the use of the visual and the tangible. At the start of a unit in social studies, for example, pictures, reproductions, and various realia may be exhibited to

Note commas

Question for interest, followed by imperative "consider"

stimulate interest. What child fails to respond to a colorful illustration such

<u>POINT-SCORING ELEMENTS</u>   <u>PARAGRAPH NUMBER</u>

	as a scene from history, a map or portrait of a hero? Consider the appeal of real Indian arrowheads, old coins, battle equipment, and antique household articles. With su stimuli as these, the child plunges into the past and roams **in far place** He is lead eventually to draw his ow maps, to compose his own Indian book or to build his own pioneer cabin or canoe.
Note diction: trip, excursion, visit, bus ride *Use of capitals*	(6) An occasional <u>trip</u> gives great impet to the search for knowledge. An <u>excursion</u> to the Museum of Natural History or to the Hayden Planetarium opens up the world of science; a <u>vis</u> to the Philharmonic nurtures the see of music appreciation and skill; a <u>bus ride</u> to a zoo or to an arboretum kindles love of nature and lays the groundwork for experiences in art.
Summary sentence to round out paragraph	This kind of linkage of the world of the school with the outside world gi meaning and inspiration to pupils' classroom lives.
Key word: lastly *Compound sentence with three main clauses*	(7) <u>Lastly,</u> the big events of the school year are centers of natural interest Thanksgiving and Christmas spur acti vities in choral music; Lincoln's Birthday encourages brotherhood them and learnings; Decoration Day offers
Idiomatic and imaginative presentation	opportunities for patriotic fervor a for appreciation of our country's history. On the local scene, Open School Night and the preparations fo it lead to the kind of bee-hive acti vity which keeps the children engros in studies and eager to show themsel at their best.
Direct and simple sentences	(8) Such motivational devices as these p the way to successful learning. Goo teachers are good ad-men.

QUESTION 4 - UNITED COMMUNITY ACTION

In an article in a recent publication of the Board of Education, the following statement was made: *"The united efforts of all agencies in the community are needed if the school is to achieve the goals for which it has primary responsibility."*

In a well-organized essay of *at least 450 words*, explain in detail the part played by community agencies in developing the child as a social and moral being and as a healthy, useful, and productive citizen. Include in your discussion a consideration of any or all of the following: the home, the church, community groups, communications media, industry, labor, and government.

ANALYSIS OF THE QUESTION

It should be noted that this essay is to be an expository one -- *explain in detail* -- setting forth the *part played by community agencies* in education CONSIDERED BROADLY. Although this is a question in a test for a specific license or certificate, its terms are NOT LIMITED TO THAT LEVEL.

The quotation from the recent publication of the Board of Education indicates that the efforts of all agencies should be *united*. The model essay recognizes and includes this idea.

Note, too, that *the goals for which it has primary responsibility* are detailed later on in the question: social competency, moral strengthening, good health, personal development according to ability (useful and productive), good citizenship.

PLAN OF THE ESSAY

The agencies themselves are listed and provide the framework of the essay. The model which follows adopts a simple plan of paragraphing:

Par. 1. Introduction, stating the relationship of the school and other agencies
Par. 2. The influence of the home
Par. 3. The church
Par. 4. Community agencies (clubs, teams, services, etc.)
Par. 5. Communications media
Par. 6. Government
Par. 7. Conclusion, containing summary

MODEL ANSWER

POINT-SCORING ELEMENTS	PARAGRAPH NUMBER

Mature thought and vocabulary

Direct reference to main theme of the question

(1) It is a truism that education is the business of the school, but this sta ment is also an oversimplification. The school cannot handle all the con of education. While it assumes prim responsibility for clearly recognize goals, it depends markedly on other community agencies for success.

Point No. 1 - the home

Sentence variety; simple introductory sentence followed by complex sentence with a multiple subject and an interrupted construction

(2) The home is certainly a heavily infl ential factor in a child's education development. The stature of parents siblings, the level of the cultural milieu, the maintenance of standards dress and deportment, the attention given to matters of health -- the ex to which these elements conform to praiseworthy criteria will determine the readiness of the child and his a tude toward the educational approach provided in the school.

Transitional sentence links previous paragraph (home) to this one (church)

Point No. 2 - the church

First three sentences of this paragraph are:
1. simple
2. complex
3. compound

(3) The church (synagogue) adds to the c tribution of the home in its own par cular way. While it is an accepted that parents imbue their children wi moral and spiritual values both by instruction and example, it is the c (synagogue) which gives added emphas: by virtue of its superior knowledge inspiration. Its representatives re codes of conduct to deep moral and t logical concepts; moreover, they act: vate these through religious ceremon and planned social action. The acti ties of the church and the synagogue develop the character of the child i a functional pattern.

Transition to Point No. 3 - community agencies
Thus introduces illustrations
Parallel structure in clauses separated by semi-colons

(4) Still, other community groups lend t support. Clubs provide outlets for variety of talents and thereby help their exercise and improvement. Thus musical interests are discovered and cultivated; dramatics ability is per fected; scouting activities are giver direction; hobbies are encouraged. Neighborhood teams and "Little League organizations contribute their benefi in the area of health, sportsmanship and character building. In addition to these well-known instruments, the are the family agencies, such as the Jewish Family Service and Catholic Charities, which take it upon themsel

In addition provides transition within paragraph
Examples answer request for details

14

POINT-SCORING ELEMENTS	PARAGRAPH NUMBER

Point No. 4 - communications
Identification of media and their concomitant elements.
Three simple sentences varied in structure

Maturity of judgment indicated

Balanced structure

(5) to give relief in cases of hardship and social maladjustment

(5) The impact of our ever-present communications media is certainly a potent force visited upon our young. They learn about life through television, the movies, the radio, and the newspapers. In these media, mixed in with the factual are the many imaginative creations of artistry, the lure of entertainment, and the blandishments of persuasive advertising. The quality of this kind of influence is often regarded as debatable, but an influence it most certainly is. As such, a responsible nation must have a constant concern that it plays its role well, setting forth truth rather than error, excellence rather than shoddiness, worth rather than waste.

Transition to Point No. 5 - government Answering direction to be specific

(6) Last consideration of all, but not least, is the hand that government plays in education. It provides museums and parks, its police give direction in living amid the unavoidable hazards of traffic and crime, it sends its firemen to counsel concerning the dangers of fire, its sanitation department pursues a policy of active education in the maintenance of clean streets and neighborhoods, its hospitals stand ready with emergency services and clinics to preserve bodily health.

Final paragraph providing summary

Return to the main theme: united community action for a definite goal

(7) The union of all such agencies as these cited here can give fulfillment to the broad objectives of education. The home, the church, clubs, centers, teams, family services, the media of communication, government itself -- each has its own contribution to make. Working and planning together provides the best product -- honest, healthy, useful, well-educated citizens.

NOTE: If you elected to describe, in addition, the part played by industry and labor, you would specify the following: the influences of steady employment upon family living, the suggestions given by industry for the improvement of curricula in line with technological advancement, the protection of rights, and the prevention of exploitation.

Among proposals for increased utilization of school facilities and extension of educational guidance is the suggestion that the school day be changed to an eight-to-four o'clock schedule and that no homework be assigned.

In a well-organized essay of *at least 450 words*, discuss your reactions to this proposal for a lengthened school day. Consider advantages and disadvantages for both pupils and teachers.

ANALYSIS OF THE QUESTION

The question deals with two educationally provocative problems of perennial interest -- the lengthening of the school day and the elimination of homework. In this question, the two are co-joined. Be sure to include both of these items in your answer.

Your answer should be a *balanced* one -- the advantages and disadvantages of each course advocated should be given temperately in respect to BOTH pupils and teachers.

Select and present only the most general and outstanding outcome and features for the topic can be (and has been) engaged at great length and in a variety of expositions.

PLAN OF THE ESSAY

Par. 1. The proposal for a lengthened school day is stated succinctly in the opening sentence. The idea of *advantages and disadvantages* is used as the *division* of the topic.

Par. 2. Discussion of *advantages to pupils*: more time for instruction in basics; provision for special subjects.

Par. 3. Discussion continued: a *varied program* possible through related experiences; the homework activities improved through supervision.

Par. 4. *Advantages to teachers*: guidance services, clerical responsibilities; reduction of tension.

Par. 5. Transition to disadvantages to both pupils and teachers: danger of over-long sessions; personal factors.

Par. 6. Discussion of disadvantages continued: possibility of poor planning because of limited facilities for play; teacher programming a real consideration.

Par. 7. Concise conclusion, summarizing main theme and calling for wise study before implementation.

MODEL ANSWER

POINT-SCORING ELEMENTS	PARAGRAPH NUMBER

Use of question for interest
Complex sentence

(1) Shall the school day be lengthened from six to eight hours? Before such a proposal is put into effect, it would be wise to consider what advantages and disadvantages would be present for both pupils and teachers.

Complex sentence with _that_ *clause*
Complex sentence with _which_ *clause*

(2) It is clear that in some ways the proposed plan would be profitable for pupils. They would have more time in which to receive instruction in their studies. There would be greater opportunity for the full development of skills and concepts in the basic areas of reading and arithmetic. In addition, provision may be made for science, social studies, and foreign language instruction. Since these areas have grown in importance in recent years, they should be included in the elementary program. The additional time of the longer school day would make their inclusion feasible.

Transitional expression, _In addition_
Complex sentence starting with _since_ *clause*

Simple sentence

Use of _also_ *as transition*

(3) An eight-to-four day would also allow for a more varied school program. Assembly programs, remedial instruction, visual aid activities, art and music, physical fitness training -- all these, and other, aspects of a rich school experience can be realized when an ample quota of time is available. Even the ordinary homework responsibilities may be planned within the school day. Thus, the work can be done under expert supervision and with the aid of classroom libraries and reference materials.

Compound subject for variety (use of dash before all)
Attractive diction: _aspects_, _rich_, _ample quota_
Balance phrase

(4) Teachers would also find some advantage in the longer day. They would find additional opportunities for guidance services, studying pupil problems and working out solutions. Moreover, they would have more time for the performance of clerical duties, such as the collection of milk money, the keeping of school records, and the handling of reports and correspondence. The pace of the day's activities would be relieved of undue tension, and happier personalities might result.

Moreover *as transition*

Reference to examples found in question

POINT-SCORING ELEMENTS	PARAGRAPH NUMBER
Contrast (comma after introductory phrase)	(5) On the other hand, there may be real disadvantages for both pupil and teacher. Long sessions in school ma be excessively tiring. Starting as
Variety in use of gerund as subject	early as eight o'clock can impose a further burden on the family which i sending its child (or children) off
Commas before and after parenthetical expressions: too, as a result	school. Teachers, too, may have con siderable traveling to do before reaching the classroom. It is conce
Sums up the idea of the paragraph	able that, as a result, neither chil nor teacher may be in the best frame of mind for the work of the day.
Further as transition *Simple sentence*	(6) Without careful planning, further di advantages may eventuate. Pupils ma not be given opportunities to partic
	pate in a varied program and to enjo free play out-of-doors. Teachers ma
Simple sentence	be expected to devote an excessive amount of time to contact with pupil in the classroom. If the concept of
Complex sentence starting with if clause	the longer school day means an exten teaching day, one wonders about the effect on teacher morale and physica
	resources.
Final summation *Use of infinitive phrase, set off by comma*	(7) All in all, there is much to be said on both sides of this stimulating question. To devise the perfect sch day, one must seek to incorporate every advantage and plan to avoid every possible defect.

TEST OF STANDARD WRITTEN ENGLISH *(ESSAY)*

QUESTIONS AND MODEL ANSWERS

CONTENTS

TEST OF STANDARD WRITTEN ENGLISH *(ESSAY)*

QUESTIONS AND MODEL ANSWERS

QUESTION 1

In an experimental project in selected schools in low socio-economic areas, it was found that when the children were taken to theatres, museums, and other places of cultural enrichment and were given special help in school to develop latent interests and to express special talents, marked improvement resulted. Many of the children developed greater interest in academic subjects and began plans to continue their education in college.

In a well-organized essay of *at least 450 words*, discuss the advantages, and possible disadvantages, of extending such a program to other schools in the city. You may include in your answer one or both of the following aspects of the topic:

1. The role of community resources in carrying out a program of this type.

2. A plan for determining the degree of success in attainment of the desired goal of such a program.

ANALYSIS OF THE QUESTION

The response to this question may well emphasize the many advantages of the cultural enrichment opportunities in a city like New York. The item of *possible disadvantages* may be slighted since the implication is that they may not be great. The model essay takes this tack. Moreover, it slights the plan for determining success since, according to the instruction, it is not necessary to deal with both aspects.

PLAN OF THE ESSAY

Par. 1. Topic an important and interesting one. The program of enrichment identified through various examples. Fine effects noted.
2. Brief, transitional paragraph.
3. Opportunities in the arts.
4. Science: natural history, astronomy.
5. Literature, the newspaper, the theatre.
6. The business world: manufacture, automation, commerce, transportation.
7. Summary of advantages: knowledge, experience, interest in study, personal traits of good manners, responsibility, civic-mindedness. A few dangers dealt with.
8. A yardstick for judging the value of extra-school visits: pupil interest.

POINT-SCORING ELEMENTS	PARAGRAPH NUMBER

1. *Puts topic in perspective*
 	
  Two simple sentences
 	
  Relates closely to the question by using its terminology
 	
  Compound sentence
	(1) The problem of the culturally depri
	child has been one of absorbing
	interest in the last decade. Among
	possible solutions, the direct prov
	sion of programs of cultural enrich
	ment has proved most worthwhile.
	Through the education attained by
	means of out-of-school visits to
	museums, theatres, and the like, pu
	have developed greater interest in
	their school subjects and they have
	even begun to prepare themselves fo
	college training later on.

Short transitional paragraph	(2) Varied community resources may be u to effect the desired result. In a city as large as New York, there ar a tremendous number of such resourc
Discussion of the role of community resources (aspect #1 of the topic): *The arts* *Note commas* *Complex sentence-noun clause introduced by* <u>how</u> *series* *Use of example* *Use of capitals for specific orchestra*	(3) First, in the field of music and ar concert halls, theatres, and museum play a major role. The pupil may b introduced to the works of the mast both classic and modern, in the are of painting, sculpture, tapestry, a ceramics. He may see for himself h these arts have originated and developed down through the centurie As for music, special trips may be arranged to the opera house, the ballet performance, and the concert orchestra. It is even possible to see a rehearsal of the Philharmonic Symphony under one of its outstandi conductors.

2. *Science*
 	
  Two simple sentences
 	
  Examples
  Complex sentence (adjective clauses)
  Effective diction: <u>wonders</u>, <u>fascination</u>, <u>learning process</u>
	(4) Science education, a field of incre
	ing performance, may also receive a
	impetus through visits to places o
	cultural enrichment. Two favorite
	objectives in recent years have bee
	the Museum of Natural History and
	Planetarium. The wonders of living
	things and the fascination of the
	universe fill the child's mind with
	impressions he carries back to scho
	where the learning process goes
	forward with growing interest and
	intensity.

POINT-SCORING ELEMENTS	PARAGRAPH NUMBER

3. Literary
   a. libraries
Complex sentence
 	
Simple sentence
 	
  b. newspaper plants
Complex sentence
 	
  c. theatre
Simple sentence
	(5) The world of books and the printed word may be examined at close range, too. The neighborhood library is often a source of pleasure, which when once experienced becomes a continuing source of intellectual development and delight. A visit to the great library at 42nd Street and 5th Avenue is an unforgettable experience of the same type. In addition, trips can be arranged to newspaper plants, where the excitement of the daily press fills the onlooker both with knowledge and with inspiration. The great world of the theatre is but another sphere in which the word becomes a concrete, living thing.

4. Business *Simple sentence* *Complex sentence (adjective clause)* *Use of examples* *Effective use of imperative* <u>*Think*</u>	(6) Even the industrial and commercial areas of the city contribute to the child's education. A plant which contains a multi-phased process, such as the assembly line of the Ford Motor Company, or which makes use of the machinery of automation, such as the Sperry-Rand Corp., becomes an informative experience. Think, too, of the breadth of vision which New York harbor or JFK Airport can provide.
Summary and transition *Advantages* *Simple sentences* *Balanced infinitive phrases* *Possible disadvantages* *Effective alliterative expression,* <u>*pure profit*</u>	(7) The advantages of this type of introduction to learning are clearly many. The pupils gain knowledge and experience. They are stimulated to return to school with an increased appetite for book learning. Moreover, they have an opportunity to develop and exercise good manners in public, to accept responsibility, and to grow in civic appreciation and loyalty. The only dangers to be avoided are lack of relatedness to the school program of studies and loss of time from basic subjects. With good planning, the *trip* can become pure profit.
States reasoned preference for the advantages *Apt diction:* <u>*diminution,*</u> <u>*runs off-course*</u>	(8) To judge the success of such a program, the teacher should concentrate on the determination of evidences of growth, both personal and social. If the program runs off-course, a diminution in pupil response and behavior will be obvious. The chances of success, however, are great, for there is a clear connection between experience and education.

3

QUESTION 2

Criticism has been levelled at the schools because of time taken from *regular* work for such activities as school banking, milk distribution, class trips, book fairs, bazaars, evening dance or song festivals, and operettas. Teachers, too, have complained of feeling frustrated by the encroachments of such non-teaching duties on the teaching day. They feel that their energies are dissipated with bus firms, the collection of money, and the keeping of records.

In a well-organized essay of *at least 450 words*, discuss the problem of non-teaching assignments referred to in the above passage. Express clearly your own thinking on the subject, touching on one or more of the following aspects:

1. The burden of non-teaching assignments upon the teacher
2. The point of view that non-teaching activities are *frills* which encroach upon the teacher's real work of teaching the basic skills
3. The value of using voluntary or paid assistants to take care of non-teaching duties.

ANALYSIS OF THE QUESTION

In this question, you are invited to express *your own* ideas and you are required to *touch upon* one or more of the suggestions given. Thus, it would be sufficient to develop a whole composition on *frills* (1) or on the use of assistants (3) as long as you stay on the general topic of *the problem of non-teaching assignments*. The essay which follows makes use of all the aspects presented.

PLAN OF THE ESSAY

Par. 1. Presents the topic in the light of the *hectic* life of the teacher. Cites the need of determining who will best perform the *non-teaching* assignments.

2. Refers to the history of modern educational development. Raises question of necessity of the extra responsibilities mentioned; justifies their inclusion with reasons for each; banking and thrift, milk sales and health, book fairs and reading, etc.

3. Moves to consideration of the relative value of the teacher and the specialized assistant; the inherent authority of the teacher; the peculiar knowledge and interest of the special teacher or expert. The attempt to make efficient use of both.

4. The reaction of individual teachers to demands and opportunities; the cry for equality of treatment; the malcontent; factors in faculty morale.
5. Comparison of the teacher's day with that of the present-day worker. The role of the budget-maker and the administrator in solving the problem.

TOPIC: THE NON-TEACHING ASSIGNMENT

POINT-SCORING ELEMENTS	PARAGRAPH NUMBER
Presents topic as having two sides: some ...... others ...... *Balanced structure of <u>that</u> clauses* *Suggests solution broadly*	(1) One hears much these days about the hectic day of the elementary school teacher. Some say that it is too busy and call for a re-appraisal of the situation with lessening of the load a prime objective. Others feel that the teacher is the best one to handle the many activities which fl in and through the normal day's work Perhaps it is all in the point of v
Discusses (2) at length *Complex sentence with <u>when</u> clause* *Question lends interest* *Compound sentence (four independent clauses)* *Note use of semi-colons* *Commas for words in series* *Conclusion of (2)*	(2) At one time, it was thought that th only concern of the teacher was tha of teaching the basic skills. When other duties, such as school bankir and milk distribution, were added, these were regarded as *frills*. But are they? School banking is a way of developing the necessary habit thrift; milk sales and accounting make a contribution to health and number work; book fairs stimulate interest in books and leisure read bazaars develop loyalty to the sch through a building-wide or, at lea grade-wide activity. Dances, song festivals, and operettas promote their own special kind of learning the form of culminating long-range activities, chiefly in the arts. There are few educational theorist today who would deny the value of these co-curricular interests.
Discusses (3) at length *Compound question* *Simple sentences* *Note connecting words (underlined)* *Compound complex sentence* *Simple sentence*	(3) The question is, Shall the classro teacher be expected to handle all the details of such activities or should assistants of some sort be employed to take care of non-teach assignments? In some schools, the PTA or a hired monitorial staff pe forms eating and lunchroom chores. <u>Such</u> an arrangement may work well. It is a fairly common experience, <u>however</u>, to find that there is a loss of authority in some cases: pupils may not respect the casual employee as much as they would the teacher. <u>Another</u> device, of cours is to have the specialist instruct

6

Simple sentence with compound subject

Complex sentence (adverbial indicating time)

in such areas as music and dance. Book fairs and bazaars may be run by the representatives of companies especially skilled in such enterprises. When such an arrangement is set up with proper scheduling and safeguards, the complaints about excessive burdens tend to diminish

Discusses (4) at length Complex sentence

Simple sentence Complex sentence with adjective clause

Complex sentence (conditional)

Compound element introduced by but

Effective diction: sympathetically conceived principles, unhappy few, deaf ears
Balanced phrases

(4) No matter what assignments are given to the various teachers on a school staff, there is bound to be some inequality. This is inevitable in the nature of things. There are malcontents here and there who feel that this is an evidence of favoritism or prejudiced planning. If faculty morale is low generally because of other factors of wide and great importance, such a charge may be an incisive blow to school administration, but in a normal situation where the principal enjoys good relationships with the staff because of broad and sympathetically conceived principles of cooperative action, the cries of the unhappy few should fall on deaf ears. Actually, the extra assignment given to a teacher is best taken as a sign of trust and confidence and as a stepping-stone to promotion.

Compound sentence Brief summary reference to (1)

Effective close

(5) We are living in an age of shorter working days and lighter responsibilities, but the work of the teacher has appeared to grow in intensity and complexity. Wise attention to this situation on the part of the budget-makers and the school administrators should result in the best possible day-to-day performance in the classroom.

QUESTION 3

In recent discussions of American education, many suggestions have been made for enriching and accelerating education. One proposal which has had a warm reception among educators and the public is to lengthen the school year to permit full-time use of school facilities and to eliminate the alleged education *waste* of the long summer vacation. As a prospective member of the educational profession, you will have some reactions to this proposal.

Write an essay of *at least 450 words* on the advantages and disadvantages of the all-year school. You may include in your discussion consideration of some of the following aspects of this topic:

A. The effect of such a program upon
   1. intellectually gifted children
   2. slow learners
   3. children with special talents in music, art, or dramatics
   4. children who do not adjust well to school.
B. The effect of such a program upon traditional summertime activities, such as travel, camping, etc.
C. The advantages and disadvantages of shortening the twelve-year period normally required to prepare for college
D. The economy of using educational facilities on a full-time basis
E. The effect upon present and prospective teachers of a possible curtailment of the traditional vacation period
F. Possible effects of *voluntary* summer service upon basic salary schedules of teachers.

ANALYSIS OF THE QUESTION

This question calls for the reaction of a prospective teacher. Many such reactions are, of course, possible. Full-length essays could be written on any one of the suggestions given or on several of them combined, such as A, E, and C since they deal with the effect on children, or E and F since they concern teachers. The sample essay given attempts to consider the topic in all aspects and sets up a criterion for making a decision between the advantages and disadvantages -- certainly an acceptable collating of ideas.

PLAN OF THE ESSAY

Following are the pertinent lines of development:

Par. 1. Introduces topic, relates it to traditional schedule, raises question as to advantages and disadvantages
   2. Advantages: maximum use of plant (D); effect on children (A); acceleration (C); teacher compensation (F

3. Disadvantages: need for change of routine (B); shortening of college preparatory period (C); curtailment of teacher improvement (E); effect on plant (D).
4. Consideration of possible motives for a change to the twelve-month scheme. Call for caution. Citing of a recommended criterion: the service to children.

POINT-SCORING ELEMENTS	PARAGRAPH NUMBER
Striking diction: <u>*staple*</u>, <u>*envision*</u>, <u>*revolutionary*</u>	(1) The summer-long vacation has been s a staple of American education that is difficult to envision the revolu tionary idea of the all-year school Nevertheless, this concept is being widely discussed. What are the advantages and the disadvantages of keeping our schools open for twelve months of the year?
Complex sentence *Leads easily to the main topic and its two-fold division* *Brief simple sentence*	
Question *Discusses advantages* *1. plant (D)* *Compound sentence with semi-colon* *2. children (A), (C)* *Simple sentence* *Complex sentence (adjective clause)* *Complex sentence* *Note connectives from sentence to sentence (underlined)* *3. teachers (F)*	(2) Some advantages are immediately ide tifiable. The school plant, an expensive construction, is put to maximum use; it does not stand idle for two whole months. In addition, the talents and skills of children need not lie dormant during this period. They may blossom and grow under expert supervision, as in art and music. At the other end of the spectrum, children who need special remedial help in basic subjects wil receive instruction. The slow lear ers and maladjusted may find within the pace of the new summer school period the kind of opportunity they need to improve themselves. <u>Finall</u> some pupils may utilize the summer time to move ahead in basic subject areas and in this way accelerate their progress through school. <u>As for the teaching staff</u>, the year- round school should mean more pay, an outcome all critics will applauc
Transition to disadvan- tages, Topic (B) *Complex sentence (adver- bial indicating time)* *Comma for series* *Complex sentence* *Connective (underlined)*	(3) On the other hand, it is possible t cite a number of disadvantages. Ma feel that a full vacation during th summer is a needed change of pace. After he has spent ten months in daily classroom routine, the pupil ready for travel, for rest, for camping, in short, for the activiti that will restore and refresh his physical and mental powers. A summ program which would make these activities difficult or impossible actuate may be detrimental to educa tion in the long run. <u>Again</u>, con- tinued application to school tasks

*Apt diction: acceleration,
propel*

*Topic (C)
Use of also as connective*

*Topic (E)
Complex sentence (causal
clause)*

*Use of even to move to
next idea
Effective diction: traffic,
toll, obliterated, weekend,
week*

*Citing of specific tasks
relevant to (D)*

*Summing up and leading to
conclusion
Noun clauses in parallel -
a mature style*

Simple connective

*A key to resolution of the
discussion
Complex sentence*

*Use of gerund as subject
A sense of conclusion*

and resultant acceleration may propel the pupil at an immature age into the advanced studies of college and eventually graduate school. The life of the teacher would also be affected adversely by the newly proposed plan. Opportunities to travel and to take summer courses for personal enrichment would be fewer, since the young teacher may rightly feel the need of making money rather than engaging in study. Even the school plant may suffer from constant use. The daily traffic of hundreds, maybe thousands, of youngsters takes a toll of the physical structure which cannot be obliterated in a weekend or even a week. The building custodian usually requires a much longer period of time for repairing, painting, floor polishing, and cleaning.

(4) Where does the wisdom of the situation lie? Those who fear the Russians and wilt under their claims of superior education, those who feel they may squeeze the most return out of the taxpayer's dollar, those who consider that teachers have too easy an existence at present -- all these may advocate the twelve-month school. But we should be most discerning in weighing both their motives and their arguments. The best criterion is surely that of the advantages which may accrue to the children; that is, whatever suits them best by answering their needs, abilities, and interests. Applying such a criterion will test the knowledge and skill of educators everywhere.

QUESTION 4

Everybody has heard in past years that the schools are *soft*. The children do not work hard, or long enough. Schools must be toughened up and speeded up or *the Russians will get us. Now it is the Japanese.* As someone has said, *The responsibility for national survival has been placed squarely upon the shoulders of the children.*

The barrage of destructive criticism of education (and of children and their supposedly soft-living and indulgent parents) has put great pressure upon the schools. In some instances, this pressure has resulted in unwise practices.

In a well-organized essay of *at least 450 words*, discuss the current controversy over *softness* in American education. You may include in your discussion personal experiences, case studies, or recent books and articles on the subject to substantiate your opinions.

ANALYSIS OF THE QUESTION

The answer to this question must deal with the impact of adverse criticism, stimulated first by *the Russians* and now by the Japanese upon our schools. You are directed to discuss the alleged *softness* of American education. You are free to include personal experiences, case studies of specific areas, and books and articles. These will help to *substantiate your opinions*. The model essay makes use of all these briefly as space permits.

PLAN OF THE ESSAY

The scheme of development is as follows:

Par. 1. Introduction of the topic, a broad picture of the rise of recent criticism as related to modern scientific developments. Gradual arrival at key point of *softness*
   2. A prominent area of controversy-reading instruction. The battle between the *whole word* and *phonics* methods. Books projecting the attack.
   3. Effects of this criticism: theories compared; methods and materials examined; the view of practical educators; recognition of importance of reading standards and reading achievement
   4. Briefer references to other areas: two new subjects added to elementary curriculum to *beef up* the program; namely, science and foreign language; impact on the program
   5. Value of the controversy: our faith in free discussion and eventual improvement of the schools.

TOPIC: *SOFTNESS* IN AMERICAN EDUCATION

POINT-SCORING ELEMENTS	PARAGRAPH NUMBER

Complex sentence with adverbial clause

(1) Ever since the Russian Sputnik blazed its trail through the skies, American educational patterns and practices have become the object of sustained critical appraisals. The reason is a compelling one. We who had always considered ourselves supreme in science found that we were outstripped and outsmarted in the race into space. Where did the fault lie? Inevitably, the accusing finger was pointed at the schools. From elementary to college grades, the whole system has been adjudged by some to be too full of mistaken theories, too lacking in direction and purpose, and, fundamentally, too *soft*.

Short effective simple sentence arousing interest
Complex sentence with adjective and noun clauses

Question for interest
Simple sentence with directness
Climactic series reaching central point

Simple transition to prime example
Complex sentence with adverbial and noun clauses

(2) One of the most violent areas of attack has been that of basic reading instruction. The opening gun was fired even before Sputnik when the book WHY JOHNNY CAN'T READ made the charge that the phonics system should be restored to its proper place in the primary grades. The allegation was made that this method of teaching reading has been supplanted in the last few decades by the *whole word* method and that this latter method was erroneous in its assumptions and unproductive in its results. In subsequent books came the inevitable comparison between American and Russian techniques as in WHY IVAN KNOWS WHAT JOHNNY DOESN'T, and the quality of our educational output was denoted even in the title of a book, TODAY'S ILLITERATES.

Complex sentence with noun clauses

Note balanced predicate phrases

Inverted structure
Compound sentence

Transition through question
Simple sentence

(3) What has been the result? There has been a concentration of attention on the whole problem of reading readiness, methods of instruction, materials, and remedial techniques. Sharp differences of opinion have been delineated and defended by the theorists; the practical educators have done their best to choose wisely from all that research can offer.

POINT-SCORING ELEMENTS	PARAGRAPH NUMBER

Simple sentence with compound verb

Simple sentence

Simple sentence with infinitive phrase
Complex sentence with noun clause

Simple sentence, effective because of periodic structure

Simple sentence, conclusive in tone

Parents have become alerted to the situation and have become more cogn zant of the standing and progress c their children. School administrat have set minimum reading grades as absolute standards for promotion. Special reading teams have been add to school staffs to care for reveal needs. In all this, it is apparent that the need to cope with the written and printed word has been underscored. Despite the rise of radio, television, and other forms of oral communication, the place of reading has retained its importance It will remain basic and will receive more and more emphasis in t schools.

Transition through <u>also</u>

Complex sentence with noun clause

Simple sentence

Simple sentence with infinitive phrase
Compound complex structure

Simple sentence

(4) Science and foreign language study have also received a tremendous amount of attention. Statistics revealed that in most schools these were hitherto unknown in the lower grades. Now, syllabi in science ca for the introduction of simple con cepts and experiments very early i the educational program. Common branch teachers have had to learn to teach this kind of material. I addition, outside the city, as I know from personal experience, tea chers of foreign language have bee added to elementary school staffs, and *oral-aural* instruction begins as early as the fourth grade. The need for communicating with the other peoples of the world has bee recognized.

Effective diction in this final paragraph
Inverted order in this noun clause

Optimistic prognosis

Effective climax in series

(5) Our country has always distinguish itself by preserving the individua right to free discussion. It is o faith that out of the exchange of knowledge and opinion comes the mo perfect instrument. In education, we look forward with the hope that out of stern criticism will rise stronger schools, with better tea ching techniques and materials, an with an improved educational produ

In Russia, before the overthrow of communism in 1991, the State attempted to decide through its planning mechanism what skills were needed and in what proportion they were needed for the most efficient development of the State. For example, the State decided that a certain number of ballet stars were needed to entertain the people. In turn, aspiring children throughout the USSR competed for enrollment in the few ballet schools. Of those permitted to enroll, only those judged best according to Soviet standards survived the years of study and practice necessary to become stars for the State.

Similarly, exacting admission requirements applied to the university or the engineering institute, the excellence of whose graduates was considered to be fundamental to the advancement of the Soviet State both economically and militarily. Whatever the type of training or whatever the kind of school or educational program the individual was permitted to enter, it was his duty to contribute his maximum to the State in return for State-provided education.

Soviet education aims at education for excellence with freedom of choice resting with the State to the end that the State may be developed to the optimum.

> Taken from *Education in the USSR*
> U.S. Department of Health, Education, and Welfare

In a well-organized essay of *at least 450 words*, discuss the above passage, pointing out how the principles set forth therein differ from those which are fundamental to our system of education.

ANALYSIS OF THE QUESTION

The excerpt from the document *Education in the USSR* provides a bird's-eye view of the fundamental tenets of Soviet education. You will note the elements of this doctrine: strict planning by a totalitarian State, limitation upon human aspiration, control of the individual by the State, the ultimate functioning within a Communist dominated society. In answer, the American creed must be detailed and illustrated

PLAN OF THE ESSAY

Following are the pertinent lines of development:

Par. 1. Broad contrast between the USSR and the USA, mentioning various differences in education and proceeding to the heart of the matter: the purpose of education. This is then related to the State and society.

2. Russian objectives and principles, developed as in the excerpt explained above. At the end, a preparation for transition by reference to the effect on the individual qualities we in the USA esteem.
3. American beliefs and goals: education for all according to potential; an informed public the basis of democracy; personal freedom of choice in life and work; the ultimate value of man in society.
4. Concrete demonstration of the American philosophy in action: free schools; scholarship aids; types of schools and courses; varying standards of achievement according to interest and ability.
5. The contrast drawn again in terms of ultimate conflict.

TOPIC: SOVIET AND AMERICAN EDUCATION COMPARED

POINT-SCORING ELEMENTS	PARAGRAPH NUMBER

Broad approach to topic
Complex sentence with
noun clause

Contrasts in the schools -
an effective series

Simple sentence stressing
main idea

Question to elicit interest
Indication of broad lines of
inquiry

(1) In the competitive spirit of today's world, it was inevitable that our system of education would be compared with that of other nations and, particularly, with that of Russia. A finger has been pointed at contrasts in curricula, in materials, in teaching techniques, and even in the length of the school year. Beneath these considerations, however, lies the fundamental idea of purpose. How did the schools of the USSR and the USA differ in purpose? The answer to this inquiry is imbedded in the political theory of the State and the relationship of the individual to society.

Simple-direct statement
Compound-complex sentence

Introducing examples
Complex sentence with ad-
verbial and adjective
clauses

Simple sentence

Short complex sentence

Long, well-developed
simple sentence

Use of figurative language

Complex sentence with an
effective series

(2) The Russian idea stemmed from its concept of totalitarianism. The State was the all-important element and all individuals were subject to the service they may contribute to the government. Thus, as authoritative sources revealed, the schools were permitted to produce only the number of engineers, of lawyers, of technicians, and of artists, that the State could have utilized. Rigid examination procedures limited sharply the number of aspirants in each skill area. The rest were forced into occupations as the need indicated. This sort of planned preparation for life had a natural concomitant. Once trained for a particular niche in society, each growing citizen devoted all his talents, training, and energy to the development of the State. The whole process is a kind of mathematical equation in which people become numbers and symbols, losing the qualities of personal freedom, ambition, inventiveness, and interest which we, of the Western world, hold so dear.

17

POINT-SCORING ELEMENTS	PARAGRAPH NUMBER

Transition

Simple sentence

Complex sentence with adjective clause
Note coherence in <u>such</u>, <u>Moreover</u>, *and* <u>This exercise</u>

Summary in effective diction and parallel predicate elements

(3) Our fundamental belief in the value of each individual results in school patterns quite different from that of Russia. We subscribe to the theory of full education for all to the best of each one's ability. Out of <u>such</u> development will come the informed citizenry that will make a success of our democratical functioning society. <u>Moreover</u>, we urge each person to select the way of life which appeals to him and suits his talents and interests, -- the profession, the occupation, the goals that he envisions for himself. This exercise of freedom will engender respect for the country which provides opportunity for sel advancement and will elicit that participation in society which is characterized by good-will and cooperation.

Simple sentence

Compound sentence without connective

Simple sentence

Complex sentence with adjective clause

(4) To implement these ideals, we have educational programs for all: the bright, the average, the slow. Education is free up through the high school; many concessions and grants are given to the deserving to go on through college and advan study. Both academic and vocation courses are provided, depending up interest and ability. The slow, a even the handicapped of all kinds, have the opportunity of progressiv schooling at their own rate and according to their own potential. Remedial helps are offered at ever level to salvage those whom sickne and adverse fortune have kept from successful participation earlier.

Complex sentence with conditional clause
Question
Echo of condition but now given as answer

(5) If the opposing forces of society eventually to clash, the weapons are being forged now. Shall we be free or slaves? If our schools do their job well, the processes whic give man his full stature of digni worth, and freedom, will triumph over those which deny him these fundamental rights and desires.

BASIC PRINCIPLES AND PRACTICES IN EDUCATION
THE NEW PROGRAM OF EDUCATION

CONTENTS

—

BASIC PRINCIPLES AND PRACTICES IN EDUCATION
THE NEW PROGRAM OF EDUCATION

I. PHILOSOPHY AND OBJECTIVES

A. PHILOSOPHY
   1. An analysis of the aims and purposes of education
   2. An appraisal of current educational practices
   3. A statement of the "ideal" to be attained
   4. A justification of the means to be employed
B. CONCEPTS OF EDUCATION
   1. Education as knowledge
      a. Emphasis on factual learning
      b. Transmitting the past heritage
      c. Excessive use of texts
   2. Education as discipline
      a. Training the memory, imagination, etc.
      b. Emphasis on rote memory, drill, frequent tests, etc.
      c. Reliance on theory of transfer of training
   3. Education as growth
      a. Developing latent capacities and realization of child's
         potentialities
      b. Experiential and functional learning
      c. Emphasis on attitudes, appreciations, and interests
      d. Child-centered curriculum
      e. Stress on social relationships and democratic living
         procedures
C. OBJECTIVES
   1. Character - ethical living in a society promoting the common
      welfare
   2. American Heritage - faith in American democracy and respect
      for dignity and worth of the individual regardless of race,
      religion, nationality or socio-economic status
   3. Health - sound body and wholesome mental and emotional
      development
   4. Exploration - discovery and development of individual aptitudes
   5. Thinking - develop ability to reason critically, using facts
      and principles
   6. Knowledges and skills - command of common integrating knowledges
      and skills
   7. Appreciation and expression - appreciation and enjoyment of
      beauty and development of powers of creative expression
   8. Social relationships - develop desirable social relationships
      at home, in school, in the community
   9. Economic relationships - appreciation of economic processes and
      of contributions of all who serve in the world of work

MNEMONIC DEVICE FOR REMEMBERING THESE OBJECTIVES

T hinking	K nowledges and skills
E xploration	A ppreciation
A merican heritage	S ocial relationships
C haracter	E conomic relationships
H ealth	

1

D. METHOD OF ACHIEVING THESE OBJECTIVES
1. Former emphasis on content with limited worthwhile, real experiences. Present stress on experiences with content used as a means to an end rather than as an end in itself.
2. This calls for a reorganization of our courses of study. Organization will now be in related areas rather than in separate isolated syllabi.
   These areas include:
   a. Pupil participation - to include planning, routines, and housekeeping, responsibilities, exploring school and community activities.
   b. Health - to include health instruction and guidance, safety education, rest, recreation, emotional adjustment, nutrition.
   c. Art - to include experimenting, use of various media as means of expression, practical applications in home, school, and community.
   d. Music - vocal, instrumental, rhythmic for enjoyment, expression, and understanding.
   e. Language Arts - reading, literature, composition, spelling, penmanship, speech, listening, dramatization.
   f. Social Studies - history, geography, civics, character, famil relationships, consumer problems, intercultural education, citizenship and concepts of democracy.
   g. Science - nature study, weather, plants and soil, animals, earth and sky, food and water, tools and instruments, simple machines and electrical devices, flightcraft.
   h. Arithmetic - size, space, distance, time, weight, concepts, computations, problem solving.

MNEMONIC DEVICE FOR THESE AREAS

H ealth	L anguage Arts
A rithmetic	A rt
S ocial Studies	M usic
	P upil participation
	S cience

E. ORGANISMIC PSYCHOLOGY *(our current program is based chiefly on thes principles)*
1. The principle of continuous growth - This emphasizes the flexibl experimental, emergent nature of the individual and of society; it stresses the continuity of experience. (Aspects: continuous progress plan; constant curriculum revision.)
2. The principle of experience as the method of learning - This emphasizes learning through functional, real experiences as opposed to memorization, drill, dictated assignments, etc. (Aspects: excursions; planning; research; reporting.)
3. The principal of integration - This emphasizes the wholeness and unity of individuals and of society. It stresses the interactio between the learner and the learning situation and demands maxim life-likeness in learning situations. (Aspects: units; use of community resources; large areas of instruction; larger time-blc

F. UNDERLYING TENETS OF THE PROGRAM
1. Education of the whole child - social, civic, intellectual, ethi vocational
2. Learning through real, functional experiences (activity vs. passivity)

2

3. The "intangibles" as an important end of education (interests, attitudes, character, etc.)
4. The concept of the child-centered school as opposed to the subject-centered school
5. The inclusion of the nine objectives of education as a part of educational planning at every step

G. WHAT DOES THE NEW PROGRAM MEAN?
 1. These things are basic:
    a. Socialization of procedures
    b. Integration of personality (before integration of subject matter)
    c. Increased pupil-teacher participation in planning and evaluating the educative process
    d. Group procedures
    e. A program to meet the individual's time-table of growth as well as a general development time-table
    f. First-hand experiencing as a "must" in education
    g. A mental hygiene viewpoint for the teacher
    h. Closer relationship between school-life and life in the world outside
    i. An acceptance of the view that concomitant learnings can some-times be more important than the original learnings to be taught
 2. It is NOT merely:
    a. Unit development
    b. Correlation of subject matter
    c. Working through committees
    d. Provision for research activities
    e. Emphasis on reporting and discussion
    f. Planning for a culmination
    g. Keeping diaries and logs

H. ADVANTAGES AND DISADVANTAGES
 1. Proponents of the New Program maintain that this program:
    a. Provides a flexible content
    b. Encourages individual aptitudes
    c. Permits much practice in social behavior
    d. Encourages independent learning
    e. Encourages creative expression
    f. Provides a vitalized curriculum
    g. Permits greater integration of subject matter
    h. Provides for leisure-time activities
    i. Provides a success program for each child
    j. Makes greater provision for diagnosis, guidance, and in-dividual remedial treatment
    k. Contributes abundantly towards the development of good character
 2. Opponents of the New Program maintain that:
    a. There is no gradation of the difficulties of different units of work
    b. It is not true to life (since life is not a series of activities)
    c. Too much reliance is placed on incidental learning
    d. There is no provision for participation by every child
    e. Teachers have not been trained sufficiently
    f. Equipment is underemphasized
    g. The interests of children are not sufficient as a guide for subject matter

h. The superficial aspects are overemphasized

i. Many important "learnings" are omitted

j. No provision is made for duplication in the case of pupils who are transferred or admitted

I. TRADITIONAL VS. PROGRESSIVE EDUCATION

TRADITIONAL   *PROGRESSIVE*

1. PHILOSOPHY

TRADITIONAL	PROGRESSIVE
a. School is a preparation for life	a. School is "life itself"
b. Emphasis on social heritage	b. Development of whole personality-knowledge, attitudes, morals, health
c. Adjust pipil to society that arises	c. School aims to improve society

2. CURRICULUM

TRADITIONAL	PROGRESSIVE
a. Factual curriculum laid out in advance for all	a. Subject matter - vital, purposeful, integrated, flexible, follows child's interests
b. Subjects clearly separated and isolated	b. Long units, integration and correlation of subject matter
c. Emphasis on memorization	c. Learning through experiences
d. Slavish use of text books	d. Use of a variety of reference and source materials

3. ROLE OF TEACHER

TRADITIONAL	PROGRESSIVE
a. Dominant factor in the learning process	a. Teacher is a guide and helper
b. Pupil passivity	b. Socialization and maximum pupil participation

4. METHODS

TRADITIONAL	PROGRESSIVE
a. Stressed mastery of subject matter	a. Adjustment of curriculum to needs, interests, and capacities of each child
b. Isolated drills. Extrinsic	b. Functional learning. Individualized drill at the point of error. Intrinsic
c. Rigid, formal discipline	c. A hum of activity. Self-discipline. Social adjustment
d. Inside of schoolroom	d. Excursions and field trips

5. SUPERVISION

TRADITIONAL	PROGRESSIVE
a. Dictatorial and inflexible	a. Democratic, scientific, creativ
b. Teachers rated according to ability in achieving grade standards (standardized tests)	b. Teachers judged on basis of their ability to promote desirable attitudes - interests, appreciations, etc. (attitude tes and case histories)

J. GENERAL PRINCIPLES IN ANY MODERN PHILOSOPHY OF ELEMENTARY EDUCATION

1. Education must be democratic, universal, and compulsory

2. There must be a unifying philosophy for the school system as a whole

3. This philosophy must be essentially a social philosophy; the school must adjust children to a changing social order

4. The curriculum must be flexible and must be subject to frequent (continuous) revision

5. There must be flexibility in classroom procedures

6. Adequate equipment must be provided

7. Adequate provision must be made for the mentally and physically handicapped

4

A. DEFINITIONS
  1. The *CURRICULUM* consists of all the experiences, including all
     the subject matter and skills, which are utilized and inter-
     preted by the school to further the aims of education. These
     experiences result from interaction between persons, influences,
     and material facilities. Some of the factors which effect the
     curriculum are:
     a. The political, economic, and social structure of the sur-
        rounding society
     b. The public opinion toward education
     c. The aims and philosophies of those operating the educational
        system
     d. The decisions concerning methods and materials, teacher
        selection, sarlaries, and physical plant
     e. The course of study, or,more properly,the documents made
        available to the teachers
  2. Early *COURSES OF STUDY* usually consisted only of a subject-matter
     outline; later ones included also some suggested learning activi-
     ties, teaching procedures, diagnostic devices, and evaluation
     techniques. The emphasis, in all instances, was on "prescribed"
     subject matter to be covered, and some courses of study even
     specified the number of minutes per day to be devoted to each of
     the segments and the specific fact questions to be used.
  3. Modern *GUIDES* for teachers are not usually called courses of
     study. They suggest a wealth of materials and experiences; far
     from minimizing subject matter, they suggest more of it better
     adapted for use with varying levels of abilities and interests.
     They include bulletins on:
     a. the teaching of various subjects
     b. the organization of experience units with subject lines dis-
        regarded
     c. the characteristics of children
     d. varied learning experiences
     e. teaching procedures
     f. ways of using different types and amounts of subject matter
     g. sources of instructional aids
     h. evaluational techniques
     i. bibliographies, etc.
B. GENERAL CONSIDERATIONS
  1. A curriculum develops in answer to the needs of a group of
     learners and to the demands of a given society.
  2. A curriculum is made by a teacher and her pupils as they work
     together in the school.
  3. The development of a specific curriculum is a cooperative activi-
     ity in which many persons participate (superintendents, principals,
     teachers,subject-matter specialists,consultants,school psychologists,
     pupils, parents, social agencies, advisory commissions, etc.)
  4. A program of curriculum improvement involves a study of:
     a. the political, economic, and social structure of the sur-
        rounding society
     b. public opinion toward education
     c. advice or information for the public
     d. the aims and philosophy of current educational practice

      e. the abilities, needs, purposes and individual differences among the learners

      f. the origin and nature of subject matter

      g. the development of present curriculums

      h. the nature of modern outcomes of learning

      i. the many new techniques of evaluation

  5. A program of curriculum improvement is far broader than the writing of a course of study or series of teachers' guides; it is concerned with the improvement of living and learning conditions in the school and in the community of which it is a part.

  6. A program of curriculum improvement should result in changes of attitudes, appreciations, and skills on the part of the participants and in important changes in the learning situation.

C. CONDITIONS THAT COMPEL CURRICULAR CHANGES

  1. Technological developments – In a society where most people work for someone else, it is important that the curriculum emphasize the attitudes and skills of cooperation.

  2. International problems – The curriculum must emphasize international understanding as well as the defense of America and other freedom-loving nations.

  3. Social change – The curriculum must prepare children for living in a complex and changing world, and must emphasize moral responsibility for one's acts both as an individual as well as a member of a group.

  4. Educational progress – The increase of available materials of instruction and the expanding role of the teacher call for a redistribution of teachers' time and energies in terms of a new set of values.

D. CHANGES THAT RESULT FROM CURRICULUM IMPROVEMENT

  1. In the professional staff-cooperative planning; working together on educational problems; experimentation with promising procedure study of human growth and development.

  2. In the teaching-learning situation – improvement in the school plant, equipment, and supplies; use of community resources; available community services; opportunities for children to participate in community life.

  3. In improved pupil behavior – ability to define and solve meaningful problems: development of new interest; self-evaluation; skill in communication; skill in human relations; initiative; creativeness.

  4. In community relationships – participation by lay citizens; public support; public relations.

  5. In school organization – plan of organization; staff selection procedures; school size; class size; daily schedules; district services; faculty conferences.

  6. In instructional materials – cooperative production of instructional materials; more effective use of commercial materials; better selection of teaching aids; establishment of a "materials center"; development of a professional library.

  7. In ways of working together – teacher-pupil planning; group dynamics; sociometric techniques; intergroup education.

E. MAIN PROBLEMS IN CURRICULUM DEVELOPMENT

  1. The determination of educational directions

  2. The selection of experiences comprising the educational program

  3. The selection of a pattern of curriculum organization

4. The determination of principles and procedures by which the curriculum can be evaluated and changed

F. FACTORS AFFECTING CURRICULUM DEVELOPMENT
1. The existing political, economic, and social structure
2. Pressure exerted by minority groups or vested interests
3. Legislation
4. Tradition
5. Influence of logically organized subject matter and compartmentalization
6. Textbooks

G. CONSIDERATIONS FOR CURRICULUM PROGRAMS
1. The improvement program is to be developed with the aid of supervisors, teachers, pupils, parents, and community.
2. The curriculum should be readily adaptable to individual differences, needs, and interests and to the special needs of groups, schools and communities.
3. There should be provision for articulation between and among the various divisions and levels of the school system.
4. There must be provision for continuous experimentation and research.
5. There must be flexibility and allowance for interpretation and change to meet new situations and conditions.
6. There must be provision for evaluation of principles, practices, and outcomes, as well as for appraisal of the curriculum improvement program itself.
7. The curriculum must provide conditions, situations, and activities favorable to the continuous growth and progress of each individual.
8. Curriculum policies and practices should encourage friendly understanding and democratic relations among supervisors, teachers, pupils and parents.
9. The success of a curriculum is dependent on competent leadership. (Supervision interprets and implements the curriculum and seeks to improve teaching and learning; teachers' attitudes and understandings determine the effectiveness of the curriculum; community aims, purposes, and resources exert an important influence on the curriculum; pupils help in developing a wholesome pattern of democratic living in which the curriculum operates most effectively.)

H. QUESTIONS RELATED TO CURRICULUM DEVELOPMENT
1. Why is the traditional curriculum, used with seeming success for years, now under such criticism, analysis, and change?
2. Is the curriculum an instrument of social progress?
3. Should the aims of education and the content of the curriculum be determined with some definiteness in advance of actual teaching-learning situations?
4. Is all, none, or a given part of the curriculum to be required of all learners - regardless of origin, present status, and very probable destiny?
5. How shall the curriculum be organized - scope and sequence determined?
6. How shall the curriculum content be selected?
7. What are the desired outcomes of learning experiences?
8. How much of the curriculum can be formulated by the pupils?
9. What stand shall the curriculum take on "indoctrination?"

10. What procedures should be used in reconstructing the curriculum?
11. What are the criteria for evaluating a curriculum?

III. GROUPING AND COMMITTEE WORK

A. ORGANIZING GROUPS FOR INSTRUCTION
1. Know the children before you group
    a. General level of achievement (standardized tests)
    b. Individual problems in the area (everyday performance)
    c. Capacity to achieve (expectancy)
    d. Personal and social adjustment (sociogram)
2. Develop a "readiness" for grouping
    a. Teach the techniques that will be the basis for independent activity later
    b. Be familiar with the types of exercises to be used for group work later; anticipate some of the skills which will be required
    c. Develop work-skills (choosing something, sharing materials, working independently, etc.)
3. Launch the best group first
    a. The first group will be those children most advanced intellectually and socially
    b. The remainder of the class learns to work independently as the teacher works with the first group
    c. As both these groups learn to work simultaneously, the teacher notes the point at which further subdivision becomes necessary (for example, the slower group may be broken down into a normal and slow group)
4. Group standards should be set cooperatively by the teacher and class
5. Some abilities to aim for:
    a. Working alone
    b. Working quietly
    c. Completing a job
    d. Moving to the next job when the present one is completed
    e. Finding and correcting one's errors
    f. Evaluating one's own work
6. Arrangement of pupils
    a. Reduce to a minimum the interference of one group with anothe (through location of groups in the room, allocation of blackboard space, etc.)
    b. Have a group's materials placed near to where that group work
B. CRITERIA FOR GROUP WORK
1. Are the procedures used in accordance with the techniques advocated in the program of education?
    a. What is the basis on which the groups are set up? (Common weaknesses, sociogram, etc.)
    b. Is the goal for each group set and understood?
    c. Have these goals been set by cooperative planning?
    d. In what type of activity is the group engaged - individual or group? Is there a free interplay of minds at all times?
    e. Are there evidences of evaluation within the group - by individuals and by the group?
    f. What is the extent and variety of materials used?
2. Are there evidences of individual contributions by children in the group?

3. Are there evidences of committee work of children (charts, etc.)?
4. Are there evidences of teacher-supervision of group procedures?
5. Are there evidences of the growth of social skills, attitudes, and understandings of social living?

C. COMMITTEE WORK
1. Group dynamics as a factor in committee work
    a. Sociograms and friendship charts
    b. Place of the "stars"
    c. Working the isolates into the committee
2. As in grouping, the teacher starts with a single-committee and develops committee techniques with the members
3. Selection of a chairman and a secretary by the committee - importance of leadership and followership
4. Contributions of the members of a committee toward the solution of a problem - working together and all that it implies
5. Place of the teacher
    a. She never "abdicates her position;" she advises and guides when indicated
    b. She watches closely those members with personal problems
    c. She anticipates difficulties in human relations
    d. She assigns a place for the committee to work comfortably
    e. She displays charts listing the committees, with leaders starred
    f. She makes available materials for research, including pictorial material and special materials for the non-reader or retarded reader
    g. She checks the progress of the group and of the individuals in the group regularly (before a reporting period, etc.)
6. Standards for group work periods
    NOTE: These are suggestions for charts
    a. For a Group Leader
        a.1 Know what work to do each day
        a.2 Keep the group working
        a.3 Do not be too bossy
    b. For the Group
        b.1 We will speak softly
        b.2 We will talk only to our own group
        b.3 We will talk only about our own work
        b.4 We will try to find our own materials
        b.5 We will use our time wisely
        b.6 We will clean up when we have finished
    c. For Groups preparing a report
        c.1 Skim books for stories on the topic of your report
        c.2 Plan an outline of the whole topic
        c.3 Choose sub-topics for study
        c.4 Work on topics - make an outline, do some research, make something, etc.
        c.5 Give your report to the group for criticism
        c.6 Give the report to the class

IV. EVALUATION

. ITEMS TO BE EVALUATED
1. Mental development *(traditionally, this has been almost the sole emphasis)*
2. Physical aspects

3. Social aspects
4. Emotional aspects
B. REASONS FOR EVALUATING
1. It is a means of discovering group and individual growth
2. It is a means of discovering whether children are developing at a rate commensurate with their general capacity (expectancy)
3. To discover children's strengths and weaknesses, and necessity for specific help (diagnostic) in particular cases
4. To indicate to the school how it can best provide the conditions of growth that make learning most economical and most effective
5. Children learn more effectively when they take part in evaluation
   a. As members of a group, they learn to become aware of group needs (through learning they must acquire for a specific purpose)
   b. They learn how to plan for group needs (through practice in evaluating possible courses of action)
   c. They learn to take stock as they proceed with their tasks (through evaluating progress periodically)
   d. They learn ways of deciding when their project has reached a satisfactory conclusion (through practice in evaluating their achievements in the light of their original objectives)
C. WHEN TO EVALUATE
1. It is a continuing activity, taking place at every stage of the learning process (*Evaluation is not concerned solely with end products*)
2. The teacher evaluates situations as they occur
3. "The quality of living" that goes on in a classroom is evaluated as an indication of class morale
4. The amount of communication that takes place is, at all times, a significant evaluative factor
5. The need for recording social adjustments, emotional maturity, attention span, language development, interests, and enthusiasms of children makes continuous evaluation a necessity
6. Check lists and anecdotal records may be used to record what is observed
D. WHO EVALUATES?
1. Everyone concerned in the educative process should take part in evaluation
   a. The children, with or without the guidance of the teacher, make valid judgments
   b. The teacher evaluates herself, the effectiveness of her procedures, the progress of her class and the individuals therein, the climate of her room, and the classroom situation
   c. The school, as a composite of teachers and supervisors, evaluates its curriculum, its services to children, its growth of teachers and supervisors, and its relationship to the life of the community
   d. Members of the community, especially parents, evaluate the school, its program and its teachers (The school should provide such information so as to make possible an intelligent evaluation on the community's part)
E. EVALUATION IN A UNIT OF WORK
1. The unit should be evaluated in light of its objectives
2. The primary objective is not absorption of a mass of facts, but the development of attitudes, understandings, and appreciations

3. The evaluation of desirable social relationships, the development of good habits of work and thought, and the imparting of basic concepts are our major social studies goals
4. Measurement of the so-called intangibles, while admittedly difficult, is possible (Formal tests, such as the California Tests of Personality and Winnetka Behavior Rating Scale are not so valuable as teacher observation and judgment)
5. The teacher, by recording objectively significant behavior, can observe the developmental pattern of growth in chidren (anecdotal records, etc.)
6. Teacher-made checklists and tests are helpful in determining growth and progress
   a. Tests in ascertaining places where information is available (A test of this type may be administered before and after a unit is taken. Growth may be measured by comparing results)
      a.1 Whom would you ask where to find a certain building if you were downtown?
      a.2 How would you locate a certain book if you were in the library?
      a.3 If you weren't sure whether a word ended in "ant" or "ent," how could you find out?
      a.4 Where would you look to find out something about an explorer?
      a.5 How could you tell, by looking at a map, whether New York is closer to Connecticut than it is to Virginia?
   b. Tests involving the relevancy of data to particular problems and tests involving the relevancy of statements to a conclusion
      b.1 Does a person's race or religion have any bearing on his athletic or musical ability?
      b.2 Since your city uses great amounts of food, does that mean that your city produces huge amounts of meat, grain, etc.?
   c. Tests involving the reliability of various sources, the matching of persons with the fields of their probable competence
      c.1 Would Mickey Mantle necessarily be an authority on international relations?
   d. Checklists of instances of voluntary cooperation (Does the child of his own accord clean up the area around his seat? Does the child bring materials from home?, etc.)
7. Methods of evaluation of a unit
   a. Objective tests *(prepared by teachers and pupils)*
   b. Teacher's written accounts and criticisms
   c. Teacher's anecdotal reports on individual and group work
   d. Matching achievement against predetermined objectives
   e. Comparison of activities and skills of this unit with those of preceding units
   f. Noting observations made by parents and community
8. Children's evaluation in a unit
   a. Charts: "Did I Do a Good Job?",etc.
   b. Evaluation "envelopes," in which children retain samples of their work and note-progress
   c. Children (and teacher) appraise:
      c.1 What have we learned?
      c.2 What should we remember?
      c.3 Did we do everything we set out to do?
      c.4 What must still be done?

c.5 What could we have done better?
c.6 What questions should be included on a "test of all the important things we learned?"
c.7 How can we make further use of the things we learned?
9. Evaluation is a means of discovering:
   a. Group and individual growth
   b. Teacher-effectiveness or weakness
   c. Group needs
   d. Curriculum strengths or deficiencies
   e. Objectives realized
   f. Experience gained
   g. Subject matter acquired
   h. Skills mastered
   i. Evidences of creative expression
   j. Evidences of growth toward desirable habits, attitudes, and appreciations
   k. Activities not yet completed
   l. Subject matter not covered

V. DISCIPLINE

A. MEANING
   1. Broad Meaning - The attainment by the individual of such knowledges, skills, habits, and attitudes as will promote the well-being of himself and of his social group.
   2. Narrow Meaning - The creation of classroom conditions to provide a wholesome environment for the best functioning of the individual and the group.
B. DISCIPLINE VS. ORDER
   1. Difference
      a. Discipline: Based on self-direction; maintained by building habits of self-control and by stressing the social need for desirable conduct. It aims at a self-directed class that works quietly and efficiently even though the teacher is temporarily too busy to supervise the class.
      b. Order: Based on instant obedience to commands emanating from above; depends on the teacher's ability to exercise constant surveillance and to use the pupils' fear of detection as a deterrent to undesirable action. Order reaches its height when the teacher can make the meaningless boast that she "can hear a pin drop."
   2. As a means toward discipline, order is sometimes essential. It may be a legitimate aid to discipline. As a goal in itself, it has little justification.
C. THE DIFFERENCE BETWEEN CONDUCT AND BEHAVIOR
   1. Conduct: The adult's reaction to the child's acts. It is considered "good" or "bad." Depends on adult's standards or values
   2. Behavior: The child's reaction to stimuli (physical, mental, or social). It is "normal" or "abnormal." Depends on child's personality.
D. PLANES OF DISCIPLINE
   1. Obedience - military concept
   2. Personal domination by the teacher - "good order" concept
   3. Social pressure - living and working with others
   4. Self-discipline - living and working alone

E. GENERAL PRINCIPLES OF CLASSROOM DISCIPLINE
  1. Self-control is achieved through proper habit formation
     (psychological principles)
  2. Desirable discipline is social control within the school group
  3. Discipline should be positive and constructive, rather than
     negative and destructive
  4. It should appeal to the highest motives of which the pupil is
     capable
  5. It should impress pupils as being fair, reasonable, and social-
     ly necessary
F. POSITIVE VS. NEGATIVE DISCIPLINE
  1. The essential difference is one of attitude and approach
     a. Present conformity to rule vs. cultivating motives for sound
        action in later years
     b. Getting children to do the right thing vs. preventing them
        from doing the wrong thing
  2. Examples:

POSITIVE	NEGATIVE
a. Stimulating attention.	a. Coping with inattention. Scolding.
b. Creating desire to come to school because of meaningful activities.	b. Devising measures to curb truancy. Scolding.
c. Encouraging children to come early by starting promptly with interesting work and duties.	c. Devising new procedures to curb lateness. Scolding.
d. Awakening the desire to do things for the good of the school.	d. Compelling observance of class and school rules. Punishment.
e. Giving children opportunities of participating in class and school administration.	e. Teacher does everything. Doing things for children which they can be trained to do for themselves.

  3. Caution: It is impossible to dispense with negative discipline
     entirely, but the emphasis should be placed on the positive plane.
G. WHY SOME TEACHERS HAVE DISCIPLINARY TROUBLES
  1. Pedagogical Reasons
     a. Failure to employ appropriate subject matter and materials
     b. Poor teaching techniques
     c. Failure to consider the individual pupil's capacities,
        talents, and interests
  2. Classroom Management
     a. Failure to mechanize routines
     b. Unattractive, physically uncomfortable surroundings
  3. Personality
     a. Lack of tact   b. High strung manner
     c. Idiosyncrasies in dress   d. High pitched voice
     e. Lack of a sense of humor
  4. Psychological
     a. Lack of sympathy with children
     b. Procrastination in handling cases (not facing the issue)
     c. Lack of a fair disciplinary policy
H. CLASS MORALE AS A FACTOR IN CLASSROOM DISCIPLINE
  1. Meaning of morale or class spirit

a. "Morale is the feeling among members of a group that stimulate them to work happily together toward the realization of shared aims"

b. "The personality of the group born of common attitudes"

2. How Developed

L a. *Leadership* of the teacher - she sets the tone

a.1 Her personality - ability to fire others with enthusiasm for ideals and service; to arouse faith of pupils in her

a.2 Her educational qualifications

a.3 Her understanding of children

A b. Stressing of strong social *attitudes* - work of the group more important than that of the individual - team work of pupils

C c. Situations arousing *common* loyalties - participation in joint efforts

c.1 Class projects - making things for the class or the school (posters, art objects, Christmas gifts to soldiers or destitute children, class newspaper, class party, help with parents' bazaar)

c.2 Assembly programs, pageants

c.3 Athletic teams

c.4 Friendly competition with other classes (attendance records, contributions to the Red Cross)

P d. Situations arousing *pride* as a result of achievement and recognition

d.1 Service to the class and school

d.2 Records - attendance, punctuality, neatness, cleanliness, etc.

d.3 Good deeds and accomplishments of classmates

d.4 Accomplishment of learning goals (New Program)

S e. Attractive surroundings - contribution of pupils to the appearance of the room

(Mnemonic - S C A L P)

I. THE USE OF INCENTIVES

1. Distinction between incentives and motives

a. Incentive - An environmental object or condition, the attainment or avoidance of which motivates behavior (external) - praise, blame, reward, punishment, rivalry

b. Motive - The process within an organism which energizes or directs it toward a specific line of behavior (internal) - interest, need, urge, drive, desire

c. Incentive is the stimulus; motive is the reaction, though the terms, including "motivation," are used loosely and interchangeably.

2. Real vs. Artificial Motivation (intrinsic vs. extrinsic)

a. Real Motivation - Gives purpose and direction to the learning process, is part of the task, arises from the value of the task for its own sake, is related to the life of the child (aroused by problems or challenges to which the child desires the answer or solution)

b. Artificial Motivation - attempts to make uninteresting material attractive by sugarcoating; is based on traditional attitude that every lesson is a unit in itself; is usually unrelated or only slightly related to the task (stores, games, marks, rewards)

14

c. The new program vs. the traditional program from the point of view of motivation

d. Some examples of real and artificial motivation:

REAL

1. Arithmetic: Learning percents through computing class averages in attendance or the standing of athletic teams
2. Spelling: Learning words by writing a real letter
3. Geography: Learning the geography of the city through trips and excursions
4. Science: Learning about plants through growing them
5. Social Studies: Learning the industries of a country through a study of how people live and work
6. Art: Learning color and perspective through illustrating a unit by murals

ARTIFICIAL

1. Learning by reference to father's bank account
2. Learning through the desire to get a better mark
3. Learning in order to do well on a quiz
4. Learning through a reference to the flower shop around the corner or to a picture
5. Learning through reference to the work children's parents do
6. Learning in order to get a good mark, to have work displayed, or to obtain the approval of the teacher

(*NOTE: Extrinsic motivation is sometimes justifiable or desirable, but it should be subordinated to intrinsic drives wherever possible.*)

3. Incentives in the Classroom
   a. Principles
      a.1 The best incentive is one which makes a task significant to the child
      a.2 It should influence future as well as present actions and attitudes
      a.3 It should make doing an act a satisfying process
      a.4 It should encourage the social point of view
   b. Motives to which the teacher can appeal
      b.1 The desire to do the right for its own sake should always be the ultimate goal even with very young children
      b.2 The desire for self-respect - knowledge of progress, recognition of abilities or status
      b.3 The desire to win the approval of one's fellow - displaying good work, posting lists of children doing well, monitorships
      b.4 The desire to gain the approval of the teacher or one's parents - praise succeeds better than blame, recognizing the good better than scolding the bad, letters to parents
      b.5 The desire for new experiences - problems, excursions, class clubs, projects
      b.6 The desire to win a reward - need not be of material value - praise, exhibition of work, monitorships should be within reach of all - avoid bribery

(*NOTE: The lowest form of incentive is better than the best form of punishment.*)

J. CLASSROOM PUNISHMENTS
   1. The Basis for Punishment
      a. What should be the aim? Retributive, deterrent, or corrective?
      b. Punishment may be justified if it is *corrective*
         b.1 It must be a means of removing a tendency to unsocial behavior

15

          b.2 It must not be a separate entity, but part of the educa-
               tion process
          b.3 It must aid in the process of adjusting behavior in a
               positive direction
    c. Criteria of effective punishment
          c.1 The child should be shown that he is being punished for
               a social transgression
          c.2 The teacher's personal feelings must not be a considera-
               tion
          c.3 Punishment is to be used only when the child fails to
               respond to incentives
          c.4 It should be adapted to the child (not uniform)
          c.5 It must not be unduly severe
          c.6 It must not leave a residue of antagonism or resentment
          c.7 It must not constitute the complete treatment for problem
               behavior
2. Punishment by Natural Consequence
    a. It is sound in theory but difficult in practice in the class-
       room (copying, cheating, failing to do work, obscene language)
    b. The principle can be followed, by making punishment seem to
       be a natural consequence wherever possible
3. Punishment by Fear
    a. Fear is an inhibiting rather than a stimulating force. It has
       a paralyzing harmful effect on development. It should rarely
       be used
    b. Corporal punishment is the lowest form of the use of fear. If
       ever administered, it should be for its shocking effect, rather
       than for punitive or corrective reasons
4. Evaluation of Classroom Punishments
    a. Minor punishments, such as staring at a child or calling his
       name - effective in nipping trouble in the bud
    b. Deprivation of position - effective if the door is held open
       for reinstatement
    c. Reprimands - effective, if given unemotionally and child is
       shown how his act interferes with others (must be used spar-
       ingly)
    d. Doing a written task - ineffective because it avoids the true
       causes of the trouble (I must come to school on time) and
       builds wrong associations (writing spelling words twenty five
       times)
    e. Picking up papers, etc. - effective if used as a means of mak-
       ing up for an offense, doing a positive deed in place of a
       negative
    f. Detention - generally ineffective because it leads to wrong
       associations with school
    g. Isolation - of doubtful value. The practice of having a child
       stand in a corner or in the corridor has no justification
    h. Social disapproval - effective if public humiliation does not
       result
    i. Saturation - ineffective and dangerous (it may backfire)
    j. Sarcasm - dangerous because mistaken for humor, builds resent-
       ment instead of cooperation (of doubtful value even with
       "smart alecks")
    k. Epithets - unjustified
    l. Sending for parent - effective if designed to understand causes
       and to devise program for cooperation between home and school

16

K. SOME PRACTICAL SUGGESTIONS FOR TEACHERS *(CHARACTERISTIC OF TRANSI-TION FROM ORDER TO DISCIPLINE)*
1. Give pupils the impression that you expect perfect order
2. Learn the names of all pupils as soon as possible
3. Give no unnecessary orders or directions - no repetitions
4. An explanatory statement, preparatory to giving a direction or order, reduces the possibility of confusion or disobedience
5. Insist upon a reasonable compliance with those directions which are given
6. Don't let little things go *(Nip disorder in the bud)*
7. Keep the machinery of class management simple
8. Plan lessons and all work well
9. Keep the class busy on worthwhile work and activities
10. Use rewards and punishments judiciously - watch for and reward desirable actions
11. Avoid punishing in anger (It's the child, not the offense, that must be considered)
12. Don't punish the group for the offense of an individual
13. Don't make threats
14. Severe penalties should not be used for minor offenses
15. The teacher should never give the impression that she has exhausted her supply of punishments or rewards
16. Avoid forcing an issue with a disobedient pupil before the class
17. When a child is punished, keep the door open for him to return to the good graces of the class and the teacher
18. Have a sense of humor
19. Be fair and consistent in your decisions
20. Have an element of surprise - something new - in class work
21. Seat pupils so that opportunities for infraction are lessened
22. The voice should be subdued, but audible enough to be heard clearly throughout the room
23. Primarily, the handling of discipline cases is the responsibility of the teacher
24. In handling discipline cases, the teacher may have reasonable recourse to the parents
25. When a teacher has exhausted her own resources, or in the cases of emergency, she should call upon the supervisor for help

VI. *BASIC FUNDAMENTALS OF EDUCATIONAL PSYCHOLOGY*

A. CONDITIONING
Learning takes place as a result of experience with outside stimuli. Responses are established by means of fixed associations.
1. Principles of Conditioning *(for use by teachers)*
   a. Learners' responses must be systematically studied
   b. Records of progress indicate need for change of pace, concentration on difficult parts, return to basic skills, new motivation, variations in use of cues
   c. Learner should make own records of progress
   d. Unlearning takes place rapidly; support and repeated reinforcement are required to consolidate and maintain habitual performance
   e. Teacher must control stimulating conditions (motivation)
   f. Teacher must help learner by providing varying conditions and extended practice
   g. Forced pacing methods are a poor substitute for adequate motivation

17

B. LEARNING BY TRIAL AND ERROR (CONNECTIONISM)
Learning involves the making of new mental and neural connections and the discarding or strengthening of old connections.
1. Concerned with what takes place between S-R to the neural connections
   a. Atomistic analysis of behavior
   b. Development is from hereditary instincts and reflexes to acquired habits
   c. Intellect and intelligence are quantitative
2. Thorndike's Laws of Learning
   a. Readiness - When a conduction unit is ready to act, conduction by it is satisfying and failure to conduct or being forced when not ready is annoying.
   b. Exercise - (Use and Disuse) Repetition with satisfaction strengthens the connection; disuse weakens the connection.
   c. Effect - Satisfaction strengthens the connection which it follows and to which it belongs. (Importance of motivation)
3. Thorndike's Five Characteristics of Learning
   a. Multiple responses to the same external situation pervade nine tenths of learning.
   b. The responses made are the product of the "set" or "attitude" of the learner. The satisfaction or annoyance produced by a response is conditioned by the learner's attitude.
   c. Partial Activity: One or another element in the situation may be prepotent in determining the response.
   d. Law of Assimilation or Analogy: If one element in the situation resembles another, it will call forth a corresponding response.
   e. Associative Shifting - Omitting elements of a situation and still getting the same response. (Conditioned response)
4. The Significance of "Cues" in Learning
   a. The learner tends to respond to loud sound, intense, brilliant or rapidly changing cues.
   b. Conspicuous stimuli may receive undue attention. Important stimuli may thus be overlooked.
   c. Cues help emphasize important stimuli.
   d. The teacher must discover when to use proper cues, and how much guidance to give the learner.
C. LEARNING BY INSIGHT: GESTALT PSYCHOLOGY
1. Constant striving to make sense out of a situation
2. The learner's efforts are not purely random
3. Understanding is enhanced by responding to total patterns, to relation between things
4. Motivation helps create perception of the problem
5. The learner's background of experience aids in insight, in perceiving figurations, in seeing the relationships of the parts to the whole, and in acquiring meaning and value
D. THE FIELD THEORY (ORGANISMIC, HOLISTIC THEORY)
1. Derived from the Gestalt theory
2. Insight is the alteration of organic structure within an area of the "whole organism"
3. Significances
   a. Breakdown of atomistic views
   b. Importance of chemical function of neural mechanisms
   c. Fundamental role of "feelings and emotions" in learning

d. Muscular coordination of the complete organism is a factor in skill acquisition
e. Recognition of the principle of maturation
f. Best motivation derives from needs of learners

E. TRANSFER OF TRAINING
1. Recognized as significant in educational theory and practice
    a. Traditional Concept - Doctrine of Formal Discipline: the mind gains strength through use, and this strength is automatically available in all situations. (Faculties of the Mind)
    b. Current Concept - No faculties as such. Transfer is a fact of mental life occurring under certain mental conditions, not because of external causes.
2. Factors Influencing Transfer
    a. Methods of procedure in learning and teaching
    b. Attitude of readiness set up by instructions given
    c. Degree of mastery of the material learned
    d. Integration of the initial learning - as to content and method
    e. Extent to which generalization and application are applied - "psychological organization"
3. Current Theories of Transfer
    a. Theory of Identical Elements (Thorndike)
        a.1 Identity of content
        a.2 Identity of procedure
        a.3 Identity of aims or ideals
        These identical elements make use of the same neural bonds.
    b. Theory of Generalization or Abstraction or Relationship
        Transfer takes place to the extent that one generalizes his experiences and is able to apply general principles to different situations. (Scientific method)
4. Implications for the Supervisor
    a. Materials used should have real value for children, not for mental discipline.
    b. A subject which has slight transfer value in a large field may be of more value than a subject which has a greater transfer value, but in a very limited field.
    c. The difficulty of a subject is not any indication of its transfer value.
    d. Recognition of child growth and development is the basic aim.
    e. The position accorded any subject in the school curriculum should be decided by the value of the special training it affords and by the social significance of its content rather than by its promise to develop general intellectual capacities.
5. Implications for the Teacher
    a. The most effective use of knowledge is assured, not through acquisition of any particular item of experience but only through the establishment of associations which give it general value.
    b. Transfer is most common at the higher levels of intellectual activity.
    c. Children should receive training in methods of memorizing, acquiring skills, and in solving problems.
    d. If transfer value is slight, then it is most economical to practice directly those habits and skills we wish to develop.
    e. An individual's ability to apply knowledge is not in proportion to his knowledge of facts.

  f. The teacher should know what it is that she wants the
    children to transfer to other fields, and she must learn by
    experience or experiment how to teach for transfer.
  g. The theory of transfer is recognized by all schools of
    psychology. More research is necessary before teachers can
    be guided by the theory to any great extent.

F. HABIT
 1. Meaning - A learned response made automatically to the appropriate stimulus.
 2. Principles of Habit Formation (Bagley)
  a. Focalize consciousness (Motivation)
   a.1 Give clearest possible idea of habit to be formed
   a.2 Use demonstration   a.3 Make it vivid
   a.4 Arouse motivation
   a.5 Give instruction in how habits are formed
   a.6 Multiple sense appeal
  b. Attentive repetition
   b.1 Vigorous, short, definite drill b.2 Use devices
   b.3 Have a definite goal (focalization)
   b.4 Watch for lag in attention
   b.5 Vary the number of repetitions
   b.6 "Practice makes perfect" only if with attention
  c. No exceptions
   c.1 Analyze habit in advance to prepare for likely slips
   c.2 Give special drill on difficult parts
   c.3 Put child on his guard c.4 Remove opposing stimuli
   c.5 Avoid forming similar habits at the same time
   c.6 Punishment, if necessary, should follow wrong act
  d. Automatization
   d.1 Attention to weak elements
   d.2 Distribution of practice (optional length)
 3. Values and Limitations
  a. Diminishes fatigue because habit mechanizes reactions so tha
   they accomplish their function with directness and minimum
   time and effort
  b. Releases consciousness for the guidance of other activities
  c. Makes responses reliable and accurate
  d. Complete domination, however, retards progress
  e. Sensibilities often deadened, lessening normal emotional ton
  f. Difficult to break bad habits
 4. Breaking Bad Habits
  a. Avoid the situation which will result in the undesirable hab
  b. Avoid opportunity for its practice
  c. Concentrate on one or two bad habits at a time
  d. Follow the principles of habit formation for developing the
   reverse of the bad habit (Substitution)
  e. Attach unpleasant feeling tone
 5. Significance for Teaching
  a. Dependence of habit on sensory stimulation *(Habits never
   initiate themselves)*
  b. Importance of gradation of subject matter to develop mechani
   cal habits
  c. In skills, improvement is very rapid at first
  d. Attention to physical and psychical conditions (time of day,
   length of period, etc.)

e. Recognition of possible periods of lapse and plateau
   e. 1 Need for rest
   e. 2 Attention and interest misdirected
   e. 3 Conflict in habits
   e. 4 Minor causes - indisposition, irritation
f. Recognition of individual differences in habit formation
g. Rate of forgetting high at first
h. Consideration of Speed vs. Accuracy
i. Recognition of three sets of habits (Mechanical;Subject Matter; Mental)

G. INDIVIDUAL DIFFERENCES
  1. Principles
    a. Pupils differ in degree of ability, not in the ability itself
    b. Individuals differ in degree of difficulty of tasks which they can learn; also in the method of learning
    c. Pupils of the same age and grade differ greatly - there is considerable overlapping of successive grades
    d. No one class can ever be entirely homogeneous - variations are continuous
    e. There are no readily available and fixed categories which the school can employ for the purpose of differentiated instruction
    f. Provision for individualization presents teaching and administrative difficulties
    g. Chronological age alone cannot be the determinant of an individual's capacity
  2. Conclusions for the School
    a. Administrative
      a. 1 Vary the time element
      a. 2 Flexible grouping
      a. 3 Testing programs
      a. 4 Modification of the curriculum
      a. 5 Provision for educational guidance
      a. 6 Flexible promotions
      a. 7 Supervision of proper teaching practices
    b. Curricular
      b. 1 Individualization of instruction
      b. 2 Diagnostic testing and remedial teaching
      b. 3 Provision for individual methods of learning
      b. 4 Grouping within the class
      b. 5 Record of needs, progress, and evaluation

VII. HISTORY OF EDUCATION

A. LEADERS
  1. Socrates (5th century B.C.)(469-399 B.C.)(Athens, Period of Sophists)
    (1) Writings - Left no writings, is studied in works of Plato and Xenophon.
    (2) Emphasis-Highest formulation of principles of moral life up to his time.
    (3) Contributions - His starting point:"Man is the measure of all things" (Protagoras).
    (4) Developed opinion into true or universal knowledge.
    (5) Aid of education: Not sophist brilliancy of speech, but knowledge arising from power of thought, analysis of experience.
    (6) Method: Dialectic, skillful questioning, distinguishing between permanent form and changing appearance, forming concepts from percepts.

2. Plato (4th century B.C.) (429-348 B.C.) (Athens, Academy)
   (1) Writings - "Republic," "Dialogues."
   (2) Three social classes: philosophers, warriors, workers.
   (3) Six major concerns of life: psychology, knowledge, soul,
       state, politics, ethics.
   (4) The ideal *State*, which exists for the realization of *justice*
       consists of three classes of people: philosophers, soldiers,
       and workers.
       These classes of society correspond to the soul (or *psycholo*
       of the individual: intelligence or reason; the passions, spi
       or will; and the desires, appetites, or sensations.
       The *ethics* of the classes embraces the traits of character w
       they should exhibit: wisdom, or correctness of thought; hono
       courage, energy of will, or justice of the heart; and temper
       self-control, or justice of the senses.
       Politics indicates the duties of the classes: the philosophe
       are to rule, the soldiers to protect and defend the State, a
       the workers to obey and support those above them.
   (5) Aim of education: To discover and develop individual qualifi
       tions to fit into classes of society; harmony of individual
       social motives.
3. Aristotle (3rd century B.C.) (384-322 B.C.)(Athens, Lyceum)
   (1) Writings - "Organon," "Politics," "Ethics," "Metaphysics."
   (2) Like Plato, he believed the highest art of man to be to dire
       society so as to produce the greatest good for mankind.
   (3) Education is subject to politics, each kind of state having
       appropriate kind of education.
   (4) Education is a life activity.
   (5) Method: Objective and scientific ; used inductive method, and
       thus founded practically all the modern sciences.
   (6) Education democratic, although all could not reach the same
       point.
   (7) Greatest systematizer of knowledge.
   (8) Formulated deductive reasoning; dialectic given form and uni
       sal influence.
   (9) Gave vocabulary of reasoning to the world.
4. Comenius (17th century)` (1592-1670)
   (1) Writings - "Orbus Pictus," "Vestibulum,""Janua,""School of
       Infancy," "The Great Didactic"
   (2) Sense - realist
       a. The teacher should appeal through sense-perception to und
          stand the child
   (3) Contributions
       a. Forerunner of 18th and 19th century educational theory
       b. Reformed Latin textbooks
5. John Locke (17th century) (1632-1704)
   (1) Writings - "Essay on Conduct of the Human Understanding,"
       "Thoughts"
   (2) Founder of modern psychology; advocate of faculty psychology
   (3) Empiricism; induction
   (4) Conception of the child's mind as a "tabula rasa" (blank sla
   (5) His influence strong up to the middle of the 19th century
6. Rousseau (18th century) (1712-1778)
   (1) Writings - "La Nouvelle Heloise," "Emile"
   (2) Education is life, not preparation for life
   (3) Importance of the child
   (4) Functional education
   (5) Individual differences

7. Johann Bernard Basedow (18th century)(1723-1790)
    (1) Writings -"Elementarwerk," "Book of Method"; established school called Philanthropinum, at Dessau.
    (2) Belongs to the line of Sense-Realists following Rousseau and forerunner to Pestalozzi.
    (3) Made first attempt since Comeniums to improve the work of the school through the use of appropriate textbooks.
    (4) Ideas embodied:
        (a) Children to be treated as such, not as adults.
        (b) Each child taught a handicraft for educational and social reasons.
        (c) Vernacular rather than classical languages chief subject matter of education.
        (d) Instruction connected with realities rather than with words.
        (e) Rich and poor educated together.
    (5) Contributions
        (a) Trained teachers.
        (b) Milder form of discipline.
        (c) Broader and more philanthropic view of man's duty to his fellow-man.
8. Pestalozzi (18th and early 19th century)(1746-1827)
    (1) Writings - "How Gertrude Teaches Her Children," "Leonard and Gertrude"
    (2) Sense impression
    (3) Respect for the individuality of the child
    (4) Discipline based upon love
    (5) Education for the subnormal
    (6) Normal schools
9. Herbart (19th and first half of the 19th century)(1776-1841)
    (1) Writings - First to write a textbook on psychology,"Testbook of Psychology"; Psychology as a Science"
    (2) Rejected the faculty psychology of Pestalozzi
    (3) Substituted his own method - the Five Formal Steps:
        (a) Preparation   (b) Presentation   (c) Comparison
        (d) Generalization (e) Application
    (4) Organization and technique of classroom instruction
    (5) Emphasis on environment in education
10. Froebel (first half of 19th century)(1782-1852)
    (1) Writings - "Education of Man," "Mutter," "Kose Lieder"
    (2) Founder of the kindergarten and the kindergarten idea
    (3) Education by doing
11. Spencer, Herbert (19th century) (1820-1903)
    (1) Writings - "Principles of Psychology," "Synthetic Philosophy," "Essays on Education"
    (2) Not originator but developer of the best in democratic education of his predecessors
    (3) Emphasis on scientific knowledge
12. Mann, Horace (19th century) (1796-1859)
    (1) Reference: Mary T.Mann, ed.,"The Life and Works of Horace Mann" (5 vols.-1891)
    (2) First secretary of the first Board of Education of Massachusetts (1817)
    (3) Conception of education as universal,secular,public,free, and compulsory
    (4) Outstanding organizer in education

13. Barnard, Henry (19th century) (1811-1900)
    (1) Writings - Edited "The American Journal of Education"(1855-1?
    (2) Held positions in Connecticut and Rhode Island similar to th?
        of Horace Mann in Massachusetts, i.e., Secretary of the Boar?
        of Education in Connecticut, 1838-1842, 1851-1855; and State
        Superintendent of Education in Rhode Island, 1845-1849.
    (3) First United States Commissioner of Education 1867-1870
14. Dewey, John (19th and 20th century) (1859-1952)
    (1) Writings - "The School and Society,""Democracy and Education,"
        "Experience and Nature," "Freedom and Culture"
    (2) Education is life, not a preparation for life
    (3) Learning takes place by doing
    (4) The bases of education are psychological and sociological
    (5) Father of progressive education ("activity" program)

B. CONCEPTUALIZED DEFINITIONS AND AIMS OF EDUCATION
   1. Character, morality: Plutarch (Spartans), Herbart
   2. Perfect development: Plato,Rabelais,Montaigne,Comenius,Locke,
      Parker,Pestalozzi
   3. Happiness: Aristotle, James Mill
   4. Truth: Socrates
   5. Citizenship: Luther, Milton
   6. Mastery of nature: Bacon, Huxley
   7. Religion: Comenius
   8. Mental power, discipline: Locke, Van Dyke, Ruediger
   9. Preparation for the future: Kant
  10. Habits: Rousseau, William James
  11. Unfolding: Froebel, Hegel
  12. Holy life: Froebel
  13. Interests: Herbart
  14. Knowledge: L.F. Ward
  15. Complete living: Spencer
  16. Culture, liberal education: Dewey
  17. Skill: Nathaniel Butler, E.C. Moore
  18. Inheritance of culture: N.M. Butler
  19. Socialization: W.T. Harris, Dewey
  20. Social efficiency: Dewey, Bagley
  21. Adjustment: Dewey, Ruediger, Chapman and Counts
  22. Growth: Dewey
  23. Organization of experience: Dewey
  24. Self realization: Dewey and Tufts
  25. Satisfying wants: Thorndike and Gates
  26. Insight: Gentile

———

ANSWER SHEET

ST NO. _____ PART _____ TITLE OF POSITION _____

(AS GIVEN IN EXAMINATION ANNOUNCEMENT - INCLUDE OPTION, IF ANY)

ACE OF EXAMINATION _____ DATE_____

(CITY OR TOWN) (STATE)

RATING

USE THE SPECIAL PENCIL. MAKE GLOSSY BLACK MARKS.

Make only ONE mark for each answer. Additional and stray marks may be counted as mistakes. In making corrections, erase errors COMPLETELY.

ANSWER SHEET

TEST NO. _____ PART _____ TITLE OF POSITION _____
(AS GIVEN IN EXAMINATION ANNOUNCEMENT - INCLUDE OPTION, IF ANY)

PLACE OF EXAMINATION _____ DATE _____
(CITY OR TOWN)   (STATE)

RATING

USE THE SPECIAL PENCIL.   MAKE GLOSSY BLACK MARKS.

Make only ONE mark for each answer.   Additional and stray marks may be
counted as mistakes.   In making corrections, erase errors COMPLETELY.